Vulnerable Witnesses and Defendants in Criminal Proceedings

VULNERABLE WITNESSES AND DEFENDANTS IN CRIMINAL PROCEEDINGS

MIRIAM DELAHUNT
BL, PhD

CLARUS
PRESS

Published by
Clarus Press Ltd,
Griffith Campus,
South Circular Road,
Dublin 8.
www.claruspress.ie

Typeset by
Gough Typesetting Services,
Dublin

Printed by
CPI Antony Rowe,
Chippenham,
Wiltshire

ISBN
978-1-911611-90-5

A catalogue record for this book is available from the British Library

For Mary Delahunt Egan and the Delahunt/Egan siblings

FOREWORD

The main principles and procedures underpinning the criminal justice system in Ireland were developed for the prosecution of offences largely committed by adults and those considered to have reached the age of criminal responsibility. From the age of twelve, children may be the subject of a criminal prosecution. Children who are much younger may be called as witnesses in criminal trials at any level. Other witnesses may require protection or assistance when giving their evidence due to particular vulnerabilities arising out of a mental disorder or illness, an intellectual or physical disability or because of intimidation or fear. That prospect is a daunting one even for an adult. This book is a very important compendium and analysis of how Irish society over the last forty years has sought to address these complex problems. It provides an incisive analysis of the legislation and case-law which are the forensic tools necessary to facilitate such witnesses in furnishing the best evidence available to courts of trial and the effect of that legislation on received legal norms.

It took a considerable time for society to recognise that the adversarial system of justice was not only inadequate in the manner in which it dealt with children and vulnerable persons but that such a process was likely having a damaging effect on them. It diminished their capacity and opportunity to deliver their testimony as fully as possible. Gradually, there was a realisation that the special needs of children and vulnerable persons required special measures whereby their ability to tell their stories and give their testimony – their ability to communicate as clearly and effectively as possible with the judge and/or jury–should be enhanced to the greatest possible extent.

In 1970, the late District Judge Eileen Kennedy produced a ground-breaking report on the inadequacies of how children were dealt with by the criminal law. In 1977 the Director of Public Prosecutions commissioned a short study by the late Denis Mitchell SC, QC, which summarised the legal principles applicable to the prosecution of young offenders. Since that time others have expanded our knowledge of how the rights of our children may be more effectively enhanced and vindicated within our system of justice in a manner consistent with our increasing understanding of child development and psychology and the many different ways other conditions affect vulnerable witnesses.

These developments were facilitated and encouraged by the international recognition of the rights of the child by the United Nations and the European Convention on Human Rights and Fundamental Freedoms, the work of the Council of Europe in this area and the acceptance of these international standards and obligations by the State. Change was not easily achieved and occurred in a somewhat piecemeal fashion. Even when statutory change was effected, it took years in some instances before the legislation was made operative and the appropriate facilities were physically provided in the courtroom. It also gave rise to a number of legal challenges in which the effect of these changes on the fairness of the criminal trial and in particular the constitutional rights of those accused of offences to challenge a witness's testimony were litigated. One such example was the Supreme Court's interpretation of legislation providing for video-link testimony and whether such a scheme would diminish the fundamental right to a fair trial in accordance with law. The Supreme Court held that the legislation struck a proportionate balance between the rights of children and vulnerable persons with those of the accused. More recently, the Court of Appeal reviewed other aspects of child testimony given by way of a visually recorded interview, and how such interviews should be conducted together with the effect of delays between such interviews and the cross-examination of the witness at trial and the use of intermediaries.

In addition these changes also required all involved within the system to educate ourselves as to how each of us should act in respect of children and vulnerable witnesses.

Judges at all levels were required to adapt their approach to children accused of offences and child and vulnerable witnesses. The District Court in many ways led the way. It has the greatest case-load involving children accused of offences. In trials on indictment, courts had to adapt procedures which were designed for the trial of adults to accord with best human rights practice in respect of children and their best interests without legislative guidance. Judges and practitioners had to learn new skills as to how children and vulnerable persons should be questioned. In fairness, many practitioners have honed and adapted their skills over the years in the conduct of examination and cross-examinations when questioning such witnesses. However, despite best endeavours it is clear that appropriate questioning was by no means the norm and in many instances lacked the insight into the negative effect that inappropriate questions and presentation of matters had on the giving of testimony by such witnesses and their welfare. It is fair to say that there is greater and continuing development at all levels of an understanding of these issues amongst criminal lawyers and judges gleaned both from growing experience and courses and guidance now available from professional bodies and the Judicial Council. The practice of law whether as solicitor, barrister or judge is always a process of continuing education.

This book is a very important step in that education and in enhancing our understanding of these issues. It chronicles and explains these ground-breaking changes -how the courts and legislature endeavoured to address the problems posed and create an environment in which the rights of the most vulnerable in society are enhanced within the adversarial criminal trial. It also highlights the problems that remain and suggests how they might be addressed in the future. This area of law presents enormous challenges for practitioners and judges and other professionals engaged with children and vulnerable persons, but more especially, for those children or vulnerable witnesses, who did not choose but are obliged to engage with the criminal justice process in a surrounding that may be both unfamiliar, intimidating and/or challenging in other ways for them. It is an area that is extremely demanding on those who work within it. In completing this work Miriam Delahunt has done an enormous service for those children and vulnerable witnesses and the legal practitioners, judges and other professionals engaged in this difficult area by providing ready access to the law which is to be found in disparate sources and statutes and offer explanations of its nature and effect in a manner that is of great practical value. She has also deftly crossed what is often seen as a divide between the professional practitioner and academia in sharing her insights into the day-to-day application of the law and identifying issues which may merit future consideration by the Oireachtas or the judiciary and the extent to which that law may require further shaping and improvement in the future.

Paul Mc Dermott
The Central Criminal Court
Criminal Courts of Justice
Dublin
16 November 2023

PREFACE

Introduction

This book came about as a result of the PhD '*Support Measures for Child Witnesses in Criminal Proceedings*', which I began in 2009 in Trinity College, Dublin, under the supervision of Dr Liz Heffernan. Since that time, the criminal courts have seen radical changes such as the implementation of recorded testimony and intermediaries as well as further legislative developments such as the Criminal Justice (Victims of Crime) Act 2017 and Criminal Law (Sexual Offences) Act 2017. As a criminal practitioner, I've been very privileged to have been either involved with or observed certain cases which have been at the forefront of changes in the way that the legal system treats vulnerable witnesses and defendants in Ireland.

Format of the Book

This book is an attempt to gather and present current information relating to vulnerable witnesses and defendants in the criminal justice system in Ireland. Questions and issues that have come up in the years since completing the PhD have been added and the goal of the book was that it would be of practical assistance. The book started out as a 'practitioner's handbook' but in order to include as much as possible that is relevant to the topic, the book has become a mixture of areas and styles. It has been divided into four parts: Investigation, Pre-Trial, Trial and General Issues and approaches in certain sections may differ greatly. For example, a large part of the chapter on preliminary trial hearings summarises the Criminal Procedure Act 2021 as it's a relatively recent legislative development with not a great deal of case law to cite as yet. However, chapters on support measures such as video link, recorded testimony and intermediaries address relevant case law in detail where such case law exists. The areas of anonymity and restrictions on reporting are an attempt to gather, in one place, the many legislative provisions and so they are listed in chronological form with the relevant legislation in the footnote for easy access. The size of a given chapter ranges from one to many pages as appropriate to the relevance and size of the content. This all gives a somewhat inconsistent and sometimes repetitious style but it is hoped that the overall book is of assistance.

References are also made to other textbooks which deal with other areas to which this book cannot do justice, e.g. sexual offences, sentencing and evidence, and so the reader will be referred to the excellent works of O'Malley, McGrath and Heffernan.

Use of the words 'victim' and 'vulnerable'

It should be noted that there is no definition of 'vulnerable witness' or 'vulnerable defendant' in the legislation in Ireland.[1] For the purposes of this book, it is a wide

1 Liz Heffernan, *Evidence in Criminal Trials* (2nd edn, Bloomsbury 2020), para 2.127: 'The term "vulnerable witness" has no formal place in Irish law although it is often used in social discussion and academic discourse. Special measures have been extended, instead, to certain categories of

definition but is dependent on legislation and case law. Legislation may provide assistance to a person under 18 so we may deem a child to be vulnerable because of his or her age. A person may be vulnerable because of an intellectual disability. A person who has been the victim of a sexual or violent offence may be vulnerable because that offence has particular characteristics which we feel, as a society, should be treated with greater sensitivity in the courts. A person may be vulnerable because he or she has personally experienced an alleged offence rather than witnessed it or committed it. A defendant may be vulnerable because although deemed fit to plead he or she may still need further assistance in order to participate fully and follow his or her trial. Unfortunately, it is not within the scope of this work to analyse and address in any depth the difficulties that a person with a physical disability must face if he or she must engage with the courts. Hopefully this may be addressed in the future.

The definition of 'victim' is contained in s 2 Criminal Justice (Victims of Crime) Act 2017 which outlines that a victim is 'a natural person who has suffered harm, including physical, mental or emotional harm or economic loss, which was directly caused by an offence.' In addition, s 30(a) of that Act inserted a new s 12 into the Criminal Evidence Act 1992 which defines victim as above and also as a family member where the victim has died and where the family member is not charged or under investigation for that death. Interestingly, s 12(2) Criminal Evidence Act 1992 now also states:

> The application of this Part (Part III of the Act- 'Evidence in Certain Proceedings') is not dependent on the commission of an offence having to be established (nor is it dependent on establishing whether the person concerned suffered any harm caused by an offence)

The use of the word 'victim' as used in the relevant legislation indicates the origin, perhaps, of the EU law on which it is based but it is a word which presupposes certain factors which appear to impact on a defendant's presumption of innocence and to that end, it is suggested, that the word 'complainant' would have been preferable in that context.

The provisions that exist for vulnerable witnesses and defendants that come before the court may overlap and sometimes there are odd exclusions and inconsistencies.

---

witness through piecemeal legislation. The groups in question include children, persons with some forms of intellectual disability, and intimidated witnesses.'

See also Criminal Justice (Withholding of Information on Offences against Children and Vulnerable Persons) Act 2012, s 1 which does include an interpretation of 'vulnerable person' as:

> 'a person (including, insofar as the offences specified at paragraph 8 of Schedule 2 are concerned, a child aged 17 years old)—
>
> (a) who—
>
> (i) is suffering from a disorder of the mind, whether as a result of mental illness or dementia, or
>
> (ii) has an intellectual disability,
>
> which is of such a nature or degree as to severely restrict the capacity of the person to guard himself or herself against serious exploitation or abuse, whether physical or sexual, by another person, or
>
> (b) who is suffering from an enduring physical impairment or injury which is of such a nature or degree as to severely restrict the capacity of the person to guard himself or herself against serious exploitation or abuse, whether physical or sexual, by another person or to report such exploitation or abuse to the Garda Síochána or both.'

In addition, while a complainant may be a witness in respect of certain legislation, a witness cannot be a complainant/victim and this may be confusing. Also, some obvious vulnerabilities are not provided for e.g., why is a child who witnesses a murder not able to avail of recorded testimony? Why are vulnerable defendants excluded in the legislation which provides support measures? Why are certain provisions such as video link and screens not included in the legislative provision which facilitates support measures for persons with an intellectual disability? Why is the use of an intermediary connected to the use of video link obliging the eligible witness or victim to give evidence through a camera?

Revised, New and Future Legislation

The Criminal Evidence Act 1992, the core legislation for vulnerable victims and witnesses and the Children Act 2001, the core legislation for child defendants, innovative and excellent as they were when enacted, need significant revision and not piecemeal amendments. The Criminal Evidence Act 1992 has been amended consistently, perhaps most significantly by the Criminal Justice (Victims of Crime) Act 2017, and is now a complicated mix of aspirational legislative goals. The wording is also confusing. When the Criminal Justice (Victims of Crime) Act 2017 expanded legislative provisions for victims for certain support measures, the legislation doesn't say 'any offence' but states 'other than a relevant' offence in certain sections. The Explanatory Memorandum of the Act confirms the expansion to all offences when it says that the relevant section 'amends the Criminal Evidence Act 1992 by extending the application of Part III — Evidence in Certain Proceedings from the current list of specified offences to victims of all offences.' The differentiation between 'relevant offence' and 'other than a relevant offence' appears to exist in order to oblige the court , in certain sections, to 'have regard to the need to protect the victim from secondary and repeat victimisation, intimidation, or retaliation' in relation to the latter offences. However, it must be questioned as to whether this type of differentiation could not be put in a more general way to avoid confusion or whether the differentiation needs to exist at all.

Existing legislation is consistently being amended with new legislation. Whatever may be said as to the necessity and use of new legislation as opposed to its political expediency, what the new provisions will definitely do is make the law more confusing as they continue to amend existing legislation. At time of writing, certain sections of the Criminal Justice (Miscellaneous Provisions) Act 2023 have been commenced amending a range of legislation. The Criminal Law (Sexual Offences and Human Trafficking) Bill 2023 and the Domestic, Sexual and Gender Based Violence Agency Bill 2023 have started making their way through the Oireachtas. New legislative proposals such as the Court Proceedings (Delay) Bill 2023, Criminal Justice (Juvenile Offenders) Bill 2023, and the Criminal Justice (Engagement of Children in Criminal Activity) Bill 2023 may or may not be enacted. At time of writing, the Garda Síochána (Powers) Bill 2021 is at a 'General Scheme' stage.

With all of this legislation, new and proposed, it is clear that practitioners and the judiciary are obliged to wrestle with on the one hand, an onslaught of new legislation which may or may not address the relevant circumstance they are dealing with. On the other, there is an absence of legislative provisions and /or guidance in certain areas. For example, there are no equivalent legislative support measures at court for vulnerable defendants as there are for vulnerable witnesses or victims. In addition, there appears to be no guidance in respect of the use of intermediaries in criminal proceedings and yet the criminal courts avail of their services on a consistent basis. The guidance that does exist for recorded testimony under s 16(1)(b) of the Criminal Evidence Act 1992, the '*Good Practice Guidelines*', was drafted in 2003 and is now in urgent need of updating.

Practitioners and the judiciary have recognised the need for, and are putting in place, greater opportunities for education and training. As Judge McDermott has stated in the foreword, the practice of law whether as solicitor, barrister or judge is always a process of continuing education. The adversarial system may be more damaging to vulnerable members of society and there are consistent media reports of those who have been through the courts criticising the effect on them. It is difficult to know how to work within such a system while ensuring no harm is caused. However, a thorough knowledge of the law and procedures may minimise confusion, errors and delays which will in turn assist the position of the vulnerable witness or defendant. While increased advocacy training has been implemented by the Honorable Society of Kings Inns and the Bar Council of Ireland, specialised training for those dealing with vulnerable persons in court is still required. Ireland has not gone down the road of 'ticketing' in terms of ensuring that prosecution counsel[2] or judges[3] have the required experience or relevant training before taking on certain cases involving vulnerable persons. But it is something we might consider when we have a situation in Ireland in which there is a significantly inconsistent range of practitioner knowledge and skill, confusing legislation and inadequate and outdated procedural guidance.

For many years, we have looked to neighbouring jurisdictions for developments in this area and many of our legislative provisions are reflective of that. We are now the only adversarial legal system in the European Union. How we reconcile these facts and chart a course for vulnerable defendants and witnesses remains to be seen. In this book, I have tried to focus on relevant Irish case law and Irish legislation. While there have been enormous changes in case law and legislation in this country, there is still a need for an overview of where we are and what we need for vulnerable witnesses, victims and defendants. We seem to be creating changes at considerable speed without consideration as to how those changes are to be resourced, whether they can be fully implemented and what impact they are having at a local and national level on witnesses, victims, defendants, practitioners and the judiciary.

Legislation which is overly specific may be too restrictive while overly general legislation places significant discretion on the trial judge which may result in an inconsistency across court rooms in different jurisdictions and counties. This balancing exercise is an impossible task. However, perhaps we are excessively dependent on our good fortune of having experienced and knowledgeable practitioners and judges who create good practices and case law which benefit both witness and defendant. Consistent and centralised legislation for vulnerable witnesses and defendants underpinned by current and detailed guidance must surely be the goal for consistent practice across Ireland in case our good fortune ever runs out.

---

2 'Every rape case that comes to the CPS (Crown Prosecution Service) is dealt with by a specialist prosecutor in a dedicated rape and sexual offences unit. Recruitment into these units is of highly trained staff, with requisite skills and experience, to ensure we deliver justice in every possible case and provide a high-quality service to victims.'
End to End Rape Review Progress Update, (Ministry of Justice December 2022).

3 CPD Authorisation of Judges, Criminal Practice Directions, England and Wales (November 2023) para.5.9, p 36.

I have hoped to state the law as accurately as possible as of the 17 November 2023 and all errors and omissions are mine and mine alone.

Miriam Delahunt
1 December 2023

ACKNOWLEDGEMENTS

I am not so much the author of this book as the conduit of it. I have had the good fortune to be exposed to the knowledge, experience and encouragement of friends and colleagues in the Law School in Trinity and the Law Library in the Criminal Courts of Justice. I have so many people to thank without whom this book would have fallen by the wayside. In naming individual people there is always a risk of failing to mention a particular person and I apologise if anyone has been forgotten. I have found that writing is a lonely, anxiety ridden and often boring process and every kind word and gesture is deeply appreciated.

From the Law School, Dr Caoimhín MacMaoláin, Catherine Finnegan, Dr Eoin O'Connor BL and Dr Neville Cox BL have been a fount of thoughtfulness and practical assistance.

I have to give particular thanks to Dr Liz Heffernan who guided me with unending patience and kindness through the PhD and I still benefit from her thoughtfulness and advice. She has set the bar very high both personally and professionally.

Will Maher BL was very inspiring and of huge practical support. He also regularly asked how the book was coming along and was very patient with the abusive responses he received.

I would also like to acknowledge the support and constructive feedback of Marc Thompson Grolimund BL who encouraged me when there was no evidence that merited encouragement. In addition, and in no particular order, thanks are due to Oisín Clarke BL, Eoin Lawlor BL, John Berry BL, Diarmuid Collins BL, Maurice Coffey SC, Mark Nicholas SC, Niamh Gaughan BL, Conor Devally SC, Ger Small SC, John Byrne SC, James Dwyer SC, Lorcan Staines SC, John Moher BL, Barry Ward BL, Ann Rowland SC, Ronan Monro SC, Seamus Clarke SC, Garnet Orange SC, Paul Carroll SC, Grainne Mullan BL, Giollaíosa Ó Lideadha SC, Cathleen Noctor SC, Niall Nolan BL, Damien Colgan SC, Patrick Gageby SC, Padraig Dwyer SC, Kevin White BL, Fiona Murphy SC and Barry Murphy BL. Noel Whelan SC was a constant source of support and a wonderful Master and I am sorry he is not here to give his usual kind-hearted feedback on this book.

I have constantly availed of the skill and kindness of Michael Bowman SC and I want to thank him for his time and knowledge.

Dean Kelly SC spent a great deal of time discussing practical issues with me which were directly relevant to the book and for that I'm in his debt. I benefited hugely from his skill and generosity of spirit.

Brendan Grehan SC has been particularly helpful and generous with his time and wisdom from the very start of the PhD right through to the publication of this book and I will be forever thankful to him.

I am so grateful to the members of the judiciary who have made such an impact on this book and these include Judge Aileen Donnelly, Judge Caroline Biggs, Judge Tony Hunt, Judge Siobhan Lankford, Judge Patricia Ryan, Judge Martina Baxter, Judge Karen O'Connor, Judge Mary Ellen Ring, Judge Mary Rose Gearty, Judge Elma Sheahan and Judge John O'Connor who I would like to thank for their expertise and kindness.

Judge Úna Ní Raifeartaigh has not only been an inspiration but an amazing source of practical help and encouragement and I am very grateful to her.

I would like to especially thank Judge Paul McDermott for his wisdom and kindness and I am honoured that he has given so much of his time to write the foreword to this book.

I am indebted to Caroline Cosgrave who has been instrumental in developing the role of intermediaries in Ireland. I am also extremely grateful to Inspector Jennifer Molony whose practical experience and kindness were invaluable.

I would like to thank Damien Grenham, Magalie Guignon, Lucy Sheridan, Wesley Smith, Sean Ryan, James Harrington, Eamonn Doherty and Michelle Smith in the Criminal Courts of Justice for their constant help and encouragement.

I am not alone in knowing David McCartney of Clarus Press to be a gifted editor and I cannot thank him enough for his kindness, patience and hard work. Marsha Swan of Clarus Press also deserves huge praise for her helpful and patient revisions and corrections as does Shane Gough for his helpful comments and typesetting the work and for Jacob McCartney for compiling the tables of cases and legislation.

Special mention must be given to Sinéad McMullan BL who read every single word of an awful, early draft and who has given me invaluable advice and practical help from the first day to the last. I owe her a debt that is impossible to repay but I am going to try.

Without Mary Delahunt Egan, Adrienne Egan, Peter Delahunt and Stephen Egan, this book would not have been possible. Their support and kindness have meant so much to me and I am only sorry that Mary is not here to see the final published book.

TABLE OF CONTENTS

PART III: TRIAL

CHAPTER 16
IDENTIFICATION AT TRIAL

CHAPTER 17
INTERMEDIARIES

PART IV: GENERAL ISSUES

TABLE OF CASES

TABLE OF LEGISLATION

[Note: Paragraph references in bold denote reproduction of the section.]

UK Secondary Legislation

Other Jurisdictions

PART I
INVESTIGATION

Chapter 1

MANDATORY REPORTING

Introduction

Legislative provisions provide for mandatory reporting of abuse in order to protect children and vulnerable persons. The Criminal Justice (Withholding of Information on Offences against Children and Vulnerable Persons) Act 2012 and the Children First Act 2015 create responsibilities for persons and organisations to report abuse, be it neglect, emotional, physical or sexual abuse.[1] **[1–01]**

Criminal Justice (Withholding of Information on Offences against Children and Vulnerable Persons) Act 2012

The Act creates a criminal offence of withholding information relating to the commission of a serious offence, including a sexual offence, against a person under 18 years or a vulnerable person. Under s 1 'Interpretation' of the Act, a vulnerable person means: **[1–02]**

> [A] person (including, insofar as the offences specified at paragraph 8 of Schedule 2 are concerned, a child aged 17 years old) –
> (a) who –
> (i) is suffering from a disorder of the mind, whether as a result of mental illness or dementia, or
> (ii) has an intellectual disability, which is of such a nature or degree as to severely restrict the capacity of the person to guard himself or herself against serious exploitation or abuse, whether physical or sexual, by another person, or
> (b) who is suffering from an enduring physical impairment or injury which is of such a nature or degree as to severely restrict the capacity of the person to guard himself or herself against serious exploitation or abuse, whether physical or sexual, by another person or to report such exploitation or abuse to the Garda Síochána or both.

The offence arises where a person knows or believes that a specified offence has been committed against a child or vulnerable person and he or she has information which would be of material assistance in securing the apprehension, prosecution or conviction of another person for that offence and fails without reasonable excuse to disclose that information as soon as it is practicable to do so to a member of the Garda Síochána.[2] **[1–03]**

---

1 For more information see Citizens Information <https://www.citizensinformation.ie/en/birth-family-relationships/services-and-supports-for-children/child-abuse/> accessed 13 October 2023.
2 Criminal Justice (Withholding of Information on Offences against Children and Vulnerable

The Children First Act 2015

[1–04] The Children First Act 2015 was enacted on 19 November 2015 and was fully commenced on 11 December 2017. The Act places additional obligations on providers of certain services to children. Mandated persons are people who have contact with children and/or families and who, because of their qualifications, training and/or employment role, are in a key position to help protect children from harm. According to the Children First guidance,[3] mandated persons include professionals working with children in the education, health, justice, youth and childcare sectors. Certain professionals who may not work directly with children, such as those in adult counselling or psychiatry, are also mandated persons. The list also includes registered foster carers and members of the clergy or pastoral care workers of a church or other religious community.

HSE Guidance on Mandatory Reporting

[1–05] HSE guidance is contained in the HSE Child Protection and Welfare Policy document.[4] This is available on the HSE website and was originally published in 2019. In addition, Children First National Guidance is available through Tusla and was published in 2017 by the Dept of Children and Youth Affairs.[5]

McGrath v HSE – mandatory reporting – historic child abuse

[1–06] In *McGrath v HSE*[6] the issue before the court in relation to s 14(1)(a) Children First Act 2015 was the statutory interpretation of mandatory reporting obligations created under that section in respect of historic child abuse. Phelan J concluded that s 14(1) imposes a reporting obligation in the following circumstances:

> a. Information has been received or acquired by a mandated person;
> b. Based on that information the mandated person has reasonable grounds to suspect that a child has been harm [*sic*], is being harmed or is at risk of being harmed.[7]

[1–07] Phelan J went on to clarify:

> Section 14(1)(a) of the 2015 Act properly construed requires that mandated persons to (sic) notify Tusla where an adult discloses past harm suffered as a child where that harm falls within the definition of harm set out in s. 2 of the 2015 Act.[8]

Persons) Act 2012. Dept of Justice, Information re Criminal Justice (Withholding of Information on Offences against Children and Vulnerable Persons) Act 2012 <https://www.gov.ie/en/publication/95eda-criminal-justice-withholding-of-information-on-offences-against-children-and-vulnerable-persons-act-2012/> accessed 13 October 2023.

[3] HSE Child Welfare Protection Policy https://www.hse.ie/eng/services/list/2/primarycare/childrenfirst/resources/hsecpwpolicy.pdf accessed 13 October 2023..

[4] ibid.

[5] *Children First: National Guidance for the Protection and Welfare of Children Dept of Children and Youth Affairs* (2017) <https://www.tusla.ie/uploads/content/Children_First_National_Guidance_2017.pdf> accessed 13 October 2023.

[6] *McGrath v HSE* [2022] IEHC 541.

[7] ibid [56].

[8] ibid [58].

Chapter 2

PRE-TRIAL IDENTIFICATION

Accommodation for a Vulnerable Witness

McGrath notes that the procedure for holding an identification parade is well settled. [1] It involves placing the suspect among eight or nine persons of the same sex and of similar age, height, appearance and dress as the suspect and who come from the same socio-economic background (termed 'foils'). The suspect or his or her solicitor can object to the composition of the parade and any reasonable objections should be addressed. If a witness indicates that he or she has made an identification, he or she will generally be asked to touch the person identified on the shoulder. McGrath notes that if a witness is a child or an old person or is frightened it will suffice if he or she makes the identification by pointing at and describing the person in question. However, in addition, certain legislative supports may be of assistance at trial. **[2–01]**

Facilitation for children and persons with a mental disorder in respect of evidence of identification during trial is provided for in s 18 Criminal Evidence Act 1992 in relation to certain offences for witnesses/victims giving evidence through video link or a screen.[2] **[2–02]**

1 Declan McGrath and Emily Egan McGrath, *McGrath on Evidence* (3rd edn, Round Hall 2020) paras 4.237, 274.

2 See 'Identification at Trial' para [16-01].

CHAPTER 3

ASSESSMENT OF VICTIM / TAKING OF EVIDENCE IN A DEDICATED SPACE

Assessment of Victim by An Garda Síochána for 'Protection Measures' – s 15 Criminal Justice (Victims of Crime) Act 2017

The Criminal Justice (Victims of Crime) Act 2017 outlines obligations to the victim making a complaint under Part 2 which includes s 7 'Information on first contact', s 8 'Information regarding investigations and criminal proceedings', s 9 'Decisions regarding prosecution of offences', s 10 'Review of decisions in relation to prosecutions'. **[3–01]**

Information in relation to the decisions regarding prosecutions of offences is examined in the DPP's *Guidelines for Prosecutors* [1] and *How to request reasons and reviews.*[2] **[3–02]**

Section 15 Criminal Justice (Victims of Crime) Act 2017 sets out the obligation of An Garda Síochána to be aware that, during investigation and beyond, support measures may be required for a victim, which may include the use of an intermediary.[3] It is the responsibility of a member of An Garda Síochána, when a complaint is made, to consider whether the witness/victim has cognitive or communication needs that will require protection measures to facilitate communication during the investigation of the offence in line with s 16 Criminal Justice (Victims of Crime) Act 2017[4] or s 17 Criminal Justice (Victims of Crime) Act 2017.[5] **[3–03]**

The Garda shall carry out on assessment of the victim for the purpose of: **[3–04]**

(a) identifying the protection needs, if any, of the victim,
(b) ascertaining whether and to what extent the victim might benefit from protection measures, and
(c) ascertaining whether and to what extent the victim might, due to his or her particular

---

1 Office of the Director of Public Prosecutions, *Guidelines for Prosecutors* (5th edn, December 2019) The Rights of Victims of Crime, ch.12, 44. <https://www.dppireland.ie/app/uploads/2021/01/Guidelines-for-Prosecutors-5th-Edition-eng.pdf> accessed 9 May 2022.

2 Office of the Director of Public Prosecutions, *How to request reasons and reviews* (November 2015) https://www.dppireland.ie/app/uploads/2022/09/English-How-to-Requets-Reasons-and-Reviews-September-2022.pdf accessed 13 October 2023

3 Criminal Justice (Victims of Crime) Act 2017, s 15, Assessment of Victim.

4 ibid s 16, Application of protection measures and special measures during investigations.

5 ibid s 17, Special measures during investigations (interviews).

vulnerability to secondary[6] and repeat victimisation, intimidation and retaliation, benefit from—

(i) special measures during the course of an investigation of the alleged offence, and

(ii) special measures during the course of any criminal proceedings relating to the alleged offence.

[3–05] Under s 15(2) A member of the Garda Síochána or an officer of the Ombudsman Commission, as the case may be, shall, when carrying out an assessment, have regard to the following matters:

(a) the type and nature of the alleged offence
(b) the circumstances of the commission of the alleged offence
(c) whether the victim has suffered considerable harm due to the severity of the alleged offence
(d) the personal characteristics of the victim, including his or her age, gender, gender identity or expression, ethnicity, race, religion, sexual orientation, health, disability, communications difficulties, relationship to, or dependence on, the alleged offender and any previous experience of crime
(e) whether the alleged offence appears to have been committed with a bias or discriminatory motive, which may be related to the personal characteristics of the victim, including such characteristics as are referred to in paragraph (d)
(f) the particular vulnerability of victims of terrorism, organised crime, human trafficking, gender-based violence, violence in a close relationship, sexual violence or exploitation and victims with disabilities.

[3–06] Under s 15(4) where a member of the Garda Síochána or an officer of the Ombudsman Commission, as the case may be, assesses that a victim has specific protection needs and that in order to protect the victim from any secondary or repeat victimisation, intimidation or retaliation—

(a) the victim would benefit from protection measures
(b) the victim would benefit from any special measure the member or officer, as the case may be, carrying out the assessment shall—
  (i) consult with the victim in relation to that assessment, and
  (ii) take into account the views of the victim in relation to any protection measures or special measures identified further to the assessment concerned.

[3–07] In relation to the assessment of a child victim, it will be presumed that he or she will have protection needs and the following factors will be taken into consideration:

(i) the best interests of the child
(ii) any views and concerns raised by the child taking into account his or her age and level of maturity
(iii) any views and concerns raised by a parent or guardian of the child or any other person duly authorised to act on his or her behalf provided that such parent, guardian or other person has not been charged with, or is not under investigation for, an alleged offence relating to the child.

S.15 (5) obliges the member of the Garda Síochána or an officer of the Ombudsman Commission, as the case may be, to report the results of an assessment referred to in subsection (4) to a member of the Garda Síochána not below the rank of superintendent

6 Criminal Justice (Victims of Crime) Act 2017, s 2, Interpretation. Secondary victimisation is interpreted in the Act as '*victimisation that occurs indirectly through the response of institutions and individuals to the victim*'.

or an officer of the Ombudsman Commission authorised for that purpose by the Ombudsman Commission, as the case may be. The contents of the assessment must be communicated to the member of Garda Síochána who is carrying out the investigation.

Section 15(9) of the Act states that 'a record shall be kept by the Garda Síochána and the Ombudsman Commission of any assessments or reports made, or directions or notifications given, under this section.' Anecdotal evidence would suggest that s.15 assessments will be examined in court as to their detail and relevance and may be challenged by the defence as to their relevance. Undue responsibility appears to be placed on a member of Garda Síochána to conduct a complete assessment of a victim which may then be challenged at court particularly in light of the complexities that such an assessment involves. However, s.15(3) does state that the extent of an assessment may be adapted having regard to the severity of an alleged offence and any apparent harm suffered by a victim. **[3–08]**

Section 19 of the Criminal Justice (Victims of Crime) Act 2017 states that where a victim has been the subject of an assessment under s 15: **[3–09]**

> the Garda Síochána or the Director of Public Prosecutions, as the case may be, shall, in determining whether to make an application to the court for a special measure specified in subsection (2) during the course of any criminal proceedings related to the alleged offence, have regard to the specific protection needs identified under section 15 in relation to the victim concerned.

This would seem to potentially limit the granting of protection measures where no assessment has been carried out or if an assessment does not pick up on a particular issues. However, it would seem inconsistent with the objective and the rights granted not only by the Act but its originating EU legislation, the EU 'Victims Directive'[7] if, where issues arise at a later stage of proceedings, an assessment and application for appropriate support measures could not be made. A person with particular communication or cognitive difficulties may mask issues to hide social discomfort and issues and an issue may not come to light during the first or only assessment by a member of Garda Síochána. **[3–10]**

It is also worth noting that s 15 allows for the wishes of the victim to be taken into account in relation to the protection measures that may be used. Anecdotal evidence suggests that this is not something that is emphasised at a later stage in proceedings and for example, there may be an assumption that a child witness will give evidence via video link rather than being physically present in the court room. This is something which practitioners should be aware of as the case progresses through the court in terms of the individual needs of the witness. **[3–11]**

Section 16, 'Application of protection measures and special measures during investigations' of the Criminal Justice (Victims of Crime) Act 2017 detail further procedures in relation to the application of protection and support measures. **[3–12]**

It may be noted that the Guideline for Prosecutors states that it is the responsibility of the prosecutor: **[3–13]**

---

[7] Directive 2012/29/EU of The European Parliament and of the Council (25 October 2012) Establishing minimum standards on the rights, support and protection of victims of crime, and replacing Council Framework Decision 2001/220/JHA.

j) To work with the Garda Síochána and the Courts Service to ensure that the victim can understand and be understood in the criminal proceedings, including having regard to the following where applicable:
   a. the assessment of the victim carried out by the Garda Síochána under section 15 of the Criminal Justice (Victims of Crime) Act 2017 including the identification of any special measures required during the course of criminal proceedings
   b. Assistance by way of interpretation and/or translation in accordance with sections 22 to 25 of the Criminal Justice (Victims of Crime) Act 2017[8]

Taking of Evidence in a Dedicated Space

[3–14] Conventional interview rooms may not be conducive for vulnerable victims in relation to the investigation of an offence and certain legislative provisions and policy documents reflect this. In addition, certain initiatives such as *Barnahus Ireland* may assist in putting the goals of the legislation into practice. [9]

Adapted premises / trained personnel – s 17 Criminal Justice (Victims of Crime) Act 2017

[3–15] Section 17, 'Special measures during investigations' outlines protections which may be implemented in respect of a victim during the course of an investigation. These include:

(a) that any interview with the victim—
   (i) be carried out in premises designed or adapted for that purpose,
   (ii) be carried out by or through persons who have been trained for that purpose, and
   (iii) where there is more than one interview, be carried out, where possible, by the same member or members of the Garda Síochána or the same officer or officers of the Ombudsman Commission, as the case may be;

(b) where the alleged offence involves sexual violence, gender-based violence or violence in a close relationship, that the victim be informed of his or her right to request that interviews are carried out by a person of the same sex as him or her.

---

8 Office of the Director of Public Prosecutions, *Guidelines for Prosecutors* (5th edn, December 2019) Responsibilities of Prosecutors to Victims in Criminal Proceedings para 12.21, 46. <https://www.dppireland.ie/app/uploads/2021/01/Guidelines-for-Prosecutors-5th-Edition-eng.pdf> accessed 13 October 2023.

9 Barnahus ('Children's House') is a recent European Union assisted initiative that allows various services to be provided in one space for children who have suffered abuse. The Barnahus Network website outlines the goal of the programme: *Barnahus works rather as a child-friendly office, under one roof, where law enforcement, criminal justice, child protective services, and medical and mental health workers cooperate and assess together the situation of the child and decide upon the follow-up.* Promise Barnahus Network, '*About Barnahus: A Scandinavian Word for "Children's House"*' https://www.barnahus.eu/en/about-us/> accessed 13 October 2023.

The pilot Barnahus project in Galway was commenced and then became operational in January 2022. The progamme as described, attempts to obtain and share information amongst relevant agencies thus limiting possible traumatisation. As outlined by Barnahus-Ireland, the objective is to widen the scheme with two additional locations, Barnahus South in Cork and Barnahus East in Dublin. The project is co-funded by the European Union and the Council of Europe, and is implemented by the Council of Europe's Children's Rights Division in co-operation with the Irish Department of Children, Equality, Disability, Integration and Youth (DCEDIY) from 12 August 2022 to 11 February 2025.

Barnahus Galway, Tusla Child and Family Agency <https://www.tusla.ie/barnahus/> accessed 13 October 2023. https://www.barnahus.eu/en/about-barnahus/> accessed 13 October 2023 Council of Europe, 'Support the Implementation of the Barnahus Project in Ireland' <https://www.coe.int/en/web/children/barnahus-ireland> accessed 13 October 2023.

s.17(2) provides that the special measures shall be made available to the victim unless there are particular reasons why this may not occur. **[3–16]**

The taking of evidence under s 16(1)(b) Criminal Evidence Act 1992

The taking of evidence under s 16(1)(b) of the Criminal Evidence Act 1992 is mentioned in certain relevant policy documents. **[3–17]**

Garda Síochána Policy

The Garda Síochána Policy on the Investigation of Sexual Crime, Crimes against Children and Child Welfare[10] states: **[3–18]**

> A number of dedicated interview suites have been secured at strategic locations throughout the country designed to provide appropriate facilities for interviewing complainants in accordance with the provisions of section 16(1)(b) of the Criminal Evidence Act, 1992. The interview suites have the capacity to record witness statements on DVD. The recording equipment produces three copies of the videorecorded interview on three DVD's. The interview suites are independently located away from Garda Stations and their locations are listed on the Garda Síochána Portal.
>
> Interviews conducted at these suites in accordance with Section 16(1)(b) of the Criminal Evidence Act, 1992 will only be conducted by trained Specialist Interviewers.
>
> The interview suites may also be used for the interviewing of complainants of other serious crime when deemed appropriate by the District Officer in charge of the investigation and in consultation with the District Officer in whose area the suite is located. The interviewing of children and persons with an intellectual disability will at all times take precedence over other interviews. The interview suites will not be used for any purpose other than the interviewing of complainants.[11]

The significance of the interview suites being independently located away from Garda stations is that hopefully a complainant or witness will feel less intimidated knowing that he or she will not be identified going into a police station to give evidence. In addition, the environment of a dedicated interview space may be less intimidating as the surroundings generally consist of comfortable couches and armchairs rather than the usual office furniture of an interview room. A less stressful environment will hopefully assist in reducing potential for further trauma and may contribute to gathering better quality evidence for the trial itself. **[3–19]**

Good Practice Guidelines

The procedural guidance for taking evidence under s.16(1)(b) of the Criminal Evidence Act 1992, the 'Good Practice Guidelines', sets out important criteria for the interview rooms/suites: **[3–20]**

> The interview suite/facilities should be located in a reasonably quiet location away from noisy traffic or other sources of local noise such as offices, toilets, banging doors, etc. It should not be possible to hear the interview in any adjoining rooms or corridors. The

---

10 Garda Síochána Policy on the Investigation of Sexual Crime, Crimes against Children and Child Welfare (2013) <https://www.garda.ie/en/about-us/publications/policy-documents/> accessed 13 October 2023.

11 ibid paras 33.4.1–33.4.3.

suite should have a carpeted floor and curtains on the windows. Ideally, the interview room should be rectangular (not square) and no larger than 5m by 4m. The furniture in the room should not convey a loud and cluttered image on the screen and should be arranged prior to the interview to maximise the camera angles and light source. It may be helpful to mark the position of the furniture on the floor for future reference.

Care should be taken to ensure that neither furniture nor toys are noisy. Children's furniture, filled with polystyrene chips (e.g. bean bags), should not be used. Care should be taken to avoid intrusive noise from any other source, for example, mobile phones, rustling papers.[12]

[12] Good Practice Guidelines for Persons Involved in Video Recording Interviews with Complainants under 14 Years of Age (or with Intellectual Disability) for Evidential Purposes in Accordance with Section 16(1)(b) of the Criminal Evidence Act, 1992, in Cases involving Sexual and/or Violent Offences (July 2003) 'Annex C, Technical Guidance 'Interview Room', paras 1V, V, p 54.

PART II

PRE-TRIAL MATTERS

Chapter 4

BAIL

Introduction

[4–01] The core principles of bail are dealt with in greater detail elsewhere.[1] However, certain aspects in relation to bail may be specific to children, such as ss 68 and 90 Children Act 2001, 'Release on bail by member of An Garda Síochána' and 'Conditions of bail'. Other provisions contained in legislation relating to bail specifically mention children and include provisions which attempt to accommodate their needs. Under s 9A of the Bail Act 1997 'Hearing the child victim or a person with a mental disorder in a bail hearing', a parent or a family member, as appropriate, may give evidence on behalf of a child victim or a victim with a mental disorder. Relevant provisions are outlined below.

Section 68 Children Act 2001

Release on bail by member of An Garda Síochána

[4–02] This section provides for station bail for a child where he or she is arrested and brought to a Garda Síochána station by a member of the Garda Síochána. In that case, the member in charge of the station may, if he or she considers it prudent to do so and there is no warrant in force, release the child on bail. A recognisance may be taken, with or without sureties, to ensure the child's next appearance in court.

Section 89 Children Act 2001

Payment of monies into court (s 5 Bail Act 1997) does not apply to children

[4–03] This section amends s 5 of the Bail Act 1997 ('Payment of monies into court') providing that this section shall not apply in relation to a person under the age of 18 years.

---

1 See Thomas O'Malley, *The Criminal Process* (Round Hall 2009); Declan McGrath and Emily Egan McGrath, *McGrath on Evidence* (3rd edn, Round Hall 2020); Liz Heffernan, *Evidence in Criminal Trials* (2nd edn, Bloomsbury 2020); Dermot Walsh, *Walsh on Criminal Procedure* (2nd edn, Round Hall 2016).

Section 90 Children Act 2001

Conditions of bail for child

[4–04] This section allows the court, when a releasing a child on bail, to make one or more of the following conditions:

(a) that the child resides with his or her parents or guardian or such other specified adult as the Court considers appropriate,
(b) that the child receives education or undergoes training, as appropriate,
(c) that the child reports to a specified Garda Síochána station at a specified time at such intervals as the Court considers appropriate,
(d) that the child does not associate with a specified individual or individuals,
(e) that the child stays away from a specified building, place or locality except in such circumstances and at such times as the Court may specify,
(f) such other conditions as the Court considers appropriate.

[4–05] If found guilty of an offence, the court can take into account any noncompliance with the conditions and the circumstance in which it occurred.

Section 100 Children Act 2001

Remand for preparation of report or other reason.

[4–06] The Court may remand a child on bail for the preparation of a report for a period not exceeding 28 days. One extension of not more than 14 days may be allowed by the Court. In addition, the report should be submitted four working days before the end of the remand period.

Section 101 Children Act 2001

Availability of child on bail for preparation of report

[4–07] Section 101 allows the court, where the child is remanded on bail, to order where the child may reside in anticipation of the report and also facilitate the attendance of the child or the person preparing the report at any location required for the preparation of that report.

Section 52 Children Act 2001

Consent of DPP not necessary for children under 14 for remand in custody or on bail

[4–08] Where a child under 14 is charged with an offence, no further proceedings other than any remand in custody or on bail, shall be taken except by or with the consent of the Director of Public Prosecutions.

Section 9 Bail Act 1997

Estreatment of recognisance and forfeiture of monies paid into court

Where bail conditions are not complied with, s 9(13) of the Bail Act 1997,[2] which deals with the estreatment of recognisance and forfeiture of monies paid into court, refers to s 110 of the Children Act 2001 '[d]efault in payment of fine, costs or compensation'[3] as alternative orders for children as opposed to those outlined in s 9 of the Bail Act 1997. **[4–09]**

Section 9A Bail Act 1997

Hearing the child victim or a person with a mental disorder in a bail hearing

Section 9A was inserted into the Bail Act 1997 by s 8 of the Criminal Justice Act 2017. **[4–10]** It allows the victim to give evidence in relation to the direct, indirect or attempted interference by the accused person with the victim or his or her family as well as the nature and seriousness of any danger to any person that may be presented by the release of the accused person on bail. Under s 9A(2), if the victim is under 14 years of age, he or she may give evidence or his or her parents may do so on his or her behalf.[4] If the victim has a mental disorder,[5] he or she or a family member[6] may give evidence on his or her behalf. Mental disorder is defined under the Mental Health Act 2001.[7]

---

2 Bail Act 1997, s 9(13):
'Where the person referred to in subsection (12) is a child within the meaning of section 110 of The Children Act 2001, non-compliance with an order under subparagraph (i) of subsection (1) or with any variation of it under subsection (10) shall be treated as a default in payment of a fine, costs or compensation under the said section 110 and the provisions of that section shall apply accordingly.'

3 Children Act 2001, s 110, Default in payment of fine, costs or compensation:
> '(1) Where a court orders a child to pay a fine, costs or compensation and the child is in default – (a) the court shall not order that the child be detained in any case where, if the child were a person of full age and capacity, he or she would be liable to be committed to prison, and (b) in lieu of such an order, the court may make one or more than one of the following orders: (i) in the case of a fine, an order reducing its amount, (ii) an order allowing time, or further time, for payment of the fine, costs or compensation, (iii) an order imposing a community sanction appropriate to the age of the child. (2) An order under subsection (1)(b) shall be deemed for the purposes of this or any other Act to be an order made on a finding of guilt.'

4 Bail Act 1997, s 9A(2)(a).

5 ibid s 9A(2)(b).

6 ibid s 9A outlines that a family member means:
> '(a) a spouse or partner of the person, (b) a child, grandchild, parent, grandparent, brother, sister, uncle, aunt, nephew or niece of the person, (c) a person who is acting in loco parentis to the person, (d) a dependant of the person, or (e) any other person with whom, in the opinion of the court, the person has a close connection'.

7 Mental Health Act 2001, s 3:
> '(1) In this Act "mental disorder" means mental illness, severe dementia or significant intellectual disability where – (a) because of the illness, disability or dementia, there is a serious likelihood of the person concerned causing immediate and serious harm to himself or herself or to other persons, or (b) (i) because of the severity of the illness, disability or dementia, the judgment of the person concerned is so impaired that failure to admit the person to an approved centre would be likely to lead to a serious deterioration in his or her condition or would prevent the administration of appropriate treatment that could be given only by such admission, and (ii) the reception, detention and treatment of the person concerned in an approved centre would be likely to benefit or alleviate the condition of that person to a material extent.'

Extern Bail Supervision Scheme for Children

[4–11] The Extern Bail Supervision Scheme[8] is an initiative based in Limerick, Cork and Dublin which allows for a bail framework providing multi-systemic therapy as an option where a child might otherwise be remanded in custody. The scheme facilitates the child's home and school routines while working to reduce criminal behaviour. The objective of the scheme is to 'prevent young people being detained in a youth justice facility and preventing them from entering further down the path of criminality'.[9]

[4–12] In *DPP v TC*,[10] O'Connor J outlined the benefits of the Extern Bail Supervision Scheme in relation to the child defendant:

> Extern is a social justice charity which was awarded a contract by the Irish Youth Justice Service [which operates as [sic] through the Department of Children and Youth Affairs] to deliver a 'Bail Supervision Scheme'. Currently, this is a pilot scheme in the Children Court Dublin, working alongside the Irish Youth Justice Service, to ensure young people on bail and their families are supported through a dedicated scheme to address their needs. The scheme provides an intensive support through the use of Multisystemic Therapy (MST), an Evidence-Based approach, which seeks to understand the factors that contribute to the young person's behaviour.
>
> MST is an internationally recognised Evidence Based Programme. MST interventions start out by identifying the causes of offending, and then builds itself around treating them. It is called 'multi-systemic' because it works across the different social systems that the young person moved in; family, school, peer group and community. MST addresses risk factors that lead to offending, and works with the family as well as the offender, coming to the family's environment in their time, and asking what the family needs. It works in the four social environments of the young person, being family, school, peer group and community. It works in the community with chronic young offenders who are detention bound. Since being admitted to Bail JC [*sic*] has worked well with the Bail Support Scheme.[11]

---

[8] Extern Bail Supervision Scheme <https://www.extern.org/bail-supervision-scheme-ireland> accessed 13 October 2023.

[9] ibid.

[10] *DPP v TC* [2017] IEDC 7.

[11] ibid [3]–[4].

Chapter 5

PRELIMINARY TRIAL HEARINGS

Introduction

The delay and uncertainty attached to applications made during a trial impacts significantly on both vulnerable victims and defendants. Prior to the introduction of preliminary trial hearings, important aspects of the trial such as the admission of evidence and the use of support measures had to be determined when the jury were in charge, ie when the trial had commenced. Where necessary, long and difficult arguments were then made in the absence of the jury who were obliged to stay in their jury room until matters had been resolved. The trial judge was obliged to consider and rule on complex issues under significant time pressures. These included not only the availability of the jury but also the trial judge's future trial calendar as well as that of the practitioners in the case at hearing. As noted by TJ McIntyre,[1] there has been significant judicial commentary in favour of preliminary hearings and the arguments for them were outlined in *Cruise v O'Donnell*[2] by Hardiman J: **[5–01]**

> It has, unfortunately, become all too common for juries to be sent away for long periods during the course of a criminal trial. Indeed, it has become quite common for a case to be opened and the jury sent away immediately while issues … are determined. The judge will normally send the jury away with some words of apology and attempt at an explanation but the fact is that the present system makes little or no attempt to minimise the time for which the jury's absence from their ordinary avocations and duties is required. We live in an era of case management, when a serious attempt is being made to deal with all litigation, civil or criminal, in an efficient manner. The most superficial consideration of efficiency will lead to the conclusion that it is considerably more efficient to deal with matters, which must by their nature be dealt with without a jury in any event, before the jury is sworn and taken away from their ordinary occasions rather than afterwards. I accord the fullest possible respect to Chief Justice Ó Dálaigh's statement about the essential unity and continuity of a criminal trial and entirely agree with it. Disposing

1 TJ McIntyre, 'Annotations to the Criminal Procedure Act 2021', Sutherland School of Law, UCD, September 2021.

2 *Cruise v Judge O'Donnell* [2007] IESC 67. The case involved preliminary examinations under s 4E Criminal Procedure Act 1967.

of evidential issues before the jury is sworn will assist and emphasise, rather from [sic] detracting from, that unity and continuity.[3]

[5–02] Attempts to resolve these difficulties have been made through practice directions and the preliminary trial hearings procedure under the Criminal Procedure Act 2021.

Pre-Trial Procedures Prior to Criminal Procedure Act 2021

[5–03] Preliminary applications and hearings under Criminal Practice Directions have existed in Ireland, in certain jurisdictions, for some time. [4] In addition, prior to the commencement of the Criminal Procedure Act 2021, pre-trial applications had been made before designated trial judges in the Central Criminal Courts. As the designated trial judge would be unlikely to overrule his or her own ruling, unless there was new evidence before the Court, there was an evident consistency in these rulings. [5] However, the value of pre-trial hearings in their previous forms has been undermined by the fact that it was possible for any matter to be re-litigated before the trial judge, there being no issue estoppel in Irish criminal law.[6] Preliminary trial hearings under the Criminal Procedure Act 2021[7] are now placed within the unity of the trial itself.[8]

Criminal Procedure Act 2021

Preliminary trial hearings

[5–04] Preliminary trial hearings under s 6 of the Criminal Procedure Act 2021 apply to indictable offences. The court may hold a preliminary hearing in respect of an indictable offence before it[9] but where the offence carries a maximum sentence of ten years or life imprisonment, if the prosecution or defence apply for a preliminary hearing, the court is obliged to hold one.[10] There is also provision for the Minister for Justice to designate other offences as requiring preliminary hearings.[11] Superior[12] and

---

[3] ibid [29]–[30].

[4] PD CC12: Pre-trial procedure – Dublin Circuit
PD CC13: Pre-trial procedure – Midland Circuit
PD CC14: Pre-trial procedure – South Eastern Circuit
PD CC27: Pre-trial directions hearings in criminal matters – Midland Circuit

[5] Miriam Delahunt, 'The Trial of Children in the Central Criminal Court' (2020) 25(1) Bar Review 19.

[6] *Lynch v Judge Moran & DPP* [2006] 3 IR 389; *Ryan v DPP* [1988] IR 232.

[7] The Criminal Procedure Act 2021 was commenced on 28 February 2022.

[8] Criminal Procedure Act 2021, s 6(14):

> 'Subject to subsection (15) and section 7, where the trial court makes an order at a preliminary trial hearing or under subsection (11) –
> (a) the order shall –
> (i) have binding effect, and
> (ii) where the court considers it appropriate and so directs, have effect as though it had been made in the course of the trial of the offence, and
> (b) without prejudice to the generality of paragraph (a)(ii), no appeal shall lie against the order, pending the conclusion of the trial of the offence.'

[9] ibid s 5, Relevant offence for purposes of Part.

[10] ibid s 6, Preliminary trial hearing.

[11] ibid s 5, Relevant offence for purposes of Part.

[12] RSC Ord 85A (under SI No 122/2022 – Rules of the Superior Courts (Criminal Procedure Act 2021) 2022 (commenced on 16 March 2022)). RSC Form 7 'Particulars of application for

Circuit Court Rules[13] have been amended to allow for preliminary trial hearings to be implemented in the courts.

Objective–'Expeditious and efficient conduct of the proceedings'

The aim of the Act is to facilitate preliminary trial hearings where the court is satisfied that it would be conducive to the expeditious and efficient conduct of the proceedings and it is not contrary to the interests of justice for the hearing to be held. Under s 6(4) of the Act, in deciding when to hold a preliminary trial hearing, the trial court must ensure that the timing of the hearing is likely to achieve the purposes of the Act in a manner that is consistent with the interests of justice and, in particular, is likely to: **[5–05]**

- facilitate the expeditious and efficient conduct of the proceedings;
- result in the least disruption to the jury and witnesses in the trial of the offence; and
- best protect the interests of any victim of the offence.

Definitions and interpretations

Part 2 of the Act relates to preliminary trial hearings and begins with ss 2 'definitions' and 3 'interpretations. Section 3(1) states that 'preliminary trial hearing' shall be construed in accordance with s 6(1), which merely states that the trial court may hold a hearing pursuant to this section. However, the detail of the overall section and in particular the assessments and orders relating to general matters under s 6(7) or more specific orders under s 6(8) allows for a wide and expansive understanding of the term 'hearing' in relation to any matter that might be relevant to the trial process. **[5–06]**

'Relevant offence' is construed under s 5 and comprises an offence which carries a sentence of life imprisonment or a maximum of 10-year imprisonment or relevant inchoate offences. **[5–07]**

'Relevant order' is significant as it is an order as to the admissibility of the evidence, including an order under or pursuant to s 16 of the Criminal Evidence Act 1992. Section 16 Criminal Evidence Act 1992 provides for the admission of pre-recorded interviews of examination in chief testimony of vulnerable complainants and witnesses. **[5–08]**

'Trial court' is to be construed in accordance with s 6(1), which outlines that it is the court before which the accused is to stand trial. **[5–09]**

Section 3(2)(a) also outlines that a reference to a person being sent forward for trial includes, where appropriate, reference to a person being sent forward to the Special Criminal Court and s 3 (2)(b) states that a reference to a trial of an accused in respect of an offence shall include a reference to a retrial of an accused in respect of an offence. **[5–10]**

---

preliminary trial hearing (pth)' and Form 8 'Notice of application to vary/discharge order made at preliminary trial hearing (pth)'.

13 RCC Ord 68C (under SI No 453/2022 – Circuit Court Rules (Criminal Procedure Act 2021) 2022 (commenced on 16 September 2022)). RCC – Schedule 2, Form 56 'Particulars of application for preliminary trial hearing (pth)' and Form 57 'Notice of application to vary/discharge order made at preliminary trial hearing (pth)'.

Application

[5–11] 'Section 4 (Part 2)' applies Part 2 in respect of proceedings where the accused has been or is sent forward for trial and the trial has not commenced. The section then applies to all trials on indictment which have not already commenced, whether or not the accused was sent forward for trial prior to the commencement of this Part.

Relevant Offence for Purposes of Part 2 of Act

[5–12] Section 5 outlines that a relevant offence is one where a person of full capacity and not previously convicted, or by virtue of any enactment or the common law, may be sentenced to imprisonment for life or a maximum term of imprisonment of 10 years or more or a relevant inchoate offence.

[5–13] Section 5(2) allows the Minister for Justice to specify an indictable offence as a relevant offence if the Minister considers that it is proper to do so for the purposes of facilitating 'the just, expeditious and efficient conduct of the prosecution of such indictable offence' and, 'in particular', for the avoidance of delays in such prosecution.

[5–14] An offence may also be specified as a relevant offence to prevent the disruption to juries and witnesses that could arise in the trial of such indictable offence where no preliminary trial hearing was held in respect of such trial or reducing the impact on victims of such indictable offence of orders to which s 6(8) applies being made during the course of the trial of the offence, where those orders could appropriately have been made at a preliminary trial hearing. In making an order under s 2 the Minister shall take into account a) the nature of the offence concerned; b) any relevant complexities that generally arise in the prosecution of such an offence.

Preliminary Trial Hearing

[5–15] Section 6 of the Act deals with the substantive provision of Part 2, ie preliminary trial hearings.

[5–16] Section 6(1) sets out that that court before which the accused is to stand trial may, of its own motion or upon the application of the prosecution or the accused, hold one, or more than one, preliminary trial hearing where the court is satisfied that:

> [i]t would be conducive to the expeditious and efficient conduct of the proceedings and it is not contrary to the interests of justice for the hearing to be held.

[5–17] It seems likely that 'the court before which the accused is to stand trial' means the jurisdictional court rather than the trial judge as provision for which judge will deal with preliminary hearings and trials is dealt with later at ss 6(12) and (13).

[5–18] Section 6(2) obliges the trial court to hold a preliminary trial hearing where the accused is charged with a relevant offence, the prosecution or the accused make an application to the court for one to be held, and no preliminary trial hearing has previously been held.

[5–19] Section 6(3) states that where a trial court directs a preliminary trial hearing to be held the hearing may be held at any time before the jury is sworn in (Circuit Court or

Central Criminal Court) or before the trial commences (Special Criminal Court). As the section says 'may', a decision to hold a hearing after the jury is sworn in or after the trial commences seems to be possible.

Section 6(4) relates to the timing of the preliminary trial hearing. The principles in determining this are that the timing of the hearing should be consistent with the interests of justice and, in particular, facilitate the expeditious and efficient conduct of the proceedings, result in the least disruption to the jury and witnesses in the trial of the offence, and best protect the interests of any victim of the offence. **[5–20]**

Section 6(5) allows for the trial court to direct that preliminary trial hearing be held as close in time to the date of the trial where it considers it appropriate and just in the circumstances. **[5–21]**

Section 6(6) allows for the accused to be arraigned at the commencement of a preliminary trial hearing where he or she has not been arraigned prior and where the trial court considers it appropriate. **[5–22]**

Section 6(7) is a general provision which allows the trial court to assess and make orders to ensure the 'just, expeditious and efficient conduct of the trial of the offence concerned' in relation to the availability of witnesses for the trial, any practical or technological equipment required for the trial, the extent to which the trial is ready to proceed, including any outstanding disclosure issues, and the likely length of the trial. This section appears to place, on a statutory basis, the ability of the trial court to assess the information before it as to what length and form the trial might take. **[5–23]**

Section 6(8) outlines more specific orders that the trial court may make: **[5–24]**

> (8) Without prejudice to the generality of subsection (7), the trial court may, at a preliminary trial hearing, make any one or more of the following orders:
>
> (a) where two or more persons are charged in the same proceedings, an order that the persons be tried separately;
>
> (b) any order that may be made under or pursuant to:
>
> (i) section 6 of the Criminal Justice (Administration) Act 1924; (Orders for amendment of indictment, separate trial, and postponement of trial)
>
> (ii) section 15A of the Juries Act 1976 (Provision for additional jurors.)
>
> (iii) section 21 or 22 of the Criminal Justice Act 1984 (Proof by written statement/formal admission)
>
> (iv) section 3 of the Criminal Law (Rape) Act 1981 (Restrictions on evidence at trials for rape offences)
>
> (v) section 13, 14, 14A, 14C, 19A or 29 of the Criminal Evidence 1992 (Video link, intermediary, screens, Protection against cross-examination by accused, disclosure of counselling notes, evidence through television link by persons outside the State.)
>
> (vi) section 39 of the Criminal Justice Act 1999 (Video link for witnesses in fear or subject to intimidation.)
>
> (vii) section 181 of the Criminal Justice Act 2006 (Anonymity of certain witnesses with a medical condition)
>
> (viii) section 67 of the Criminal Justice (Mutual Assistance) Act 2008 (Evidence via video link where criminal proceedings have been instituted in the State against a person, a witness in the proceedings is in a designated state, and it is not desirable or practicable for the witness to give evidence in person.)

(ix) section 34 of the Act of Criminal Procedure Act 2010 (Expert evidence adduced by defence.)
(x) section 21 of the Criminal Justice (Victims of Crime) Act 2017 (Questioning in respect of private life of victim)
(xi) section 25 of the Civil Law and Criminal Law (Miscellaneous Provisions) Act 2020 (Evidence through live video link[14])

(c) a relevant order; (i.e. an order as to the admissibility of the evidence, including an order under or pursuant to section 16 of the Criminal Evidence Act 1992. (Section 16 provides for the admission of pre-recorded depositions and interviews of examination in chief testimony of vulnerable complainants and witnesses.))
(d) in the case of proceedings before the Circuit Court or the Central Criminal Court, any other order that could be made by the court in the absence of the jury.
(e) in the case of proceedings before the Special Criminal Court any other order that could be made by the court during the course of the trial. This appears to be a catch all provision for non-jury trials.
(f) any other order relating to the conduct of the trial of the offence concerned as appears necessary to the court to ensure that due process and the interests of justice are observed.

[5–25] Section 6(8)(f) appears to be another catch all provision which gives the court greater latitude but relates to the conduct of the trial and the goal of ensuring due process and the interests of justice.

[5–26] Section 6(9) This provision allows for such orders with regard to the conduct of the preliminary trial hearing itself which the trial court may consider appropriate and in accordance with the interests of justice, including making submissions in writing. The Superior Court Rules have followed this by providing for procedures involving Preliminary Trial Hearing Notices.

[5–27] Section 6(10) This section allows for flexibility in relation to which judge may preside over the preliminary trial hearing and the trial itself.

[5–28] Section 6(11) Nevertheless, this section allows for the trial court to direct that a subsequent preliminary trial hearing be presided over by the same judge who presided over the previous one where it is in the interests of justice to do so.

[5–29] Section 6(12) This provision provides that where there is a relevant order at a preliminary hearing, the same judge who presided over the preliminary trial hearing shall preside over any future preliminary trial hearings as well as the trial of the offence, subject to s 6(13), which states that s 6(12) shall not apply where the original judge is not available or there is other good reason why the subsection shall not apply.

[5–30] Section 6(14) This section provides that subject to s 15 (which allows for the varying of

[14] Civil Law and Criminal Law (Miscellaneous Provisions) Act 2020, s 25:
'Evidence through live video link
(1) Without prejudice to sections 13 and 29 of the Criminal Evidence Act 1992, in an application of a type specified in section 23(2) in criminal proceedings or in an application in relevant proceedings to which section 24 applies, a person other than the relevant person may, with the leave of the court give evidence, whether from within or outside the State, through a live video link.
(2) Evidence given under subsection (1) shall be videorecorded or otherwise recorded in such manner as is provided for by the court or in rules of court.'

an order made during a preliminary trial hearing) and s 7 (which allows for an appeal by the prosecution in certain circumstances), an order made during a preliminary trial hearing shall have a binding effect and where, considered appropriate, have effect as though it had been made in the course of the trial of the offence and no appeal shall lie against the order pending the conclusion of the trial of the offence.

Section 6(15) The trial court may of its own motion or on application by the prosecution or the accused vary or discharge the order where it is in the interests of justice to do so. However, under s 6(16) an application may not be made by the prosecution or the accused, unless there has been, since the making of the order the subject of the application, a material change in circumstances relevant to that order. **[5–31]**

Section 6(17) provides that where the prosecution or the accused is seeking an order under s 6(8)(a)(b)or (c), the court shall be informed at the first available opportunity in order to facilitate the court in making a decision as to whether or not to direct that a preliminary trial hearing shall be held.[15] **[5–32]**

Section 6(18) This section confirms that nothing in s 6 affects the right of the accused to appeal against conviction in respect of an offence including insofar as any ground of appeal relates to matters arising from a preliminary trial hearing in respect of the trial of the offence concerned. This confirms the unity of the trial which now comprises preliminary trial hearings. **[5–33]**

Section 6(19) This section is without prejudice to the power of the trial court to delay matters referred to in s 6(7) or to make an order to which s 8 applies other than at a preliminary trial hearing. **[5–34]**

Section 6(20) General provision that says that the trial court in holding a preliminary trial hearing has all the powers it would have in conducting a trial, including the power to receive evidence. **[5–35]**

Section 6(21) A legal aid certificate extends to any preliminary trial hearing held in respect of the offence to which the certificate relates. **[5–36]**

Payment under criminal legal aid is a significant difference between pre-trial hearings under relevant Practice Directions and the procedure under s 6 Criminal Procedure Act 2021. The fact that extensive work could be done but not paid for under the Practice Directions hearings meant that the practice had little effect particularly in light of the fact that any ruling given might be overruled or amended by the trial judge. **[5–37]**

Appeal of Certain Orders Made at Preliminary Trial Hearing

Section 7 is a significant provision as it allows appeal of certain orders made in a preliminary trial hearing. Where evidence has been ruled inadmissible, the prosecution may appeal the matter on a question of law to the Court of Appeal or, where the order has been made by the Central Criminal Court, the Court of Appeal or the Supreme Court under Article 34.5.4° of the Constitution. Under s 7(2) the criterion for the **[5–38]**

---

15 RSC Rule 85A, r 2(2): 'Where it is practicable to do so, a PTH Notice shall be served at least two months prior to the trial.' RCC Ord 68C, r 2(2) also states: 'Where it is practicable to do so, a PTH Notice shall be served at least two months prior to the trial.'

appeal lies only where the evidence concerned is reliable, of significant probative value and where it is such 'that when taken together with the relevant evidence proposed to be adduced in the proceedings a jury, or in the case of an offence being tried before a Special Criminal Court, that court, might reasonably be satisfied beyond a reasonable doubt of the accused's guilt in respect of the offence concerned'.

[5–39] Section 7(3) sets out that the accused should be given notice of the appeal within 28 days but not later than 56 days from the day of the ruling.[16]

[5–40] Section 7(4) states that if the accused does not appear before the 'appeal court' the court may proceed to hear and determine the appeal in his or her absence.

[5–41] Section 7(5) sets out that the 'appeal court' will hear argument from counsel for the prosecution, counsel for the accused and in circumstances where the accused is not represented but counsel has been assigned to represent him or her for the purposes of the ruling under s 7(6) by that counsel.

[5–42] Section 7(6) elaborates that the 'appeal court' shall assign counsel to argue in support of the exclusion of the evidence if the accused doesn't wish to be represented or heard under s 7(5)(b).

[5–43] Sections 7(7), (8) and (9) deal with the legal aid aspects of the appeal hearing in the 'appeal court'.

[5–44] Section 7(10) states that on appeal the Supreme Court or the Court of Appeal, as the case may be, may affirm or quash the order under appeal.

[5–45] Section 7(11) sets out a number of definitions in respect of the section and of significance is the definition of 'relevant evidence', which states:

> in relation to an accused, means the proposed evidence contained in such of the following as have been served on the accused or his or her solicitor pursuant to section 4B or 4C of the Criminal Procedure Act of 1967:
> (a) the documents specified in section 4B(1)(b) of that Act;
> (b) the exhibits listed in the list of exhibits referred to in section 4B(1)(b)(vii) of that Act;
> (c) the documents specified in section 4C(1) of that Act;
> (d) the exhibits listed in the list of exhibits referred to in section 4C(1)(g) of that Act.

[5–46] The appeal in respect of an order regarding inadmissibility of evidence lies only with the prosecution. There is no similar appeal provision in respect of the accused who

[16] RSC Rule 85A, r 12: 'Where an appeal is made to the Court of Appeal under section 7 of the 2021 Act, a copy of the notice of appeal shall be lodged with the Registrar and the prosecution shall mention the matter to the Court on notice to the accused (or, where the accused is represented by a solicitor, the solicitor for the accused) as soon as practicable after notice of appeal has been given for the purposes of the making of further orders or giving of further directions consequent on the making of the appeal.' RCC Ord 68C, r 12 states: 'Where an appeal is made to the Court of Appeal under section 7 of the 2021 Act, a copy of the notice of appeal shall be lodged in the Office and the prosecution shall mention the matter to the Court on notice to the accused (or, where the accused is represented by a solicitor, the solicitor for the accused) as soon as practicable after notice of appeal has been given for the purposes of the making of further orders or giving of further directions consequent on the making of the appeal.'

must follow the normal procedural appeals mentioned in s 6(18) of the Act and which the preliminary trial hearing encompasses.[17]

Trial Not to Proceed Pending Appeal Under s 7

Section 8 of the Act provides that where an appeal has been brought under s 7, the trial will not commence until the appeal is determined or withdrawn. **[5–47]**

Power to Exclude Public

Section 9 sets out that preliminary trial hearings should be in public but gives the trial court power to exclude members of the public as well as specific persons bar members of the bona fide press and persons under relevant legislative provisions who are entitled to remain.[18] **[5–48]**

Hearings Not to be Published or Broadcast

Section 10(1) sets out clear and detailed reporting restrictions in relation to preliminary trial hearings. **[5–49]**

No information may be published or broadcast regarding a preliminary trial hearing except: **[5–50]**

> (a) a statement of the fact that such a hearing is to be, or is being, conducted, or such an appeal is being brought, as the case may be, in respect of proceedings for an offence against a named person, or
> (b) where an order has been made by the court at a preliminary trial hearing or in an appeal under section 7, as the case may be, and that court is satisfied that such publication or broadcast is not contrary to the interests of justice, a statement of the fact that such an order has been made.

This restriction will apply until the conclusion of the trial of the offence or until the trial judge or another court hearing the appeal may direct. **[5–51]**

Notice of contravention of the provision is made through application by the prosecution, to a judge of the District Court who, if it appears that s 10(1) has been contravened, may certify to that effect to the High Court. The High Court may then inquire further into the matter and may punish or take steps to punish the person concerned as if he or she had been guilty of contempt of court. There appears to be no means by which the accused can apply to a judge of the District Court for a certificate. **[5–52]**

Section 10(5) provides that this section does not affect the operation of any other enactment that imposes further reporting restrictions. The section goes on to define **[5–53]**

---

17 Criminal Procedure Act 2021, s 6(18): 'Nothing in this section shall affect the right of the accused to appeal against conviction in respect of an offence, including insofar as any ground of such appeal relates to matters arising from a preliminary trial hearing in respect of the trial of the offence concerned.'

18 See Chapter 8, p 49.

broadcast, which is the same as the definition given in the Broadcasting Act 2009, and 'publish' means to publish to the public or a portion of the public.

Rules of Court[19]

[5–54] Section 11 provides that rules of court may further specify procedural matters regarding preliminary trial hearings. However, it also allows the court to make provision in the absence of such rules.

[5–55] Such rules may include any one or more of the following:

- (a) the manner and form in which an application for a preliminary trial hearing is to be made;
- (b) the manner and form in which notice of the making of such an application is to be given;
- (c) the manner and form in which evidence is to be heard at a preliminary trial hearing;
- (d) the timing of the holding of a preliminary trial hearing;
- (e) other matters ancillary to the holding of a preliminary trial hearing;
- (f) matters ancillary to the hearing of an appeal under section 7.

[5–56] The Superior and Circuit Court Rules have been amended to facilitate preliminary trial hearings as follows:

Superior Court Rules

Rules of the Superior Courts – Order 85A

(SI No 122/2022 – Rules of the Superior Courts (Criminal Procedure Act 2021) 2022 (commenced on 16th day of March 2022))

Forms

Rules of the Superior Courts – Schedule 2

Form 7 '*Particulars of application for preliminary trial hearing (pth)*'

Form 8 '*Notice of application to vary/discharge order made at preliminary trial hearing (pth)*'

Circuit Court Rules

Circuit Court Rules – Order 68C

(SI No 453/2022 – Circuit Court Rules (Criminal Procedure Act 2021) 2022 (commenced on 16th day of September 2022))

---

19 RSC Ord 85A (under SI No 122/2022 – Rules of the Superior Courts (Criminal Procedure Act 2021) 2022 (commenced on 16 March 2022).

RSC Form 7 'Particulars of application for preliminary trial hearing (pth)' and Form 8 'Notice of application to vary/discharge order made at preliminary trial hearing (pth)'.

Circuit Court Rules – Order 68C under SI No 453/2022 – RCC (Criminal Procedure Act 2021) 2022 (commenced on 16 September 2022).

RCC – Schedule 2, Form 56 'Particulars of application for preliminary trial hearing (pth)' and Form 57 'Notice of application to vary/discharge order made at preliminary trial hearing (pth)'.

Forms

Circuit Court Rules – Schedule 2

Form 56 'Particulars of application for preliminary trial hearing (pth)'

Form 57 'Notice of application to vary/discharge order made at preliminary trial hearing (pth)'

CHAPTER 6

PRE- TRIAL EVIDENCE

Introduction

A deposition is a statement on oath of a witness in a judicial proceeding[1] and it may be admitted as evidence at trial only in specific circumstances.[2] The general legislative procedure for the taking and admission of pre-trial depositions is contained in ss 4F and 4G of the Criminal Procedure Act 1967. This includes a specific provision for the admission of a child complainant's evidence under ss 4F and 4G and s 255 of the Children Act 2001 where a judge of the District Court is satisfied on the evidence of a medical practitioner 'that the attendance before a court of any child, would involve serious danger to the safety, health or wellbeing of the child'.[3] The s 255 provision was undoubtedly prompted by the loss of the deposition procedure with the repeal of s 28 of the Children Act 1908 as well as the previous recommendation for the taking of depositions outlined in the Law Reform Commission *Report on Child Sexual Abuse*.[4] **[6–01]**

Section 16(1)(a) Criminal Evidence Act 1992

Section 16(1)(a) of the Criminal Evidence Act 1992 provides that a recording of any evidence given in relation to a relevant offence by a person under 18 years of age through a live television link in proceedings under Part IA of the Criminal Procedure Act 1967 (which includes ss 4F and 4G) will be admissible at the trial of the offence as evidence of any fact stated therein of which direct oral evidence by him would be admissible. **[6–02]**

---

1 Murdoch and Hunt, *Encyclopedia of Irish Law* (Bloomsbury 2021).

2 See generally RSC O 39; RCC O 23; RDC O 8;

3 Children Act 2001, s 255.

4 Irish Law Reform Commission, *Report on Child Sexual Abuse* (32–1990) Recommendation 7.14, 73:

> 'We recommend that the Criminal Procedure Act, 1967 should be amended to provide for the video-recording of any District Court deposition taken from a witness aged under 17 years in these cases, unless the Court, for special reason, rules that the deposition be taken in the ordinary way. The video-recording would be presented as the child's evidence at all trials on indictment, as the normal procedure, unless the court decides, on an application by the accused that, in the interests of justice and fair procedures, the child should give evidence at the trial. In that event, the evidence could be given on closed circuit television or from behind a screen.'

Sections 4F and 4G Criminal Procedure Act 1967

[6–03] Sections 4F and 4G(3) Criminal Procedure Act 1967 mirror s 16(1)(a) of the Criminal Evidence Act 1992. The sections permit a videorecording of evidence given through a live television link in proceedings under s 4F to be admitted at the trial of the offence with which the accused is charged in certain circumstances. These are outlined in s 4G(2) which states that the deposition may be admitted in evidence at the trial of the accused if it is proved that:

> (a) the witness—
> (i) is dead,
> (ii) is unable to attend to give evidence at the trial,
> (iii) is prevented from so attending, or
> (iv) does not give evidence at the trial through fear or intimidation,
> (b) the accused was present at the taking of the evidence, and
> (c) an opportunity was given to crossexamine and re-examine the witness;
> unless the court is of opinion that to do so would not be in the interests of justice.

[6–04] The recording is evidence of any fact stated therein of which direct oral evidence by the witness would be admissible. The provision contains a stipulation that it will be admitted unless the court is of the opinion that in the interests of justice the videorecording ought not to be admitted. There is a further caveat that the recording will only be admissible if the accused was present at the taking of the evidence and an opportunity was given to cross-examine and re-examine the witness.

[6–05] Both the provisions contained in s 4G(3) of the Criminal Procedure Act 1967 and s 16(1)(a) of the Criminal Evidence Act 1992 indicate that the deposition procedure under ss 4F and 4G of the Criminal Procedure Act 1967 is restricted to indictable offences and therefore does not apply to the District Court. In addition s 16(1)(a) of the Criminal Evidence Act 1992 is limited to a relevant offence as defined by the legislation.[5] It is also important to note that perjury offences attach to the provision.[6]

[6–06] The procedure under s 4F(3) of the Act includes the requirement that evidence must be taken in the presence of the accused and a District Court judge.[7] The section outlines that the witness may be cross-examined and re-examined.[8] Where the evidence is taken by way of sworn deposition, the deposition itself and any cross-examination and re-examination of the deponent (the person who has made the deposition shall be recorded), read to the deponent and signed by the deponent and the judge.[9]

---

[5] Criminal Evidence Act 1992, s 16:

> 'Videorecording as evidence at trial (1) Subject to subsection (2)(a) a videorecording of any evidence given, in relation to a relevant offence, by a person under 18 years of age through a live television link in proceedings under Part IA of the Criminal Procedure Act, 1967'.

[6] Children Act 2001, s 255(5):

> 'If any child whose evidence is taken as aforesaid makes a statement material in the proceedings concerned which he or she knows to be false or does not believe to be true, the child shall be guilty of an offence and on being found guilty shall be liable to be dealt with as if he or she had been guilty of perjury.' This offence is provided for in Schedule 2 the Criminal Justice (Perjury and Related Offences) Act 2021.

[7] Criminal Procedure Act 1967, s 4F(3)(a).

[8] ibid s 4F(3)(c).

[9] ibid s 4F(3)(d).

Section 255 Children Act 2001[10]

Power to take deposition where attendance at court would endanger 'safety, health or well being' of child victim

Section 255 of the Children Act 2001, in conjunction with s 4G(3) of the Criminal Procedure Act 1967, facilitates the evidence of a child where the health of the witness is at risk. Section 255 of the Children Act 2001 was commenced in 2002.[11] However, there are no reported cases of the provision having been used and anecdotal evidence suggests that the provision is rarely used. This may be due to a number of factors. The procedure is limited in its application, applying only to indictable offences. There may also be a reluctance on the part of practitioners to sever the testimony from the trial. This may be the case in circumstances where the pre-trial deposition procedure available at present under the Criminal Procedure Act 1967 may be of limited assistance to the child witness as it has all the characteristics of a formal trial. It is possible, though, that the format of the procedure may be modified to have a more child-friendly circumstance while maintaining all the essential characteristics of the pre-trial deposition procedure. The modifications could include personnel seated in a more informal setting, not wearing court attire, calling personnel by their first names, the introduction of toys or comfort animals into the procedure, etc. Modifications to the procedure can be done by suggestion to or by the relevant judge and under his or her auspices and so the process by which the evidence is taken can be done in a manner more conducive to the needs of the witness. **[6–07]**

In addition, with other support measures, such as screens, video link and intermediary under the Criminal Evidence Act 1992 and under the auspices of the Criminal Justice (Victims of Crime) Act 2017, it is still a procedure which may be useful in respect of certain vulnerable witnesses. There are substantial advantages to the deposition procedure. The taking of the evidence of the child witness in its entirety provides greater opportunities for more detailed evidence to be admitted at trial if such evidence was taken closer to the time of the incident. It also allows the child witness to put the incident itself behind him or her and the child will not have to wait to give evidence at trial. **[6–08]**

Reform of the deposition procedure is a moot point insofar as the procedure has been overtaken somewhat by the enactment of s 16(1)(b) of the Criminal Evidence Act 1992. It is only with the commencement of s 16(1)(b) of the Criminal Evidence Act 1992 that recorded testimony in any meaningful form has begun to be utilised in respect of vulnerable witnesses and children. There appear to be no plans as yet to place full **[6–09]**

---

10 The Children Act 2001, s 255:

> '(1) Without prejudice to section 4F of the Act of 1967, where a judge of the District Court is satisfied on the evidence of a registered medical practitioner that the attendance before a court of any child, in respect of whom an offence under this Part, or any offence mentioned in Schedule 1, is alleged to have been committed, would involve serious danger to the safety, health or wellbeing of the child, the judge may take the evidence either – (a) by way of sworn deposition, or (b) in case the evidence is to be given through a live television link pursuant to Part III of the Criminal Evidence Act, 1992, or section 39 of the Criminal Justice Act, 1999, through such a link. (2) The rules mentioned in section 4F(3) of the Act of 1967 shall apply and have effect in relation to the taking of evidence under subsection (1). (3) A deposition taken under subsection (1) or a videorecording of evidence given by a child under paragraph (b) of that subsection shall be deemed to have been taken under section 4F of the said Act of 1967, and section 4G (admissibility of deposition or videorecording) shall apply and have effect accordingly.'

11 Children Act 2001 (Commencement) Order 2002 (SI No 151 of 2002), art 2(p) (1 May 2002).

recorded testimony, including cross-examination and re-examination, on a legislative basis for the vulnerable witness. In England and Wales, recorded cross-examination under s 28 of the Youth Justice and Criminal Evidence Act 1999 has been piloted and rolled out on a national basis.[12] While examined in the *Review of Protections for Vulnerable Witnesses in the Investigation and Prosecution of Sexual Offences*, the 'O'Malley Report', full recorded testimony was not recommended due to disclosure and other issues which, according to the report, would need to be addressed before the measure could be introduced.[13]

12 'Case Management in Criminal Cases when a Witness or a Defendant is Vulnerable' (*The Advocate's Gateway*, 2 September 2019) Toolkit 1a <https://www.theadvocatesgateway.org/_files/ugd/1074f0_cbed7b4162c8468aa9cd7dc3c4ddffb6.pdf> accessed 13 October 2023.

13 Dept of Justice and Equality, *Review of Protections for Vulnerable Witnesses in the Investigation and Prosecution of Sexual Offences* (August 2020). 'The Trial of Sexual Offences' ch 6, para 6.28, 73.

CHAPTER 7

PRE-TRIAL ISSUES – VULNERABLE DEFENDANTS

Introduction

Regulation 13 'Interviews (persons under eighteen years)' Criminal Justice Act 1984 (Treatment of Persons in Custody in Garda Síochána Stations) Regulations, 1987[1] set out the protections and supports which must be given to a child during his or her arrest and detention. In relation to persons with an intellectual disability, Regulation 22 'Mentally Handicapped Persons' states: **[7–01]**

> The provisions of these Regulations relating to persons under the age of eighteen years shall apply, in addition to any other applicable provisions, in relation to a person in custody not below that age whom the member in charge suspects or knows to be mentally handicapped.[2]

Part 6 'Treatment of Child Suspects in Garda Síochána Stations' of the Children Act 2001 sets out the protections for child suspects. Section 55 states: **[7–02]**

> In any investigation relating to the commission or possible commission of an offence by children, members of the Garda Síochána shall act with due respect for the personal rights of the children and their dignity as human persons, for their vulnerability owing to their age and level of maturity and for the special needs of any of them who may be under a physical or mental disability, while complying with the obligation to prevent escapes from custody and continuing to act with diligence and determination in the investigation of crime and the protection and vindication of the personal rights of other persons.

Part 6 also outlines that children should not associate with adult detainees and should **[7–03]**

1 Criminal Justice Act 1984 (Treatment of Persons in Custody in Garda Síochána Stations) Regulations 1987 (SI No 119 of 1987) reg 13 'Interviews (persons under eighteen years)'.

2 Criminal Justice Act 1984 (Treatment of Persons in Custody in Garda Síochána Stations) Regulations 1987 (SI No 119 of 1987) reg 22 'Mentally Handicapped Persons'.

not be kept in a cell unless no other accommodation is available,[3] that the child should be notified as to the nature of the offence and his or right to a solicitor,[4] that the child's parent or guardian should be notified,[5] that the 'health board' be notified where the member in charge has reasonable cause to believe the child in custody may be in need of care or protection,[6] and that a solicitor be notified where a child has asked for one.[7]

[7–04] In relation to questioning or the taking of a written statement, s 61 of the Act states that a child shall not be questioned or asked to make a statement unless in the presence of a parent or guardian, or another adult as appropriate. However, a proviso allows for questioning or a written statement in the absence of the appropriate adult where the member in charge has reasonable grounds for believing that to delay the questioning would involve a risk of death or injury to persons, serious loss of or damage to property, destruction of or interference with evidence or escape of accomplices. An adult may be excluded where he or she may be complicit in the offence or may obstruct the course of justice. Section 62 sets out the obligations of the member in charge in relation to furnishing copies of the charge sheet and the information regarding the child suspect's first appearance in court. Section 63 provides that this information can be given to another relative or adult as appropriate. Section 64 provides that a summons may be sent to the child's parents or guardian whose presence may be required and s 65 provides that where the whereabouts of the parents or guardian are unknown, the summons may be sent to another nominated adult. Release on bail is provided for under s 68 of the Act.

[7–05] Practice Direction DC 04 for the Dublin Metropolitan District also sets out a number of objectives underpinning the legislation in respect of the treatment of children in criminal proceedings.[8] These provisions will be further reinforced by the provisions contained in the Garda Síochána (Powers) Bill, still at General Heads of Bills stage at time of publication.[9]

[7–06] The Supreme Court has noted in *People (DPP) v Wilson*:

> We accept that a person in detention is, for a variety of reasons, in a particularly vulnerable position. Apart from other potential issues, the Court of Criminal Appeal was correct in pointing out that he or she will be dependent on the gardaí for the supply of all necessary things and facilities for the duration of the detention. It is partly for that reason that the courts will give extra scrutiny to events occurring during detention, to ensure that the rights of a vulnerable person are not breached.[10]

---

3 Children Act 2001, s 56.

4 ibid s 57.

5 ibid s 58.

6 ibid s 59.

7 ibid s 60.

8 PD, DC 04, Children Court, Dublin Metropolitan Children Court, 17 January 2014 <https://www.courts.ie/content/children-court> (accessed 13 October 2023).

9 General Scheme of Garda Síochána (Powers) Bill: 'Special measures to be taken for suspects who are children, and suspects who may have impaired capacity[:] The Bill will place fundamental rights principles on a statutory basis and make provision for the use of powers in respect of children and persons with impaired capacity (whether because of an intellectual disability, mental illness, physical disability or intoxication). This is to reflect the fact that such persons may lack capacity to make decisions for themselves for example.' <https://www.gov.ie/en/press-release/6ed9f-garda-powers-to-be-modernised-and-updated-under-new-bill-from-minister-humphreys/> accessed 13 October 2023.

10 *People (DPP) v Wilson* [2019] 1 IR 96, 110.

It should be noted, however, that in *People (DPP) v Wilson*, the suspect did not have any particular vulnerabilities and the Supreme Court dismissed the appeal which had been based on a challenge to the admissibility of DNA recovered from items used by the suspect in detention. **[7–07]**

The area of arrest and detention is superbly covered in other works[11] but certain issues, recently addressed by the courts such as delay after a child has been arrested, are worth attention here. **[7–08]**

Prosecutorial Delay

The obligation for expediency where a child has been charged with an offence has given rise to significant judicial review judgments. Applications for a restraint of prosecution may be made on the basis of unfairness and, in particular, that certain statutory provisions under the Children Act 2001 will be lost when the child turns 18 years of age. The lack of legislative provisions in respect of children who 'age out' in the course of prosecution was noted in the case of *Michael Ward v Judges of the Circuit Court.*[12] The balancing of issues by the courts in terms of age at time of offence, responsibility as to delay, seriousness of offence, and whether admissions had been made or not juxtaposed with the loss of benefits under the Children Act 2001 require legislative action in order to ensure transparency and consistency. **[7–09]**

Donoghue v DPP

Blameworthy prosecutorial delay/prejudice caused by delay / public interest in prosecution

In *Donoghue v DPP*,[13] the applicant was successful in the High Court in his application for an injunction by way of judicial review to have the prosecution of a drug offence prohibited. The applicant had made immediate admissions to the charge and Birmingham J in the High Court had concluded that there had been significant, culpable prosecutorial delay in the case. The DPP appealed the ruling and the Supreme Court dismissed the appeal. **[7–10]**

Examining the High Court judgment, Dunne J observed that the trial judge, Birmingham J, had noted that had the case come before the court when it ought to have done that Mr Donoghue would have benefited from the provisions of s 93 of the Act, as substituted by s 139 of the Criminal Justice Act 2006, which provides for anonymity in respect of a child defendant. Dunne J acknowledged that the trial judge was of the view that that section was particularly significant when considered in combination with the provisions of s 258 of the Act allowing for convictions to be spent after three years in certain circumstances. Birmingham J had stated that: **[7–11]**

> The ability to expunge the record of conviction is particularly valuable if the original conviction did not and could not receive publicity.

---

11 Vicky Conway and Yvonne Daly, *Criminal Defence Representation at Garda Stations* (Bloomsbury 2023) chs 6 and 7; Garnet Orange, *Police Powers in Ireland* (Bloomsbury 2014) para 7.35.

12 [2021] IEHC 819.

13 *Donoghue v DPP* [2014] 2 IR 762.

[7–12] Dunne J went on to observe that, in addition, had the case come to court when Mr Donoghue was still a child, he would have been entitled to the benefit of s 96 of the Children Act 2001 which provides that a sentence of detention should be imposed only as a measure of last resort. He would also have had the benefit of s 99 of the Act which mandates the obtaining of a probation report where a court is of opinion that the appropriate sanction is detention.

[7–13] Birmingham J had also referred to s 75 of the Act which relates to the determination of the jurisdiction of the court to deal summarily with indictable offences and in particular to the provisions of s 75(2) which states:–

> In deciding whether to try or deal with a child summarily for an indictable offence, the Court shall also take account of –
> (a) the age and level of maturity of the child concerned, and
> (b) any other facts that it considers relevant.[14]

The delay had meant that the possibility of the matter staying in the District Court was significantly reduced.

Special duty owed to child/young person for a 'speedy trial'

[7–14] The Supreme Court found that there had been blameworthy prosecutorial delay but that, as in any such case, something more had to be put in the balance to outweigh the public interest in the prosecution of offences. In upholding the injunction preventing the DPP from prosecuting, Dunne J observed:

> The special duty of State authorities owed to a child or young person over and above the normal duty of expedition to ensure a speedy trial is an important factor which must be considered in deciding whether there has been blameworthy prosecutorial delay. That special duty does not of itself and without more result in the prohibition of a trial. As in any case of blameworthy prosecutorial delay, something more has to be put in the balance to outweigh the public interest in the prosecution of offences. What that may be will depend upon the facts and circumstances of any given case. In any given case, the age of the young person before the courts will be of relevance. Someone close to the age of 18 at the time of an alleged offence is not likely to be tried as a child no matter how expeditious the State authorities may be in dealing with the matter. On the facts of this case, had the prosecution of Mr. Donoghue been conducted in a timely manner, he could and should have been prosecuted at a time when the provisions of The Children Act 2001 would have applied to him. The trial judge correctly identified a number of adverse consequences that flowed from the delay. Accordingly, I am satisfied that the trial judge was correct in reaching his conclusion that an injunction should be granted preventing the DPP from further prosecuting the case against Mr. Donoghue.[15]

Cerfas v DPP

Certain benefits lost when child becomes adult still available at discretion of trial judge

[7–15] In the judicial review proceedings in *Cerfas v DPP*,[16] Hyland J found that there had been culpable prosecutorial delay, but that the public interest in permitting the trial

---

[14] ibid [16]–[17].
[15] ibid [56].
[16] [2022] IEHC 70.

to go ahead outweighed the disadvantage to the applicant in not having the benefit of the Children Act 2001, particularly where some, though not all, of those benefits were still available to him, albeit now at the discretion of the trial judge. The judgment detailed the effect of the prosecutorial delay and the statutory benefits, which might have been unavailable to the defendant, were detailed in the applicant's legal submissions. These included:

- a. The right to make submissions on the issue of jurisdiction i.e. to have the case dealt with summarily in the Children Court (s 75).
- b. The requirement to be accompanied to Court by parent or guardian (s.91).
- c. Reporting restrictions and requirement of anonymity (s 93 and s 252).
- d. An in-camera hearing (s 94).
- e. That any sentence should cause as little interference as possible with the child's legitimate activities and pursuits (s 96(2)).
- f. That any sentence should take the least restrictive form (s 96(2)).
- g. That detention be imposed only as a measure of last resort (s 96(2)).
- h. The stipulation that a Court may take into consideration as mitigating factors a child's age and level of maturity in determining penalty (s 96(3)).
- i. The stipulation that when dealing with a child a Court shall [sic] due regard to inter alia the child's best interests (s 96(5)).
- j. The possibility of a conditional discharge order upon a finding of guilt (s 98).
- k. The mandatory referral for a Probation and Welfare Report (s 99).
- l. The possibility of Community Sanction (s 115).
- m. The possibility of a deferment of any detention order (s 144).
- n. The prohibition on imprisonment (s 156).[17]

In considering the public interest in prosecuting the case, Hyland J noted that the applicant had made certain admissions, and also examined the nature of the offences and the injuries sustained. She observed: [7–16]

> In those circumstances, it is difficult to avoid the conclusion that it would not be in the public interest if the applicant avoided trial for this matter. In coming to this conclusion, I have considered the following factors: the length of the delay, the age of the applicant at the time of the offence and now, the fact that he would have benefited from the regime under the Children Act had the delay not taken place, the nature of the prejudice and the seriousness of the offence.[18]

Forde v DPP[19]

Section 75 Children Act 2001

Hearing re jurisdiction eligibility only up to 18 years of age

The judgment involved a consultative case stated to the High Court in relation to whether a s 75 hearing (a District Court hearing to determine jurisdiction of indictable offences[20]) could take place after the defendant had reached 18 years of age at time of charge. The case stated posed two questions as to: [7–17]

a) whether the words 'child charged' with an indictable offence appearing under s 75(1) of The Children Act 2001 included a child who was under 18 years at the time of

---

17 ibid 70 [16].
18 ibid [39]–[40].
19 *Forde v DPP* [2017] IEHC 799.
20 Children Act 2001, s 75, 'Jurisdiction to deal summarily with indictable offences'.

the date of alleged offence but over 18 years at the time of the actual charging of that offence.

b) whether the said judge was correct in determining that the words 'child charged' under s 75(1) of the 2001 Act referred to the date on which the child had been actually charged.

[7–18] In the course of the judgment, Faherty J noted that it may be the custom and practice of certain District Court judges to allow s 75 hearings to take place for an adult who was a child at the time of the offence but was satisfied that the Children Act 2001 did not require that to be the case.

> While finding as I have as to what is the plain meaning of s. 75(1), I accept entirely that it may well be the custom and practice of the Children's Court to afford the benefit of s. 75(1) to persons over 18 years of age once they were under 18 years at the time of charge. However, I am satisfied that the 2001 Act does not require that to be the case.[21]

[7–19] In answering both questions posed in the negative, Faherty J stated:

> The reference to "a child charged" in s. 75(1) of the 2001 Act does not include a child who was under 18 years of age at the time of the alleged offence but over 18 at the time of the actual charging of the alleged offence.
>
> I would also answer "no" to the second question. The reference to "a child charged" in s. 75(1) of the 2001 Act must be construed as a person who was a child at the time of charging and who is a child at the time of the s. 75(1) hearing.[22]

Furlong v DPP[23]

Loss of opportunities of s 75 Children Act 2001 not determinative

[7–20] In *Furlong v DPP*,[24] Birmingham P noted the loss of the opportunity for a s 75 of the Children Act 2001 hearing and stated:

> I approach the case on the basis that the judge was correct to conclude that if there had been a s. 75 hearing, there was a reasonable prospect of the judge in the District Court accepting jurisdiction. To the extent that the accused's solicitor and Garda O'Reilly expressed views as to what the likely outcome would have been, I take the position that both were doing so on the basis of their experience from appearing in the Children's Court, even though it was not stated expressly by Garda O'Reilly.
>
> In my view, the combined loss of anonymity and a potential s. 75 hearing does amount to a significant disadvantage. However, that conclusion is itself not determinative. In *DPP v. LE* [2020] IECA 101, I commented:
>
> > "I do accept that the loss of anonymity is a significant disadvantage. However, it is necessary to put in the balance against that the seriousness of the case..."[25]

---

21 *Forde v DPP* [2017] IEHC 799 [45].

22 ibid [60].

23 [2022] IECA 85.

24 ibid.

25 ibid [33–[34].

Where defendant contributed to delay

In *Furlong,*[26] while delay had been caused by the Gardaí, it was found that delay was also materially contributed to by the suspect. The Court of Appeal was of the view that the balancing exercise required, led to a conclusion that the interests of justice were served by permitting the prosecution to proceed. Birmingham J observed: [7–21]

> Overall, I am of the view that while there was delay on the part of the Gardaí, the chronology which played out was materially contributed to by the suspect. That being so, having regard to the seriousness of the offence and the public interest that there is in having offences of such seriousness prosecuted, I find myself coming to a different view than the judge did in the High Court. I am of the view that the balancing exercise required leads to a conclusion that the interests of justice are served by permitting the prosecution to proceed. Therefore, I would allow the appeal.[27]

DPP v LE[28]

'Pockets of delay'

Birmingham P in the Court of Appeal decision in *DPP v LE*[29] noted where, while there had been 'pockets of delay', there had been no blameworthy or culpable prosecutorial delay. The Court also held that the overall cause of the delay lay at the feet of the applicant. The applicant in that case was a minor in 2015, when she allegedly committed offences, including assault causing harm, threats to kill and violent disorder. The Court of Appeal upheld the finding of the High Court that there had been no culpable or blameworthy prosecutorial delay. This was in circumstances which concerned a complex investigation with a number of suspected offenders and no admission of guilt. The High Court had held that although there had been 'pockets of delay', when looking at the matter overall, there had been no blameworthy or culpable prosecutorial delay. [7–22]

Cash v DPP[30]

Relevant periods relating to prosecutorial delay do not include periods after defendant reaches majority

In judicial review proceedings in *Cash v DPP*[31] where the applicant was 17 years and 9 days old on the date of the offence, White J noted: [7–23]

> There was prosecutorial delay from 2nd February, 2015 up to the date of charge on 7th January, 2016. The applicant reached his majority on 8th July, 2015. I do not consider any delay subsequent to 8th July, 2015 as being relevant to the applicant's challenge in these proceedings. I would not regard the delay as significant culpable prosecutorial delay. Even if the respondent prosecuted the matter without undue prosecutorial delay, it would not have concluded by way of indictable trial by jury before the applicant's eighteenth birthday.[32]

---

26 ibid.
27 ibid [40]–[41].
28 [2020] IECA 101.
29 ibid.
30 [2017] IEHC 234.
31 ibid.
32 ibid [12].

[7–24] Similarly to *Cash*, in the case of *TG v DPP*[33] the applicant was 17 years of age at the time of the offence.

> In performing the balancing exercise mandated by the Supreme Court in Donoghue, it is necessary to weigh this prejudice against the public interest in the prosecution of offences. There are a number of aspects of the present case which point strongly in favour of allowing the prosecution to proceed. First, the offences occurred at a time when the applicant was 17 years of age. As noted in Donoghue, the age of the applicant is something to be taken into account. Secondly, the offences alleged are very serious offences. They include a charge of arson under the Criminal Damage Act 1991. The offence of arson under subsection 2(1) carries a maximum penalty of imprisonment for life. Thirdly, there is a particular public interest in the prosecution of these alleged offences as they involve a disturbance at a children detention centre. It is essential to the rule of law to ensure that discipline and order are maintained at prisons and other places of detention.

[7–25] The implications of delay and the lack of legislative provisions where a child defendant is involved was highlighted by Meenan J in the case of *Michael Ward v Judges of the Circuit Court*.[34] The matter involved judicial review proceedings in which Meenan J, in refusing the reliefs sought, examined the principle of *Donoghue v DPP* and stated:

[7–26] These principles have been applied more recently in judgments given by Simons J in *Dos Santos v DPP* [2020] IEHC 252 and *Wilde v DPP* [2020] IEHC 385. Simons J makes the observation in both that it:

> [is] surprising that the legislation (the Act of 2001) 'does not expressly address the position of an alleged offender who has transitioned from being a 'child' (as defined) to an adult between the date on which the offences are said to have occurred and the date of the hearing and determination of criminal charges arising from those alleged offences. Such an interregnum will arise in a significant number of cases, even allowing for prompt Garda investigations. …' I endorse this observation.

[7–27] In *Wilde v DPP* Simons J states:

> (4) The case law indicates that the existence of blameworthy prosecutorial delay will not automatically result in the prohibition of a criminal trial. Rather, something more has to be put in the balance to outweigh the public interest in the prosecution of offences. What that may be will depend upon the facts and circumstances of any given case. Factors to be considered include inter alia (i) the length of delay itself; (ii) the age of the accused at the time the alleged offences occurred; (iii) the loss of statutory safeguards under The Children Act 2001; (iv) the stress and anxiety, if any, caused to the child as a result of the threat of prosecution hanging over them; and (v) any prejudice caused to the conduct of the defence.[35]

Wilde v DPP[36]

Public interest issues in prosecution proceeding

[7–28] In these judicial review proceedings the case involved, amongst other issues, an attempted escape from custody in a courthouse setting and an assault on three members of An Garda Síochána. The Court held that there was a public interest in ensuring

33 [2019] IEHC 303 [70].
34 [2021] IEHC 819.
35 ibid [7]–[8].
36 [2020] IEHC 385.

the integrity of court proceedings, and the health and safety of those involved in transporting detainees to and from courthouses. It also held that it was essential to the rule of law to ensure that discipline and order are maintained at courthouses and that it would tend to undermine the rule of law if the respondent, the Director of Public Prosecutions, were to be restrained from pursuing prosecutions for offences such as those alleged in this case. This was especially so where there had been no suggestion that the applicant's ability to defend the proceedings had been prejudiced by the delay.[37]

DPP v DK, *DPP v DK* and *DPP v JS*

General outline of relevant case law

Three judgments from Barr J were published on the same date, one of which (*DPP v DK* [2023] IEHC 273) arose from a money laundering offence, and two of which (*DPP v DK* [2023] IEHC 274 and *DPP v JS* [2023] IEHC 275) concerned an assault. The judgments are extremely similar and so confusion may arise. In the first two cases, the applicant, DK, was the same person although the offences are different and occurred on different dates. In *DPP v JS*[38] the applicant was slightly younger and in that case a s 75 application was made but jurisdiction was refused. In all three cases, the applicants were successful in the reliefs sought and the prosecutions were prohibited. **[7–29]**

In *DPP v DK* [2023] IEHC 273, the applicant was charged with money laundering offences which were alleged to have occurred around April 2019 when the applicant was approximately 16 years of age. The applicant brought judicial review proceedings on the grounds of delay. Having made admissions in May 2019, the applicant was arrested in July 2020 and made further admissions. He was then charged in October 2021 having already reached his majority in February of that year. The District Court judge (Zaidan J) refused jurisdiction determining the offence to be non-minor in nature. **[7–30]**

Barr J noted the words of O'Malley J in *G v DPP* concerning minor offenders: **[7–31]**

> Children differ from adults, not just in their physical development and lesser experience of the world, but in their intellectual, social and emotional understanding. It is for this reason that it has long been recognised that it is unfair to hold a child to account for his or her behaviour to the extent that would be appropriate when dealing with an adult.[39]

Barr J differentiated the case *SA v DPP*,[40] which had been cited by the respondent, in which Hardiman J had noted that a significant factor against prohibiting the trial where there had been delay was the fact that admissions had been made. The judge found that that those *dicta* were made in a very different factual context where in a case of historic child abuse the applicant was seeking to prohibit the trial on the basis that the delay meant that he could no longer obtain a fair trial. **[7–32]**

The judge found that the respondent's submission that the loss of the right to s 75 of the Children Act 2001 was somewhat ameliorated by the fact that the District Court judge had refused jurisdiction due to the seriousness of the offence was compelling.[41] **[7–33]**

---

37 ibid [54].
38 [2023] IEHC 275.
39 [2014] IEHC 33.
40 [2007] IESC 43.
41 *DPP v DK* [2023] IEHC 273 [80]: 'Turning to the consideration of these matters in this particular case, I find that the submission that was put forward by Mr. Clarke BL in relation to the theoretical

The loss of anonymity linked with the possibility of having the convictions deemed spent under s 258 of the Children Act 2001 was very significant in this case, particularly in the current situation where a report on the internet is to all intents and purposes permanent.

> In former times, where the reporting of cases only took place in hard copy versions of newspapers, the phrase "Today's newspaper, is tomorrows fish and chip wrapping", was apposite. It meant, that for a young person who was convicted of a criminal offence in the past, when there was only reporting in hard copy news format, there was a good chance that his conviction would be forgotten within a relatively short period of time. Now, once the matter is reported on the internet, that matter will remain accessible and searchable against the person's name forever. That is a significant handicap to impose on a young person, both in his or her future employment prospects and also in the social and other aspects of his life; because a future partner, a friend, or even children and grandchildren, who do a search against his or her name on the internet, will forever be informed of the conviction. As such, I hold that the loss of anonymity is a significant prejudice for a young man in the applicant's position.[42]

[7–34] The judgment outlines the significant case law in relation to these issues. Having considered it and the issues in the case, Barr J stated:

> Notwithstanding the public interest in the prosecution of serious offences, in carrying out the balancing exercise in this case, I have come to the conclusion that the appropriate order to make is an order prohibiting the future prosecution of the applicant in this matter. I have reached that conclusion due to the fact that the applicant was considerably less than the age of majority at the time that he allegedly committed these offences; the investigation was all but complete within a short number of months after the date of the offences and no credible excuse has been forthcoming why the gardaí and the prosecuting authorities did not bring this matter to trial well in advance of the applicant attaining his majority.
>
> In the present case, the key issue is whether there was undue delay in concluding the prosecution of the case, such that the applicant 'aged out' of certain procedural benefits that would have been available to him under the 2001 Act. The fact that he made admissions, made the investigation of the offence easier for the gardaí. The making of admissions does not weigh against the applicant's case to have the trial halted because he has lost benefits under the 2001 Act due to delay on the part of the prosecuting authorities. In this case, it is accepted that the applicant did not contribute to any delay that arose in the investigation and prosecution of the case against him.[43]

[7–35] In *Yui Orobor v DPP*[44] judicial review proceedings failed to halt the prosecution where there had been a delay during which the accused had reached his majority. O'Regan J set out the factors that had to be weighed in considering whether the prosecution should continue and these included whether the matter was going to be tried summarily, the length of the interval between the date of offence and the hearing, the special duty to expedite the prosecution in respect of children or young adults, the workload of the

---

nature of the loss of the right to make a s. 75 application in this case, is compelling. Owing to the fact that the district court judge had already declined to accept jurisdiction in the case, when the DPP had consented to summary disposal of the matter; I find that on the balance of probabilities, any s. 75 application that would have been made by the applicant to have the matter dealt with summarily, would probably have been unsuccessful. Accordingly, the loss of the right to make this application, which undoubtedly arose as a result of the prosecutorial delay this case, does not in reality amount to a significant prejudice suffered by the applicant.'

42 *DPP v DK* [2023] IEHC 273 [82].

43 ibid [92]–[95].

44 *Yui Orobor v DPP* [2023] IEHC 384.

investigating Garda, the prejudice to the applicant, the complexity of the investigation, the age of the applicant at the time of the offence, the loss of anonymity, whether a fair trial might have been impaired by the delay, the public interest in prosecution of the offences, the likelihood of a non-custodial sentence, the loss of the statutory right to a probation report, whether admissions had been made, and prosecutorial delay and any prejudice arising from it. In relation to the loss of anonymity under the Children Act 2001, O'Regan noted:

> However, unlike the applicant in *JS v DPP* [2023] IEHC 275, such loss is not as oppressive or prejudicial than if the applicant since his majority had not come to the attention of An Garda Síochána or was not convicted or charged with other offences which might be recorded or reproduced in the media or online. This is not, as contended for by the applicant in submissions, an additional penalty for those subsequent offences, but rather, a reflection of the reality of the situation.[45]

It was accepted that the onus was on the applicant to tip the balance in favour of prohibition of the trial as opposed to allowing the trial to proceed. However, O'Regan J stated that, having regard to the relevant circumstances of the case, it appeared to her that the applicant had not established that the preponderance of the factors favoured a prohibition of the applicant's trial and she refused the relief sought.[46] **[7–36]**

CL v DPP[47]

Pre-emptive application for order to limit sentence unsuccessful

In *CL v DPP*,[48] Mulcahy J ruled against granting the reliefs sought in an application for prohibition on prosecution due to delay. In considering the relevant case law, and conducting a balancing exercise in relation to the public interest in prosecution against the prejudice to the defendant having turned 18, the Court held that while there had been culpable delay it was on the lower end of the scale. The Court also refused the applicant's argument that the Court should seek to ameliorate any prejudice by making an order limiting the sentencing jurisdiction of the Circuit Court to that of the District Court; the Court stated that in effect, the applicant was asking the Court to mirror certain of the potential effects of a s 75 of the Children Act 2001 hearing (in relation to whether the matter could be heard summarily). The applicant contends that the jurisdiction to make such an order exists and relies in that regard on the decision of the High Court (Hogan J) in *BG v Judge Murphy (No 2)*.[49] In that case a fitness to plead hearing was required to be carried out in the Circuit Court, although summary disposal of the case was deemed appropriate, the defendant thereby losing the advantages of any relevant sentencing provisions. The High Court made the order in order to address a legislative lacuna, which Mulcahy J noted, in refusing the application, was not the case before him which involved wholly different circumstances.[50] **[7–37]**

---

45 ibid 384[17].
46 ibid 384[18]–[19].
47 *CL v DPP* [2023] IEHC 331.
48 ibid.
49 [2011] 3 IR 748.
50 *CL v DPP* [2023] IEHC 331 [57].

PART III
TRIAL

CHAPTER 8

IN CAMERA/ANONYMITY/ REPORTING RESTRICTIONS/ EXCLUSION OF THE PUBLIC/ OTHERWISE THAN IN PUBLIC/ CLEARING OF THE COURT

Introduction

[8–01] The need to balance the requirement to have criminal trials conducted in public with that of negotiating the sensitivities in proceedings involving vulnerable witnesses and defendants is a difficult one. Article 34.1 of the Constitution of Ireland states:

> Justice shall be administered in courts established by law by judges appointed in the manner provided by this Constitution, and, save in such special and limited cases as may be prescribed by law, shall be administered in public.

[8–02] Legislation regulating anonymity and reporting restrictions is an embodiment of Article 34.1. International law, including Article 6 European Convention on Human Rights,[1] Article 10 UN Declaration of Human Rights,[2] and the EU Charter of Fundamental Rights,[3] also underpins the principle that justice must be administered in public.

[8–03] There can be confusion and overlap between the meaning of the terms of '*in camera*', 'anonymity', and 'reporting restrictions' and the range of eligible provisions. The situation is made more challenging with the advent of social media and questions such as who may be deemed to be the author of the content or the publisher. In addition, terms such as 'broadcast' and 'media' require updating in an online context.

1 European Convention on Human Rights Art 6.1: 'In the determination of his civil rights and obligations or of any criminal charge against him, everyone is entitled to a fair and public hearing within a reasonable time by an independent and impartial tribunal established by law.'

2 Universal Declaration of Human Rights Art 10: 'Everyone is entitled in full equality to a fair and public hearing by an independent and impartial tribunal, in the determination of his rights and obligations and of any criminal charge against him.'

3 EU Charter of Fundamental Rights Art 47: 'Right to an effective remedy and to a fair trial'; 'Everyone is entitled to a fair and public hearing within a reasonable time by an independent and impartial tribunal previously established by law.'

In Camera

[8–04] The term '*in camera*', literally 'in chambers', may be defined as proceedings where only the judge and the parties to the hearing are present. It has perhaps come to be used interchangeably with circumstances where the public is excluded and other parties, including members of the bona fide press, are allowed to be physically present in the court. It may then be used in place of other terms such as 'exclusion of the public' or 'otherwise than in public'.[4] As a catch-all term, *in camera* generally indicates that the case is one in which the subject matter or a party involved in the proceedings is vulnerable and so will be accorded anonymity or reporting restrictions. The term *in camera* literally signifies that only the interested parties are allowed to be present in the course of the hearing and no reporting of any aspect of the case is permitted only subject to the relevant legislative provisions.

[8–05] For a child defendant, anonymity under s 93 of the Children Act 2001 may protect him or her from public scrutiny and provide for some aspects of normal life to continue while the criminal proceedings take place. Anonymity may also significantly link to s 258 of the Children Act 2001 which allows for the expunging of convictions in certain circumstances. Without anonymity, s 258 of the Children Act 2001 would not be an effective rehabilitation mechanism.[5]

[8–06] In relation to the anonymity of vulnerable complainants and witnesses, the protections afforded by it may assist a less stressful courtroom environment, which will not only protect the witness from the distress of giving evidence but may also assist the quality of the evidence.

[8–07] Generally, the statutory provisions which provide for criminal cases to be held '*in camera*' may also use the terms 'otherwise than in public' or 'exclusion of the public'. They may provide for officers of the court, persons directly concerned in the proceedings, bona fide representatives of the press and such other persons (if any) as the judge, or 'the court', as the case may be, may in his, her or its discretion permit to remain. Parents, relatives, and support workers, as appropriate, may be permitted to remain. The Criminal Justice (Victims of Crime) Act 2017 acknowledged the evolving need for support but also of privacy by providing a general exclusion provision while extending the category of support persons who may remain.[6]

[8–08] The presence of bona fide members of the press indicates that the case may be reported

---

4 The term *in camera* was examined in the case of *DPP v WM* [1995] 1 IR 226 where Carney J considered the provisions of the then existing s 5 of the Punishment of Incest Act 1908 and whether it had survived Art 34 of the Constitution of Ireland, which provides that justice be done in public save in certain circumstances. His ruling held that it did (through the benefit of the Courts Supplemental Provisions Act 1961) and led to the establishment of the Criminal Law (Incest) Proceedings Act 1995, which has since been repealed by the Criminal Law (Sexual Offences) Act 2017.

5 *Donoghue v DPP* [2014] 2 IR 762 (SC).

6 Criminal Justice (Victims of Crime) Act 2017, ss 20(2) and 20(3), Power to exclude public: '(2) Subsection (1) is without prejudice to – (a) the right of – (i) a parent, relative or friend of the victim, (ii) a support worker of the victim's choice, (iii) where the accused person is under the age of 18 years, a parent, relative or friend of the accused person, or (iv) an appropriate person under section 18, to remain in court, and (b) the power of a court to exclude the public or any person from the court under any other enactment or rule of law. (3) In this section, "support worker" means a volunteer of, or an individual employed under a contract of service or under a contract for services by, an organisation which provides support to victims of crime.'

on, subject to legislative provisions for anonymity and reporting restrictions, such as that no information be published which may lead to the identification of the protected person.

Anonymity/reporting restrictions

Certain legislative provisions explicitly provide for the anonymity of the child, defendant or complainant. This may be further expanded in terms of 'reporting restrictions'. For example, s 252 of the Children Act 2001 provides expressly for the anonymity of a child in court proceedings in relation to any proceedings for an offence against a child or where a child is a witness in any such proceedings.[7] But the section also sets out reporting restrictions in terms of the information that may be published, ie (a) no report which reveals the name, address or school of the child or includes any particulars likely to lead to his or her identification, and (b) no picture which purports to be or include a picture of the child or which is likely to lead to his or her identification, shall be published or included in a broadcast. Additionally, under s 93 of the Children Act 2001, child defendants are entitled to '[r]estrictions on reports of proceedings in which children are concerned' but states, in similar terms to s 252, that a) no report revealing the name, address or school of any child concerned in the proceedings or including any particulars likely to lead to the identification of any such child shall be published or included in a broadcast or any other form of communication, and (b) no still or moving picture of or including any such child or which is likely to lead to his or her identification shall be so published or included. [8–09]

Exclusion of the public/ otherwise than in public

In order to both minimise the anxiety and stress of the complainant or defendant and also to ensure the anonymity of the complainant, certain provisions allow for the court to exclude persons from being physically present in the court unless they are connected with the case under the provision, eg support persons and bona fide members of the press. Section 20 of the Criminal Justice (Victims of Crime) Act 2017[8] gives the courts wider powers to exclude persons not involved with criminal proceedings from the courtroom in certain circumstances. When the public is excluded or the matter is *in camera*, signs on the doors of the courtroom should state that the proceedings are *in camera*, indicating that only persons connected with the proceedings will be permitted to be present. [8–10]

Legislative provisions

Legislative provisions providing for anonymity/reporting restrictions are taken from various Acts which may overlap depending on the nature of the offence, the age of the witness/defendant and whether the provision attaches to a complainant, witness or defendant. The provision may also lapse on the conviction of the defendant. As the relevant legislation may originate from various provisions, the following is an attempt to gather relevant provisions which may affect vulnerable witnesses and defendants. [8–11]

7 Children Act 2001, s 252 was amended by Children (Amendment) Act 2021, s 1 to allow for reporting in regard to the death of a child within certain parameters.

8 Criminal Justice (Victims of Crime) Act 2017, s 20, Power to exclude public.

Legislative Provisions – *In Camera*/ Anonymity/Reporting Restrictions

Section 7 Criminal Law (Rape) Act 1981[9]

Anonymity of complainants'

[8–12] After a person is charged with a sexual offence, nothing that might identify the complainant may be published or broadcast except as authorised by the section. The restriction may be lifted before or during the trial (if there was good reason for not doing so previously) if the judge is satisfied that the lifting is necessary to induce witnesses to come forward who may be needed at trial and that the conduct of the applicant's defence is likely to be adversely affected if the direction to lift the restriction is not given.

[8–13] The judge may lift the order if satisfied that the order for anonymity imposes a substantial and unreasonable restriction on the reporting of proceedings at the trial and that it is in the public interest to remove or relax the restriction. But the trial judge shall not give such a direction by reason only of the outcome of the trial. On conviction, a similar order may be applied for to the appellate court if required for the purpose of obtaining evidence in support of the appeal, and if the applicant is likely to suffer injustice if the direction is not given.

[8–14] The provision is activated after charge of a sexual assault offence. A 'sexual assault offence' under s 1 'Interpretation' Criminal Law (Rape) Act 1981 means:

> a rape offence, aggravated sexual assault, attempted aggravated sexual assault, sexual assault,

---

9 Criminal Law (Rape) Act 1981, s 7:

'(1) Subject to subsection (8)(a), after a person is charged with a sexual assault offence no matter likely to lead members of the public to identify a person as the complainant in relation to that charge shall be published in a written publication available to the public or be broadcast except as authorised by a direction given in pursuance of this section.

(2) If, at any stage before the commencement of a trial of a person for a sexual assault offence, he or another person against whom the complainant may be expected to give evidence at the trial applies to a judge of the High Court or Circuit Court for a direction in pursuance of this subsection and satisfies the judge –

(a) that the direction is required for the purpose of inducing persons to come forward who are likely to be needed as witnesses at the trial, and

(b) that the conduct of the applicant's defence at the trial is likely to be adversely affected if the direction is not given, the judge shall direct that subsection (1) shall not, by virtue of the charge alleging the offence aforesaid, apply to such matter relating to the complainant as is specified in the direction.

(3) If at a trial of a person for a sexual assault offence he or another person who is also charged at the trial applies to the judge for a direction in pursuance of this subsection and satisfies the judge –

(a) that the direction is required for the purpose of inducing persons to come forward who are likely to be needed as witnesses at the trial,

(b) that the conduct of the applicant's defence at the trial is likely to be adversely affected if the direction is not given, and

(c) that there was good reason for his not having made an application under subsection (2) before the commencement of the trial, the judge shall direct that subsection (1) shall not, by virtue of the charge alleging the offence aforesaid, apply to such matter relating to the complainant as is specified in the direction.

[…]

It should be noted that this section will be amended by Criminal Law (Sexual Offences and Human Trafficking) Bill 2023, s.11 when/if commenced to expand eligibility and update the definitions of 'publish' and 'broadcast'.

> attempted sexual assault, aiding, abetting, counselling and procuring aggravated sexual assault, attempted aggravated sexual assault, sexual assault or attempted sexual assault, incitement to aggravated sexual assault or sexual assault and conspiracy to commit any of the foregoing offences

A 'rape offence' under s 1 'Interpretation' Criminal Law (Rape) Act 1981 means: **[8–15]**

> rape, attempted rape, burglary with intent to commit rape, aiding, abetting, counselling and procuring rape, attempted rape or burglary with intent to commit rape, and incitement to rape and, other than in sections 2(2) and 8 of this Act, rape under section 4 [s 4 Criminal Law (Rape) (Amendment) Act 1990], attempted rape under section 4, aiding, abetting, counselling and procuring rape under section 4 or attempted rape under section 4 and incitement to rape under section 4

DPP v DH,[10] a decision of the Court of Appeal, addressed circumstances where the complainant had not been informed of her right to waive her anonymity but wished to do so. The Director of Public Prosecutions appealed to the Court of Appeal against an order of the High Court (White J), sitting in the Central Criminal Court, of 17 May 2019, as well as an appeal from an order of the same judge of 14 November 2019. The effect of the orders sought to be appealed was that there was in place a prohibition on naming the respondent, a person who had been convicted and sentenced following a trial in the Central Criminal Court for a number of offences of rape and sexual assault of a child. It was held that the orders were superfluous and ought not to have been made. It also held that if such an order was under consideration, it was appropriate that the parties would be given an opportunity to consider the matter and express views in relation to it. The Court allowed the appeal insofar as it related to the order of 17 May 2019 and the Court removed any reference in a court order to an ongoing restriction on the identification of the respondent. The judgment underlined the right of the complaint to waive his or her anonymity following the conviction of the defendant.[11] The anonymity of the defendant is protected until conviction under s 8 Criminal Law (Rape) Act 1981. **[8–16]**

Section 11 of the Criminal Law (Rape) Act 1981 'Penalty for publication of unauthorised matter' provides for the penalty in respect of the section. **[8–17]**

> 11. – (1) A person guilty of an offence under section 7(6) (including an offence under that section as applied by section 8(6)) shall be liable on conviction on indictment to a fine not exceeding £10,000 or, at the discretion of the court, to imprisonment for a term not exceeding 3 years or to both such fine and such imprisonment.[12]

Section 36 Domestic Violence Act 2018[13]

'Prohibition on publication or broadcast of certain matters'

Where a person is charged with an offence under s 33 of the Domestic Violence Act **[8–18]**

---

10 *DPP v DH* [2020] IECA 321.

11 See Orla O'Donnell '*Waiving Right to Anonymity a Difficult Choice, Survivors Say*' RTE <https://www.rte.ie/news/analysis-and-comment/2023/0730/1397066-right-to-anonymity-analysis/> accessed 13 October 2023.

12 The Irish Law Reform Commission Criminal Law (Rape) Act 1981 Annotated Act notes that a 'fine of £10,000 converts to €12,697.38'.

13 Domestic Violence Act 2018, s 36: 'Prohibition on publication or broadcast of certain matters':
'(1) Subject to subsection (2) and any direction given under subsection (4), where a person is charged with an offence under section 33, a person who publishes or broadcasts information

2018, a person who publishes or broadcasts information about, or a photograph, depiction or other representation of the physical likeness of the person charged or a dependent person of either of them that is likely to enable the identification of the relevant person or the person charged commits an offence under this Act. Section 33 of the Domestic Violence Act 2018 sets out offences in relation to the contravention of:

- a safety order
- a barring order
- an interim barring order
- an emergency barring order
- a protection order

[8–19] A relevant person under s 33 of the Act means the applicant for the order referred to in s 33(1) to which the offence relates.

[8–20] Penalties are outlined in s 37 of the Domestic Violence Act 2018:

> (1) A person who commits an offence under subsection (1) of section 36 is liable –
> (a) on summary conviction, to a class A fine or to imprisonment for a term not exceeding 12 months, or both, or
> (b) on conviction on indictment, to a fine not exceeding €50,000 or to imprisonment for a term not exceeding 3 years, or both.
>
> (2) A person who contravenes a direction or a condition specified in a direction given under subsection (4) of section 36 commits an offence and is liable – (a) on summary conviction, to a class A fine or imprisonment for a term not exceeding 12 months, or both,

---

about, or a photograph, depiction or other representation of the physical likeness of, the relevant person, the person charged or a dependent person of either of them that is likely to enable the identification of the relevant person or the person charged commits an offence.
(2) A person does not commit an offence under subsection (1) where –
(a) the relevant person consents in court to being identified or to the person charged being identified, or both, and
(b) the court, having considered the effect of identification on a dependent person of either the relevant person or the person charged, consents to that identification.
(3) If any matter is published or broadcast in contravention of subsection (1), the following persons commit an offence:
(a) in the case of matter published in a newspaper or periodical publication, the proprietor, the editor and the publisher thereof;
(b) in the case of matter published in any other written publication, the publisher thereof;
(c) in the case of matter broadcast, each person who transmits or provides the programme in which the broadcast is made and each person who performs functions in relation to the programme corresponding to those of the editor of a newspaper.
(4) The judge of the court in which proceedings for an offence under section 33 are brought may, where he or she considers that the interests of justice so require, direct that such information to which subsection (1) applies as he or she shall specify in the direction, may be published or broadcast in such manner and subject to such conditions as he or she may specify in the direction.
(5) In this section –
"broadcast" has the same meaning as it has in the Broadcasting Act 2009;
"publish" means publish, other than by way of broadcast, to the public or a portion of the public;
"relevant person" means the applicant for the order referred to in section 33(1) to which the offence relates.'

and (b) on conviction on indictment, to a fine not exceeding €50,000 or imprisonment for a term not exceeding 3 years, or both.[14]

Harassment, Harmful Communications and Related Offences Act 2020[15]

Anonymity of victim of offence under ss 2 or 3[16]

The Harassment, Harmful Communication and Related Offences Act 2020 was commenced in February 2021 and, amongst other matters, provides for offences where intimate images are shared without consent. **[8–21]**

Section 5 provides that where a person is charged in relation to ss 2 or 3 of the Act, no information, photographs or information of the victim may be broadcast. However, under s 5(2) where a judge of the court considers that the interests of justice so require, he or she may, having taken into account the views of the alleged victim of the offence, direct that such information, photograph or representation referred to in subsection (1) as he or she specifies may be published or broadcast in such manner and subject to such conditions (if any) as he or she specifies in the direction. **[8–22]**

---

[14] A 'Class A' fine means a fine not greater than €5,000 (Fines Act 2010, ss 3, 4(1)).

[15] Harassment, Harmful Communications and Related Offences Act 2020, Anonymity of victim of offence under ss 2 or 3:

> '5.(1) Where a person is charged with an offence under section 2 or 3, any person who publishes or broadcasts –
>
> (a) any information,
>
> (b) a photograph of, or a photograph that includes a depiction of, the alleged victim of the offence, or
>
> (c) any other representation of the physical likeness, or any representation that includes a depiction of the physical likeness, of the alleged victim of the offence,
>
> that is likely to enable the identification of the alleged victim of the offence, is, subject to any direction under subsection (2), guilty of an offence.
>
> (2) Where a judge of the court in which proceedings for an offence under section 2 or 3, as the case may be, are brought considers that the interests of justice so require, he or she may, having taken into account the views of the alleged victim of the offence, direct that such information, photograph or representation referred to in subsection (1) as he or she specifies may be published or broadcast in such manner and subject to such conditions (if any) as he or she specifies in the direction.
>
> (3) A direction given under subsection (2) shall be in writing.
>
> (4) A person who contravenes a direction given under subsection (2) , including a condition in such a direction, is guilty of an offence.
>
> (5) A person who is guilty of an offence under subsection (1) or (4) is liable –
>
> (a) on summary conviction to a class B fine or to imprisonment for a term not exceeding 12 months, or both, or
>
> (b) on conviction on indictment to a fine or to imprisonment for a term not exceeding three years, or both.
>
> (6) It shall be a defence for a person who is charged with an offence under subsection (1) or (4) to prove that at the time of the alleged offence the person was not aware, and neither suspected nor had reason to suspect –
>
> (a) in the case of an offence under subsection (1), that the information, photograph or other representation published or broadcast was information, a photograph or other representation referred to in that subsection, or
>
> (b) in the case of an offence under subsection (4), that the information, photograph or other representation was published or broadcast in contravention of a direction given under subsection (2), including a condition in such a direction.'

[16] Harassment, Harmful Communications and Related Offences Act 2020,
s 2 'Distributing, publishing or threatening to distribute or publish intimate image without consent with intent to cause harm or being reckless as to whether harm is caused').
s 3 'Recording, distributing or publishing intimate image without consent'

Criminal Procedure Act 2021[17]

'Hearings not to be published or broadcast'

[8–23] Section 10(1) restricts reporting in relation to preliminary trial hearings for matters under the Criminal Procedure Act 2021. No information may be published or broadcast regarding a preliminary trial hearing except:

(a) a statement of the fact that such a hearing is to be, or is being, conducted, or such an appeal is being brought, as the case may be, in respect of proceedings for an offence against a named person, or
(b) where an order has been made by the court at a preliminary trial hearing or in an appeal under section 7, as the case may be, and that court is satisfied that such publication or broadcast is not contrary to the interests of justice, a statement of the fact that such an order has been made.

[8–24] This restriction will apply until the conclusion of the trial of the offence or until the trial judge or another court hearing the appeal may direct.

[8–25] Notice of contravention of the provision is made through application by the prosecution to a judge of the District Court who, if it appears that s (10)(1) has been contravened, may certify to that effect to the High Court. The High Court may then inquire further into the matter and may punish or take steps to punish the person concerned as if he or she had been guilty of contempt of court.

---

[17] Criminal Procedure Act 2021, s 10, Hearings not to be published or broadcast:
'(1) No person shall publish or broadcast or cause to be published or broadcast any information about a preliminary trial hearing or an appeal under section 7 other than –
(a) a statement of the fact that such a hearing is to be, or is being, conducted, or such an appeal is being brought, as the case may be, in respect of proceedings for an offence against a named person, or
(b) where an order has been made by the court at a preliminary trial hearing or in an appeal under section 7, as the case may be, and that court is satisfied that such publication or broadcast is not contrary to the interests of justice, a statement of the fact that such an order has been made.
(2) Subsection (1) shall apply until the conclusion of the trial of the offence concerned or until such other time as the trial judge or the court hearing the appeal concerned, as the case may be, may direct.
(3) If, on application by the prosecution, it appears to a judge of the District Court that a person has contravened subsection (1), the judge may certify to that effect to the High Court.
(4) On receiving a certificate under subsection (3), the High Court may –
(a) inquire into the matter to which the certificate relates, and
(b) after hearing any witnesses and after considering any statement that may be offered in defence of the person alleged to have contravened subsection (1), punish, or take steps for the punishment of, that person in the like manner as if he or she had been guilty of contempt of the court.
(5) This section shall not affect –
(a) the operation of any other enactment that imposes further restrictions on the extent to which information relating to court proceedings may be published or broadcast, or
(b) any power conferred on a court by such an enactment to make an order authorising the publication or broadcast of such information.
(6) In this section –
"broadcast" has the same meaning as it has in the Broadcasting Act 2009;
"publish" means publish to the public or a portion of the public.'

Section 252 Children Act 2001[18]

'Anonymity of child in court proceedings'

Section 252 of the Children Act 2001 restricts reporting, publishing or broadcasting of any details which would lead to the identification of a child in any proceedings in relation to a child victim or a child witness. **[8–26]**

The section was amended to allow for the reporting of details in relation to children who had died following the Court of Appeal decision in *DPP v C*[19] in which the Court had interpreted the legislation as restricting the identification of a deceased child who was the victim of murder. **[8–27]**

---

[18] Children Act 2001, s 252, Anonymity of child in court proceedings:

'(1) Subject to this section in relation to any proceedings for an offence against a child or where a child is a witness in any such proceedings – (a) no report which reveals the name, address or school of the child or includes any particulars likely to lead to his or her identification, and (b) no picture which purports to be or include a picture of the child or which is likely to lead to his or her identification, shall be published or included in a broadcast.

(1A) Subsection (1) shall not apply to the publication or inclusion in a broadcast of a report or picture referred to in paragraph (a) or (b) of that subsection relating to a child where – (a) the proceedings concerned relate to the death of the child, and (b) such publication or inclusion in a broadcast would not result in a contravention of – (i) that subsection in so far as it relates to another child who is alive, or (ii) section 93.

(1B) Subsection (1) shall not apply to the publication or inclusion in a broadcast of a report or picture referred to in paragraph (a) or (b) of that subsection relating to the person against whom the offence concerned is alleged to have been committed where –

(a) the person has attained the age of 18 years on or before the date on which the proceedings commence,
and

(b) such publication or inclusion in a broadcast of the report or picture would not result in a contravention of – (i) that subsection in so far as it relates to another person, who is a child and is alive, or (ii) section 93.

(1C) Subsection (1B) is without prejudice to any other enactment or rule of law applicable to proceedings referred to in subsection (1) that operates to prohibit the publication or inclusion in a broadcast of a report or picture referred to in paragraph (a) or (b) of that subsection relating to any person.

(2) The court – (a) shall, subject to such conditions (if any) as it considers appropriate, dispense with the requirements of subsection (1) in relation to a child referred to in that subsection where the proceedings concerned relate to the death of that child unless it is satisfied that to do so would –

(i) not be in the best interests of another child referred to in that subsection who is alive, or

(ii) contravene section 93, and

(b) may, subject to such conditions (if any) as it considers appropriate, dispense with the requirements of subsection (1) in relation to a child referred to in that subsection where the proceedings concerned do not relate to the death of a child and where the court is satisfied that to so do –

(i) is appropriate having regard to the best interests of that child,

(ii) would not be contrary to the best interests of another child referred to in that subsection who is alive, and

(iii) would not contravene section 93.

(3) Where the court dispenses with the requirements of subsection (1), the court shall explain in open court why it is satisfied it should do so.

(4) Subsections (3) to (6) of section 51 shall apply, with the necessary modifications, for the purposes of this section.

(5) Nothing in this section shall affect the law as to contempt of court.'

[19] [2020] IECA 292.

[8–28] The section restricts the reporting, publishing or broadcasting of any report which reveals the name, address or school of the child or includes any particulars likely to lead to his or her identification, and any picture which purports to be or include a picture of the child or which is likely to lead to his or her identification. The section allows for the publication or inclusion of a report or picture in relation to the death of a child where the publication wouldn't result in a contravention of the section insofar as it relates to a child who is alive or a child defendant under s 93 of the Children Act 2001.

[8–29] The restrictions on reporting don't apply where the person has reached 18 on or before the date on which the proceedings commence and where any contravention wouldn't affect a child who is alive or a child defendant under s 93 of the Children Act 2001. The court may dispense with the provision but must give reasons in open court as to why it is doing so.

[8–30] The penalty provisions for a breach of s 252 are contained in s 51 of the Children Act 2001, which provides the following penalties:

(i) on summary conviction, to a fine not exceeding £1,500 or imprisonment for a term not exceeding 12 months or both, or
(ii) on conviction on indictment, to a fine not exceeding £10,000 or imprisonment for a term not exceeding 3 years or both.

Section 181 Criminal Justice Act 2006[20]

'Anonymity of certain witnesses' (medical condition)

[8–31] Where in any criminal proceedings it is proposed to call a person to give evidence and the person has a medical condition, an application may be made for an order under this section prohibiting the publication of any matter relating to the proceedings which would identify the person as having that condition.

[8–32] The order may be made where the judge concerned is satisfied that

(a) the person concerned has a medical condition,
(b) his or her identification as a person with that condition would be likely to cause undue distress to him or her, and

---

[20] Criminal Justice Act 2006, s 181:

'(1) Where in any criminal proceedings –

(a) it is proposed to call a person to give evidence, and
(b) the person has a medical condition,

an application may be made for an order under this section prohibiting the publication of any matter relating to the proceedings which would identify the person as a person having that condition.

(2) An application for such an order may be made at any stage of the proceedings and shall be made –

(a) in case the accused person has been sent forward for trial, to the trial judge,
(b) in case the proceedings are proceedings on appeal, to the judge, or a judge, of the appeal court,
(c) in any other case, to a judge of the District Court.

(3) An order under this section may be made only where the judge concerned is satisfied that –

(a) the person concerned has a medical condition,
(b) his or her identification as a person with that condition would be likely to cause undue distress to him or her, and
(c) the order would not be prejudicial to the interests of justice.'

(c) the order would not be prejudicial to the interests of justice.

There is no definition of the term 'medical condition' in the Act. **[8–33]**

The extent of the anonymity is slightly ambiguous as to whether the person called to give evidence will retain complete anonymity or whether only the facts of the medical condition remain unreported.[21] The wording of the section would imply that the circumstances will dictate to what extent the anonymity provision will apply, ie 'any matter relating to the proceedings which would identify the person as having that condition'. **[8–34]**

Section 181(8) provides for the penalty for a breach of the provision: **[8–35]**

> Each of the following persons who publishes or broadcasts any matter in contravention of an order under this section is guilty of an offence and is liable on conviction on indictment to a fine not exceeding €25,000 or imprisonment for a term not exceeding 3 years or both: (a) if the matter is published in a newspaper or periodical, any proprietor, editor or publisher of the newspaper or periodical; (b) if the matter is published otherwise, the person who publishes it; or (c) if the matter is broadcast, any person transmitting or providing the programme in which the broadcast is made and any person having functions in relation to the programme corresponding to those of an editor of a newspaper.

Section 11 Criminal Law (Human Trafficking) Act 2008[22]

'Anonymity of victims of trafficking' (also child exploitation)

Where a person is charged with an offence under ss 2 or 4, or s 3 (other than subsections **[8–36]**

---

[21] Declan McGrath and Emily Egan McGrath, *McGrath on Evidence* (3rd edn, Round Hall 2020) para 3–66, 115.

[22] Criminal Law (Human Trafficking) Act 2008, s 11, Anonymity of victims of trafficking:

'(1) Where a person is charged with an offence under section 2 or 4, or section 3 (other than subsections (2A) and (2B)) of the Act of 1998, any person who publishes or broadcasts any information, including –

(a) any photograph of, or that includes a depiction of, the alleged victim of the offence, or

(b) any other representation of the physical likeness, or any representation that includes a depiction of the physical likeness, of the alleged victim of the offence,

that is likely to enable the identification of the alleged victim of the offence, shall, subject to any direction under subsection (2), be guilty of an offence and shall be liable upon conviction on indictment to a fine, or imprisonment for a term not exceeding 10 years, or both.

(2) The judge of the court in which proceedings for an offence under section 2 or 4, or section 3 (other than subsections (2A) and (2B)) of the Act of 1998, are brought may, where he or she considers that the interests of justice so require, direct that such information to which subsection (1) applies as he or she shall specify in the direction may be published or broadcast in such manner and subject to such conditions as he or she may specify in the direction.

(3) A direction under this section shall be in writing.

(4) A person who contravenes a direction under this section, including a condition in such a direction, shall be guilty of an offence and shall be liable upon conviction on indictment to a fine, or imprisonment for a term not exceeding 10 years, or both.

(5) In this section –

"broadcasts" means transmits, relays or distributes by wireless telegraphy or by any other means, or by wireless telegraphy in conjunction with any other means, of communications, sounds, signs, visual images or signals intended for reception by any person whether such communications, sounds, signs, visual images or signals are received by that person or not;

(2A) and (2B)) of the Child Trafficking and Pornography Act 1998, any person who publishes or broadcasts any information, including (a) any photograph of, or that includes a depiction of, the alleged victim of the offence, or (b) any other representation of the physical likeness, or any representation that includes a depiction of the physical likeness, of the alleged victim of the offence, that is likely to enable the identification of the alleged victim of the offence, shall, subject to any direction under subsection (2), 'be guilty of an offence and shall be liable upon conviction on indictment to a fine, or imprisonment for a term not exceeding 10 years, or both.'

[8–37] The relevant provisions are:

- Section 2 Criminal Law (Human Trafficking) Act 2008 – 'Trafficking, etc., of children';
- Section 4 Criminal Law (Human Trafficking) Act 2008 – 'Trafficking of persons other than children';
- Section 3 Child Trafficking and Pornography Act 1998 (other than 2A and 2B of the Act) – 'Child trafficking and taking, etc., child for sexual exploitation'.

[8–38] Section 11(4) of the Criminal Law (Human Trafficking) Act 2008 contains the provisions that a person who contravenes a direction under this section, including a condition in such a direction, shall be guilty of an offence and shall be liable upon conviction on indictment to a fine, or imprisonment for a term not exceeding 10 years, or both.

[8–39] It should be noted that s 3(2)(a) of the Child Trafficking and Pornography Act 1998 (other than 2A and 2B of the Act) – 'Child trafficking and taking, etc., child for sexual exploitation' created the offence of child exploitation.[23]

Section 30 Criminal Law (Sexual Offences) Act 2017 (Punishment of Incest Act 1908)[24]

'Anonymity of person charged with offence under Act of 1908 and person to whom offence relates'

[8–40] After a person is charged with an offence under the Punishment of Incest Act 1908,

---

"publishes" means publishes to any person, and includes publishes on the internet'.

23 *DPP v LS and PS* [2021] IECA 308.

24 Criminal Law Sexual Offences Act 2017, s 30, Anonymity of person charged with offence under Act of 1908 and person to whom offence relates:

'(1) Subject to subsection (4), after a person is charged with an offence under the Act of 1908 no matter likely to lead members of the public to identify that person as the person charged or to identify any other person as a person in relation to whom the offence is alleged to have been committed shall be published in a publication available to the public or broadcast.

(2) If any matter is published or broadcast in contravention of subsection (1), the following persons shall be guilty of an offence namely:

(a) in the case of matter published in a newspaper or periodical publication, the proprietor, the editor and the publisher thereof;

(b) in the case of matter published in any other publication, the publisher thereof; and

(c) in the case of matter broadcast, any person who transmits or provides the programme in which the broadcast is made and any person who performs functions in relation to the programme corresponding to those of the editor of a newspaper.

(3) Nothing in this section shall be construed as –

no matter likely to lead members of the public to identify that person as the person charged, or to identify any other person as a person in relation to whom the offence is alleged to have been committed, shall be published or broadcast.

Where a person is charged with an offence under the Punishment of Incest Act 1908 and also a sexual assault offence, and the offence under the 1908 Act is not proceeded with or if the person is acquitted of it and no appeal is taken, then ss 7 ('anonymity of complainants') and 8 ('anonymity of defendants') of the Criminal Law (Rape) Act 1981 shall apply as if the charge under the 1908 Act had not been brought. **[8–41]**

The Criminal Law (Incest Proceedings) Act 1995 has been repealed under s 32 of the Criminal Law (Sexual Offences) Act 2017[25] and so s 2 of the Criminal Law (Incest Proceedings) Act 1995, which provided for the exclusion of public from hearings under the 1908 Act, is no longer relevant to those offences. **[8–42]**

Penalties for s 31 are contained in s 31 of the Criminal Law (Sexual Offences) Act 2017: **[8–43]**

> (1) A person guilty of an offence under section 30 shall be liable –
> (a) on summary conviction, to a class B fine or to imprisonment for a term not exceeding 12 months or both, or
> (b) on conviction on indictment, to a fine or to imprisonment for a term not exceeding 3 years or both.
>
> (2) It shall be a defence for a person who is charged with an offence under section 30 to prove that at the time of the alleged offence the person was not aware, and neither suspected nor had reason to suspect, that the matter alleged to have been published or broadcast was a matter specified in the said section 30.

(a) prohibiting the publication or broadcast of matter consisting only of a report of legal proceedings other than proceedings at, or intended to lead to, or an appeal arising out of, a trial of a person for an offence under the Act of 1908, or

(b) affecting any prohibition or restriction imposed by virtue of any other enactment upon the publication or broadcasting of any matter.

(4) Notwithstanding the provisions of subsection (1), where a person is charged with both an offence under the Act of 1908 and a sexual assault offence and the charge relating to an offence under the Act of 1908 is not proceeded with or the person is acquitted of the charge under the Act of 1908 and no appeal is taken under section 23 of the Criminal Procedure Act 2010, the provisions of sections 7 and 8 of the Act of 1981 shall apply as if the charge under the Act of 1908 had not been brought.

(5) In this section –

"a sexual assault offence" has the meaning assigned to it by section 1(1) of the Act of 1981 (amended by section 12 of the Act of 1990);

"broadcast" means the transmission, relaying or distribution by wireless telegraphy or by any other means or by wireless telegraphy in conjunction with any other means of communications, sounds, signs, visual images or signals, intended for direct reception by the general public whether such communications, sounds, signs, visual images or signals are actually received or not;

"published" means published to any person, and includes published on the internet;

"publication" includes a film, sound track or any other record in permanent form (including a record that is not in a legible form but which is capable of being reproduced in a legible form) but does not include an indictment or other document prepared for use in particular legal proceedings.'

[25] Part 5 'Incest' (ss 28–32) Criminal Law (Sexual Offences) Act 2017 was commenced on 2 September 2019 (SI No 434/2019).

Section 10A Non-Fatal Offences Against the Person Act 1997[26] as inserted by Section 24 Criminal Justice (Miscellaneous Provisions) Act 2023

'Prohibition on publication or broadcast of certain material' (harassment or stalking)

[8–44] Section 10A provides anonymity protections in respect of s 10 Non-Fatal Offences Against the Person Act 1997. Previously, the latter section dealt with the offence of harassment. However, s 23 Criminal Justice (Miscellaneous Provisions) Act 2023 will widen the offence to include stalking.[27]

Section 46 Criminal Justice (Miscellaneous Provisions) Act 2023

'Prohibition on publication or broadcast of certain material relating to offence under section 44'

[8–45] Section 44 of the Criminal Justice (Miscellaneous Provisions) Act 2023, when commenced, provides the offence for a contravention of a civil order in respect of 'relevant conduct' under s 27 of the Act. Section 46 provides anonymity in respect of those proceedings. 'Relevant conduct' is outlined under s 27 as:

> conduct engaged in, without lawful authority or reasonable excuse, by the respondent towards the applicant or, where relevant, a person connected to the applicant, that would reasonably be considered likely to cause the applicant—
>
> (a) to fear that violence will be used against the applicant or person, or
>
> (b) serious alarm or distress that has a substantial adverse impact on his or her usual day-to-day activities.

---

[26] Non-Fatal Offences Against the Person Act 1997, s 10A.

s.10A (1) Subject to this section, a person (other than the alleged victim) who, where a person is charged with an offence under section 10, publishes or broadcasts identifying material shall be guilty of an offence.

(2) Subsection (1) shall not apply where the alleged victim consents in court to being identified.

(3) The court in which proceedings for the offence are brought may, where satisfied that it is in the interests of justice to do so, direct that such information, photograph, depiction or other representation to which subsection (1) applies as the court may specify may be published or broadcast in such manner, and subject to such conditions, as may be specified in the direction.

(4) Before giving a direction under subsection (3), the court shall take into account—

(a) the views of the alleged victim, and

(b) the nature or circumstances of the case, and in particular the effect of the publication or broadcast concerned on the alleged victim.

(5) A direction given under subsection (3) shall be in writing.

(6) A person who contravenes the terms of a direction given under subsection (3) shall be guilty of an offence.

(7) A person who is guilty of an offence under subsection (1) or (6) is liable—

(a) on summary conviction to a class B fine or to imprisonment for a term not exceeding 12 months, or both, or

(b) on conviction on indictment to a fine or to imprisonment for a term not exceeding three years, or both.

[27] Non-Fatal Offences Against the Person Act 1997 as amended by Criminal Justice (Miscellaneous Provisions) Act 2023, s 23 'Harassment or stalking'.

Section 55 Criminal Justice (Miscellaneous Provisions) Act 2023

'Anonymity of witnesses in criminal proceedings'

Part 7, s 55 of the Criminal Justice (Miscellaneous Provisions) Act 2023, when commenced, provides a general anonymity provision which applies in criminal proceedings. It provides the trial court with wide discretionary powers in terms of what anonymity measures may be applied to proceedings. **[8–46]**

Section 55 (1) states: **[8–47]**

> Without prejudice to any enactment or rule of law, a court may order such measures (referred to in this section as "anonymity measures") to be taken in relation to a witness in criminal proceedings as the court considers appropriate to ensure that the identity of the witness is not disclosed in or in connection with the proceedings.

Use of a pseudonym, screening and alteration of the witness' voice are amongst some of the measures which the court may adopt to preserve the anonymity of the witness. However, the section also sets out that the anonymity measures shall not include measures to prevent the witness from being visible to the judge or judges, or to the jury (if any) or that the witness's unaltered voice being heard by the judge, judges or by the jury. In addition, the section also sets out a range of factors that the court should have regard to in considering what anonymity measures to apply including the general principle that a defendant should know the identity of witnesses. **[8–48]**

Legislative Provisions–Exclusion of the Public/ Otherwise than in Public/Clearing of the Court

Section 20 Criminal Justice Act 1951[28]

'Clearing of court and prohibition of reports of proceedings'

The section provides for the exclusion of the public in proceedings 'of an indecent or obscene nature'. Persons permitted to remain are: **[8–49]**

---

[28] Criminal Justice Act 1951, s 20, 'Clearing of court and prohibition of reports of proceedings, ((1), (2) repealed by Criminal Procedure Act 1967), s 3:

> 'In any criminal proceedings for an offence which is, in the opinion of the Court, of an indecent or obscene nature, the Court may, subject to subsection (4), exclude from the Court during the hearing all persons except officers of the Court, persons directly concerned in the proceedings, bona fide representatives of the Press and such other persons as the Court may, in its discretion, permit to remain.
>
> (4) In any criminal proceedings –
>
> (a) where the accused is a person under the age of twenty-one years, or
>
> (b) where the offence is of an indecent or obscene nature and the person with or against whom it is alleged to have been committed is under that age or is a female,
>
> a parent or other relative or friend of that person or a support worker chosen by a person referred to in paragraph (b) shall be entitled to remain in Court during the whole of the hearing.
>
> (5) A person who contravenes an order or direction of the Court under this section shall, without prejudice to his liability for any other offence of which he may be guilty, be guilty of an offence under this section and shall be liable on summary conviction thereof to a fine not exceeding one hundred pounds or, at the discretion of the Court, to imprisonment for a term not exceeding six months or to both such fine and imprisonment.

— Officers of the court;
— Persons directly concerned in the proceedings;
— Bona fide representatives of the press;
— Such other persons as the court may, in its discretion, permit to remain.

[8–50] Section 20(4) states proceedings:

> (a) where the accused is a person under the age of twenty-one years, or
> (b) where the offence is of an indecent or obscene nature and the person with or against whom it is alleged to have been committed is under that age or is a female,
>
> a parent or other relative or friend of that person or a support worker chosen by a person referred to in paragraph (b) shall be entitled to remain in Court during the whole of the hearing.

[8–51] Section 20 of the Criminal Justice Act 1951 was amended by s 27 of the Criminal Justice (Victims of Crime) Act 2017 to allow for a support worker chosen by the person to remain and under that section support worker means a volunteer of, or an individual employed under a contract of service or under a contract for services by, an organisation which provides support to victims of crime.[29]

[8–52] Section 20(5) of the Criminal Justice Act 1951 states:

> A person who contravenes an order or direction of the Court under this section shall, without prejudice to his liability for any other offence of which he may be guilty, be guilty of an offence under this section and shall be liable on summary conviction thereof to a fine not exceeding one hundred pounds or, at the discretion of the Court, to imprisonment for a term not exceeding six months or to both such fine and imprisonment.

Section 6 Criminal Law (Rape) Act 1981[30]

'Exclusion of the public'

[8–53] The section provides for the exclusion of the public in relation to the following offences/hearings:

---

(6) The powers conferred by this section are in addition to any other power of the Court to do all or any of the things which this section authorises.

(7) In this section, "support worker" means a volunteer of, or an individual employed under a contract of service or under a contract for services by, an organisation which provides support to victims of crime.'

29 Criminal Justice (Victims of Crime) Act 2017, s 27: 'Section 20 of the Criminal Justice Act 1951 is amended – (a) in subsection (4), by the substitution of "of that person or a support worker chosen by a person referred to in paragraph (b)" for "of that person", and (b) by the insertion of the following subsection after subsection (6): "(7) In this section, 'support worker' means a volunteer of, or an individual employed under a contract of service or under a contract for services by, an organisation which provides support to victims of crime."'

30 Criminal Law (Rape) Act 1981, s 6, Exclusion of the public:

'(1) Subject to subsections (2), (3) and (4), in any proceedings for a rape offence or the offence of aggravated sexual assault or attempted aggravated sexual assault or of aiding, abetting, counselling or procuring the offence of aggravated sexual assault or attempted aggravated sexual assault or of incitement to the offence of aggravated sexual assault or conspiracy to commit any of the foregoing offences, the judge, the justice or the court, as the case may be, shall exclude from the court during the hearing all persons except officers of the court, persons directly concerned in the proceedings, bona fide representatives of the Press and such other persons (if any) as the judge, the justice or the court, as the case may be, may in his or its discretion permit to remain.

(2) Subject to subsection (3), during the hearing of an application under section 3

— rape offence[31];
— aggravated sexual assault;
— attempted aggravated sexual assault or of aiding, abetting, counselling or procuring the offence of aggravated sexual assault or attempted aggravated sexual assault or of incitement to the offence of aggravated sexual assault or conspiracy to commit any of the foregoing offences;
— an application under s 3 Criminal Law (Rape) Act 1981 – restricting evidence regarding previous sexual history;
— an application under s 4 Criminal Law (Rape) Act 1981 relating to –
  - the dismissal of a charge of a sexual assault offence; or
  - the taking of a person's evidence by way of deposition in the case of a sexual assault offence.

It will be noted from the above that sexual offences are not included in this section. **[8–54]**

The court shall exclude the public but allow to be present: **[8–55]**

— officers of the court;
— persons directly concerned in the proceedings;
— bona fide representatives of the press;
— and such other persons (if any) as the judge, the justice or the court, as the case may be, may in his, her or its discretion permit to remain;
— a parent, relative, friend or support worker chosen by the complainant;
— if the accused is under 18 a parent, relative or friend.

Section 19A Criminal Evidence Act 1992[32]

'*Disclosure of third-party records in certain trials*'

In a hearing in respect of an application for the disclosure of counselling records, s 19(15) provides that all persons other than the officers of the court, persons directly concerned in the hearing and such other persons (if any) as the court may determine, shall be excluded from the court during the hearing. Bona fide members of the press are not mentioned in the section. **[8–56]**

Counselling records are defined in the section as **[8–57]**

> 'any record, or part of a record, made by any means, by a competent person in connection with the provision of counselling to a person in respect of whom a sexual offence is alleged to have been committed ('the complainant'), which the prosecutor has had sight of, or

---

(including that section as applied by section 5) or under section 4 (2), the judge, the justice or the court, as the case may be, shall exclude from the court all persons except officers of the court and persons directly concerned in the proceedings.'

[31] Criminal Law (Rape) Act 1981, s 1(1): '"a rape offence" means any of the following, namely, rape, attempted rape, burglary with intent to commit rape, aiding, abetting, counselling and procuring rape, attempted rape or burglary with intent to commit rape, and incitement to rape and, other than in sections 2(2) and 8 of this (Criminal Law (Rape) Act 1981) Act, rape under section 4 (Criminal Law (Rape) (Amendment) Act, 1990), attempted rape under section 4 (Criminal Law (Rape) (Amendment) Act, 1990), aiding, abetting, counselling and procuring rape under section 4 or attempted rape under section 4 (Criminal Law (Rape) (Amendment) Act, 1990) and incitement to rape under section 4 (Criminal Law (Rape) (Amendment) Act, 1990)'.

[32] Criminal Evidence Act 1992, s 19A(15): 'For the purposes of a hearing pursuant to subsection (8), all persons, other than officers of the court, persons directly concerned in the hearing and such other persons (if any) as the court may determine, shall be excluded from the court during the hearing.'

about which the prosecutor has knowledge, and in relation to which there is a reasonable expectation of privacy'.

[8–58] Counselling is also defined in the section as 'listening to and giving verbal or other support or encouragement to a person, or advising or providing therapy or other treatment to a person (whether or not for remuneration)'.

Section 94 Children Act 2001[33]

'Persons entitled to be present at hearing'

[8–59] This is a general provision in relation to hearings before the Children Court. It states:

> The Court shall exclude all persons from the hearing of any proceedings before it except –
> (a) officers of the Court,
> (b) the parents or guardian of the child concerned,
> (c) an adult relative of the child, or other adult who attends the Court pursuant to section 91(6),
> (d) persons directly concerned in the proceedings,
> (e) bona fide representatives of the Press, and
> (f) such other persons (if any) as the Court may at its discretion permit to remain.

[8–60] Where the location of the parents or guardian of the child is unknown, or where for any reason, neither a parent nor a guardian attends the proceedings, s 91(6) of the Children Act 2001 allows for a child to be accompanied by 'an adult relative or other adult.'

[8–61] Section 94(2) states that the order or decision of the Court (if any) in any such proceedings shall be announced in public.

Section 257 Children Act 2001[34]

'Clearing of court in certain cases' (when a child is giving evidence)

[8–62] The section allows the court, when a child is giving evidence, where exclusion provisions

---

33 Children Act 2001, s 94, Persons entitled to be present at hearing: '(1) The Court shall exclude from the hearing of any proceedings before it all persons except – (a) officers of the Court, (b) the parents or guardian of the child concerned, (c) an adult relative of the child, or other adult who attends the Court pursuant to section 91(6), (d) persons directly concerned in the proceedings, (e) bona fide representatives of the Press, and (f) such other persons (if any) as the Court may at its discretion permit to remain.

(2) The order or decision of the Court (if any) in any such proceedings shall be announced in public.'

34 Children Act, s 257, Clearing of court in certain cases:

'(1) Where in any proceedings for an offence a person who, in the opinion of the court, is a child is called as a witness, the court may exclude from the court during the taking of his or her evidence all persons except officers of the court, persons directly concerned in the proceedings, bona fide representatives of the Press and such other persons (if any) as the court may in its discretion permit to remain.

(2) The powers of a court under this section shall be in addition and without prejudice to any other power of the court to hear proceedings *in camera* or to exclude a witness until his or her evidence is required or to Part III (which relates to evidence through a television link in certain proceedings) of the Act of 1992.

(3) The said Part III and section 22 (which relates to compellability of spouses to give evidence at instance of prosecution in certain cases) of the Act of 1992 are hereby amended

do not already apply, to exclude all persons except for those persons connected with the case or allowed by the court to remain.

The section is also notable as it extended the original upper age limit of 17 to the age of 18 in Part III Criminal Evidence Act 1992. **[8–63]**

Section 8 Criminal Justice (Female Genital Mutilation) Act 2012[35]

'Exclusion of the public from hearing.'

The provision relates to any proceedings for an offence under s 2 ('Offences of female genital mutilation, etc'), s 3 ('Offence of removal from State for purpose of female genital mutilation'), or s 4 ('Acts, etc., done outside State') Criminal Justice (Female Genital Mutilation) Act 2012. **[8–64]**

The following may remain in court: **[8–65]**

- officers of the court;
- persons directly concerned in the proceedings;
- bona fide representatives of the press and such other persons as the court may, in its discretion, permit to remain;
- a parent, relative, friend or support worker chosen by the complainant;
- where the accused is under 18, a parent, relative or friend;

Under s 8(3), in any proceedings to which subsection (1) applies, the verdict or decision and the sentence (if any) shall be announced in public. **[8–66]**

Section 29 Criminal Law (Sexual Offences) Act 2017 (Punishment of Incest Act 1908)[36]

'Exclusion of public from hearings of proceedings under Act of 1908'

In any proceedings for an offence under the Punishment of Incest Act 1908, the court shall exclude all persons except: **[8–67]**

---

by the deletion of "17 years" wherever it occurs and the substitution of "18 years". (4) In this section "the Act of 1992" means the Criminal Evidence Act, 1992.'

[35] Criminal Justice (Female Genital Mutilation) Act 2012, s 8, Exclusion of the public from hearing: '(1) Subject to subsections (2) and (3), in any proceedings for an offence under section 2, 3 or 4, the judge or the court, as the case may be, shall exclude from the court during the hearing all persons except officers of the court, persons directly concerned in the proceedings, bona fide representatives of the Press and such other persons (if any) as the judge or the court, as the case may be, may in his or her or its discretion permit to remain.

(2) Subsection (1) is without prejudice to the right of –

(a) a parent, relative or friend of the girl or woman in respect of whom the offence is alleged to have been committed or, where the accused person is not of full age, of the accused person, or

(b) a support worker chosen by the girl or woman referred to in paragraph (a), to remain in court.

(3) In any proceedings to which subsection (1) applies, the verdict or decision and the sentence (if any) shall be announced in public.

(4) In this section, "support worker" means a volunteer of, or an individual employed under a contract of service or under a contract for services by, an organisation which provides support to victims of crime.'

[36] Criminal Law (Sexual Offences) Act 2017, s 29, Exclusion of public from hearings of proceedings under Act of 1908:

— officers of the court;
— persons directly concerned in the proceedings;
— bona fide representatives of the press;
— and such other persons (if any) as the judge or the court as the case may be, may, in 'his, her or its discretion', permit to remain.

[8–68] Under s 29(2) of the Criminal Law (Sexual Offences) Act 2017, the verdict or decision and the sentence shall be announced in public

Section 20 Criminal Justice (Victims of Crime) Act 2017[37]

'Power to exclude public'

[8–69] In any proceedings relating to an offence where a court is satisfied that the nature or circumstances of the case are such that there is a need to protect a victim of the offence from secondary and repeat victimisation, intimidation or retaliation and that it would not be contrary to the interests of justice, the judge may exclude the public or any particular person or persons but the following may remain:

— officers of the court;
— bona fide members of the press;
— a parent, relative or friend of the victim;
— a support worker of the victim's choice;
— where the accused person is under the age of 18 years, a parent, relative or friend of the accused person;
— an 'appropriate person' under s 18 of the Act,[38] which provides for an appropriate

---

'(1) In any proceedings for an offence under the Act of 1908, the judge or the court, as the case may be, shall exclude from the court during the hearing all persons except officers of the court, persons directly concerned in the proceedings, bona fide representatives of the press and such other persons (if any) as the judge or the court, as the case may be, may, in his, her or its discretion, permit to remain.

(2) In any proceedings to which subsection (1) applies the verdict or decision and the sentence (if any) shall be announced in public'.

[37] Criminal Justice (Victims of Crime) Act 2017, s 20, Power to exclude public:

'(1) In any proceedings relating to an offence, where a court is satisfied –

(a) that the nature or circumstances of the case are such that there is a need to protect a victim of the offence from secondary and repeat victimisation, intimidation or retaliation, and

(b) it would not be contrary to the interests of justice in the case, the court may, on the application of the prosecution, exclude from the court during such proceedings –

(i) the public or any portion of the public, or

(ii) any particular person or persons,

except officers of the court and bona fide representatives of the Press.

(2) Subsection (1) is without prejudice to –

(a) the right of –

(i) a parent, relative or friend of the victim,

(ii) a support worker of the victim's choice,

(iii) where the accused person is under the age of 18 years, a parent, relative or friend of the accused person, or

(iv) an appropriate person under section 18, to remain in court, and

(b) the power of a court to exclude the public or any person from the court under any other enactment or rule of law.

(3) In this section, "support worker" means a volunteer of, or an individual employed under a contract of service or under a contract for services by, an organisation which provides support to victims of crime.'

[38] Criminal Justice (Victims of Crime) Act 2017, s 18, Appropriate persons:

person to be present during interviews or court proceedings where his or her parent or guardian is precluded or unable to do so.

In the section, 'support worker' means a volunteer of, or an individual employed under a contract of service or under a contract for services by, an organisation which provides support to victims of crime. **[8–70]**

Section 20 is also specifically mentioned as a special measure under s 19(2)(a) of the Criminal Justice (Victims of Crime) Act 2017 – 'Special measures during criminal proceedings'. **[8–71]**

Under s 20(1)(b) of the Act, the application is made by the prosecution. **[8–72]**

Section 34 Domestic Violence Act 2018[39]

'Restrictions on those present in courtroom in proceedings under section 33'

The judge shall exclude from the court all persons except: **[8–73]**

— officers of the court;
— persons directly concerned with those proceedings;
— bona fide representatives of the press; and
— such other persons (if any) as the judge may in his or her discretion permit to remain.

The proceedings under s 33[40] comprise contraventions of: **[8–74]**

'(1) Where –
(a) a victim is a child, and
(b) a parent, guardian or any other person duly authorised to act on the victim's behalf –
(i) has been charged with, or is under investigation for, an offence in connection with the victim,
(ii) is, for any other reason, precluded from accompanying the victim,
(iii) is unavailable or cannot be contacted,
(iv) indicates that he or she does not wish to accompany the victim, or
(v) cannot be identified,
the Garda Síochána or the Ombudsman Commission, as the case may be, shall arrange for the victim to be accompanied by an appropriate person when attending any interviews and court proceedings at which the victim is required to be present.

(2) A member of the Garda Síochána or an officer of the Ombudsman Commission, as the case may be, shall, in determining who is to be the appropriate person to accompany a child to an interview or court proceedings pursuant to subsection (1), have regard to any views expressed by the child taking into account his or her age and level of maturity.

(3) Where an appropriate person is appointed to accompany a victim, he or she shall be entitled to remain in court during the whole of any hearing.

(4) In this section, "appropriate person" means –
(a) a relative of the child, or
(b) any other person,
who is 18 years or over.'

39 Domestic Violence Act 2018, s 34, Restrictions on those present in courtroom in proceedings under section 33: 'In proceedings relating to an offence under section 33, the judge shall exclude from the court during those proceedings all persons except officers of the court, persons directly concerned with those proceedings, bona fide representatives of the press and such other persons (if any) as the judge may in his or her discretion permit to remain.'

40 Domestic Violence Act 2018, s 33, Offences:
'(1) A respondent who –
(a) contravenes a safety order, a barring order, an interim barring order, an

— a safety order;
— a barring order;
— an interim barring order;
— an emergency barring order; or
— a protection order.

Section 9 Criminal Procedure Act 2021[41]

'Power to exclude public'

[8–75] The section states that preliminary trial hearings or their hearings shall be conducted in open court subject to any other enactment. However, the judge has a right to exclude the public, a portion of the public or any particular person or persons where he or she is satisfied that because of the nature or circumstances of the case or otherwise in the interests of justice that it is desirable to do so.

[8–76] The section allows for:

(a) a parent, relative or friend of the accused or of an injured party; or
(b) a support worker chosen by an injured party, to remain in accordance with the following provisions:
  — s 20(4) of the Criminal Justice Act 1951,
  — s 6 of the Criminal Law (Rape) Act 1981,
  — s 8 of the Criminal Justice (Female Genital Mutilation) Act 2012, or
  — s 20 of the Criminal Justice (Victims of Crime) Act 2017.

[8–77] The section outlines that 'support worker' means a volunteer of, or an individual

---

emergency barring order or a protection order, or (b) while a barring order, an emergency barring order or an interim barring order is in force, refuses to permit the applicant or a dependent person to enter in and remain in the place to which the order relates or does any act for the purpose of preventing the applicant or dependent person

from so doing, commits an offence and shall be liable on summary conviction to a class B fine or to imprisonment for a term not exceeding 12 months, or both.

(2) Subsection (1) is without prejudice to the law relating to contempt of court or any other liability, whether civil or criminal, that may be incurred by the respondent concerned.'

41 Criminal Procedure Act 2021, s 9, Power to exclude public:

'(1) Subject to this section and any other enactment, a preliminary trial hearing or the hearing of an appeal under section 7 shall be conducted in open court.

(2) Where a court conducting a preliminary trial hearing or the hearing of an appeal under section 7, as the case may be, is satisfied, because of the nature or circumstances of the case or otherwise in the interests of justice, that it is desirable to do so, it may exclude from the court during the hearing –

(a) the public or any portion of the public, or
(b) any particular person or persons,

except bona fide representatives of the Press.

(3) Subsection (2) is without prejudice to the right of –

(a) a parent, relative or friend of the accused or of an injured party, or
(b) a support worker chosen by an injured party,

to remain in court in any case to which section 20(4) of the Criminal Justice Act 1951, section 6 of the Criminal Law (Rape) Act 1981, section 8 of the Criminal Justice (Female Genital Mutilation) Act 2012 or section 20 of the Criminal Justice (Victims of Crime) Act 2017 applies.

(4) In this section, "support worker" means a volunteer of, or an individual employed under a contract of service or under a contract for services by, an organisation which provides support to victims of crime.'

employed under a contract of service or under a contract for services by, an organisation which provides support to victims of crime.

Section 37 Criminal Justice (Miscellaneous Provisions) Act 2023

'Hearing of proceedings'

When commenced, s 37 of the Criminal Justice (Miscellaneous Provisions) Act 2023 '[H]earing of proceedings' provides that the public will be excluded from the court during applications under ss 28, 29 and 30 of the Act in relation to civil orders in respect of 'relevant conduct'.[42] However, s 40 of the Act does provide for court accompaniment as appropriate. **[8–78]**

The defendant – in camera /anonymity/ restrictions on reporting /exclusion of the public/otherwise than in public /clearing of the court

Certain provisions may overlap, for example where the defendant is a child[43] and where the offences may carry reporting restrictions such as rape offences.[44] **[8–79]**

Section 20 Criminal Justice Act 1951[45]

'Clearing of court and prohibition of reports of proceedings'

The section provides for the exclusion of the public in proceedings 'of an indecent or obscene nature'. Persons permitted to remain are: **[8–80]**

---

42 Criminal Justice (Miscellaneous Provisions) 2023, s 27.

> s 27 (1) In this Part, "court" means the District Court, or, on appeal from the District Court, the Circuit Court. (2) For the purposes of this Part, "relevant conduct" means conduct engaged in, without lawful authority or reasonable excuse, by the respondent towards the applicant or, where relevant, a person connected to the applicant, that would reasonably be considered likely to cause the applicant— (a) to fear that violence will be used against the applicant or person, or (b) serious alarm or distress that has a substantial adverse impact on his or her usual day-to-day activities.

43 Children Act 2001, s 93, Restrictions on reports of proceedings in which children are concerned.

44 Criminal Law (Rape) Act 1981, s 8, Anonymity of accused.

45 Criminal Justice Act 1951, s 20, Clearing of court and prohibition of reports of proceedings ((1), (2) repealed by Criminal Procedure Act 1967, s 3):

> '(3) In any criminal proceedings for an offence which is, in the opinion of the Court, of an indecent or obscene nature, the Court may, subject to subsection (4), exclude from the Court during the hearing all persons except officers of the Court, persons directly concerned in the proceedings, bona fide representatives of the Press and such other persons as the Court may, in its discretion, permit to remain.
>
> (4) In any criminal proceedings –
>
> (a) where the accused is a person under the age of twenty-one years, or
>
> (b) where the offence is of an indecent or obscene nature and the person with or against whom it is alleged to have been committed is under that age or is a female,
>
> a parent or other relative or friend of that person or a support worker chosen by a person referred to in paragraph (b) shall be entitled to remain in Court during the whole of the hearing.
>
> (5) A person who contravenes an order or direction of the Court under this section shall, without prejudice to his liability for any other offence of which he may be guilty, be guilty of an offence under this section and shall be liable on summary conviction thereof to a fine not exceeding one hundred pounds or, at the discretion of the Court, to imprisonment for a term not exceeding six months or to both such fine and imprisonment.

- officers of the court;
- persons directly concerned in the proceedings;
- bona fide representatives of the press;
- such other persons as the court may, in its discretion, permit to remain.

[8–81] Section 20(4)states proceedings:

> (a) where the accused is a person under the age of twenty-one years, or
> (b) where the offence is of an indecent or obscene nature and the person with or against whom it is alleged to have been committed is under that age or is a female,
>
> a parent or other relative or friend of that person or a support worker chosen by a person referred to in paragraph (b) shall be entitled to remain in Court during the whole of the hearing.

[8–82] Section 20 of the Criminal Justice Act 1951 was amended by s 27 of the Criminal Justice (Victims of Crime) Act 2017 to allow for a support worker chosen by the person to remain, and under that section support worker means a volunteer of, or an individual employed under a contract of service or under a contract for services by, an organisation which provides support to victims of crime.[46]

[8–83] Section 20(5) of the Criminal Justice Act 1951 states:

> A person who contravenes an order or direction of the Court under this section shall, without prejudice to his liability for any other offence of which he may be guilty, be guilty of an offence under this section and shall be liable on summary conviction thereof to a fine not exceeding one hundred pounds or, at the discretion of the Court, to imprisonment for a term not exceeding six months or to both such fine and imprisonment.

Section 6 Criminal Law (Rape) Act 1981[47]

'Exclusion of the public'

[8–84] The section provides for the exclusion of the public in relation to the following offences/hearings:

---

(6) The powers conferred by this section are in addition to any other power of the Court to do all or any of the things which this section authorises.

(7) In this section, "support worker" means a volunteer of, or an individual employed under a contract of service or under a contract for services by, an organisation which provides support to victims of crime.'

46 Criminal Justice (Victims of Crime) Act 2017, s 27.
27. s 20 of the Criminal Justice Act 1951 is amended – (a) in subsection (4), by the substitution of "of that person or a support worker chosen by a person referred to in paragraph (b)" for "of that person", and (b) by the insertion of the following subsection after subsection (6): "(7) In this section, 'support worker' means a volunteer of, or an individual employed under a contract of service or under a contract for services by, an organisation which provides support to victims of crime.".

47 Criminal Law (Rape) Act 1981, s 6, Exclusion of the public:
'(1) Subject to subsections (2), (3) and (4), in any proceedings for a rape offence or the offence of aggravated sexual assault or attempted aggravated sexual assault or of aiding, abetting, counselling or procuring the offence of aggravated sexual assault or attempted aggravated sexual assault or of incitement to the offence of aggravated sexual assault or conspiracy to commit any of the foregoing offences, the judge, the justice or the court, as the case may be, shall exclude from the court during the hearing all persons except officers of the court, persons directly concerned in the proceedings, bona fide representatives of the Press and such other persons (if any) as the judge, the justice or the court, as the case may be, may in his or its discretion permit to remain.

- rape offence[48];
- aggravated sexual assault;
- attempted aggravated sexual assault or of aiding, abetting, counselling or procuring the offence of aggravated sexual assault or attempted aggravated sexual assault or of incitement to the offence of aggravated sexual assault or conspiracy to commit any of the foregoing offences;
- an application under s 3 Criminal Law (Rape)Act 1981 – restricting evidence regarding previous sexual history;
- an application under s 4 Criminal Law (Rape) Act 1981 relating to –
  - the dismissal of a charge of a sexual assault offence; or
  - the taking of a person's evidence by way of deposition in the case of a sexual assault offence.

The court shall exclude the public but allow the following to remain: **[8–85]**

- officers of the court;
- persons directly concerned in the proceedings;
- bona fide representatives of the press;
- and such other persons (if any) as the judge, the justice or the court, as the case may be, may in his, her or its discretion permit to remain;
- a parent, relative, friend or support worker chosen by the complainant;
- if the accused is under 18 a parent, relative, or friend.

Section 8 Criminal Law (Rape) Act 1981[49]

'Anonymity of accused'

After a person is charged with a rape offence, no matter likely to lead members of **[8–86]**

---

(2) Subject to subsection (3), during the hearing of an application under section 3 (including that section as applied by section 5) or under section 4 (2), the judge, the justice or the court, as the case may be, shall exclude from the court all persons except officers of the court and persons directly concerned in the proceedings.'

48 Criminal Law (Rape) Act 1981, s 1(1): '"a rape offence" means any of the following, namely, rape, attempted rape, burglary with intent to commit rape, aiding, abetting, counselling and procuring rape, attempted rape or burglary with intent to commit rape, and incitement to rape and, other than in sections 2 (2) and 8 of this (Criminal Law (Rape) Act 1981) Act, rape under section 4 (Criminal Law (Rape) (Amendment) Act, 1990), attempted rape under section 4 (Criminal Law (Rape) (Amendment) Act, 1990), aiding, abetting, counselling and procuring rape under section 4 or attempted rape under section 4 (Criminal Law (Rape) (Amendment) Act, 1990) and incitement to rape under section 4 (Criminal Law (Rape) (Amendment) Act, 1990)'.

49 Criminal Law (Rape) Act 1981, s 8(1):

'After a person is charged with a rape offence no matter likely to lead members of the public to identify him as the person against whom the charge is made shall be published in a written publication available to the public or be broadcast except – (a) as authorised by a direction given in pursuance of this section or by virtue of section 7 (8) (a) as applied by subsection (6) of this section, or (b) after he has been convicted of the offence. (2) If a person charged with a rape offence applies in that behalf to a judge of the High Court before the commencement of the trial or to the judge at the trial, the judge shall direct that subsection (1) shall not apply to the person in relation to the charge: Provided that, if it appears to the judge that, if the direction were given, the publication of any matter in pursuance of the direction might enable members of the public to identify a person as the complainant in relation to the charge, the judge shall not give the direction unless he is satisfied that a direction could properly be given in relation to that person in pursuance of section 7. (3) If, at any stage before the commencement of a trial of a person for a rape offence, another person who is to be charged with a rape offence at the trial applies to a judge of the High Court for a direction in pursuance of this subsection and satisfies the judge – (a) that the direction is required for the purpose of inducing persons to come

the public to identify him as the person against whom the charge is made, shall be published in a written publication available to the public or be broadcast except under certain circumstances under the section. A rape offence is outlined in s 1 of the Act, which states:

> rape offence means any of the following, namely, rape, attempted rape, burglary with intent to commit rape, aiding, abetting, counselling and procuring rape, attempted rape or burglary with intent to commit rape, and incitement to rape and, other than in sections 2(2) and 8 of this Act, rape under section 4, attempted rape under section 4, aiding, abetting, counselling and procuring rape under section 4 or attempted rape under section 4 and incitement to rape under section 4.

[8–87] The anonymity provisions will end for the defendant on the conviction of the offence.

Section 51 Children Act 2001[50]

'Protection of identity of children' (admitted to the diversion programme)

[8–88] The section restricts publishing or broadcast of any report in respect of a child admitted

---

forward who are likely to be needed as witnesses at the trial, and (b) that the conduct of the applicant's defence at the trial is likely to be adversely affected if the direction is not given, the judge shall direct that subsection (1) shall not, by virtue of the charge alleging the offence aforesaid, apply to such matter relating to the first-mentioned person as is specified in the direction. (4) If at a trial of a person for a rape offence another person who is also charged at the trial applies to the judge for a direction in pursuance of this subsection and satisfies the judge – (a) that the direction is required for the purpose of inducing persons to come forward who are likely to be needed as witnesses at the trial, (b) that the conduct of the applicant's defence is likely to be adversely affected if the direction is not given, and (c) that there was good reason for his not having made an application under subsection (3) before the commencement of the trial, the judge shall direct that subsection (1) shall not, by virtue of the charge alleging the offence aforesaid, apply to such matter relating to the first-mentioned person as is specified in the direction. (5) If at a trial at which a person is charged with a rape offence the judge is satisfied that the effect of subsection (1) is to impose a substantial and unreasonable restriction on the reporting of proceedings at the trial and that it is in the public interest to remove or relax the restriction in respect of that person, the judge shall direct that subsection (1) shall not, by virtue of the charge alleging the offence aforesaid, apply to such matter relating to that person as is specified in the direction. (6) Subsections (6) to (9) of section 7 shall have effect for the purposes of this section as if for references to that section there were substituted references to this section. (7) If, after the commencement of a trial of a person for a rape offence, a new trial of the person for that offence is ordered, the commencement of any previous trial of that person for that offence shall be disregarded for the purposes of subsections (2), (3) and (4).

(8) If, at any time after a person is charged with a rape offence, the Director of Public Prosecutions applies in that behalf to a judge of the High Court, the judge, if he is satisfied that it is in the public interest to do so, shall direct that subsection (1) shall not apply to such matter relating to the person charged with the offence as is specified in the direction.'

This section will be amended by Criminal Law (Sexual Offences and Human Trafficking) Bill 2023, s 12 when/if commenced to expand eligibility and update the definitions of 'publish' and 'broadcast'.

[50] Children Act 2001, s 51, Protection of identity of children:

'(1) Subject to subsection (2), no report shall be published or included in a broadcast –

(a) in relation to the admission of a child to the Programme or the proceedings at any conference relating to the child, including the contents of any action plan for the child and of the report of the conference, or

(b) which reveals the name, address or school of the child or any other information, including any picture, which is likely to lead to identification of the child.

(2) Subsection (1) does not apply to the publication or broadcast of –

(a) statistical information relating to the Programme, and

to the Diversion Programme. Section 51 also sets out the penalties in respect of the more general provision under s 252 of the Children Act 2001 in relation to child victims or child witnesses. These are:

(i) on summary conviction, to a fine not exceeding £1,500 or imprisonment for a term not exceeding 12 months or both, or
(ii) on conviction on indictment, to a fine not exceeding £10,000 or imprisonment for a term not exceeding 3 years or both.

Section 93 Children Act 2001[51]

'*Restrictions on reports of proceedings in which children are concerned*'

Under s 93 of the Children Act 2001, child defendants are entitled to reporting restrictions. The sections states, in similar terms to s 252, that a) no report revealing **[8–89]**

(b) the results of any bona fide research relating to it.

(3) If any matter is published or broadcast in contravention of subsection (1), each of the following persons, namely –

(a) in the case of publication of the matter in a newspaper or periodical, any proprietor, any editor and any publisher of the newspaper or periodical,
(b) in the case of any other such publication, the person who publishes it, and
(c) in the case of any such broadcast, any body corporate which transmits or provides the programme in which the broadcast is made and any person

having functions in relation to the programme corresponding to those of an editor of a newspaper,

shall be guilty of an offence and shall be liable –

(i) on summary conviction, to a fine not exceeding £1,500 or imprisonment for a term not exceeding 12 months or both, or
(ii) on conviction on indictment, to a fine not exceeding £10,000 or imprisonment

for a term not exceeding 3 years or both.

(4) (a) Where an offence under subsection (3) –

(i) has been committed by a body corporate, and
(ii) is proved to have been committed with the consent or connivance of, or to be attributable to any neglect on the part of, any director, manager, secretary or other similar officer of the body corporate or any person who was purporting to act in any such capacity,

he or she as well as the body corporate shall be guilty of the offence and be liable to be proceeded against and punished accordingly.

(b) Where the affairs of a body corporate are managed by its members, paragraph (a) shall apply in relation to the acts and defaults of a member in connection with his or her functions of management as if he or she were a director of the body corporate.

(5) Where a person is charged with an offence under subsection (3), it shall be a defence to prove that at the time of the alleged offence the person was not aware, and neither suspected nor had reason to suspect, that the publication or broadcast in question was of a matter referred to in subsection (1).

(6) In this section –

"broadcast" means the transmission, relaying or distribution by wireless telegraphy of communications, sounds, signs, visual images or signals, intended for direct reception by the general public whether such communications, sounds, signs, visual images or signals are actually received or not;

"publish" means publish to the public or a section of the public, and cognate words shall be construed accordingly.'

[51] Children Act 2001, s 93:

'(1) In relation to proceedings before any court concerning a child –

(a) no report which reveals the name, address or school of any child concerned in the proceedings or includes any particulars likely to lead to the identification of any such child shall be published or included in a broadcast or any other form the name, address or school of any child concerned in the proceedings or including any particulars likely to lead to the identification of any such child shall be published or included in a broadcast or any other form of communication, and (b) no still or moving picture of or including any such child or which is likely to lead to his or her identification shall be so published or included.

[8–90] In terms of anonymity beyond the age of 18, where proceedings have been completed before his or her 18th birthday, the courts have indicated that it is clear that the protection conferred by s 93 continues for life.[52]

[8–91] In relation to a child defendant, anonymity is an important aspect of the benefit of being dealt with in the Children's Court and under the protections of the Children Act 2001. It gives the child defendant with convictions an opportunity to deal with the sentences up and until he or she is an adult without the convictions affecting any opportunities which may be impacted by a publicised verdict and sentence. The Children Act 2001 also allows for a 'spent conviction' under s 258, and the value of this would be undermined if the verdict and sentence were published.[53]

---

of communication, and (b) no still or moving picture of or including any such child or which is likely to

lead to his or her identification shall be so published or included.

(2) A court may dispense, in whole or in part, with the requirements of this section in relation to a child if satisfied that to do so is necessary –

(a) where the child is charged with an offence –

(i) to avoid injustice to the child,

(ii) where the child is unlawfully at large, for the purpose of apprehending the child, or

(iii) in the public interest, or

(b) where the child is subject to an order under section 257D –

(i) to avoid injustice to the child, or

(ii) to ensure that the order is complied with.

(3) Where a court dispenses with any requirements of this section, it shall explain in open court the reasons for its decision.

(4) Subsections (3) to (6) of section 51 of this Act shall apply, with the necessary modifications, to matters published or included in a broadcast or other form of communication in contravention of subsection (1).

(5) This section shall apply in relation to proceedings on appeal from a court, including proceedings by way of case stated.

(6) This section shall not affect the provisions of any enactment concerning the anonymity of an accused or the law relating to contempt of court.'

52 *INM v IA* [2018] IEHC 120 [43], in which McDermott J observed: 'While it is clear that the protection conferred by s. 93 continues for life in respect of a child who is prosecuted, convicted and sentenced under the age of eighteen, there is no specific provision extending those benefits when a child passes the threshold age limit of eighteen years in the course of the criminal proceedings. Thus for example, a child whose eighteenth birthday occurs in the middle of criminal trial or is convicted the day after his eighteenth birthday would not have the protection of s. 93 or the sentencing regime that would apply to a child. These specific protections under The Children Act 2001 only apply to a child – a person under eighteen years of age. In cases where offences committed by a child are only detected when they enter adulthood, he/she does not obtain the benefit of any of the provisions of s. 93 or any other provisions of the Children Act. There may be good policy reasons to vest in a court a discretion to extend the protections of anonymity in cases which overlap the transition between childhood and adulthood but this has not been addressed by the Oireachtas which has confined the protections to those under eighteen years. This is consistent with the well-established principles of sentencing applicable to an adult who has committed an offence as a child but comes to be sentenced as an adult considered in the case law set out above.'

53 *DPP v Donoghue* [2014] 2 IR 762.

As with s 252 ('Anonymity of child in court proceedings'), breaches under s 93 are dealt with under s 51 ('Protection of identity of children' (in the Diversion programme) of the Act.[54] **[8–92]**

Section 93(4) states: **[8–93]**

> Subsections (3) to (6) of section 51 of this Act shall apply, with the necessary modifications, to matters published or included in a broadcast or other form of communication in contravention of subsection (1).

Legislative provisions may be underpinned by an order of the court which may be punished under contempt of court proceedings.[55] **[8–94]**

Section 94 Children Act 2001[56]

'Persons entitled to be present at hearing'

Under s 94, the court shall exclude from the hearing of any proceedings before it all persons except: **[8–95]**

> (a) officers of the court;
> (b) the parents or guardian of the child concerned;
> (c) an adult relative of the child, or other adult who attends the court pursuant to s 91(6);
> (d) persons directly concerned in the proceedings;
> (e) bona fide representatives of the press; and
> (f) such other persons (if any) as the court may at its discretion permit to remain.

Under s 94(2), the order or decision of the court (if any) in any such proceedings shall be announced in public. **[8–96]**

---

54 Paul Neilan 'Cases of three accused of posting pictures of Kriégel murderers should not be returned to lower court, State argues' *The Irish Times* (Dublin, 23 May 2023) < https://www.irishtimes.com/crime-law/courts/2023/05/02/cases-of-three-accused-of-posting-pictures-of-kriegel-murderers-should-not-be-returned-to-lower-court-state-argues/> accessed 13 October 2023.

55 Miriam Delahunt, 'The Trial of Children in the Central Criminal Court' (2020) 25(1) Bar Review, 20.

> '… the proceedings were held in camera, and reporting restrictions were in place, augmented by an order of the court making any violation not only punishable under the Children Act 2001, but also under contempt of court proceedings.'

56 Children Act 2001, s 94, Persons entitled to be present at hearing:

> '(1) The Court shall exclude from the hearing of any proceedings before it all persons except –
> (a) officers of the Court,
> (b) the parents or guardian of the child concerned,
> (c) an adult relative of the child, or other adult who attends the Court pursuant to section 91(6),
> (d) persons directly concerned in the proceedings,
> (e) bona fide representatives of the Press, and
> (f) such other persons (if any) as the Court may at its discretion permit to remain.
> (2) The order or decision of the Court (if any) in any such proceedings shall be announced in public.'

Section 181 Criminal Justice Act 2006[57]

'Anonymity of certain witnesses' (medical condition)[58]

[8–97] Where, in any criminal proceedings, it is proposed to call a person to give evidence and the person has a medical condition, an application may be made for an order under this section prohibiting the publication of any matter relating to the proceedings which would identify the person as having that condition.

Section 8 Criminal Justice (Female Genital Mutilation) Act 2012[59]

'Exclusion of the public from hearing.'

[8–98] The provision relates to any proceedings for an offence under s 2 ('Offences of female genital mutilation, etc'), s 3 ('Offence of removal from State for purpose of female genital mutilation'), or s 4 ('Acts, etc., done outside State') Criminal Justice (Female Genital Mutilation) Act 2012.

[8–99] The following may remain in court:

- officers of the court;
- persons directly concerned in the proceedings;
- bona fide representatives of the press and such other persons as the court may, in its discretion, permit to remain;
- a parent, relative, friend or support worker chosen by the complainant;
- where the accused is under 18, a parent, relative or friend;

[8–100] Under s 8(3), in any proceedings to which subsection (1) applies, the verdict or decision and the sentence (if any) shall be announced in public.

---

57 Criminal Justice Act 2006, s 181:
'(1) Where in any criminal proceedings –
(a) it is proposed to call a person to give evidence, and
(b) the person has a medical condition,
an application may be made for an order under this section prohibiting the publication of any matter relating to the proceedings which would identify the person as a person having that condition.'

58 For civil proceedings see Civil Law Miscellaneous Provisions Act 2008, s 27.

59 Criminal Justice (Female Genital Mutilation) Act 2012, s 8, Exclusion of the public from hearing:
'(1) Subject to subsections (2) and (3), in any proceedings for an offence under section 2, 3 or 4, the judge or the court, as the case may be, shall exclude from the court during the hearing all persons except officers of the court, persons directly concerned in the proceedings, bona fide representatives of the Press and such other persons (if any) as the judge or the court, as the case may be, may in his or her or its discretion permit to remain.
(2) Subsection (1) is without prejudice to the right of –
(a) a parent, relative or friend of the girl or woman in respect of whom the offence is alleged to have been committed or, where the accused person is not of full age, of the accused person, or (b) a support worker chosen by the girl or woman referred to in paragraph (a), to remain in court.
(3) In any proceedings to which subsection (1) applies, the verdict or decision and the sentence (if any) shall be announced in public.
(4) In this section, "support worker" means a volunteer of, or an individual employed under a contract of service or under a contract for services by, an organisation which provides support to victims of crime.'

Section 20 Criminal Justice (Victims of Crime) Act 2017[60]

'Power to exclude public'

In any proceedings relating to an offence where the court is satisfied that the nature or circumstances of the case are such that there is a need to protect a victim of the offence from secondary and repeat victimisation, intimidation or retaliation, and that it would not be contrary to the interests of justice, the judge may exclude the public or any particular person or persons but the following may remain: **[8–101]**

- officers of the court;
- bona fide members of the press;
- a parent, relative or friend of the victim;
- a support worker of the victim's choice;
- where the accused person is under the age of 18 years, a parent, relative or friend of the accused person;
- an appropriate person under s 18 of the Act,[61] which provides for an appropriate

---

[60] Criminal Justice (Victims of Crime) Act 2017, s 20, Power to exclude public:
'(1) In any proceedings relating to an offence, where a court is satisfied –
(a) that the nature or circumstances of the case are such that there is a need to protect a victim of the offence from secondary and repeat victimisation, intimidation or retaliation, and
(b) it would not be contrary to the interests of justice in the case, the court may, on the application of the prosecution, exclude from the court during such proceedings –
(i) the public or any portion of the public, or
(ii) any particular person or persons,
except officers of the court and bona fide representatives of the Press.
(2) Subsection (1) is without prejudice to –
(a) the right of –
(i) a parent, relative or friend of the victim,
(ii) a support worker of the victim's choice,
(iii) where the accused person is under the age of 18 years, a parent, relative or friend of the accused person, or
(iv) an appropriate person under section 18, to remain in court, and
(b) the power of a court to exclude the public or any person from the court under any other enactment or rule of law.
(3) In this section, "support worker" means a volunteer of, or an individual employed under a contract of service or under a contract for services by, an organisation which provides support to victims of crime.'

[61] Criminal Justice (Victims of Crime) Act 2017, s 18, Appropriate persons:
'(1) Where –
(a) a victim is a child, and
(b) a parent, guardian or any other person duly authorised to act on the victim's behalf –
(i) has been charged with, or is under investigation for, an offence in connection with the victim,
(ii) is, for any other reason, precluded from accompanying the victim,
(iii) is unavailable or cannot be contacted,
(iv) indicates that he or she does not wish to accompany the victim, or
(v) cannot be identified,
the Garda Síochána or the Ombudsman Commission, as the case may be, shall arrange for the victim to be accompanied by an appropriate person when attending any interviews and court proceedings at which the victim is required to be present.
(2) A member of the Garda Síochána or an officer of the Ombudsman Commission, as the case may be, shall, in determining who is to be the appropriate person to accompany a child to an interview or court proceedings pursuant to subsection (1), have regard to any views expressed by the child taking into account his or her age and level of maturity.

person to be present during interviews or court proceedings where his or her parent or guardian is precluded or unable to do so.

[8–102] In the section, 'support worker' means a volunteer of, or an individual employed under a contract of service or under a contract for services by, an organisation which provides support to victims of crime.

[8–103] Section 20 is also specifically mentioned as a special measure under s 19(2)(a) of the Criminal Justice (Victims of Crime) Act 2017 – 'Special measures during criminal proceedings'.

[8–104] Under s 20(1)(b) of the Act, the application is made by the prosecution.

Section 30 Criminal Law (Sexual Offences) Act 2017 (for offences under the Punishment of Incest Act 1908)[62]

'Anonymity of person charged with offence under Act of 1908 and person to whom offence relates'

[8–105] The section states that after a person is charged with an offence under the Act of 1908,

---

(3) Where an appropriate person is appointed to accompany a victim, he or she shall be entitled to remain in court during the whole of any hearing.

(4) In this section, "appropriate person" means –

(a) a relative of the child, or

(b) any other person,

who is 18 years or over.'

[62] Criminal Law Sexual Offences Act 2017, s 30, Anonymity of person charged with offence under Act of 1908 and person to whom offence relates:

'(1) Subject to subsection (4), after a person is charged with an offence under the Act of 1908 no matter likely to lead members of the public to identify that person as the person charged or to identify any other person as a person in relation to whom the offence is alleged to have been committed shall be published in a publication available to the public or broadcast.

(2) If any matter is published or broadcast in contravention of subsection (1), the following persons shall be guilty of an offence namely:

(a) in the case of matter published in a newspaper or periodical publication, the proprietor, the editor and the publisher thereof;

(b) in the case of matter published in any other publication, the publisher thereof; and

(c) in the case of matter broadcast, any person who transmits or provides the programme in which the broadcast is made and any person who performs

functions in relation to the programme corresponding to those of the editor of a newspaper.

(3) Nothing in this section shall be construed as –

(a) prohibiting the publication or broadcast of matter consisting only of a report of legal proceedings other than proceedings at, or intended to lead to, or an appeal arising out of, a trial of a person for an offence under the Act of 1908, or

(b) affecting any prohibition or restriction imposed by virtue of any other enactment upon the publication or broadcasting of any matter.

(4) Notwithstanding the provisions of subsection (1), where a person is charged with both an offence under the Act of 1908 and a sexual assault offence and the charge relating to an offence under the Act of 1908 is not proceeded with or the person is acquitted of the charge under the Act of 1908 and no appeal is taken under section 23 of the Criminal Procedure Act 2010, the provisions of sections 7 and 8 of the Act of 1981 shall apply as if the charge under the Act of 1908 had not been brought.

(5) In this section –

no matter likely to lead members of the public to identify that person as the person charged or to identify any other person as a victim of the offence shall be published or broadcast.

Where a person is charged with an offence under the Punishment of Incest Act 1908 and also a sexual assault offence, and the offence under the 1908 Act is not proceeded with or if the person is acquitted of it and no appeal is taken, then s 7 ('anonymity of complainants') and s 8 ('anonymity of defendants') of the Criminal Law (Rape) Act 1981 shall apply as if the charge under the 1908 Act had not been brought. **[8–106]**

The Criminal Law (Incest Proceedings) Act 1995 has been repealed under s 32 of the Criminal Law (Sexual Offences) Act 2017[63] and so s 2 of the Criminal Law (Incest Proceedings) Act 1995, which provided for the exclusion of public from hearings under the 1908 Act, is no longer relevant to those offences. **[8–107]**

The relevant penalties are contained in s 31 of the Criminal Law (Sexual Offences) Act 2017, which states: **[8–108]**

> 31. (1) A person guilty of an offence under section 30 shall be liable –
> (a) on summary conviction, to a class B fine or to imprisonment for a term not exceeding 12 months or both, or
> (b) on conviction on indictment, to a fine or to imprisonment for a term not exceeding 3 years or both.
>
> (2) It shall be a defence for a person who is charged with an offence under section 30 to prove that at the time of the alleged offence the person was not aware, and neither suspected nor had reason to suspect, that the matter alleged to have been published or broadcast was a matter specified in the said section 30.

Section 10 Criminal Procedure Act 2021[64]

'Hearings not to be published or broadcast'

Section 10(1) restricts reporting in relation to preliminary trial hearings for matters under the Criminal Procedure Act 2021. **[8–109]**

"a sexual assault offence" has the meaning assigned to it by section 1(1) of the Act of 1981 (amended by section 12 of the Act of 1990);
"broadcast" means the transmission, relaying or distribution by wireless telegraphy or by any other means or by wireless telegraphy in conjunction with any other means of communications, sounds, signs, visual images or signals, intended for direct reception by the general public whether such communications, sounds, signs, visual images or signals are actually received or not;
"published" means published to any person, and includes published on the internet;
"publication" includes a film, sound track or any other record in permanent form (including a record that is not in a legible form but which is capable of being reproduced in a legible form) but does not include an indictment or other document prepared for use in particular legal proceedings.'

63 Criminal Law (Sexual Offences) Act 2017, Part 5 'Incest' (ss 28–32) was commenced on 2 September 2019 (SI No 434/2019).

64 Criminal Procedure Act 2021, s 10, Hearings not to be published or broadcast:
'(1) No person shall publish or broadcast or cause to be published or broadcast any information about a preliminary trial hearing or an appeal under section 7 other than –
(a) a statement of the fact that such a hearing is to be, or is being, conducted, or such an appeal is being brought, as the case may be, in respect of proceedings for an offence against a named person, or

[8–110] No information may be published or broadcast regarding a preliminary trial hearing except:

(a) a statement of the fact that such a hearing is to be, or is being, conducted, or such an appeal is being brought, as the case may be, in respect of proceedings for an offence against a named person, or

(b) where an order has been made by the court at a preliminary trial hearing or in an appeal under section 7, as the case may be, and that court is satisfied that such publication or broadcast is not contrary to the interests of justice, a statement of the fact that such an order has been made.

[8–111] This restriction will apply until the conclusion of the trial of the offence or until the trial judge or another court hearing the appeal may direct.

[8–112] Notice of contravention of the provision is made through application by the prosecution to a judge of the District Court who, if it appears that s (10)(1) has been contravened, may certify to that effect to the High Court. The High Court may then inquire further into the matter, and may punish or take steps to punish the person concerned as if he or she had been guilty of contempt of court.

Miscellaneous relevant provisions

[8–113] The following provisions may be relevant to vulnerable witnesses in relation to provisions for anonymity/reporting restrictions as appropriate.

- Section 2 of the Tribunals of Inquiry (Evidence) Act 1921 – 'Powers of tribunals of exclusion of public and granting right of audience'
- Section 30/s 30A of the Offences Against the State Act 1939 – 'Arrest and detention of suspected persons' (exclusion of public and reporting restrictions contained within the section) and 'Rearrest under section 30'

(b) where an order has been made by the court at a preliminary trial hearing or in an appeal under section 7, as the case may be, and that court is satisfied that such publication or broadcast is not contrary to the interests of justice, a statement of the fact that such an order has been made.

(2) Subsection (1) shall apply until the conclusion of the trial of the offence concerned or until such other time as the trial judge or the court hearing the appeal concerned, as the case may be, may direct.

(3) If, on application by the prosecution, it appears to a judge of the District Court that a person has contravened subsection (1), the judge may certify to that effect to the High Court.

(4) On receiving a certificate under subsection (3), the High Court may –

(a) inquire into the matter to which the certificate relates, and

(b) after hearing any witnesses and after considering any statement that may be offered in defence of the person alleged to have contravened subsection (1), punish, or take steps for the punishment of, that person in the like manner as if he or she had been guilty of contempt of the court.

(5) This section shall not affect –

(a) the operation of any other enactment that imposes further restrictions on the extent to which information relating to court proceedings may be published or broadcast, or

(b) any power conferred on a court by such an enactment to make an order authorising the publication or broadcast of such information.

(6) In this section –

"broadcast" has the same meaning as it has in the Broadcasting Act 2009;

"publish" means publish to the public or a portion of the public.'

- Section 45 of the Courts (Supplemental Provisions) Act 1961 – 'Administration of justice otherwise than in public'
  - applications of an urgent nature for relief by way of habeas corpus, bail, prohibition or injunction
  - matrimonial causes and matters
  - lunacy and minor matters
  - proceedings involving the disclosure of a secret manufacturing process
- Section 12 of the Official Secrets Act 1963 – 'Proceedings *in camera*'
- Section 2 of the Criminal Justice (Drug Trafficking) Act 1996 – 'Power of detention' – Application for detention of persons arrested for an offence under this Act (exclusion of public and reporting restrictions contained within the section)
- Section 4 of the Criminal Justice (Drug Trafficking) Act 1996 – 'Rearrest' (exclusion of public provision contained in the section)
- Section 40 of the Civil Liability and Courts Act 2004 – 'Proceedings heard otherwise than in public'
- Section 40A of the Civil Liability and Courts Act 2004 – 'Prohibition on publication or broadcast of certain matters'
- Section 50(4A) of the Criminal Justice Act 2007 – 'Powers of detention for specified offences' (exclusion of public and reporting restrictions contained within the section)
- Section 27 of the Civil Law (Miscellaneous Provisions) Act 2008 – 'Anonymity in civil proceedings in relation to medical condition of relevant person'
- Section 23 of the Domestic Violence Act 2018 – 'Hearing of civil proceedings' – Subject to s 40 of the Civil Liability and Courts Act 2004 and s 26 of the Domestic Violence Act 2018, civil proceedings under the Act shall be heard otherwise than in public
- Section 26 of the Domestic Violence Act 2018 – 'Right to be accompanied in court in certain circumstances'
- Section 23 of the Counterfeiting Act 2021 – 'Privileged legal material' – Where the Central Bank applies to the Court for a determination as to whether documentation is privileged under s 23(2), s 23(6) provides that if the Court so directs, an application under subsection (2) may be heard otherwise than in public.

Chapter 9

COMPETENCE

The Pre-1992 Position

[9–01] Prior to the commencement of s 27 of the Criminal Evidence Act 1992, vulnerable witnesses would have to swear or affirm before giving evidence. The Court had to address the difficulties of engaging with a witness who may not understand the concept of an oath, which had a moral as well as legal implication. This difficulty meant that many victims and witnesses were excluded from giving testimony, thus allowing persons to act with impunity when it came to crimes against children and persons with an intellectual disability. As part of the suite of support measures assisting vulnerable witnesses, under s 27 of the Criminal Evidence Act 1992, the Oireachtas provided for the giving of unsworn testimony for persons under 14 and for persons with 'a mental handicap', a term which has unfortunately survived in the section (s 27(3)) while being amended to 'mental disorder' in other provisions.[1]

[9–02] In the case of *Mapp v Gilhooley*,[2] a civil case where the trial judge had accepted the unsworn testimony of a child who had said he did not understand the oath, the Supreme Court ruled that there were no statutory exceptions in civil cases and ordered a retrial. Finlay CJ stated:

> It is a fundamental principle of the common law that for the purpose of trials in either criminal or civil cases viva voce evidence must be given on oath or affirmation.[3]

1 Criminal Evidence Act 1992, s 19. This section uses the term 'mental disorder', the definition of which is found under Criminal Justice Act 1993, s 5. Unfortunately, the title of the section has not been amended: 'Application of Part III to persons with mental handicap'.

2 [1991] 2 IR 253, [1991] ILRM 695.

3 *Mapp v Gilhooley* [1991] 2 IR 253 [262], [1991] ILRM 695 [700].

Competency Test in Ireland for Witnesses

[9–03] The competency test in Ireland[4] has developed from the provision which allows for the admission of unsworn evidence at trial. Section 27 of the Criminal Evidence Act 1992 provides that evidence of children under 14 and persons with an intellectual disability will be admitted otherwise 'on oath or affirmation if the court is satisfied that he is capable of giving an intelligible account of events which are relevant to those proceedings'.[5] It is this criterion, the ability to give an intelligible account of events which are relevant to the proceedings, which has emerged as the competency test in Ireland.[6] In *DPP v Campion*,[7] O'Malley J stated that 'the threshold for competency is low – an ability to understand questions and give intelligible answers on matters relevant to the issues in the trial'.[8]

Relevance of the Circumstances of the Taking of the Statement

[9–04] The court may also look to the circumstances surrounding the provision and to how the evidence was taken. In *DPP v PP*[9] the Court referred to the request for the witness to tell the truth as a factor regarding the competency of the child witness. In *DPP v O'Brien*,[10] s 16 of the Criminal Justice Act 2006 was used for the admission of recorded testimony where the complainant no longer wished to give evidence. The Court looked at how the statement, which had been recorded, had been taken. The case deals with a different legislative provision in respect of the admission of the recorded testimony. However, the guidance of the Court may be helpful:

> The starting point, however, must be the provisions of the Act of 2006 itself. It seems relatively clear that the Act, in requiring that the statement be found to be "reliable", appears to mandate the court to examine the circumstances and factors surrounding the making of the statement, to ensure this is a reliable statement in the sense that it is one which can be relied upon, rather than requiring the court to be satisfied that the actual content of the statement is reliable in the sense that it is true. The section permits the admission of a statement, under s. 16, provided it is voluntary and reliable, "as evidence of any fact mentioned therein". The weight to be attached to that evidence is, of course, a different matter, but no point is taken on that.[11]

Legislative Provisions

[9–05] **Section 27 Criminal Evidence Act 1992**

'Oath or affirmation not necessary for child etc., witness.'

> 27. –(1) Notwithstanding any enactment, in any criminal proceedings the evidence of a person under 14 years of age may be received otherwise than on oath or affirmation if

4 In contrast to England and Wales where the Youth Justice and Criminal Evidence Act, s 53, sets out the competency test.

5 Criminal Evidence Act 1992, s 27(1).

6 *O'Sullivan v Hamill* [1998] 2 IR 9; *DPP v Campion* [2018] IESC 35.[2021] 2 IR 1. See, generally, Liz Heffernan, *Evidence in Criminal Trials* (2nd edn, Bloomsbury 2020) para 2.18.

7 *DPP v Campion* [2018] IESC 35; [2021] 2 IR 1.

8 *DPP v Campion* [2018] IESC 35; [2021] 2 IR 1 [136].

9 *DPP v PP* [2015] IECA 152.

10 *DPP v O'Brien* [2011] 1 IR 273.

11 *DPP v O'Brien* [2011] 1 IR 273, 294.

> the court is satisfied that he is capable of giving an intelligible account of events which are relevant to those proceedings.
>
> (2) If any person whose evidence is received as aforesaid makes a statement material in the proceedings concerned which he knows to be false or does not believe to be true, he shall be guilty of an offence and on conviction shall be liable to be dealt with as if he had been guilty of perjury.
>
> (3) Subsection (1) shall apply to a person with mental handicap who has reached the age of 14 years as it applies to a person under that age.

The perjury offence under s 27(2) has been included in Schedule 2 of the Criminal Justice (Perjury and Related) Offences Act 2021. **[9–06]**

The Rationale for a Test of Competence

A test for competence[12] is of practical use in that it restricts the admission of evidence which is of little intrinsic value and which may be unfair to the accused.[13] The competence of vulnerable witnesses, particularly that of children, has undergone significant social and cultural changes in a legal context in recent years. In *R v Wallwork*,[14] Lord Goddard CJ 'deprecated' the calling of a child of five as a witness in a case of incest, saying that it was 'ridiculous' to suppose a jury would attach any value to it.[15] That principle has changed considerably where the case of *R v Barker*[16] saw the complainant, X, give testimony at the age of four-and-a-half years of age concerning allegations of anal rape which had occurred when she was two-and-a-half years of age. In Ireland, one of the youngest victims was six years old while giving evidence about incidents that had occurred approximately two years previously.[17] **[9–07]**

The principle of competence is not linked to the question of whether the witness is credible. The issues of competence and credibility are wholly separate issues. Hoyano and Keenan note: **[9–08]**

> The goal is not to ensure that the evidence is credible, but only that it meets the minimum threshold for being heard; the court's enquiry is into capacity to perceive, recollect, and

---

12 *DPP v Campion* [2018] IESC 35; [2021] 2 IR 1[136].

13 The Australian Law Commission stated in its 2006 Report that the 'primary rationale for the existence of tests of competence is to guard against the admission of evidence of little or no probative value': Australian Law Reform Commission, *Competence and Compellability* (ALRC Report 102, 13 February 2006) ch 4. In England and Wales, in its report Speaking Up For Justice, the Home Office stated, 'It is important to have a safeguard in place to prevent the court hearing evidence which is not only irrelevant but which, if admitted, would be unfair to the accused.' Home Office, *Speaking Up for Justice: Report of the Interdepartmental Working Group on the treatment of Vulnerable or Intimidated Witnesses in the Criminal Justice System* (1988) para 11.25, 87.

14 *R v Wallwork* [1958] 42 CAR 153.

15 *R v Wallwork* [1958] 42 CAR 153, 160.

16 *R v Barker* [2010] EWCA Crim 4, [2010] All ER (D) 126.

17 Sarah-Jane Murphy, 'The story of "Zoe", one of the youngest sex-abuse cases ever heard in Irish courts' *The Irish Times* (Dublin, 24 April 2021) <https://www.irishtimes.com/the-story-of-zoe-one-of-the-youngest-sex-abuse-cases-ever-heard-in-irish-courts-1.4537355> accessed 13 October 2023.

In the more recent case of *DPP v FN* [2021] IECA 238; [2022] IESC 22 the complainants were approximately four and six years old at the time of the alleged offences. The matter came on for trial approximately 20 months after the recording of the testimony.

communicate, not whether the witness actually perceived, recollects, and can communicate about the events in question.[18]

[9–09] In *DPP v VE*,[19] the child complainant's evidence was unsworn, which had been put forward as a cumulative factor as to why the trial judge should have given a corroboration warning. In addressing this, Ní Raifeartaigh J stated:

> … it is now almost thirty years since the Oireachtas saw fit to abolish the requirement that a child's evidence be sworn. Nothing in the legislation suggests that the unsworn evidence of a child is to be given lesser weight than sworn evidence. The weight to be given to a child's evidence depends more upon its content and the manner in which the child gives evidence and the overall circumstances than the simple fact of whether or not it was sworn.[20]

[9–10] However, child witnesses who are under 14 may still be sworn when giving testimony despite s 27 of the Criminal Evidence Act 1992 dispensing with the requirement for oath or affirmation for children under 14. In the case of *DPP v MC*,[21] the Court of Appeal judgment mentions that the witness, who was 12 at the time of the trial, gave sworn testimony.[22] As to whether a child may or may not be sworn is a factor for the court and the practitioners involved in the case. Whether the swearing of the child witness will have any bearing on the evidence in the perception of the jury is a consideration in the decision made.

[9–11] The section states that '[i]n any criminal proceedings *the evidence of a person under 14 years of age* (emphasis added) may be received otherwise than on oath or affirmation if the court is satisfied that he is capable of giving an intelligible account of events which are relevant to those proceedings'. The provision thereby applies to child defendants and, as s 27(3) of the Criminal Evidence Act 1992 allows the section to apply to a person with a 'mental handicap' who has reached the age of 14, the section may also apply to a defendant with a mental disorder. Mental handicap is not merely an outdated term but it is not defined within the section or the Act and it is submitted here that the section should be revised as soon as possible.

Presumption of Competence of Witnesses

[9–12] It is a common law presumption that all witnesses in Ireland are competent bar the accused, the accused's wife, children and persons with an intellectual disability.[23] If issues arise during the giving of evidence which challenge this presumption, the court may examine if the witness is competent to give evidence. Where a particular party submits that a witness is not competent, the responsibility is with them to show that this is the case based on the balance of probabilities.

[18] Laura Hoyano and Caroline Keenan, *Child Abuse, Law and Policy Across Boundaries* (Oxford University Press 2010) ch 8, 599, citing *R v Marquand* [1993] 4 SCR 223 (236); *R v MAM* [2001] BCCA 6 (British Columbia CA)(Rowles J).

[19] *DPP v VE* [2021] IECA 122.

[20] ibid [65].

[21] *DPP v MC* [2022] IECA 96.

[22] ibid [5]: 'The complainant was aged 12 at the time of the trial. Her evidence-in-chief consisted of a DVD recording of her interview by the Gardaí, which had been conducted by a specialist Garda interviewer. She was sworn at the trial and cross-examined after the DVD was played.'

[23] Liz Heffernan, *Evidence in Criminal Trials* (2nd edn, Bloomsbury 2020) para 2.20, 39.

In respect of vulnerable witnesses such as children and persons with an intellectual disability, even where no issues have been evident prior to trial, it appears to be the custom that the trial judge routinely assesses competency prior to the witness giving evidence at trial. This may be particularly relevant where recorded evidence has been admitted as evidence in chief testimony and there has been a significant interval between the recording of the evidence and the cross-examination of the witness. In relation to a challenge to competency of a witness, some evidence must be put forward for consideration by the Court. In *DPP v Campion*, in relation to the foundation for an allegation of incompetency, O'Malley J stated: [9–13]

> In this case the trial judge did not accede to the application for a determination of competency. Indeed, the application seems to have become subsumed to a large extent into the debate about the application to have the witness examined. In any event, I cannot see that such a procedure would have been warranted. The threshold for competency is low – an ability to understand questions and give intelligible answers on matters relevant to the issues in the trial. It is not the case that a party is entitled simply to put a witness's competency in issue by way of formal challenge, and thereby become entitled to a full hearing on the issue. Some foundation must be laid, whether by way of formal evidence or the presentation of other material, that gives rise to a genuine question for the trial judge to resolve. There was nothing in this case to indicate any doubt as to whether Mr. Cahill could pass the threshold test.[24]

Competence and the Offence of Perjury

If a child is competent and gives evidence which is proved to be deliberately false, the offence of perjury may be relevant. The offence of perjury was contained in s 30 of the Children Act 1908[25] and this provision is also included under s 27 of the Criminal Evidence Act 1992[26] and s 255 of the Children Act 2001. Indicating that these are still prosecutable offences, s 27 of the Criminal Evidence Act 1992, s 255 of the Children Act 2001 and s 28 of the Children Act 1997 (civil proceedings) are listed in the Schedules of the Criminal Justice (Perjury and Related Offences) Act 2021. [9–14]

The potential for a charge of offence of perjury for child witnesses raises a number of issues. Due to the age and offence eligibility relating to criminal responsibility in Ireland,[27] child witnesses under the age of 12 could not be prosecuted for a criminal offence including perjury.[28] Between the age of 12 and 14, an offence of perjury can only be taken with the consent of the DPP. A prosecution could still take place where the age of the witness is between 14 and 18 years of age, has given sworn testimony in court and subsequently given false testimony. There appears to be no procedural [9–15]

24 *DPP v Campion* [2018] IESC 35; [2021] 2 IR 1 [136].

25 Children Act 1908, s 30(b).

26 Criminal Evidence Act 1992, s 27(2): 'If any person whose evidence is received as aforesaid makes a statement material in the proceedings concerned which he knows to be false or does not believe to be true, he shall be guilty of an offence and on conviction shall be liable to be dealt with as if he had been guilty of perjury.'

27 Criminal Justice Act 2006, s 129, amended Children Act 2001, s 52. The section provides that the age of criminal responsibility is 12 but that a child of 10 or 11 may be responsible for the offences of murder, manslaughter, rape, or rape under s 4 of the Criminal Law (Rape)(Amendment) Act 1990, or aggravated sexual assault. Where a child under 14 years of age is charged with an offence, the Director of Public Prosecution's consent must be given to proceed beyond remand or bail proceedings.

28 A comprehensive examination of the issues regarding the age of criminal responsibility in Ireland is contained in Geoffrey Shannon, *Child and Family Law* (3rd edn, Round Hall 2020) 760–62.

guidance which indicates that the child witness should be warned where appropriate that he or she may be prosecuted for perjury if he or she gives false evidence when testifying. The guidance in the Good Practice Guidelines in relation the taking of recorded testimony outlines the necessity for the witness to tell the truth and to avoid telling lies.[29]

'Capable of giving an intelligible account'

[9–16] In *DPP v PP*,[30] counsel for the appellant cited *DPP v Mallen*[31] in relation to the requirement of a peace commissioner to be satisfied as to the relevant Garda's belief in relation to a search warrant as an analagous provision in respect of the need for an inquiry as to the competence of the witness under s 27 of the Criminal Evidence Act 1992. The statutory provision required an exercise in mental engagement of the facts as an essential part of the inquiry. The court in *DPP v PP* did not address this question as it determined that no issue regarding the witness's competence under the provision was warranted by her testimony. Sheehan J stated:

> In relation to s. 27(1) of the Criminal Evidence Act 1992 the Court has considered the submissions made by counsel for the appellant and the respondent. Evidence introduced by way of recorded DVD interview pursuant to the section does not have to be sworn. While this Court accepts the respondent's submission that s. 27 of the Act of 1992 does not prescribe the manner or form in which the inquiry should be embarked on, it is the view of this Court that it is preferable that such an inquiry be held prior to placing the evidence before the jury. The question for this Court is whether in the circumstances of this case, the failure to carry out a formal inquiry in advance rendered the trial unsatisfactory. This question must be considered in light of a number of matters. Firstly, the absence of a formal inquiry did not result in any unfairness to the appellant. Secondly, it requires to be considered in light of the cross-examination of the child witness. She was subjected to a relatively short but focused cross examination in which she was asked general questions about her family and then more specific questions about her memory, did she know

---

29 An Garda Síochána, *Good Practice Guidelines for Persons involved in Video Recording interviews with complainants under 14 years of age (or with intellectual disability) for Evidential Purposes in accordance with Section 16(1)(b) of the Criminal Evidence Act, 1992, in cases involving Sexual and/or Violent Offences* (July 2003) paras 3.8–3.10, 28.

'Establishing Ground Rules with the Complainant

The interviewer may then proceed to emphasise the necessity to tell the truth and to avoid telling lies. The complainant should be told the following:

- to tell the interviewer if he/she does not understand any question;
- to say to the interviewer if he/she does not know or does not remember the answer, and
- to correct the interviewer if the interviewer has misunderstood the complainant.

The interviewer should then explore such matters as the complainant's ability to distinguish between truth and lies; fantasy as opposed to reality; level of suggestibility and the presence of any family or other divisions/alliances which may affect the complainant's credibility during disclosure.

The interviewer may proceed by introducing some topic familiar to the complainant and develop the topic so as to allow the introduction of simple questions, such as "If I knocked over this glass and broke it, and then I told x that you did it, what would I be doing?" The complainant's response to this type of question may give the interviewer a reasonable idea of the complainant's concept and ability to distinguish between truth and lies. The interviewer may then develop the conversation into more specific matters, such as the complainant's favourite television programme or film to establish circumstances where he/she can explore the complainant's ability to determine reality from fantasy. This may be done by taking instances from a television programme or film and transposing the events or characters to a real life situation to explore the complainant's concept of real experience as opposed to imaginary situations'.

30 *DPP v PP* [2015] IECA 152.

31 *DPP v Mallen* [2011] IECCA 19.

> what pretending meant, and had she discussed the case with her mother. Following this she was then asked to view three DVD interviews in which she had been questioned by a member of the HSE. She was asked was she telling the truth in these interviews. She replied that she was and it is evident from the transcript that she answered all the other questions in a coherent manner. It is clear from this cross examination that the child witness was not only capable of giving an intelligible account but actually did so. There is no doubt that the witness satisfied the requirements of the section so there is no basis for any other conclusion. The failure to carry out a formal inquiry in advance to establish that fact cannot render the trial unsatisfactory. Accordingly this Court dismisses this ground of appeal.'[32]

The use of the word 'capable' may indicate that the child witness must have the requisite skill of giving an intelligible account of relevant proceedings but is not required to do so at all times during the course of giving evidence. In *R v Barker*,[33] a case which has been referenced approvingly in Irish case law,[34] the very young complainant's competency was unsuccessfully challenged. The Court pointed out: **[9–17]**

> The witness need not understand the special importance that the truth should be told in court, and the witness need not understand every single question or give a readily understood answer to every question. Many competent adult witnesses would fail such a competency test. Dealing with it broadly and fairly, provided the witness can understand the questions put to him and can also provide understandable answers, he or she is competent.[35]

Matter for Trial Judge to Determine Competence

In *R v Hayes*[36] where, in response to questions from the court, a 12-year-old boy stated that he had not received religious instruction and had not heard of God. However, the boy had stated that he understood the importance of telling the truth and was then sworn and gave evidence. On appeal, the Court of Appeal acknowledged that 'the divine sanction of an oath' was probably no longer recognised in society and held that the consideration to be determined was **[9–18]**

> whether the child has a sufficient appreciation of the solemnity of the occasion and the added responsibility to tell the truth, which is involved in taking an oath, over and above the duty to tell the truth which is an ordinary duty of normal social conduct.[37]

The Court also stressed that the determination of competence to take the oath was a matter for the trial judge, who was in the position of being able to personally assess the witnesses. Bridge LJ stated that an appellate court should 'hesitate long' before interfering with that decision.[38] After an assessment, a trial judge may decide that a child witness is capable of giving sworn testimony. **[9–19]**

In *AG v Kehoe*[39] the Court stated that it would follow *R v Hill*[40] in determining that it was **[9–20]**

---

32 *DPP v PP* [2015] IECA 152 [27].
33 *R v Barker* [2010] EWCA Crim 4 [38].
34 *DPP v VE* [2021] IECA 122; *DPP v MB* [2023] IECA 85; *DPP v MT* [2023] IECA 65.
35 *R v Barker* [2010] EWCA Crim 4 [38].
36 *R v Hayes* [1977] 1 WLR 234.
37 ibid 237.
38 ibid.
39 *AG v Kehoe* [1951] 1 IR 70.
40 *R v Hill* (1851) 2 Den 254.

for the trial judge to determine competence. Where there is a challenge to competency, the party tendering the witness may examine him or her to prove competency and the party making the challenge has the right to cross-examine the witness.[41] The question of competence must be determined in the case itself; the trial judge cannot rely on a previous finding of competence by him or her or any other judge in a previous case.[42]

[9–21] As mentioned above, some foundation must be laid in respect of a challenge to competency.[43]

Assessment of Competency

[9–22] In *DPP v PP*[44] recorded examination in chief testimony had been admitted as evidence under s 16(1)(b) of the Criminal Evidence Act 1992. The trial judge had made no inquiry as to whether the complainant was eligible to have such evidence admitted, ie was under 14 years of age at the time of recording. He had also omitted to assess whether the complainant was eligible to give unsworn testimony at trial under s 27 of the Criminal Evidence Act 1992. The defendant appealed on these and other grounds. The Court of Appeal accepted that s 27 of the Criminal Evidence Act 1992 does not prescribe the manner or form in which the inquiry should be embarked on. However, it was the view of the Court that it is preferable that such an inquiry be held prior to the placing of the evidence before the jury. It dismissed the appeal and, referring to these particular grounds, it stated that the absence of an inquiry did not result in an unfairness to the defendant as it was clear from her testimony that the complainant was not only capable of giving an intelligible account but did so. The Court stated that the failure to carry out a formal inquiry in advance of the complainant giving evidence did not render the trial unsatisfactory.[45]

[9–23] In the presence of the jury, prior to the child testifying either through recorded statement or live in court via video link, the judge may ask the witness general questions as to his or her age, what class he or she is in school, about a recent event, eg a sporting event, a recent birthday, whether he or she made his or her first communion/confirmation, what is happening in school, etc.

[9–24] In relation to recorded testimony, since the commencement of s 16(1)(b) of the Criminal Evidence Act 1992 and the admission of recorded testimony under that section, a responsibility to assess and monitor competence is now given to the Specialist Interviewers.[46] These trained interviewers conduct the recorded record examination in chief evidence in anticipation of its admission at trial. The *Good Practice Guidelines*[47]

---

41 *AG v Kehoe* [1951] 1 IR 70, 71 Maguire J: 'I propose to follow the practice in *R. v. Hill*, which I accept and believe to be correct. Counsel for the Attorney General will examine the witness to demonstrate her competency, and counsel for the accused will be permitted to cross-examine and to call evidence upon this issue, if he thinks proper. The final determination of the issue is for the judge alone.'

42 *People (AG) v Keating* [1953] IR 200, 201.

43 *DPP v Campion* [2018] IESC 35; [2021] 2 IR 1 [136].

44 *DPP v PP* [2015] IECA 152 [27].

45 ibid.

46 A Specialist Interviewer is the term which denotes a member of the gardaí or a person competent for the purpose who conducts a recorded interview with the appropriate witness for admission at trial at a later date under Criminal Evidence Act 1992, s 16(1)(b).

47 An Garda Síochána, *Good Practice Guidelines for Persons involved in Video Recording interviews with complainants under 14 years of age (or with intellectual disability) for Evidential Purposes in*

were drafted in 2003 as procedural guidance for use of the s 16(1)(b) of the Criminal Evidence Act 1992 and include a section regarding the assessment of competence of the witness with a view to the admission of the recorded testimony at trial.[48] As there may be a considerable interval between the taking of the recording and the commencement of the trial itself, a trial judge may assess the competence of a child witness before he or she is cross-examined.

The final determination of competence rests with the trial judge[49] and if the trial judge deems the witness to be incompetent then the recorded testimony will also be excluded. It is a requirement of the provision that the witness is available at trial for cross-examination[50] and so, if this is not possible either through absence or lack of competency, then all the evidence of the witness will be excluded. **[9–25]**

Oath Taken in Contrast to Witness' Professed Religion

Prior to giving evidence, the court registrar generally asks the witness how he or she wishes to swear, or affirm, and on which sacred text, as appropriate. In *R v Kemble*,[51] at the trial, a Muslim witness swore on the New Testament but in the appeal hearing, he swore on the Qur'an. Referencing the case, the Equal Treatment Bench Book notes: **[9–26]**

> He (the witness) told the Court of Appeal on oath that he considered himself conscience-bound by the oath he made at the trial. He added that he would still have considered the oath to be binding on his conscience whether he had taken it upon the Qur'an, the Bible or the Torah. The Court of Appeal accepted his evidence, finding that he considered all those books to be holy books, and thus that he was conscience-bound by his oath. This is despite the fact that evidence was received in that case that an oath taken by a Muslim is only binding if taken on the Qur'an. In the courtroom, the emphasis is upon receiving testimony and determining the credibility of the witness on the basis of his or her binding oath or affirmation.[52]

---

accordance with Section 16(1)(b) of the Criminal Evidence Act, 1992, in cases involving Sexual and/ or Violent Offences (July 2003).

48 ibid paras 2.14–2.18:

> '2.14 Following an assessment of the complainant's development and needs, the interview team should consider whether, in principle, the complainant is likely to be able to give a coherent account of the events under investigation.
>
> 2.15 A video recording will be able to speak to the court of any fact stated therein of which direct oral evidence by the complainant would be admissible. The issue of the competence of a complainant may therefore arise in relation to a video recording.
>
> 2.16 It is not possible to predict precisely, how the courts will treat the question of competence, if it is raised. It is reasonable for the interview team to assume that the courts will be willing to listen to the evidence of any complainant who can give a clear account of the alleged offence in a manner that the team, as a whole, can understand.'

49 *AG v Kehoe* [1951] 1 IR 70, 71.

50 Criminal Evidence Act 1992, s 16(1)(b): 'Provided that, in the case of a video recording mentioned in paragraph (b), the person whose statement was video recorded is available at the trial for cross-examination.'

51 *R v Kemble* [1990] 91 Cr App R 178.

52 *Equal Treatment Bench Book, England and Wales* (Judicial Council, February 2021 edn, April 2023 revision) 'The diversity of religious practice' paras 35–38, 278–79.

[9–27] In *Fay (A Debtor) v Personal Insolvency Acts 2012–2015*[53] McDonald J noted the case by reference to McGrath's *Evidence*[54] and observed:

> Where a witness gives evidence orally in court, the judge is in a position to ensure that the witness makes the appropriate oath or affirmation and that the witness is therefore aware of the essential importance of telling the truth. When the oath or affirmation is administered to a witness, there will always be complete silence in the courtroom so that the witness is conscious of the solemnity of the moment. There is a pause in the proceedings as both the registrar and witness stand for that purpose. At different points in the hearing, a witness may also be reminded by counsel or the court that he or she has sworn (or solemnly affirmed) to tell the truth. Often witnesses will themselves, in the course of their evidence, reaffirm that they have sworn to tell the truth.[55]

[9–28] Where a vulnerable witness is giving evidence, the manner and taking of the oath should be given attention to avoid difficulties which may impact on the evidence and on the stress of the witness. The court may also look to the circumstances surrounding how the evidence was taken.[56]

Sanction Versus Promise to Tell the Truth

[9–29] It is suggested that the offence of perjury should be revised for children under 14 years of age and rather the court should be obliged to ask the child witness to promise to tell the truth. This procedure appears to have some efficacy and an example of this is contained in s 16 of the Canada Evidence Act where a child under 14 who is giving evidence must first promise to tell the truth.[57] Lyons states that the comprehension of the child witness of truth and lies may be underestimated and a promise to tell the truth yields increased honest responses.[58] Whether or not any sanction could or should be imposed is difficult to evaluate; to communicate to the child, in an age-appropriate way, that it is important to tell the truth and to elicit from him or her a promise to do so may be more effective in terms of the quality of the evidence given. However, the Court of Appeal has outlined that a communication as to the consequences of not telling the truth may intimidate a young witness. The case of *DPP v JD*[59] involved the sexual abuse of a niece by the defendant. The complainant was approximately seven to nine years at the time of the abuse and 12 at the time of the trial. One of the grounds of the appeal was the admission of the s 16(1)(b) recording. The Appellant's case was

---

53 *Fay (A Debtor) v Personal Insolvency Acts 2012–2015* [2020] IEHC 163.

54 Declan McGrath and Emily Egan McGrath, *McGrath on Evidence* (3rd edn, Round Hall 2020) para 3–06, 95.

55 *Fay (A Debtor) v Personal Insolvency Acts 2012–2015* [2020] IEHC 163, [82].

56 *DPP v PP* [2015] IECA 152; *DPP v O'Brien* [2011] 1 IR 273.

57 Canada Evidence Act, s 16.1(6), 'Promise to tell truth': 'The court shall, before permitting a proposed witness under fourteen years of age to give evidence, require them to promise to tell the truth.'

Persons whose mental capacity is challenged under s 16(1) of the Act are also required to promise to tell the truth under the Canada Evidence Act, s 16(3) 'Testimony on promise to tell truth'

> 'A person referred to in subsection (1) who does not understand the nature of an oath or a solemn affirmation but is able to communicate the evidence may, notwithstanding any provision of any Act requiring an oath or a solemn affirmation, testify on promising to tell the truth.'

58 Thomas D Lyon, 'Assessing the Competency of Child Witnesses: Best Practice informed by Psychology and Law', in Michael E Lamb et al (eds), *Children's Testimony – A Handbook of Psychological Research and Forensic Practice* (2nd edn, Wiley-Blackwell 2011) 76.

59 *DPP v JD* [2018] IECA 232.

that no warning was given to the complainant before she participated in the interview as to the consequences of telling lies. The Court of Appeal agreed with the comments of the trial judge that a nine-year-old would be intimidated by a warning about the consequences of not telling the truth. Birmingham J stated:

> The Court agrees with the observations of the trial judge that common sense would suggest that a child of nine years would be intimidated by being warned of such consequences. In this case, it is clear from the transcript of the interview that the Gardaí went to very considerable lengths to establish that the complainant knew the difference between truth and lies and was fully aware of the importance of telling the truth.[60]

The appellant was unsuccessful on this and all grounds of appeal and the Court dismissed the appeal. However, an examination of how the offence of perjury may juxtapose with a prohibition of a warning against telling lies would be of assistance to the courts and a revision of the perjury offences for children is required to make them of practical use. **[9–30]**

No Ground for Appeal Where no Preliminary Examination of Competence

The decision in *DPP v PP*[61] underpins the decision in *AG v O'Sullivan*.[62] In the latter case, the Court stated that where the complainant gave sworn testimony which was not objected to during the course of the trial, and where it had been shown that the complainant's testimony did in no way give any foundation for such an objection, there could be no grounds of appeal on the basis that no preliminary examination was made. Although *O'Sullivan*[63] involved sworn as opposed to unsworn testimony as was the case in *DPP v PP*, it forms part of the body of jurisprudence which underscores the contention that where no objection is made and no issue arises as to competence, there is no ground for appeal merely on the basis of no inquiry having been made in advance of the evidence being given by the witness. **[9–31]**

Competency to be Assessed with the Use of Support Measures

It is to be noted that the competency of a witness will generally be assessed with the benefit of support measures such as video link, recorded testimony and, if required, with an intermediary. Although there is no statutory or procedural guidance regarding this aspect, it is significant that guidance in England and Wales mentions specifically that the competence of a witness is to be determined with the use of support measures. It states: **[9–32]**

> All people, whatever their age, are competent to act as witnesses unless they cannot understand questions asked of them in court or cannot answer them in a way that can be understood with, if necessary, the assistance of special measures (sections 53 and 54 of the 1999 Act and R v B [2010] EWCA Crim 4).[64]

---

60 ibid [7].

61 *DPP v PP* [2015] IECA 152 [27].

62 *AG v O'Sullivan* [1930] IR 552, 556–57.

63 ibid.

64 National Chiefs' Police Council, *Achieving Best Evidence in Criminal Proceedings: Guidance on Interviewing Victims and Witnesses, and Guidance on Using Special Measures* (Ministry of Justice, January 2022) para 5.20, 144–45.

[9–33] Archbold notes[65] that the incompetency of a witness may become apparent, however, only after he has commenced to give evidence[66] and, at common law, an objection may be made at any time during the trial.[67] The recording of pre-trial testimony now means that there may be a long interval between the taking of recorded examination in chief evidence and cross-examination at trial. In *R v Powell*[68] the defendant was convicted of child sexual abuse. Recorded examination in chief testimony was recorded close to the time of the offence. This had been admitted at trial under s 27 of the Youth Justice and Criminal Evidence Act 1999, played to the Court and the child witness then cross-examined. On appeal, the Court said that the test of competency should have been revisited by the trial judge at the time of cross-examination. The Court was unsure of the competency of the complainant who was three-and-a-half, particularly as the child was interviewed nine weeks after the date of the incident and there was a nine-month delay from the time of offence to date of trial. The implication of the case is that the test of competency remains live throughout the trial.

[9–34] In *R v Malicki*[69] the defendant was accused of child sexual abuse and the complainant was four years and eight months. Again, recorded examination in chief evidence taken close to the time of the incident was admitted at trial and the child witness cross-examined some time after the alleged incident. The Court of Appeal said that it could not be sure whether the complainant was remembering the details of the video of her recorded testimony or the details of the event itself. There was a delay of 14 months from the date of offence to the time of trial. Again the implication of the judgment is that competency is an issue that remains live throughout the trial, and in both *Powell*[70] and *Malicki*[71] the Court quashed the convictions and did not order a retrial.

[9–35] It is important to distinguish the separate issues of competency as opposed to difficulties in memory recall. In *DPP v MT*,[72] the Court noted that the inability of the complainant to recall the offence did not have anything to do with her competency:

> While the case does concern the issue of cross-examination of a child witness, it should be noted what the case is not about. It does not concern the issue of requiring counsel to tailor their cross-examination of a child to the age and understanding of the specific child, or whether the trial judge unfairly constrained the ability of counsel to cross-examine the child, or anything connected with "ground rules" hearings. Nor does it concern the competence of the child to give evidence in the sense of whether, in view of her age and understanding, she would have been capable of giving an intelligible account of events at the time of the interview and/or the trial. The question raised in this case is specific: it is whether, in view of the child's concession that she had little memory of the incident in question, the appellant's ability to cross-examine was so impaired as to be meaningless and that a fair trial could therefore not be achieved.[73]

---

65 *Archbold: Criminal Pleading Evidence and Practice* (ed PJ Richardson) (Sweet & Maxwell 2024) para 8.43, 1525.
66 *Jacobs v Layborn* (1843) 11 M & W 685.
67 *Stone v Blackburn* (1793) 1 ESp 37.
68 *R v Powell* [2006] 1 CAR 31.
69 *R v Malicki* [2009] EWCA Crim 365.
70 *R v Powell* [2006] 1 CAR 31.
71 *R v Malicki* [2009] EWCA Crim 365.
72 *DPP v MT* [2023] IECA 65.
73 ibid.

A significant factor of that case was that the complainant was six at the time of the alleged offence and 11 years of age at the time of cross-examination.[74] **[9–36]**

No Minimum Age of Witness

Section 27 of the Criminal Evidence Act 1992 does not specify a minimum age under which a child may not be allowed to give unsworn/sworn or unaffirmed/affirmed testimony. The prior age eligibility for the admission of unsworn testimony under s 30 of the Children Act 1908 was a child of 'tender years'. However, case law indicated a minimum age under which it was unlikely that a child would be called on to testify. In *R v Wallwork*,[75] Lord Goddard CJ 'deprecated' the calling of a child of five as a witness in a case of incest, saying that it was 'ridiculous' to suppose a jury would attach any value to it.[76] As late as 1990, the Court of Appeal in *R v Wright and Ormerod*[77] said that 'quite exceptional circumstances' would be required to justify receiving the evidence of a child of 'extremely tender years' such as six and stated that it would be a 'bold tribunal' which disregarded *Wallwork*.[78] **[9–37]**

The credibility of a child under a certain age may have been in doubt due to his or her capacity to remember and communicate details of the event to the court. There is also a doubt as to whether it is in the child's interests to give evidence where there may be a risk that he or she may be harmed by the process of giving evidence and having that testimony challenged. The evidence of very young children has been increasingly accepted by courts in this and neighbouring jurisdictions as competent and credible and given in circumstances where support measures have been used to ensure that the child witness is protected.[79] In *R v Barker*[80] the complainant, X, gave testimony at the age of four-and-a-half years of age concerning allegations of anal rape which had occurred when she was two-and-a-half years of age. She had disclosed details of the evidence when she was three-and-a-half and her examination in chief testimony had been recorded at that age under s 27 of the Youth Justice and Criminal Evidence Act 1999. Medical evidence showed that the allegation had occurred but was inconclusive as to the identity of the perpetrator. The trial had been delayed due to the fact that the defendant had also been charged with the unlawful death of X's brother, Peter Connolly, also known as Baby P, and that trial took priority. Therefore, X was cross-examined at trial when she was four-and-a-half years of age. The defendant was convicted predominantly on her testimony and subsequently challenged the decision on the basis of the competence of the complainant. The appeal court deemed the child witness competent in accordance with the parameters set down in s 53 of the Youth Justice and Criminal Evidence Act 1999 and quashed the appeal. The judgment noted that the courts had seen an increasing willingness to accommodate the witness: **[9–38]**

---

74 ibid [1].

75 *R v Wallwork* [1958] 42 CAR 153.

76 ibid 160.

77 *R v Wright and Ormerod* [1990] CAR 91.

78 *R v Wallwork* [1958] 42 CAR 153.

79 In *R v Barker* [2010] EWCA Crim 4, [2010] All ER (D) 126 the complainant was four-and-a-half years of age when cross-examined at trial. Since that trial, a child of three has given evidence in a case involving serious assault. See also: Owen Bowcott, 'Two-year-old girl gives evidence in UK abuse case: Defendant pleads guilty after intermediary helped police interview girl, believed to be youngest to give evidence in criminal case' *The Guardian* (London, 10 October 2017) <https://www.theguardian.com/law/2017/oct/10/two-year-old-girl-gives-evidence-in-uk-abuse-case> accessed 13 October 2023.

80 *R v Barker* [2010] EWCA Crim 4, [2010] All ER (D) 126.

> The trial process must, of course, and increasingly has, catered for the needs of child witnesses, as indeed it has increasingly catered for the use of adult witnesses whose evidence in former years would not have been heard, by, for example, the now well understood and valuable use of intermediaries. In short, the competency test is not failed because the forensic techniques of the advocate (in particular in relation to cross-examination) or the processes of the court (for example, in relation to the patient expenditure of time) have to be adapted to enable the child to give the best evidence of which he or she is capable. At the same time the right of the defendant to a fair trial must be undiminished.[81]

[9–39] The complainant in the case of 'Zoe' has been reported as one of the youngest witnesses to give evidence in a criminal trial in Ireland. There was an acquittal in that case and the report highlights the difficulties of delay and procedural issues in a matter such as this.[82] However, there appear to have been no difficulties in terms of the complainant's age in relation to her competency as a witness.

[9–40] In Ireland, cases such as *DPP v VE*[83] and *DPP v FN*[84] indicate to what extent the criminal courts have moved away from concerns that a young child may not be a competent witness. The individual characteristics of the victim or witness appear to be the most important consideration and whether or not he or she passes the test under s 27 Criminal Evidence Act 1992.

Fitness to Plead/Assistance to Participate – Vulnerable Defendants

[9–41] In relation to defendants, the mental health issues of a defendant may make him or her unfit to plead. If so, a hearing as to the defendant's fitness to plead may be carried out under s 4 of the Criminal Law (Insanity) Act 2006. If a judge, hearing the evidence, determines that the defendant cannot understand the charge, is unable to instruct a legal team, in relation to an indictable offence, elect for trial by jury, challenge jurors or follow the evidence, then he or she may be considered unfit to be tried. If so, a committal to a psychiatric unit or appropriate treatment may be required and a further decision taken at a later date. At time of sentencing, depending on the charge, if there is finding of mental disorder or diminished responsibility at the time of the offence, accommodation may be made in relation to the finding of guilt and the sentence imposed.[85]

[9–42] If a defendant is found fit to plead, there may still be many accommodations required in terms of the requirements mentioned above in terms of understanding the charge, instructing a legal team, challenging jurors or following evidence. In the case of *DPP v Harrison*,[86] the defendant had been found fit to plead but still had difficulties resulting from a brain injury. In the ruling of the Court, Edwards J stated that the

---

81 ibid [42].

82 Sarah-Jane Murphy, 'The story of "Zoe", one of the youngest sex-abuse cases ever heard in Irish courts' *The Irish Times* (Dublin, 24 April 2021) <https://www.irishtimes.com/the-story-of-zoe-one-of-the-youngest-sex-abuse-cases-ever-heard-in-irish-courts-1.4537355> accessed 13 October 2023.

83 *DPP v VE* [2021] IECA 122 [80].

84 *DPP v FN* [2021] IECA 238; [2022] IESC 22. The complainant was six at the time of the offence and eight at the time of trial. Examination in chief evidence was recorded under Criminal Evidence Act 1992, s 16(1)(b).

85 Thomas O'Malley, *Sentencing Law and Practice* (3rd edn, Round Hall 2016) para 6.15.

86 *DPP v Harrison* [2016] IECA 212.

Court disagreed with the trial judge's view that the Court could not assess what the defendant might require at trial.

> We disagree with that view and consider it an unjustified conclusion in the absence of a thorough, rigorous and searching exploration of the likely extent of the respondent's potential difficulties, and the range of possible measures that might be put in place to address them. The treatment of the issue at the fitness hearing was fleeting and superficial, and there was no proper engagement with the potential problems at any trial that might proceed, far less any cogent analysis. We make no criticism of the fact that that was so. The fitness hearing was not an appropriate one in which to address such issues, other than in the most general way. It was concerned with fitness to be tried in principle, not with any practical arrangements that might have to be put in place for the assurance of a fair trial of the respondent should he be found to be fit to stand trial having regard to the statutory criteria. To the extent that we are critical, it is that the trial judge considered that such practical arrangements were appropriate for consideration at that stage; then, having taken that view, failed to direct a further and more detailed exploration of the possibilities in that regard, concluding instead without a sufficiently rigorous examination of the issue that reconciling the conflicting interests of the State and the respondent was "an impossibility". It was not appropriate to use a finding of unfitness to stand trial to reflect such a view even if that view had been properly arrived at after appropriate enquiries, much less where it was arrived at after only the most superficial of enquiries. A question raised as to a person's fitness to be tried in principle must be considered and determined separately and discretely from any issue as to whether a person, having been found fit to be tried in principle, can in fact receive a fair trial in light of particular personal, mental or physical difficulties.
>
> That having been said, we adopt and approve of the statement by Lord Bingham in *Brown v. Stott* [2003] 1 A.C. 681 at 704, that it is a case of *ex facto oritur ius* (the law flows from the particular facts). Indeed, it has always been so. To give some examples, deaf people can be accommodated by sign language interpreters or induction loop facilities; blind people can be accommodated by the provision of documents in brail or the use of Optacon devices, or synthesised speech reading machines; people with speech difficulties can likewise be accommodated by various technical devices; vulnerable witnesses can be accommodated in various ways, such as by video link, screens and advance video-recording; witnesses from outside the State who are unable or unwilling to travel, and unavoidably absent witnesses within the state, can be accommodated by video link; and non-English speaking foreign nationals can be accommodated by translators and interpreters. Seriously ill persons, who might perhaps tire easily, or who must absent themselves regularly to undergo some procedure, e.g., kidney dialysis or chemotherapy, might be accommodated by shorter sittings, or breaks, or overnight adjournments. An accused person who has to temporarily absent himself or herself from the trial due to the onset of sudden acute illness might be accommodated by an adjournment, or a jury discharge with a view to starting the trial again, or by the provision of a transcript of what occurs in their absence.[87]

The Court went on to say that it was not possible to produce an exhaustive list of the many possible ways that a person who met the statutory criteria in terms of his/her fitness to be tried, but who nonetheless had particular personal mental or physical difficulties, might be assisted and accommodated. Each case would obviously depend upon its own facts. The Court stated that, assuming it is possible in a particular case to propose an accommodation or accommodations that may be efficacious to ensure that the accused concerned will receive a fair trial, the only limitation that should be put on such proposals is that they should be reasonably practical; they should be confined to what is strictly necessary, and they should not confer such an unfair advantage on the beneficiary as to render an unfairness to the other side. The Court added that the [9–43]

87 [2016] IECA 212 [53]–[54].

fact that accommodations might prolong a trial, perhaps significantly, should not be a reason in itself to discount their suitability or practicality.[88]

[9–44] In terms of child defendants, the protections under the Children Act 2001 are underpinned by the case *T v UK*, an appeal to the European Court of Human Rights, in respect of the children convicted of the murder of James Bulger.[89] It is significant in relation to requirement of the trial court to ensure that the child defendant can fully participate in criminal proceedings.

---

88 ibid [55]–[56].

89 *T v the United Kingdom* (24724/94).

CHAPTER 10

COMPELLABILITY

Introduction

Having been deemed a competent witness, the courts may also consider whether a witness is compellable to give evidence. Heffernan notes: **[10–01]**

> Whether a party may tender the evidence of a witness is governed by two related concepts: the competence of the witness and the compellability of the witness. The concept of competence relates to the personal capacity of a witness to provide information to the court. By contrast, compellability is synonymous with the authority of the trial court to enforce the attendance of a witness in court.[1]

The issue of compellability in terms of a vulnerable witness is related to the issues of prioritising the wellbeing of the witness as well as obtaining the best quality evidence possible. If a witness does not testify or 'swear up' in court, then the chance of a successful prosecution may be put in jeopardy. O'Donnell J noted in *DPP v Rattigan* in relation to s 16 Criminal Justice Act 2006, which allowed the admission of statements where witnesses resiled from giving testimony, 'The capacity of any legal system to compel the production of relevant testimony and real evidence is central to its ability to perform the function of the administration of justice.'[2] **[10–02]**

It is rare that the compellability of child witnesses in criminal cases is raised and there appears to be little reported judgment in this area. **[10–03]**

Guidance may be taken from care proceedings in judgments in England. The case of *R S (Children)*[3] concerned an appeal against a decision of a judge in care proceedings regarding two children aged four and two. Their aunt, who was 15 years of age, had made allegations of sexual abuse against her brother, who was ten years older than her. The suspect had been charged but the complainant subsequently informed the police that she did not wish to give evidence and, despite efforts to change her mind, the case was discontinued, no evidence being offered by the prosecution. **[10–04]**

In care proceedings, the judge had found the allegations proved and supervision orders were placed in respect of the appellant as a result of the allegations of his sister, who had not given evidence against him. The Court of Appeal (Civil Division) stated: **[10–05]**

> Against this background, the judge set herself the task of considering what K giving evidence would bring to the determination of the truth of the allegations that she had made and balancing that against the possible damage to her welfare that would be caused

1 Liz Heffernan, *Evidence in Criminal Trials* (2nd edn, Bloomsbury 2020) para 2.18, 38.
2 *DPP v Rattigan* [2013] IECCA 13.
3 *Re S(Children)* [2016] EWCA Civ 83.

> by the process. In so doing, she looked at a considerable number of diverse factors including: i) K's degree of maturity; ii) The availability of recorded ABE interviews; iii) The time that had elapsed since the events occurred; iv) The degree of support that K would have from her family or otherwise, and in particular the support offered by the paternal grandmother; v) The risk of delay being caused by arranging for K to give evidence; vi) K's fluctuating views about giving evidence and her feelings generally, including her sense of responsibility for the rift in her family and the situation of the appellant and his children; vii) The appellant's clear denial of the allegations, from the outset, albeit that the full detail of his case was not yet available; viii) The opportunity that there would be for the ABE evidence to be challenged in submissions; and ix) The lack of opportunity to cross-examine K if she did not give evidence.[4]

[10–06] The appeal was dismissed, the Court of Appeal having considered that the judge had taken into consideration the necessary factors in making her finding as to whether the complainant should be made to give evidence. The case may not be directly helpful in relation to criminal proceedings in Ireland but it does outline the difficulties in such a matter. In referring to the case of *Re W (Children)*[5] the Court of Appeal stated:

> When considering whether a particular child should be called as a witness, the court has to weigh two considerations, namely the advantages that calling the child will bring to the determination of the truth and the damage it may do to the welfare of this or any other child (paragraph 24 of Re W). On both sides of the equation, the court must take account of what steps can be taken to improve the quality of the child's evidence and at the same time to decrease the risk of harm to the child[6]

[10–07] In a criminal case in England,[7] a 15-year-old girl had been groomed by the defendant, who faced child sexual abuse charges, and subsequently refused to give evidence against him. In exceptional circumstances, with the complainant having absconded from the environs of the court as well as the possibility that she might influence other witnesses, the trial judge ordered her to be arrested and held in custody. She was detained for 20 hours and ultimately gave evidence, which lasted 22 minutes. The defendant was convicted. The article notes that when the witness had first arrived there was a delay of five hours and there was no courtroom available. A witness may not wish to give evidence because of loyalty, fear or intimidation. This may cause considerable difficulties for the prosecution. However, organisational issues may also exacerbate any particular difficulties the witness may be experiencing and it is suggested that appropriate planning and communication may resolve certain issues for the witness.

[10–08] The consent of the parents and guardians in relation to child witnesses is also a paramount consideration. For many reasons, a parent or guardian may not wish a child to testify, eg to save the child from a traumatising experience, to prevent reminders of the original incident resurfacing, to prevent the child being accused of being a liar or mistaken. If a child is not willing to give evidence or if a parent or guardian does not give consent, it is unlikely that the child will be compelled to give evidence. It is more likely that where a child witness or a witness with an intellectual disability refuses to give evidence, the evidence will not be available to the court. Apart from any

---

4 ibid [27].

5 *Re W (Children)* [2010] UKSC 12.

6 *Re S(Children)* [2016] EWCA Civ 83 [41].

7 Caroline Davies, 'Judge under fire after ordering detention of child sex abuse victim' *The Guardian* (London, 5 March 2014) <http://www.theguardian.com/uk-news/2014/mar/05/judge-bradford-bartfield-order-child-sex-abuse-victim> accessed 13 October 2023.

constitutional obligation of the court to protect the rights of the child,[8] the quality of any evidence given where a vulnerable witness is being forced to testify is likely to be impaired. Where a vulnerable witness did resile from giving evidence, and where a statement had been recorded, recourse has been made to s 16 of the Criminal Justice Act 2006 in *DPP v O'Brien*.[9] However, there appear to be no other circumstances in respect of the use of that legislation to support the admission of recorded evidence and that case should be seen in that context.

8 Art 42A, Constitution of Ireland.

9 [2011] IR 273.

CHAPTER 11

CORROBORATION

Introduction

Corroboration was defined by Reading LJ as follows: **[11–01]**

> We hold that evidence in corroboration must be independent testimony which affects the accused by connecting or tending to connect him with the crime. In other words, it must be evidence which implicates him, that is, which confirms in some material particular not only the evidence that the crime has been committed, but also that the prisoner committed it. The test applicable to determine the nature and extent of the corroboration is thus the same whether the case falls within the rule of practice at common law or within that class of offences for which corroboration is required by statute. The language of the statute, "implicates the accused," compendiously incorporates the test applicable at common law in the rule of practice. The nature of the corroboration will necessarily vary according to the particular circumstances of the offence charged. It would be in high degree dangerous to attempt to formulate the kind of evidence which would be regarded as corroboration, except to say that corroborative evidence is evidence which shows or tends to show that the story of the accomplice that the accused committed the crime is true, not merely that the crime has been committed, but that it was committed by the accused.[1]

While s 30 of the Children Act 1908 allowed for a child 'of tender years' to be able to give his or her evidence otherwise than on oath, a person could not be convicted on that uncorroborated evidence. In addition, if the child was able to give unsworn testimony, the judge was obliged to give a mandatory corroboration warning to the jury regarding the evidence of a child in a sexual offences case.[2] Changes under ss 27 and 28 of the Criminal Evidence Act 1992 are extremely significant not only for the practical ramifications concerning the prosecution of criminal offences which pertain to children but also regarding the perception of a child's evidence. **[11–02]**

Under s 27, a child under 14 (or a person with a 'mental handicap') is able to give evidence which is not sworn or affirmed. The requirement for that admission is that he or she can give an intelligible account of events which are relevant to the proceedings. The dispensation of the corroboration requirement under s 28 of the Criminal Evidence Act **[11–03]**

1 *R v Baskerville* [1916] 2 KB 658, 667.
2 The Children Act 1908, s 30. See also *AG v O'Sullivan* [1930] IR 552.

1992 means that where there is no corroborative evidence, a child's testimony alone can be the basis of a conviction where that child is under 14 and gives unsworn testimony. Under s 28(2), the corroboration warning was made discretionary and if a warning was given to the jury, the judge may give it in words of his or her own choosing. Under s 28(3) of the Act the unsworn evidence of a child can now corroborate the testimony of another person's testimony whether that evidence be sworn or unsworn. In cases where there are multiple child complainants this is clearly significant.

Section 28 Criminal Evidence Act 1992

[11–04] A child complainant who gives unsworn testimony does not have to have his or her evidence corroborated by other evidence.

> 'Abolition of requirement of corroboration for unsworn evidence of child, etc.
>
> 28. –(1) The requirement in section 30 of the Children Act, 1908, of corroboration of unsworn evidence of a child given under that section is hereby abolished.

[11–05] A trial judge is not obliged to give a warning about the uncorroborated evidence of a child.

> (2) (a) Any requirement that at a trial on indictment the jury be given a warning by the judge about convicting the accused on the uncorroborated evidence of a child is also hereby abolished in relation to cases where such a warning is required by reason only that the evidence is the evidence of a child and it shall be for the judge to decide, in his discretion, having regard to all the evidence given, whether the jury should be given the warning.
>
> (b) If a judge decides, in his discretion, to give such a warning as aforesaid, it shall not be necessary to use any particular form of words to do so.

[11–06] A child who gives unsworn evidence can corroborate evidence, be it sworn or unsworn, of any other person.

> (3) Unsworn evidence received by virtue of section 27 may corroborate evidence (sworn or unsworn) given by any other person.

Section 27 Criminal Evidence Act 1992

Provisions for unsworn testimony apply to a person with a 'mental handicap'

[11–07] Section 27(3) states that subsection (1) shall apply to a person with a mental handicap who has reached the age of 14 years as it applies to a person under that age.[3]

[11–08] It is not clear why the use of 'mental handicap' was not revised, particularly in light of the amendment of 'mental handicap' to that of 'mental disorder' in s 19 of the Criminal

---

3 Criminal Evidence Act 1992, s 27(2): 'Reference in subs. (2) to perjury construed (28.07.2021) by Criminal Justice (Perjury and Related Offences) Act 2021 (13/2021), s. 4(2) and sch. 2 item no. 36, SI No 378 of 2021. References to perjury or subornation of perjury 4. ... (2) A reference in an enactment specified in Schedule 2 to perjury or to subornation of perjury, howsoever described, in relation to an act committed on or after the coming into operation of this subsection, shall be construed as a reference to perjury or to subornation of perjury, as the case may be, within the meaning of this Act. SCHEDULE 2 Section 4(2) ... 36.'

Evidence Act 1992, and its definition under s 5 of the Criminal Justice Act 1993, in relation to the use of screens, intermediaries and recorded evidence. It is suggested here that this provision be revised.

Section 7 Criminal Law (Rape) (Amendment) Act 1990

Sexual offences –removal of mandatory corroboration warning

Section 7 of the Criminal Law (Rape)(Amendment) Act 1990[4] removed the requirement for mandatory corroboration warning in relation to sexual offences. The section also provided that if the trial judge should wish to give a warning, he or she was not required to use any particular form of words to do so. **[11–09]**

When the Court May Give a Corroboration Warning in Relation to Children

In the case of *DPP v VE*,[5] the Court examined the abolishment of mandatory corroboration warnings in respect of children and sexual offences. **[11–10]**

> Section 28 of the Criminal Evidence Act 1992 abolishes the mandatory requirement of a corroboration warning in cases involving children, while s. 7 of the 1990 Act abolishes the mandatory requirement of a corroboration warning in cases involving sexual offences. The previous Court of Criminal Appeal and this Court have repeatedly emphasised the discretion which inheres in the trial judge to deal with this matter, and that the purpose of the legislative provision should not be undermined by over-readiness to give such warnings. Relatively recently, the decision of this *Court in DPP v Wooldridge*[6] re-stated the principles, emphasising that the giving of a corroboration warning falls within the discretion of the trial judge and, more particularly, that the abolition of the mandatory corroboration warning must not be circumvented by a trial judge simply adopting a prudent or cautious approach of giving a corroboration warning in every case where there is no corroboration. The Court said "There must be something *special or peculiar* in the evidence which give rise to the danger of convicting the person on the uncorroborated evidence of that person before one is required" (para 14) (emphasis added).[7]

In the case of *DPP v MC*,[8] Ni Raifertaigh J noted that there were issues which could have been left for the jury to decide had the appellant chose to cross-examine on them: **[11–11]**

---

4 Criminal Law (Rape) (Amendment) Act 1990, s 7, Corroboration of evidence in proceedings in relation to offences of a sexual nature:

> '(1) Subject to any enactment relating to the corroboration of evidence in criminal proceedings, where at the trial on indictment of a person charged with an offence of a sexual nature evidence is given by the person in relation to whom the offence is alleged to have been committed and, by reason only of the nature of the charge, there would, but for this section, be a requirement that the jury be given a warning about the danger of convicting the person on the uncorroborated evidence of that other person, it shall be for the judge to decide in his discretion, having regard to all the evidence given, whether the jury should be given the warning; and accordingly any rule of law or practice by virtue of which there is such a requirement as aforesaid is hereby abolished.
>
> (2) If a judge decides, in his discretion, to give such a warning as aforesaid, it shall not be necessary to use any particular form of words to do so.'

5 *DPP v VE* [2021] IECA 122.

6 *DPP v Wooldridge* 2018 IECA 135.

7 *DPP v VE* [2021] IECA 122 [61].

8 *DPP v MC* [2022] IECA 96.

In the present case, we consider that the trial judge was well within his discretion in deciding not to give a warning. There was nothing particularly vague or unusual in any respect about the complainant's evidence in the present case, based on the Court's collective experience of the evidence of child complainants. The appellant lays particular emphasis upon the fact that the complainant said that she had discussed the matter with her mother "a couple of times a week" after the Garda interview, while her mother said they never discussed it. This was a matter for the jury to consider. It may be noted that the complainant was not cross-examined as to whether her mother had influenced her in making the allegations; nor was it was never [sic] suggested to the mother that she had influenced her daughter, improperly or otherwise, in her making of the allegations. The issue featured in the mother's cross-examination only to the extent that she was asked if she had discussed it with her daughter after the Garda interview, to which she replied that she had not, and there was then a question "so if someone were to suggest that you had discussed these matters after that date, they'd be incorrect, would they?", to which she gave an affirmative answer. In comparison to other matters which were explored in cross-examination, this was an issue on which there was a very light touch. We do not consider that this was a matter of such significance at the trial that it amounted to an error of law on the part of the trial judge not to have given the corroboration warning because of its presence on the evidence.[9]

Nature of Corroboration

[11–12] In the case of *DPP v EC*[10] where the appellant was appealing his conviction in respect of sexual offences against his three children, his points of appeal included an appeal as to whether certain evidence could have constituted corroboration. In giving the judgment of the Court and dismissing this point, Edwards J stated:

While to date it has not been considered necessary for Irish law to totally abandon the approach commended in *Rex v. Baskerville*, the decision of the Court of Criminal Appeal in *The People (Director of Public Prosecutions) v. Meehan* [2006] 3 I.R. 468 makes it clear beyond peradventure that the Baskerville approach must be applied in a nuanced and flexible way that takes appropriate account of the circumstances of the case, including the manner in which the case is run, the nature of the facts in issue in respect of which corroboration is desirable or necessary, and any defence set up by the accused. It is sufficient if there is confirmation of a material part of the witnesses' evidence implicating the accused in the offences.[11]

The appeal failed on this and all other points.

Warning Does Not Have to be in Any Particular Form of Words

[11–13] In the case of *DPP v PB*,[12] a corroboration warning was given where there had been difficulties in memory recall and inconsistencies in the evidence of the witness.[13] The defendant appealed on the basis that the corroboration warning had not been adequate in relation to the evidence in the case. The Court of Appeal stated:

The starting point for consideration of this has to be the fact that the giving of a warning

---

9 ibid [57].

10 *DPP v EC* [2016] IECA 150. See also *DPP v RO'M* [2021] IECA 243.

11 ibid.

12 *DPP v PB* [2021] IECA 152.

13 It should be noted that approximately four years had passed between the taking of the witness' evidence under s 16(1)(b) Criminal Evidence Act 1992 and the matter coming on for trial.

> is not mandatory, and that if a warning is given, the judge is not required to follow any particular form of words. In this case, the judge dealt with the issue of corroboration at two points during the course of his charge and then dealt further with the issue in response to requisitions. In the Court's view, while what the judge had to say would not be described as a textbook corroboration warning, it was, in the circumstances of the case, in our view more than adequate.[14]

While no formula exists, anecdotal evidence would suggest that the phrase 'dangerous to convict' on uncorroborated evidence which was commonly the phrase used in the warning to the jury[15] has now been overtaken by use of the word 'caution' where the evidence is uncorroborated. **[11–14]**

Warning Where Mental Health Concerns Exist in Relation to Reliability of Witness's Evidence

Coonan and Foley[16] note that the case of *People (DPP) v Molloy*[17] illustrates that where a warning as to the reliability of a witness's evidence is to be given on the basis of concerns regarding the witness's mental health, the trial judge should be careful that all factors affecting reliability are outlined to the jury.[18] **[11–15]**

---

14 *DPP v PB* [2021] IECA 152 [38]–[39].

15 See for example *DPP v MS* [2020] IECA 309.

16 Genevieve Coonan, Brian Foley *The Judge's Charge in Criminal Trials* (Thomson Reuters 2008).

17 *People (DPP) v Molloy* (Court of Criminal Appeal, 28 July 1995).

18 Geneieve Coonan, Brian Foley *The Judge's Charge in Criminal Trials* (Thomson Reuters 2008) para 32.21, 638.

Chapter 12

COURT ACCOMPANIMENT

Introduction

The need for support and assistance at court has been seen in the provision of court accompaniment services through charities such as Support After Crime,[1] Victim Support at Court, Accompaniment Support Services for Children (ASSC)[2] and Dublin Rape Crisis Centre.[3] While not offering legal advice or commenting on the evidence, volunteers can offer services to familiarise the victim/witness with the geography of the court room and court procedures before the trial and accompany him or her during the trial. **[12–01]**

The provisions which allow for the exclusion of the general public also outline who may remain. Generally, these include persons directly concerned with the matter, officers of the court, bona fide members of the press and those persons who the judge allows to remain. **[12–02]**

In addition, for certain eligible persons, based on age or gender or offence, a parent, or other relative or support worker may be allowed to remain. Terms for these may include 'accompanying adult' or 'appropriate person'. In relation to exclusion of the public/otherwise than in public, certain persons including appropriate persons and support workers may remain in order to support the witness or defendant as appropriate.[4] **[12–03]**

---

1 Support After Crime Services <https://www.supportaftercrimeservices.ie/> accessed 13 October 2023.

2 Victim Support At Court <https://www.vsac.ie/> accessed 13 October 2023; Accompaniment Support Services for Children (ASSC) https://assc.ie/ accessed 13 October 2023.

3 Dublin Rape Crisis Centre <https://www.drcc.ie/services/accompaniment/> accessed 13 October 2023.

4 See Chapter 8 – In Camera /Anonymity/Reporting Restrictions/Exclusion of the Public/ Otherwise than in Public/Clearing of the Court.

Section 20(4)(b) Criminal Justice Act 1951

Complainant under 21 or female may be accompanied during hearing where offence is of indecent or obscene nature

[12–04] Section 20(4)(b) of the Criminal Justice Act 1951 allows, for a complainant who is under 21 or a female, where the offence is of an indecent or obscene nature, for a parent or other relative or friend or a support worker chosen by the complainant to be entitled to remain in court during the whole of the hearing.

Section 91 Children Act 2001

Requirement that child defendants be accompanied by adult

[12–05] Section 91 Children Act 2001 provides a requirement for an accompanying adult to be present during investigative and court proceedings for child defendants.[5]

Section 257 Children Act 2001[6]

'Clearing of court in certain cases' (when a child is giving evidence, certain persons may remain in court)

[12–06] Under this section, the court, when a child is giving evidence, where exclusion provisions do not already apply, may exclude all persons except for bona fide members of the press, those persons connected with the case or those permitted by the court to remain. With the discretion of the court, a parent, relative, friend or support person is likely to be able to remain. In addition, it is frequently the case that a child would be giving evidence via video link and would have someone with him or her close to the video link suite in addition to the accompaniment of the court usher in that case.

Section 18 Criminal Justice (Victims of Crime) Act 2017

Appropriate persons

[12–07] For child victims, s 18 of the Criminal Justice (Victims of Crime) Act 2017 deals with the provision of appropriate persons for child victims. Section 18 outlines that where

---

5 See Chapter 8 – In Camera /Anonymity/Reporting Restrictions/Exclusion of the Public/ Otherwise than in Public/Clearing of the Court.

6 Children Act, s 257, Clearing of court in certain cases:

> '(1) Where in any proceedings for an offence a person who, in the opinion of the court, is a child is called as a witness, the court may exclude from the court during the taking of his or her evidence all persons except officers of the court, persons directly concerned in the proceedings, bona fide representatives of the Press and such other persons (if any) as the court may in its discretion permit to remain.
>
> (2) The powers of a court under this section shall be in addition and without prejudice to any other power of the court to hear proceedings in camera or to exclude a witness until his or her evidence is required or to Part III (which relates to evidence through a television link in certain proceedings) of the Act of 1992.
>
> (3) The said Part III and section 22 (which relates to compellability of spouses to give evidence at instance of prosecution in certain cases) of the Act of 1992 are hereby amended by the deletion of "17 years" wherever it occurs and the substitution of "18 years". (4) In this section "the Act of 1992" means the Criminal Evidence Act, 1992.'

a victim is a child and where a parent, guardian or any other person authorised to act on the victim's behalf has been charged, or is under investigation for, an offence in connection with the victim, or is, for any other reason, precluded from accompanying the victim, is unavailable or cannot be contacted, or indicates that he or she does not wish to accompany the victim, or cannot be identified, then An Garda Síochána or the Ombudsman Commission shall arrange for the victim to be accompanied by an appropriate person when attending any interviews and court proceedings at which the victim is required to be present.

In deciding who the appropriate person may be, the member of An Garda Síochána or an officer of the Ombudsman Commission shall have regard to any views expressed by the child taking into account his or her age and level of maturity. Where an appropriate person is appointed to accompany a victim, he or she shall be entitled to remain in court during the whole of any hearing. For the purposes of s 18 'appropriate person' means a relative of the child, or any other person, who is 18 years or over. **[12–08]**

Apart from the specific reasons outlined above, there may be other instances where an appropriate adult may be required to be appointed by An Garda Síochána or an officer of the Ombudsman Commission. For example, if a child victim's parent or guardian is also a witness in a case, it may be necessary for the adult to remain outside the court while the victim gives evidence. Depending on the circumstances of the case, the trial judge may wish for the victim to have another adult or 'appropriate adult' in court to ensure that the child victim feels secure and reassured. **[12–09]**

Section 26 Domestic Violence Act 2018

'Right to be accompanied in certain circumstances'–safety order, barring order, emergency barring order

In addition to his or her legal representative, an applicant,[7] in respect of a safety order,[8] barring order,[9] or emergency barring order,[10] may be accompanied by an individual (including a support worker) of his or her choice. The court may refuse to allow an applicant to be accompanied in court by a particular individual at any stage in the proceedings which relate to the applicant if the court considers that it would not be in the interests of justice for the individual concerned to accompany, or continue to accompany, the applicant and, where the court so refuses, it shall give reasons for such refusal. In this section, 'support worker' means a volunteer of, or an individual employed under a contract of service or under a contract for services by, an organisation which provides support to victims of domestic violence.[11] **[12–10]**

---

7 Domestic Violence Act 2018, s 2, Interpretation: '"applicant" has the meaning assigned to it by section 6, section 7 or section 9, as the case may be, and where – (a) an interim barring order has been made the applicant for the barring order to whom the interim barring order relates shall be deemed to be the applicant for that interim barring order, and (b) a protection order has been made the applicant for the safety order or the barring order to whom the protection order relates shall be deemed to be the applicant for that protection order'.

8 Domestic Violence Act 2018, s 6.

9 ibid s 7.

10 ibid s 9.

11 ibid s 26, Right to be accompanied in court in certain circumstances:

> '(1) Subject to subsection (2), an applicant may, in addition to being accompanied by his or her legal representative (if any), be accompanied in court by an individual (including a support worker) of his or her choice.

Section 20(4)(a) of the Criminal Justice Act 1951

[12–11] Section 20(4)(a) of the Criminal Justice Act 1951 allows, in any criminal proceedings, for an accused under 21 to have a parent or other relative or friend to be entitled to remain in court during the whole of the hearing.

Section 9 Criminal Procedure Act 2021[12]

'Power to exclude public' (preliminary trial hearings or appeals)

[12–12] This section states that preliminary trial hearings or their appeal hearings shall be conducted in open court subject to any other enactment. This then means that any provision which may apply shall apply to this section. Where a hearing should be conducted in open court, the judge has a right to exclude the public, a portion of the public, or any particular person or persons where he or she is satisfied that because of the nature or circumstances of the case or otherwise in the interests of justice that it is desirable to do so. Officers of the court, bona fide members of the press and persons connected with the case may remain. The section also allows for (a) a parent, relative or friend of the accused or of an injured party, or (b) a support worker chosen by an injured party to remain when

- s 20(4) of the Criminal Justice Act 1951;
- s 6 of the Criminal Law (Rape) Act 1981;
- s 8 of the Criminal Justice (Female Genital Mutilation) Act 2012; or
- s 20 of the Criminal Justice (Victims of Crime) Act 2017 applies.

[12–13] The section outlines that 'support worker' means a volunteer of, or an individual

---

(2) The court may refuse to allow an applicant to be accompanied in court by a particular individual at any stage in the proceedings which relate to the applicant if the court considers that it would not be in the interests of justice for the individual concerned to accompany, or continue to accompany, the applicant and where the court so refuses it shall give reasons for such refusal.

(3) In this section, "support worker" means a volunteer of, or an individual employed under a contract of service or under a contract for services by, an organisation which provides support to victims of domestic violence.'

12 Criminal Procedure Act 2021, s 9, Power to exclude public:

'(1) Subject to this section and any other enactment, a preliminary trial hearing or the hearing of an appeal under section 7 shall be conducted in open court.

(2) Where a court conducting a preliminary trial hearing or the hearing of an appeal under section 7, as the case may be, is satisfied, because of the nature or circumstances of the case or otherwise in the interests of justice, that it is desirable to do so, it may exclude from the court during the hearing –

(a) the public or any portion of the public, or

(b) any particular person or persons,

except bona fide representatives of the Press.

(3) Subsection (2) is without prejudice to the right of –

(a) a parent, relative or friend of the accused or of an injured party, or

(b) a support worker chosen by an injured party,

to remain in court in any case to which section 20(4) of the Criminal Justice Act 1951, section 6 of the Criminal Law (Rape) Act 1981, section 8 of the Criminal Justice (Female Genital Mutilation) Act 2012 or section 20 of the Criminal Justice (Victims of Crime) Act 2017 applies.

(4) In this section, "support worker" means a volunteer of, or an individual employed under a contract of service or under a contract for services by, an organisation which provides support to victims of crime.'

employed under a contract of service or under a contract for services by, an organisation which provides support to victims of crime.

Section 40 Criminal Justice (Miscellaneous Provisions) Act 2023

'Right to be accompanied in court in certain circumstances'

Section 37 of the Criminal Justice (Miscellaneous Provisions) Act 2023 'Hearing of proceedings', when commenced, provides that the public will be excluded from the court during applications under ss 28, 29 and 30 of the Act in relation to civil orders in respect of 'relevant conduct'. However, s 40 of the Criminal Justice (Miscellaneous Provisions) Act 2023[13] when commenced, allows for court accompaniment for applicants. Section 27 of the Criminal Justice (Miscellaneous Provisions) Act 2023 sets out the definition of 'relevant conduct' as conduct that is likely to cause the applicant or a person connected to the applicant: **[12–14]**

(a) to fear that violence will be used against the applicant or person or
(b) serious alarm or distress that has a substantial adverse impact on his or her usual day-to-day activities.

No legislative provision for 'appropriate person'/ court accompaniment for vulnerable adult witnesses (not victims)

There appears to be no specific provision which provides for an appropriate person or court accompaniment for an adult vulnerable witness who has an intellectual disability during pre-trial interviews or court proceedings. The provisions of the Criminal Justice (Victims of Crime) Act 2017 allow for protective measures for victims at investigative and trial stages including court accompaniment. However, for a witness to a crime, the provisions of the Criminal Justice (Victims of Crime) Act 2017 do not apply. Prosecution counsel, defence counsel, as well as the trial judge, may be alert to any measures which would support the witness with an intellectual disability in coming to court to give evidence as necessary and the relevant legislation and/discretion of the court may assist in allowing an appropriate support person to remain in court. **[12–15]**

---

[13] Criminal Justice (Miscellaneous Provisions) Act 2023, s 40
'Right to be accompanied in court in certain circumstances'.
s 40(1) Subject to subsection (2), an applicant may, in addition to being accompanied by his or her legal representative (if any), be accompanied in court by an individual of his or her choice.
(2) The court may refuse to allow an applicant to be accompanied in court by a particular individual at any stage in the proceedings which relate to the applicant if the court considers that it would not be in the interests of justice for the individual concerned to accompany, or continue to accompany, the applicant and where the court so refuses it shall give reasons for such refusal.

CHAPTER 13

DISCLOSURE

Introduction

The prosecution has a duty to disclose to the defence all relevant evidence.[1] This duty is in accordance with constitutional rights to a trial in due course of law[2] and to fair procedures.[3] It is also in line with Article 6 of the European Convention on Human Rights, which guarantees a person charged with a criminal offence the right to a fair trial and 'to be informed promptly, in a language which he understands and in detail, of the nature and cause of the accusation against him'. European Union Law has also conferred rights on the accused to information and right of access to relevant materials.[4] **[13–01]**

McCarthy J in *DPP v Tuite* observed: **[13–02]**

> The Constitutional right to fair procedures demands that the prosecution be conducted fairly; it is the duty of the prosecution, whether adducing such evidence or not, where possible, to make available all relevant evidence, parol or otherwise, in its possession, so that if the prosecution does not adduce such evidence, the defence may, if it wishes, do so.[5]

In *McKevitt v DPP*, Keane CJ outlined the constitutional duty on the prosecution to disclose material to the defence as follows: **[13–03]**

> the prosecution are under a duty to disclose to the defence any material which may be relevant to the case which could either help the defence or damage the prosecution and that if there is such material which is in their possession they are under a constitutional duty to make that available to the defence.[6]

1 *Guidelines for Prosecutors* (5th edn, Office of the Director of Public Prosecutions 2019) <https://www.dppireland.ie/app/uploads/2021/01/Guidelines-for-Prosecutors-5th-Edition-eng.pdf> accessed 13 October 2023.

2 Art 38.1 of the Constitution of Ireland.

3 Art 40.3 of the Constitution of Ireland.

4 The European Union Directive 2012/13/EU of 22 May 2012 on the right to information in criminal proceedings.

5 *DPP v Tuite* [1983] 2 Frewen 175.

6 Supreme Court, 18 March 2003 (*ex tempore* judgment of Keane CJ, with which Denham, McGuinness, Murray and Hardiman JJ concurred). See Irish Law Reform Commission, *Disclosure and Discovery in Criminal Cases* (112–2014) para 1.06, 8.

[13–04] The O'Malley Report[7] and the *Supporting a Victim's Journey Report*[8] both outline the issues concerning disclosure in the trial of sexual offences. In relation to disclosure, the *Supporting a Victim's Journey Report* includes a recommendation to place a positive obligation on all statutory or public bodies, voluntary bodies and independent counsellors holding counselling records to furnish those records promptly to the Director of Public Prosecutions once requested to do so.[9] It remains to be seen whether the implementation of preliminary trial hearings, which are linked to the issue of disclosure in both reports and which have been commenced since their publication under s 6 of the Criminal Procedure Act 2021, will impact on the aspect of delay in disclosure.

[13–05] The issue of delay and disclosure was outlined in an article by Mary Rose Gearty SC (now Gearty J) and Miriam Delahunt BL.[10] In many cases, disclosure may be only one of the reasons cited for delay but which may be part of a cumulative effect on the overall delay of the case. For example, in the case of *DPP v SA*,[11] where the trial took seven years to get on late disclosure was one reason for the delay, unavailability of judges and the accused remaining outside the jurisdiction before charge were other factors.

Section 16(1)(b) Criminal Evidence Act 1992/s 15 Criminal Evidence Act 1992

[13–06] The issue of disclosure in respect of recorded testimony under s 16(1)(b) of the Criminal Evidence Act 1992 is outlined in s 15 of the Act. This allows for the accused to view the video prior to the hearing only after the accused has been sent forward for trial under Part 1A of the Criminal Procedure Act 1967. The issue of pre-trial disclosure is thereby only expressly outlined for indictable offences. Disclosure concerning District Court matters will still apply under traditional District Court disclosure rules and a 'Gary Doyle Order'.[12]

Section 19A Criminal Evidence Act 1992

'Disclosure of third party records in certain trials' (counselling notes)

[13–07] Section 19A of the Criminal Evidence Act 1992 provides for the disclosure of counselling notes of the complainant to be provided to the accused in respect of a sexual offence in the Circuit Court or Central Criminal Court. Sexual offence is defined in the section itself as a sexual offence outlined in the Schedule to the Sex Offenders Act 2001.[13]

[13–08] Heffernan has examined the traditional refusal by the Irish courts to sanction third-party

7 Dept of Justice and Equality, *Review of Protections for Vulnerable Witnesses in the Investigation and Prosecution of Sexual Offences* (August 2020) 75.

8 Dept of Justice and Equality, *Supporting a Victim's Journey – A plan to help victims and vulnerable witnesses in sexual violence cases* (October 2020).

9 ibid para 5.8, 44.

10 Mary Rose Gearty, Miriam Delahunt, *Delay and Disclosure: Disaster?* (2018) 23(3) Bar Review, 83.

11 *DPP v SA* [2020] IECA 60.

12 A 'Gary Doyle Order' is the informal term for disclosure in respect of summary prosecution referred as such after the case of *Director of Public Prosecutions v Gary Doyle* [1994] 2 IR 286.

13 Sex Offenders Act 2001, Schedule, 'Sexual Offences for Purposes of Act'.

disclosure and the evolution of the legislation for third-party disclosure in limited form through s 19A of the Criminal Evidence Act 1991. Examining the provision, she notes that the section envisages the possibility that a complainant or witness might expressly waive his or her right to non-disclosure of a counselling record, thereby obviating the need for a party to invoke the s 19A procedure, but asserts that it is regrettable that the legislation did not go further in this respect and state explicitly that any waiver by a complainant must be given on the basis of fully informed consent. However, writing in 2020, she observed:

> The new procedure for disclosure of counselling records is a welcome development that provides a constructive framework for the balanced resolution of requests for disclosure of highly sensitive material in sexual offence trials. The legislation is limited in its scope and it remains to be seen how effective it will prove in protecting the respective rights of accuseds and complainants in practice.[14]

The prosecution is obliged to notify the accused that such notes exist[15] and under s 19A(10) the court shall take the following factors into consideration in determining whether the counselling notes should be disclosed to the accused: **[13–09]**

> (a) the extent to which the record is necessary for the accused to defend the charges against him;
> (b) the probative value of the record;
> (c) the reasonable expectation of privacy with respect to the record;
> (d) the potential prejudice to the right to privacy of any person to whom the record relates;
> (e) the public interest in encouraging the reporting of sexual offences;
> (f) the public interest in encouraging complainants of sexual offences to seek counselling;
> (g) the effect of the determination on the integrity of the trial process;
> (h) the likelihood that disclosing, or requiring the disclosure of, the record will cause harm to the complainant, including the nature and extent of that harm.

Representation by a barrister in respect of the application is implicitly outlined in s 19A(16) of the Act as it refers to representation by a solicitor or barrister on behalf of a complainant or witness in respect of s 11 of the Civil Legal Aid Act 1995. The O'Malley Report suggested that barristers who represent the complainant under applications under s 3 of the Criminal Law (Rape) Act 1981 in respect of evidence regarding previous sexual history should be made by appropriately experienced counsel,[16] noting that this role is often filled by junior counsel.[17] Anecdotally, since then it appears that senior counsel rather than junior counsel have been briefed not only in respect of s 3 applications but also in respect of s 19A hearings. **[13–10]**

---

14 Liz Heffernan, *Evidence in Criminal Trials* (2nd edn, Bloomsbury 2020) para 14.75, 835.

15 Criminal Evidence Act 1992, s 19A(2): 'In criminal proceedings for a sexual offence the prosecutor shall notify the accused of the existence of any counselling record but shall not disclose the content of the record without the leave of the court given in accordance with this section.'

16 Dept of Justice and Equality, *Review of Protections for Vulnerable Witnesses in the Investigation and Prosecution of Sexual Offences* (August 2020) 5; para 5.15, 60.

17 ibid para 6.13, 69.

Application for Counselling Notes – Preliminary Trial Hearing – s 6 Criminal Procedure Act 2021

[13–11] An application in respect of counselling notes under s 19A of the Criminal Evidence Act 1992 may be made under s 6(8)(b)(v) of the Criminal Procedure Act 2021, which states:

> Without prejudice to the generality of subsection (7), the trial court may, at a preliminary trial hearing, make any one or more of the following orders: (b) any order that may be made under or pursuant to:
> (i) section 6 of the Criminal Justice (Administration) Act 1924;
> (ii) section 15A of the Juries Act 1976;
> (iii) section 21 or 22 of the Act of 1984 (Criminal Justice Act);
> (iv) section 3 of the Criminal Law (Rape) Act 1981;
> (v) section 13, 14, 14A, 14C, 19A or 29 of the Act of 1992 (Criminal Evidence Act).

Admission of Social Worker Reports/Opinion Evidence

[13–12] Non-expert opinion is generally not admissible except in certain circumstances.[18] The difficulties in admission of reports of social workers in relation to assessing credibility of disclosures of young children was highlighted in a case which ended in an acquittal but which was reported in the *Irish Times*. A child of approximately three years of age made disclosures and after assessment through St Louise's Unit in Crumlin, and the disclosures were deemed credible. The suspect was charged approximately a year after the disclosures were made and was ultimately acquitted at trial. Complaints made through the HSE were not upheld on appeal.

> 'Throughout the entire process these were the only professionals qualified to determine if Zoe (the complainant) was telling the truth, and yet their report isn't admissible at trial. The jury never hears their findings because of the rule against opinion evidence. We feel a change to the law is needed in the cases of very young children, because their credibility is so open to attack.' Tom (the complainant's father) says.[19]

[13–13] However, in the case of *DPP v NR*,[20] one of the grounds of appeal involved the fact that the social worker involved with the case had stated in evidence that it was not unusual that retractions would occur. Dismissing this and all other grounds, Birmingham P stated:

> It seems to us that the appellant overstates the significance of what the social worker was doing and what the social worker was being permitted to do. The social worker was not saying that, in her opinion, the original complaint ought to be believed, but was reporting on the fact that, in her experience, children, not infrequently, do retract complaints in the run-up to a trial that is listed for hearing. In a situation where the extent of the reaction on the part of the social worker and her colleagues was likely to be in issue, we can see nothing objectionable in what she was permitted to say. Accordingly, we will reject this ground of appeal also.[21]

---

[18] Declan McGrath and Emily Egan McGrath, *McGrath on Evidence* (3rd edn Round Hall 2020) para 6.61.

[19] Sarah-Jane Murphy, 'The story of "Zoe", one of the youngest sex-abuse cases ever heard in Irish courts' *The Irish Times* (Dublin, 24 April 2021) <https://www.irishtimes.com/the-story-of-zoe-one-of-the-youngest-sex-abuse-cases-ever-heard-in-irish-courts-1.4537355> accessed 13 October 2023.

[20] *DPP v NR* [2021] IECA 121.

[21] ibid [52].

Notes of 'Clarification Meeting' – s 16(1)(b) Criminal Evidence Act 1992

Clarification meetings are mentioned in the cases of *DPP v TV*[22] and *DPP v SA*.[23] They appear to consist of Specialist Interviewers meeting the complainant after the complaint has been made to arrange recording of a statement under s 16(1)(b) of the Criminal Evidence Act 1992. The *Good Practice Guidelines*[24] were drafted in 2003 as procedural guidance for use of s 16(1)(b) of the Criminal Evidence Act 1992 but clarification meetings are not referred to in the Good Practice Guidelines. They appear to have evolved as good practice and to consist of meeting with the complainant to note the disclosures, to confirm eligibility in relation to the legislation, and to arrange the recording of any relevant testimony. **[13–14]**

In the judgment of *DPP v MT*,[25] the Court of Appeal describes the delay in respect of the trial and which may have led to the difficulties in memory recall. The conviction was ultimately quashed. As part of the timeline of the matter coming on for trial, Ní Raifeartaigh noted: **[13–15]**

> In October or November 2016 (the precise date is uncertain), two specialist interviewers attended at the child's home. No notes of this meeting were made or kept. This was described as a "clarification meeting", terminology which has apparently become common in this type of case to describe the first meeting of the Gardaí with the complainant. The fact of this meeting was not known to the appellant or his legal team prior to the first trial. (As will be seen, there were three trials: the jury were discharged in the first trial by reason of a failure to disclose the fact of, or any notes concerning, the first clarification meeting referred to; the second trial resulted in a jury discharge because of the pandemic; and the third trial resulted in the conviction of the appellant.)[26]

The failure to make notes during a clarification meeting, even where no disclosures were made, is an important evidential issue but may be rectified by subsequent statements as to what occurred in the clarification meeting: **[13–16]**

> The first trial started on 29th October 2019. The jury was discharged on the second day by reason of the absence of disclosure relating to the clarification meeting, already referred to. Statements were made by the two Gardaí in question, dated 21st November 2019, in which both stated that S made no disclosures at that first clarification meeting.[27]

22 *DPP v TV* [2017] IECA 200.
23 *DPP v SA* [2020] IECA 60.
24 An Garda Síochána, *Good Practice Guidelines for Persons involved in Video Recording interviews with complainants under 14 years of age (or with intellectual disability) for Evidential Purposes in accordance with Section 16(1)(b) of the Criminal Evidence Act, 1992, in cases involving Sexual and/ or Violent Offences* (July 2003).
25 *DPP v MT* [2023] IECA 65.
26 ibid [7].
27 ibid [12].

CHAPTER 14

DOCTRINE OF RECENT COMPLAINT

Introduction

[14–01] The origin of the principle dates back to a societal expectation that a complainant of a sexual offence would raise an immediate 'hue and cry'. The doctrine of recent complaint is an exception to the rule against narrative and allows for the admission of evidence of a complaint of a sexual offence by a complainant. It may be admitted to show consistency of the complaint but not the truth of the complaint itself and is not corroboration of the offence.[1] The purpose of the evidence must be communicated by the judge to the jury.[2]

[14–02] English case law[3] has been useful in developing the principle in Ireland. *R v Lillyman*[4] provided that evidence of complaint could be admitted to show consistency. The details of the complaint could be made and not just the fact of the complaint itself, which had been the practice prior to this. *R v Osborne*[5] also allowed evidence of the complaint to be made in circumstances where consent was not in issue, the complainant being a young girl. However, the situation in England has developed differently to that in Ireland in that the principle has been put on a legislative basis and allows for the complaint to be admitted as evidence of the truth of the matter stated and not just to show consistency.[6]

---

1 *DPP v Brophy* [1992] ILRM 709.

2 *People (DPP) v MA* [2002] 2 IR 601; *DPP v BFJ* [2023] IECA 127.

3 Archbold, *Criminal Pleading Evidence and Practice* (ed PJ Richardson) (Sweet & Maxwell 2024) ch 20, para 20-17:

> 'As to the admissibility at common law, in cases of rape and kindred offences, of the fact that a complaint was made by the victim shortly after the alleged offence and of the details thereof, see §§ 8-111 and following in the 2005 edition of this work. As to the admissibility of "recent complaint" statements under the CJA 2003, see s.120(1), (4), (7) and (8), § 11-67–11-73. It should be noted that whereas at common law, recent complaint evidence was admissible only as evidence of the consistency of the conduct of the complainant, and as tending to negative consent, under the 2003 Act, such evidence is evidence of the truth of the matter stated. The Court of Appeal in *O* [2006] EWCA Crim 556; [2006] 2 Cr. App. R. 27 has since confirmed that recent complaint evidence is admissible to prove the truth of the matter stated and not merely to demonstrate consistency of the complainant's account, as was the case prior to the 2003 Act.'

4 *R v Lillyman* [1896] 2 QB 167 (CCR).

5 *R v Osborne* [1905] 1 KB 551 (CCR).

6 Criminal Justice Act 2003, s 120. See also *The Crown Court Compendium* (Courts and Tribunals

[14–03] Heffernan argues that the doctrine of recent complaint has failed to keep pace with societal developments.[7] The O'Malley Report states:

> Nowadays, courts are willing to admit a complaint made at the first reasonable opportunity, and this in turn is to be assessed by reference to all the relevant circumstances. It may well be that some aspects of the rule could usefully be reviewed, and we understand that it will, in fact, be considered by the Law Reform Commission in its project on the consolidation and reform of the law relating to sexual offences. However, we have not been presented with any convincing argument in favour of abolishing the rule, and we recommend that it be retained.[8]

[14–04] There has been some indication that the courts will accommodate the reasons as to why a complainant may have made a complaint at a later stage,[9] or in a manner that is incomplete or varying in detail[10] and recent decisions of the Court of Appeal seem to suggest that it is adopting a more expansive approach to the doctrine However, it is still difficult to reconcile a principle which espouses stereotypical behaviour in trials of sexual offences where the nature of the offences and the characteristics and reactions of the complainant may be so diverse. Heffernan notes:

> The fact of a recent complaint tends to strengthen the inference that the complainant is being consistent and truthful at trial. Regardless of changes extrinsic to the trial process, the need for evidence of credibility in prosecutions for sexual offences has remained immutable. There are rarely eyewitnesses to the event and the ultimate issue is often whether the complainant consented to sexual activity, a matter which is unlikely to be resolved by the evidence of medical experts. The trial then becomes a contest between the conflicting accounts of the complainant and the accused. Against this contested backdrop, the timeliness of the complainant's reporting of the offence remains an important indicator of her credibility in the eyes of the law notwithstanding society's evolving understanding of the impact of sexual violence on complainants.[11]

[14–05] In a case where a previous complaint had only come to light in the victim impact statement, the Supreme Court considered the above issues in *DPP v SQ*.[12] Baker J stated:

> Immediate complaints are not always possible, and delayed complaints are not necessarily indicative of unreliability or fabrication. This could be owing to the age of the victim, the fact that the perpetrator was in a position of trust or authority, because the victim

Judiciary, 2023) p 14.28.

7 Liz Heffernan, *Evidence in Criminal Trials* (2nd edn, Bloomsbury 2020) para 7.36, 306.

8 Thomas O'Malley, *Review of Protections for Vulnerable Witnesses in the Investigation and Prosecution of Sexual Offences* (Dept of Justice and Equality 2020) para 6.26, 76. See also Irish Law Reform Commission, *Fifth Programme of Law Reform* (120–2019) paras 1.16–1.19, 7 '5. Review and Consolidation of the Law on Sexual Offences 1.16 During the public consultation process, the Commission received a large number of submissions concerning the need to review specific aspects of sexual offences law and for the consolidation of the law. 1.17 As to the specific aspects of the law, the project will examine: (1) the definition of rape; (2) sexual history evidence; (3) whether the doctrine of recent complaint ought to be abolished; (4) the discretionary corroboration warning; (5) the anonymity of accused persons in sexual assault cases; (6) whether trials for sexual assault should be heard otherwise than in public; (7) the high attrition rate in sexual offences cases, and whether procedural and other reforms could have an impact on this; and (8) separate legal representation for complainants.' <https://www.lawreform.ie/welcome/criminal-law.381.html> accessed 13 October 2023.

9 *DPP v TF* [2021] IECA 120.

10 *DPP v MA* [2020] IECA 136 and *DPP v MA* [2022] IECA 367. (The case had two appeals – the second appeal was allowed after defence counsel was discharged).

11 Liz Heffernan, *Evidence in Criminal Trials* (2nd edn, Bloomsbury 2020) para 7.36, 306.

12 *DPP v SQ* [2023] IESC 8.

often thinks he or she will not be believed, or does not have the language to voice the elements of the assault.[13]

DPP v Brophy

General principles

Heffernan notes that the core principles of the doctrine as outlined in the English cases of *R v Lillyman*[14] were affirmed by the Irish Court of Criminal Appeal in *People v Brophy*.[15] The judgment of O'Flaherty J summarised the law in this area as follows: **[14–06]**

> (a) Complaints may only be proved in criminal prosecutions for a sexual offence.
> (b) The complaint must have been made as speedily as could reasonably be expected and in a voluntary fashion, not as a result of any inducements or exhortations. Once evidence of the making of a complaint is admissible then particulars of the complaint may also be proved.
> (c) It should always be made clear to the jury that such evidence is not evidence of the facts on which the complaint is based but to show that the victim's conduct in so complaining was consistent with her testimony.
> (d) While there is mention in one of the older cases, *R. v. Osborne* (1905) 1 KB 551, of a complaint being 'corroborative of the complainant's credibility' this does not mean that such a complaint amounts to corroboration of her testimony in the legal sense of that term but as pointing to the consistency of her testimony. Corroboration in the strict sense involves independent evidence, that is evidence other than the complainant's evidence.
> (e) The law on complaints should not be confused with what takes place once the police institute their inquiries. That is a separate matter. A complaint made to the police may, as such, be admissible or not under the guidelines set out above but just because a complaint is not made at the first opportunity to the police does not, of course, inhibit their inquiries. Indeed, a complaint to the police may be made by someone other than the injured party.[16]

DPP v KM

Witnesses may give evidence which has varying detail of recent complaints

In this case, complaint evidence of a friend as well as a cousin of the child complainant had been admitted at trial. The appellant argued that the complaint evidence should not have been admitted where it was not sufficiently consistent with the evidence given by the complainant herself to come within the doctrine of recent complaint. There had been complaint evidence of molestation in contrast to the allegation of rape. Noting the difficulties that young witnesses may have in speaking about such offences, Birmingham P stated: **[14–07]**

> Here, there is no inconsistency in the accounts. What has occurred is that on one occasion, an elaborate and detailed account is given. First, over several days when providing a statement to the Gardaí, and then in the witness box during examination, cross-examination and re-examination, whereas on the other hand, the account given to Ms. L was really lacking in all detail. However, in the Court's view, that is what is in issue:

---

13 ibid [51].
14 *R v Lillyman* [1896] 2 QB 167 (CCR).
15 *People (DPP) v Brophy* [1992] ILRM 709 (CCA).
16 ibid 716.

> the distinction between an account where detail was not provided and an account where considerable detail was provided. Viewed in that light, there are no real inconsistencies. The Court does not believe that the reference to 'molesting' can be interpreted as an account involving but limited to and not going beyond inappropriate touching. It is the nature of things that individuals who have been the subject of sexual abuse, in particular, perhaps, child sexual abuse, when they first bring themselves to speak of it, that they are likely to be very reticent and to provide few details. This is a factor that trial judges are entitled to have regard to when deciding whether to admit evidence of recent complaint that is offered. In this case, so far as the evidence is concerned, the Court is satisfied that the trial judge was well within her rights to admit it.[17]

[14–08] Birmingham P went on to say:

> The Court feels that it is possible to over-parse and analyse a conversation between two children especially when one of them is in a distressed state. The reliance on the fact that the continuous past tense was used is over-analytical. Again, the reference to rapes "since moving to C" is capable of bearing the interpretation contended for by the appellant that rapes started at move time and continued thereafter, but it is equally open to the interpretation that rapes occurred from a period in time that was subsequent to the move to C. The Court is quite satisfied that such matters as the defence is in a position to point to would not have required the exclusion of the evidence [of Ms. SR.][18]

[14–09] This case was referred to in *DPP v MA*[19] where complaint evidence of a Garda and of a friend of the complainant was admitted where different details of the offences had emerged at trial.

DPP v PS

First reasonable opportunity may be flexibly interpreted

[14–10] In *DPP v PS*,[20] the appellant submitted that recent complaint evidence should not have been admitted where it was not made at the first reasonable opportunity. The appellant was convicted of offences of sexual assault against three granddaughters. Grounds of appeal were submitted in relation to two complainants where the intervals between the offences and the complaints were approximately four and two years. The appellant argued that the complaint evidence should not have been admitted due to it having been made some time after the offences. The Court of Appeal made reference to *DPP v MA*,[21] where Murray J had outlined the principle that the evidence was admissible in terms of the credibility of the victim. This was based on the natural expression of

---

17 *DPP v KM* [2018] IECA 261 [21].

18 ibid [23]–[24].

19 *DPP v MA* [2020] IECA 136 and *DPP v MA* [2022] IECA 367. In this case, there were two conviction appeals in respect of rape and sexual assault charges, the appellant having discharged his defence team after the first appeal. In both appeals, the Court of Appeal ruled on an appeal point that the evidence of a Garda to whom the complainant had made a complaint should not have been admitted into evidence when complaint evidence made at an earlier time to a friend had been admitted as evidence of recent complaint. The issue concerned the fact that evidence of oral sex had not been mentioned to the Garda but only given at trial. The evidence of the Garda was objected to on the grounds that it comprised inadmissible hearsay, there being an inconsistency as to the content of the complaints. The appeal point failed in the first appeal and in the second, the new defence team had raised a similar concern but in relation to a new point on the basis of the Garda's notebooks. However, the point did not succeed.

20 *DPP v PS* [2023] IECA 135.

21 *People (DPP) v MA* [2001] 2 IR 601.

the victim's feelings that reasonably soon after the offence she would complain to some person with whom she had a personal or confidential relationship. In dismissing the appeal, Kennedy J emphasised the word *reasonably* in that judgment[22] and outlined the issues which may arise in inter-family abuse. She noted that the complainant may not wish to complain to a parent or close relative who may have a close relationship with the abuser. The abuse itself may be prolonged and that may inhibit disclosure. In addition, there may be a reluctance to upset the extended family. Kennedy J stated:

> In these kinds of circumstances, where a complaint is made at a significant remove in time, a judge, on careful consideration of the particular circumstances may conclude that the complaint was made at the first reasonable opportunity. It is obvious that each case falls to be determined on its own facts, however, we believe there is a distinction to be drawn between cases of prolonged sexual abuse of a child, particularly inter-familial abuse, and a single incident of the rape of an adult. There are perhaps obvious reasons for this, as the circumstances will be quite different, and it is the circumstances which are pivotal to the determination of whether the complaint is made at the first *reasonable* opportunity.[23]

DPP v TF[24]

First reasonable opportunity may be some time after the alleged offence / self reported health issues may be admitted as reason for delay

In *DPP v TF*, the Court of Appeal considered the admissibility of recent complaint evidence where it had been made to the complainant's wife, Z, approximately twenty years after the sexual assault offences had taken place. The appellant contended that the complaint had not been made at the first reasonable opportunity after the offence. The Court dismissed the point stating that it was satisfied the trial judge had given careful consideration to the circumstances in which the complaint came to be made and to the background against which the complaint was made. The Court was also satisfied that the trial judge was entitled to conclude, in light of the information put before him, that even though the complaint to the first complainant's wife was made many years after the events were alleged to have taken place, that it was in fact made at the first reasonable opportunity. In dismissing the point, Birmingham P stated: **[14–11]**

> We simply wish to add that had we been persuaded that the judge's decision was not a legitimate exercise of discretion and that he was in error, we would have had to consider whether this was a case with a proviso. On one view, the complaint evidence was of limited probative value, though one cannot ignore the fact that the prosecution felt it was of sufficient value to press for its inclusion, but it seems to us that the complaint to Z was sufficiently close in time to the formal complaint to Gardaí that it did not really serve to change the dynamics of the case. There will be occasions in what might be described as historic sex cases where a complaint is made at a very considerable remove from the time of the alleged offending, but the fact of the complaint is, nonetheless, of very considerable significance in the context of the issues as they emerge at trial. We are thinking of situations where it is suggested that the complaint is being pressed because of malice or ill-will on the part of the complainant arising from a particular event occurring within the family. In such circumstances, if the prosecution is in a position to point to a complaint made before that event had occurred, that would have the potential to be very significant evidentially.[25]

---

22 ibid [41].
23 *DPP v PS* [2023] IECA 135 [48].
24 *DPP v TF* [2021] IECA 120.
25 ibid [20].

[14–12] In relation to an appeal point regarding the reason for the delay being the self-reported mental health issues of the complainant, Birmingham P observed:

> It must be said that this ground was not pressed with any vigour and understandably so, and it should be noted that we deal with it now only for the sake of completeness. The original suggestion had seemed to be that the complainant was, in effect, allowed to give expert evidence about his own health and to attribute the delay in making a complaint to the difficulties that he says he experienced. We do not believe there is any reason why someone cannot speak about their own health. While it goes without saying that they may not be in a position to offer a formal detailed diagnosis, we cannot see any reason why a witness cannot say, "I was experiencing mental health difficulties over a particular period", or, "I was experiencing restricted mobility". To the extent that the appeal ground remains live, we dismiss it.[26]

DPP v SOC

Complaint evidence admitted as rebuttal of recent fabrication

[14–13] In *DPP v SOC*[27] the evidence of two witnesses was admitted, not as recent complaint evidence, but on the basis of rebuttal of recent fabrication where the cross-examination had given rise to an impression that no one had been told of the offences. The prosecution had accepted that it would not have been possible to call the evidence by reference to the doctrine of recent complaint.[28] However, the prosecution contended that the nature of the cross-examination which put to the complainant that the allegations that she was making were untrue and fabricated meant that the accounts could be adduced because of the rule that permits prior consistent statements to be introduced in evidence in order to rebut an allegation of recent fabrication. In order to rebut the impression that no one had been told of the allegations, the prosecution counsel made an application to admit the evidence of two witnesses who had been told of the offences not on the basis of recent complaint but to rebut the allegation of recent fabrication. Birmingham J stated:

> It is clear that the judge felt that there would be a real unfairness if the jury was left with the false impression that there was no complaint until recent times. The nature of the cross examination brought the question of complaint centre stage and in those circumstances this Court cannot conclude that the judge exceeded his discretion when he permitted the jury to hear what the complainant had told her friend and the psychiatrist who was treating her. This ground of appeal therefore fails.[29]

---

[26] ibid [20]–[21].
[27] *DPP v SOC* [2017] IECA 23.
[28] There appears to be no information in the judgment as to the reasons why this was the case.
[29] *DPP v SOC* [2017] IECA 23 [14].

CHAPTER 15

GROUND RULES HEARINGS

Development with Introduction of Intermediaries

Ground rules hearings became a facet of trials involving vulnerable witnesses when intermediaries were introduced in England and Wales in the mid-2000s. While PCMHs (Plea and Case Management Hearings) were a part of the trial process, ground rules hearings were introduced as a means of familiarising the court and counsel with the individual aspects required to ensure that full communication with the witness could take place. In order to avoid interruption of the witness' evidence, aspects such as use of language, scheduling of breaks, use of support objects, arrangement of personnel in the courtroom, etc, were discussed at a hearing in the absence of the witness and jury in what became known as a 'ground rules hearing'. Although still non-statutory in England and Wales, Practice Directions and case law facilitate their use.[1] **[15–01]**

Following practice in England and Wales, ground rules hearings have become a feature of trials involving vulnerable witnesses in Ireland. Although not a reported judgment, their first use can be traced back to the case of *DPP v FE (Faisal Ellahi)* in November 2015.[2] *DPP v VE* approved the general principles of *R v Lubemba*, which stated that ground rules hearings should be used in every case involving a vulnerable witness.[3] As both intermediaries and practitioners have sought to clarify and resolve the manner in which the evidence of the victim or witness could be facilitated, ground rules hearings have become more frequent in Ireland. **[15–02]**

Ground Rules Hearings/Preliminary Trial Hearings

In Ireland, the Criminal Procedure Act 2021 provides for any further rulings to be made pre-trial or at any other time during the trial process.[4] It is suggested that the practice of ground rules hearings come under the auspices of the Criminal Procedure Act 2021.[5] However, preliminary trial hearings may differ slightly from a ground rules hearing in that the trial court may facilitate further time prior to the witness giving evidence to ensure that supplementary discussion and rulings may take place as to how **[15–03]**

---

1 *DPP v VE* [2021] IECA 122 [16]. See also 'Ground Rules Hearings and the Fair Treatment of Vulnerable People in Court' (*The Advocate's Gateway*, 2 September 2019) Toolkit 1 <https://www.theadvocatesgateway.org/> accessed 13 October 2023.

2 Caroline Biggs and Miriam Delahunt, 'Prosecutorial Challenges – Vulnerable Witnesses' (2017) 22(1) Bar Review 23, 24.

3 *DPP v VE* [2021] IECA 122 [82]; *R v JP* and *R v Lubemba* [2014] EWCA Crim 2064 [42].

4 Criminal Procedure Act 2021, ss 6(8) and 6(19).

5 ibid 6(9).

the intermediary and/or the court may interact with the trial court or to determine other facilitations by the trial court.

[15–04] The purpose of a ground rules hearing is to attempt to clarify, at an earlier stage, how the interaction with the witness will progress at trial and thereby avoid interruption, objections and delays in the course of the trial. It may also assist the vulnerable witness as it ensures that he or she knows what facilitation will be given to him or her. The practice emerged over a period of time and gained legitimacy as an established procedure in cases dealing with vulnerable witnesses. In the United Kingdom, Criminal Practice Directions now include provision for them[6] and they have been further directed through the judgment of *R v Lubemba*.[7]

> The court is required to take every reasonable step to encourage and facilitate the attendance of vulnerable witnesses and their participation in the trial process. To that end, judges are taught, in accordance with the Criminal Practice Directions, that it is best practice to hold hearings in advance of the trial to ensure the smooth running of the trial, to give any special measures directions and to set the ground rules for the treatment of a vulnerable witness. We would expect a ground rules hearing in every case involving a vulnerable witness, save in very exceptional circumstances. If there are any doubts on how to proceed, guidance should be sought from those who have the responsibility for looking after the witness and or an expert.[8]

Ground Rules Hearing without Intermediary

[15–05] Ground rules hearings could also take place where there is no application for an intermediary. The Court of Appeal in *DPP v VE*[9] referred to the paragraph in *R v Lubemba* which states that it 'would expect a ground rules hearing in every case involving a vulnerable witness, save in very exceptional circumstances'.[10] It also stated that the views expressed in *R v Lubemba*[11] and *R v Barker*[12] were apposite in Ireland.[13] The ground rules in the case of *DPP v VE*[14] are comprehensive and would not especially require the presence of an intermediary although an intermediary was appointed in that case.[15] But it is of assistance to any trial for all parties to be aware of the relevant issues, to have an opportunity to discuss them and to have them ruled on so that any issues may be resolved efficiently. Specialist and expert knowledge of the witness may be required for personalised assessment of the witness. However, many of the ground

---

6 PD 3E, General Matters: Ground Rules Hearings to plan the questioning of a vulnerable witness or defendant.

7 *R v JP and R v Lubemba* [2014] EWCA Crim 2064.

8 *R v JP and R v Lubemba* [2014] EWCA Crim 2064 [42].

9 *DPP v VE* [2021] IECA 122.

10 ibid [82]; *R v JP and R v Lubemba* [2014] EWCA Crim 2064 [42].

11 *R v Lubemba* [2014] EWCA Crim 2064.

12 *R v Barker* [2010] EWCA Crim 4.

13 *DPP v VE* [2021] IECA 122 [82, 86]; *R v JP and R v Lubemba* [2014] EWCA Crim 2064 [42].

14 *DPP v VE* [2021] IECA 122.

15 ibid [16]:

> 'At the beginning of the trial, the court conducted a "ground rules hearing" to address the manner in which the questioning of the complainant would take place. This was done at the invitation of the prosecution. Counsel for the prosecution referred the trial judge to the case of R v. Lubemba (discussed in further detail below), a judgment of the Court of Appeal of England and Wales which refers to the measures which a trial judge may legitimately take to protect a vulnerable witness without impacting adversely on the right of an accused to a fair trial. Naturally the ground rules hearing took place in the absence of the jury.'

rules contained in *DPP v VE*[16] are consistent with the objective of obtaining reliable evidence from any witness.

[16] *DPP v VE* [2021] IECA 122.

CHAPTER 16

IDENTIFICATION AT TRIAL

When Using Video Link/Screen at Trial

Section 18 Criminal Evidence Act 1992[1]

Section 18 Criminal Evidence Act 1992 provides that where a witness is giving evidence in respect of a relevant offence or gives evidence in respect of any other offence of which he or she is a victim, and is using a video link or screen to do so, then: **[16–01]**

- where evidence is given that the accused was known to the witness before the date on which the offence is alleged to have been committed, the witness shall not be required to identify the accused at the trial of the offence, unless the court in the interests of justice directs otherwise.
- in any other case, evidence by a person other than the witness that the witness identified the accused at an identification parade as being the offender shall be admissible as evidence that the accused was so identified.

1 Criminal Evidence Act 1992, s 18, Identification evidence: 'Where a person (in this section referred to as 'the witness') – (a) gives evidence in respect of a relevant offence, or (b) gives evidence in respect of any other offence of which he or she is a victim, through a live television link pursuant to section 13(1) or (1A) or using a screen or other similar device pursuant to section 14A, then – (i) in case evidence is given that the accused was known to the witness before the date on which the offence is alleged to have been committed, the witness shall not be required to identify the accused at the trial of the offence, unless the court in the interests of justice directs otherwise, and (ii) in any other case, evidence by a person other than the witness that the witness identified the accused at an identification parade as being the offender shall be admissible as evidence that the accused was so identified.'

Chapter 17

INTERMEDIARIES

Introduction

[17–01] Although Irish legislation has provided for intermediaries in criminal proceedings since 1992, their use in Ireland had been uncommon.[1] However, the DPP has, since 2016, begun to engage trained intermediaries from neighbouring jurisdictions to assist in trials involving vulnerable witnesses in Ireland.[2] The Department of Justice has also published a significant report, *Review of Protections for Vulnerable Witnesses in the Investigation and Prosecution of Sexual Offences* (commonly known as the 'O'Malley Report' chaired, as it was, by Tom O'Malley SC) in 2020.[3] It included positive recommendations for the continued use of intermediaries both at investigative and trial stages.[4]

[17–02] As a direct result of the O'Malley Report, the Department of Justice examined how its recommendations could be implemented. *Supporting a Victim's Journey*,[5] a report of the Minister for Justice, included plans to establish the training and formation of a panel of intermediaries from which the courts can draw. This plan has been implemented through the University of Limerick where a Professional Diploma in Intermediary Studies – a course for CORU-registered social workers, speech and language therapists and occupational therapists – has been established.[6]

[17–03] Section 14 of the Criminal Evidence Act 1992, which provides for intermediaries in criminal trials, has been amended by the Criminal Justice (Victims of Crime) Act 2017 and the Domestic Violence Act 2018, and allows for witnesses/victims of certain offences who are under 18 to avail of the support measure. Nonetheless, the core of the legislation remains identical to that first enacted. The current legislation provides for prosecution and defence witnesses to avail of the support measure but appears to exclude the accused through the linking of the section to the use of video link.[7] However, intermediaries for defendants have been appointed through the inherent

1 Liz Heffernan, *Evidence in Criminal Trials* (2nd edn, Bloomsbury 2020) para 5.49, 215. Heffernan notes, 'The statutory provision for intermediaries was a virtual dead letter for the two decades following the entry into force of the Act. In recent years, the special measure has been used on a limited number of occasions.'

2 An English intermediary was employed in assisting the complainant who was giving evidence via video link from the Old Bailey in England in the case of *DPP v NR* [2021] IECA 121, the trial of which took place over 33 days in April and May 2016 <https://www.theguardian.com/society/2019/mar/04/ruth-marchant-obituary> accessed 13 October 2023.

The case of *DPP v VE* [2021] IECA 122 involved the first documented use of a trained intermediary on Irish soil. The trial took place in February/March 2019.

3 Dept of Justice and Equality, *Review of Protections for Vulnerable Witnesses in the Investigation and Prosecution of Sexual Offences* (August 2020).

4 ibid 98.

5 Dept of Justice and Equality, *Supporting a Victim's Journey – A plan to help victims and vulnerable witnesses in sexual violence cases* (October 2020).

6 University of Limerick, Professional Diploma – Intermediary Studies <https://www.ul.ie/gps/courses/intermediary-studies-professional-diploma> accessed 13 October 2023.

7 See [17–17].

jurisdiction of the court. These appointments have been founded on Constitutional and ECHR rights to a fair trial which protect the defendant's right to full participation in the course of the trial.[8]

Origin and Implementation of Legislation for the Use of Intermediaries

Section 14 of the Criminal Evidence Act 1992 has its basis in the Law Reform Commission's *Consultation Paper on Child Sexual Abuse* of 1989 and the subsequent *Report on Child Sexual Abuse* of 1990. The Law Reform Commission outlined a recommendation for a 'child examiner' or intermediary to act as a conduit for all questions from the lawyers in the case, from the court or from the accused if he was representing himself, and to establish and maintain rapport and ease of communication with the child witness.[9] **[17–04]**

Legislation for Intermediaries in Ireland

Section 14 of the Criminal Evidence Act 1992 provides for the use of an intermediary in Irish criminal proceedings in Ireland at trial.[10] Provision is also available for the giving of victim impact statements through an intermediary.[11] The support measure of intermediaries is also included in other legislative provisions in civil proceedings which are outlined below.[12] **[17–05]**

> Section 14 – Evidence through intermediary
> (1) Where –
> (a) a person is accused of a relevant offence, and
> (b) a person under 18 years of age is giving, or is to give, evidence through a live television link,
>
> the court may, on the application of the prosecution or the accused, if satisfied that, having regard to the age or mental condition of the witness, the interests of justice require that any questions to be put to the witness be put through an intermediary, direct that any such questions be so put.
>
> (1A) Subject to section 14AA, where –
> (a) a person is accused of an offence, other than a relevant offence, and
> (b) a victim of the offence who is under 18 years of age, is giving, or is to give, evidence through a live television link, the court may, on the application of the prosecution or the accused, if satisfied that the interests of justice require that any questions to be put to the victim be put through an intermediary, direct that any such questions be so put.
>
> (2) Questions put to a witness through an intermediary under this section shall be either in the words used by the questioner or so as to convey to the witness in a way which is appropriate to his age and mental condition the meaning of the questions being asked.

---

8 See [17–106].

9 Irish Law Reform Commission, *Consultation Paper on Child Sexual Abuse* (CP2–1989) 205. Irish Law Reform Commission, *Report on Child Sexual Abuse* (32–1990) para 7.26, 78.

10 Criminal Evidence Act 1992, s 14 commenced 3 March 1997; Criminal Evidence Act 1992 (Sections 14 and 19) (Commencement) Order 1997, SI 1997/66.

11 Criminal Justice Act 1993, s 5B (inserted by Criminal Procedure Act 2010, s 6).

12 See [17–126]

(3) An intermediary referred to in subsection (1) or (1A) shall be appointed by the court and shall be a person who, in its opinion, is competent to act as such.

Eligibility Categories – Intermediaries under s 14 Criminal Evidence Act 1992

Section 14(1) – witness, or victim, under 18 in relation to a relevant offence

[17–06] Section 14(1) allows for a witness or a victim[13] who is under 18, and who is giving, or is to give, evidence through a live television link, to give evidence through an intermediary in relation to a relevant offence. The list of relevant offences is outlined in Part III, s 12 of the Act, and are:

(a) a sexual offence[14];
(b) an offence involving violence or the threat of violence to a person;
(ba) an offence under section 10 (amended by section 23 of the Criminal Justice (Miscellaneous Provisions) Act 2023) of the NonFatal Offences against the Person Act 1997;
(c) an offence under section 3, 4, 5 or 6 of the Child Trafficking and Pornography Act 1998;
(d) an offence under section 2, 4 or 7 of the Criminal Law (Human Trafficking) Act 2008;
(da) an offence under section 33, 38 or 39 of the Domestic Violence Act 2018;
(e) an offence consisting of attempting or conspiring to commit, or of aiding or abetting, counselling, procuring or inciting the commission of, an offence mentioned in paragraph (a), (b), (c), (d) or (da).

[17–07] The application may be made by the prosecution or the accused in respect of a witness so an intermediary may assist a prosecution or defence witness. The section appears to preclude the court of its own motion providing for an intermediary for the witness. The section appears to exclude the defendant due to the fact that the support measure is linked with the support measure of video link and available video link provisions either exclude the defendant or are inappropriate for the use of an intermediary at trial.[15]

---

13 While a witness may also mean a victim, a victim can not also mean a witness. The differentiation of s 14AA in relation to the eligibility of a victim under 18 for an offence other than a relevant offence implies that the section is only for persons against whom the alleged offence has occurred. However, s 14(1) may apply to a victim or a witness. The word 'witness' was used in the original legislation and has been used for victims in criminal trials.

14 Criminal Evidence Act 1992, s 2, Interpretation: '"sexual offence" means: rape, sexual assault (within the meaning of section 2 of the Criminal Law (Rape) (Amendment) Act 1990), aggravated sexual assault (within the meaning of section 3 of that Act), rape under section 4 of that Act or an offence under –
(a) section 3 or 6 of the Criminal Law Amendment Act 1885,
(b) section 5 of the Criminal Law (Sexual Offences) Act 1993,
(c) section 6 of the Criminal Law (Sexual Offences) Act 1993,
(d) section 1 or 2 of the Punishment of Incest Act 1908,
(e) section 4A or 5A of the Child Trafficking and Pornography Act 1998,
(f) section 249 of The Children Act 2001,
(g) the Criminal Law (Sexual Offences) Act 2006, or
(h) section 3, 4, 5, 6, 7 or 8 of the Criminal Law (Sexual Offences) Act 2017, excluding an attempt to commit any such offence.'

15 See [17–17].

The test for the provision is that the court must be satisfied that the interests of justice require that any questions to be put to the witness be put through an intermediary. [17–08]

Section 19 of the Act applies to this section in relation to the eligibility of a person with a mental disorder who has reached the age of 18.[16] [17–09]

Section 14(1A) – victims under 18 years of age of an offence other than a relevant offence

The use of an intermediary under s 14(1A) applies only to victims under 18 of an offence other than a relevant offence (as opposed to a witness to or a defendant of an offence other than a relevant offence) and this section was inserted through the Criminal Justice (Victims of Crime) Act 2017.[17] [17–10]

The application may be made by the prosecution or the accused in respect of a victim. As with s 14(1), the section appears to preclude the court, of its own motion, providing for an intermediary for the victim. [17–11]

Section 19 of the Act also applies to this section in relation to the eligibility of a person with a mental disorder who has reached the age of 18.[18] The provision under s 14(1A) is subject to the test under s 14AA,[19] which applies to victims in respect of the use of video link (s 13(1A)), intermediaries (s 14(1A)) and screens (s 14A(2)). [17–12]

Section 14 Criminal Evidence Act 1992 – Eligibility for Persons with a Mental Disorder Under s 19 Criminal Evidence Act 1992

An adult with a mental disorder may be eligible for an intermediary under s 14(1) (witness/victim to a relevant offence) or s 14(1A) (victim to an offence other than a relevant offence) under s 19 of the Criminal Evidence Act 1992. Section 19 of the Act extends the provisions for an intermediary (s 14), removal of wigs and gowns (s 14B) and recorded evidence (s 16) to persons with a 'mental disorder' as defined under s 5 of the Criminal Justice Act 1993. This section outlines that mental disorder includes a mental illness, mental disability, dementia or any disease of the mind. [17–13]

It should be noted that s 13 of the Criminal Evidence Act 1992, which allows for the use of video link, was removed from s 19 of the Criminal Evidence Act 1992 by the Criminal Justice (Victims of Crime) Act 2017.[20] The linking of the use of intermediary to the giving of evidence via video link means that an application for video link will also have to be made for that support measure so for persons with a mental disorder [17–14]

---

16 Criminal Evidence Act, s 19, Application of Part III to persons with mental handicap: 'The references in sections 14, 14B, 15 and 16 to a person under 18 years of age shall include references to a person with a mental disorder, within the meaning of section 5 of the Criminal Justice Act 1993 who has reached the age concerned.'

17 Criminal Justice (Victims of Crime) Act 2017, s 30(c)(ii), (iii), SI No 173 of 2018. Commenced on 30 May 2018.

18 Criminal Evidence Act, s 19, Application of Part III to persons with mental handicap: 'The references in sections 14, 14B, 15 and 16 to a person under 18 years of age shall include references to a person with a mental disorder, within the meaning of section 5 of the Criminal Justice Act 1993 who has reached the age concerned.'

19 See [17–20].

20 Criminal Justice (Victims of Crime) Act 2017, s 30.

under the Act, this may then be done under s 13(1)(b) or s 13(1A) of the Criminal Evidence Act 1992[21] or another appropriate legislative provision, such as s 39 of the Criminal Justice Act 1999[22] (witnesses in fear or subject to intimidation).

[17–15] The appropriate tests under the sections will apply but in respect of s 14(1), the section does outline that the court may grant the support measure if satisfied, having regard to the mental condition of the witness, the interests of justice require the use of an intermediary. This may also support the application in respect of an adult with a mental disorder under s 19 of the Criminal Evidence Act 1992.[23]

Exclusion of witness under 18/adult with a mental disorder to an offence other than a relevant offence

[17–16] It would appear that a child under 18 or an adult with a mental disorder who is a witness to an offence other than a relevant offence is excluded from this provision. It is uncertain as to why this is the case.

Exclusion of defendant from s 14 Criminal Evidence Act 1992

[17–17] Provisions for video link under s 13 of the Criminal Evidence Act 1992[24] or s 39 of the Criminal Justice Act 1999[25] exclude the accused. Other provisions for video link such as under Part 4 Civil Law and Criminal Law (Miscellaneous Provisions) Act 2020 may not accommodate trials but could accommodate an intermediary for an accused person in pre-trial hearings such as bail. The Act provides further assistance to persons in custody so procedural issues such as how the intermediary will have access

---

21 This may be made under Criminal Evidence Act 1992, s 13(1)(b) or s 13(1A), depending on whether the person with a mental disorder is a victim or witness to a relevant offence; or a victim of an offence other than a relevant offence. It would appear that a witness to an offence other than a relevant offence with a mental disorder is excluded from the provision. Criminal Evidence Act 1992, s 13:

> '1) In any proceedings (including proceedings under section 4E or 4F of the Criminal Procedure Act, 1967) for a relevant offence a person other than the accused may give evidence, whether from within or outside the State, through a live television link –
>
> (a) if the person is under 18 years of age, unless the court sees good reason to the contrary,
>
> (b) in any other case, with the leave of the court.
>
> (1A) In any proceedings (including proceedings under section 4E or 4F of the Criminal Procedure Act 1967) relating to an offence, other than a relevant offence, a court may, subject to section 14AA, grant leave for a victim of the offence to give evidence, whether from within or outside the State, through a live television link.'

22 Criminal Justice Act 1999, s 39, Witnesses in fear or subject to intimidation.

23 See *DPP v O'Driscoll* [2022] IECA 4.

24 Criminal Evidence Act 1992, s 13:

> '(1) In any proceedings (including proceedings under section 4E or 4F of the Criminal Procedure Act, 1967) for a relevant offence *a person other than the accused* (emphasis added) may give evidence, whether from within or outside the State, through a live television link –
>
> (a) if the person is under 18 years of age, unless the court sees good reason to the contrary,
>
> (b) in any other case, with the leave of the court.'

25 Criminal Justice Act 1999, s 39, Witnesses in fear or subject to intimidation: '(1) Subject to subsection (2), in any proceedings on indictment for an offence (including proceedings under Part IA of the Act of 1967) a person *other than the accused* (emphasis added) may, with the leave of the court, give evidence through a live television link.'

to the accused in custody may arise. For example, would the intermediary be able to physically sit beside the accused or would the intermediary physically stay in court?

For the substantive trial of the matter, a defendant may not be able to avail of an intermediary unless there is a video link provision which does not exclude him or her from availing of it. If it is available, such as perhaps through the inherent jurisdiction of the court, the circumstances of his or her availing of it will be limited, ie when he or she is giving evidence as the legislation states 'is giving, or is to give, evidence through a live television link'. This may be useful, but it would exclude any period beyond that, ie the duration of the trial. It would therefore not assist greatly with any further role of the intermediary to allow the defendant to follow proceedings, to participate fully in the trial and enable him or her to instruct legal representatives. **[17–18]**

However, intermediaries for defendants have been appointed in Irish courts under the inherent jurisdiction of the courts based on Constitutional and ECHR rights to a fair trial. This is examined below.[26] **[17–19]**

Test under s 14AA Criminal Evidence Act 1992 for intermediaries for victims under 18 years of age of an offence other than a relevant offence

In considering whether to grant use of the support measure, the court must have regard under s 14AA, to the need for protection: **[17–20]**

> The court, in deciding –
> (a) whether to grant leave under section 13(1A) for a victim to give evidence through a live television link,
> (b) whether, under section 14(1A), the interests of justice require that it direct that questions be put to the victim through an intermediary, or
> (c) whether, under section 14A(2), the interests of justice require that it direct that a screen or other similar device be positioned, in an appropriate place, so as to prevent the victim from seeing the accused when giving evidence,
>
> shall have regard to the need to protect the victim from secondary and repeat victimisation, intimidation, or retaliation, taking into account –
> (i) the nature and circumstances of the case, and
> (ii) the personal characteristics of the victim.[27]

The section obliges the court to consider the need to protect the victim from secondary and repeat victimisation, intimidation, or retaliation in granting the support measures of video link, intermediaries, or screens for victims of an offence other than a relevant offence. While the section obliges the court to take into account the nature and circumstances of the case and the personal characteristics of the victim, there is no legislative requirement for any evidence of victimisation, intimidation, or retaliation to be put in evidence before the court. **[17–21]**

Secondary victimisation is interpreted in the Criminal Justice (Victims of Crime) Act 2017 as 'victimisation that occurs indirectly through the response of institutions and individuals to the victim'.[28] **[17–22]**

---

26 See [17–106]

27 Criminal Evidence Act, s 14AA, Matters to be taken into account under ss 13, 14 and 14A regarding victims.

28 Criminal Justice (Victims of Crime) Act 2017, s 2, Interpretation.

[17–23] Section 12(2) of the Criminal Evidence Act 1992 states that the application of Part III of the Act, which deals with evidence in criminal proceedings, is not dependent on the commission of an offence having to be established. Nor is it dependent on establishing whether the person concerned suffered any harm caused by an offence.

[17–24] Whether this may be interpreted as relating to the original offence charged or any evidence as to whether the support measure is necessary under s 14AA in relation to secondary victimisation, intimidation or retaliation has still to be considered by the courts.

[17–25] It is possible that the requirement to protect the victim from secondary victimisation, intimidation or retaliation could be refuted on the basis that no secondary or repeat victimisation will occur or that the support measure itself will not protect from any potential victimisation, intimidation or retaliation.

[17–26] The section is in contrast to the condition in s 39(2) of the Criminal Justice Act 1999, which allows video link to be used to facilitate witnesses or victims who may be in fear or subject to intimidation. It states that the court will not grant leave 'unless it is satisfied that the person is likely to be in fear or subject to intimidation in giving evidence otherwise',[29] indicating that the court is obliged to have a degree of mental engagement with the evidence before it grants the support measure.

Section 14 Criminal Evidence Act 1992 – 'The interests of justice' requirement

[17–27] The provision of an intermediary is subject to the proviso under ss 14(1) and 14(1A) that the 'the interests of justice *require*' (emphasis added) that questions be put through an intermediary. This may imply that, in the relevant circumstances, there may be a potential breach of the interests of justice if an intermediary is not appointed. A challenge may also be made that the interests of justice do not require the use of an intermediary and that an appointment of one may breach the defendant's right to a fair trial under Article 38.1 of the Constitution. There is no definition of 'the interests of justice' within ss 14(1), 14(1A) or the Act itself.

'Mental condition' – s 14(1) Criminal Evidence Act 1992

[17–28] Section 14(1) states:

> the court may, on the application of the prosecution or the accused, if satisfied that, having regard to the age or mental condition of the witness, the interests of justice require that any questions to be put to the witness be put through an intermediary, direct that any such questions be so put.

[17–29] There is no definition of mental condition in the section. In relation to s 14(1), Heffernan notes that the 'inclusion of 'the mental condition' of the witness is likely directed not to the situation of the child witness but rather to that of a witness with

---

[29] Criminal Justice Act, s 39, Witnesses in fear or subject to intimidation:

'(1) Subject to subsection (2), in any proceedings on indictment for an offence (including proceedings under Part IA of the Act of 1967) a person other than the accused may, with the leave of the court, give evidence through a live television link.

(2) A court shall not grant leave under subsection (1) unless it is satisfied that the person is likely to be in fear or subject to intimidation in giving evidence otherwise.'

a 'mental disorder' who may potentially come within the scope of s 14 as extended by s 19'.[30]

Definition of an Intermediary

The Criminal Evidence Act 1992 does not provide a legal definition of the term intermediary nor the necessary qualifications for the role other than under s 14(3), which states: **[17–30]**

> An intermediary referred to in subsection (1) or (1A) shall be appointed by the court and shall be a person who, in its opinion, is competent to act as such.

In England and Wales, the legislative provision for intermediaries, s 29(1) of the Youth Justice and Criminal Evidence Act 1999, states: **[17–31]**

> A special measures direction may provide for any examination of the witness (however and wherever conducted) to be conducted through an interpreter or other person approved by the court for the purposes of this section ("an intermediary").

The Advocate's Gateway, an online resource for practitioners in the UK, states: **[17–32]**

> Intermediaries themselves are professionals with an expertise in facilitating the communication of those who are vulnerable.[31]

While the word 'interpreter' is contained in the legislation in England and Wales,[32] there appears to be a reluctance in the guidance to deem intermediaries as such.[33] However, in Ireland, there appears to be no such difficulty at present[34] although the establishment of training of intermediaries in Ireland may develop these distinctions further.[35] **[17–33]**

---

30 Liz Heffernan, *Evidence in Criminal Trials* (2nd edn, Bloomsbury 2020) para 5.47, n 133, 214.

31 The Advocate's Gateway <https://www.theadvocatesgateway.org/intermediaries> accessed 13 October 2023.

32 Youth Justice and Criminal Evidence Act 2009, s 29: '(1)A special measures direction may provide for any examination of the witness (however and wherever conducted) to be conducted through an interpreter or other person approved by the court for the purposes of this section ("an intermediary").'

33 The guidance in England and Wales states: 'Description of the role of a Registered Intermediary 4) A Registered Intermediary is not an expert witness, investigator, interpreter, appropriate adult or advocate for the witness.' Registered Intermediary Procedural Guidance (Ministry for Justice 2020) Appendix 2, 6.

34 Dept of Justice and Equality, *Supporting a Victim's Journey – A plan to help victims and vulnerable witnesses in sexual violence cases* (October 2020) 54 which references para 8.14, 103, Dept of Justice and Equality, *Review of Protections for Vulnerable Witnesses in the Investigation and Prosecution of Sexual Offences* (August 2020) which states: 'The sole function of an intermediary is to assist in the communication process, whether between lawyers and witnesses during trial or, earlier, during police interviews. In this respect, their role is somewhat akin to that of an interpreter. The intermediary's loyalty is to the court. Indeed in some jurisdictions, it has been suggested that intermediaries should be formally classified and treated as officers of the court. On no account, should the intermediary be, or be perceived to be, an advocate or support worker acting on behalf of the person being assisted.'

35 University of Limerick, Professional Diploma – Intermediary Studies <https://www.ul.ie/gps/courses/intermediary-studies-professional-diploma> accessed 13 October 2023.

Role of the Intermediary – s 14(2) Criminal Evidence Act 1992

[17–34] The O'Malley Report[36] cites Cooper and Mattison, who described the intermediary's role in England and Wales:

> The intermediary's role is to assist the police and the court to communicate with the witness so as to obtain the best-quality evidence from the vulnerable witness. The advice the intermediary gives is underpinned by the intermediary's assessment of the witness's communication needs; an assessment that is performed on an individual, case-by-case basis. It is usually conducted prior to the witness being interviewed by the police, although the intermediary referral can take place later in the proceedings, for example after the interview but before the witness is questioned at court. Based upon the finding of the communication assessment, an intermediary will advise police officers in the case and the advocates at court how best to communicate so that the questions they ask and the answers in reply are understood.[37]

[17–35] As the relevant legislation gives little detail to the role, the above description may best describe the functions of the intermediary in Ireland, particularly as the recommendations of the O'Malley Report are being implemented through *Supporting a Victim's Journey.*[38]

[17–36] Section 14(2) of the Criminal Evidence Act 1992 states:

> Questions put to a witness through an intermediary under this section shall be either in the words used by the questioner or so as to convey to the witness in a way which is appropriate to his age and mental condition the meaning of the questions being asked.

[17–37] The section outlines that the intermediary may either put the question asked by the questioner to the witness or put the question to the witness in a manner which has regard to the age of the witness as well as the witness' individual psychological characteristics. The utility of a question that is simply relayed by the intermediary may lie in the fact that it is being asked by someone who may be more familiar to the witness and who plays a less authoritative role in proceedings. Where the question is rephrased with regard to the age and mental condition of the witness, it would seem that the question in its original state must first be asked, causing delay and distraction, while the question is reformulated. In certain cases, questioners may work with intermediaries prior to questioning to establish how best to phrase questions to avoid confusion, upset or delay. The role of the intermediary may include assistance to the questioner prior to questioning the witness to avoid any difficulties.

[17–38] The level of involvement of the intermediary at trial will depend on the capacity of the vulnerable witness to engage in criminal proceedings as well as the skill of counsel to ask questions which the witness will understand without difficulty.[39] In the case of *DPP*

---

36 Dept of Justice and Equality, *Review of Protections for Vulnerable Witnesses in the Investigation and Prosecution of Sexual Offences* (August 2020) para 8.11, 102.

37 Penny Cooper and Michelle Mattison, 'Intermediaries, vulnerable people and the quality of evidence: An international comparison of three versions of the English intermediary model' (2017) 21(4) International Journal of Evidence and Proof, 351, 354.

38 Dept of Justice and Equality, *Supporting a Victim's Journey – A plan to help victims and vulnerable witnesses in sexual violence cases* (October 2020).

39 Emily Henderson, '"A very valuable tool": Judges, advocates and intermediaries discuss the intermediary system in England and Wales' (2015) 19(3), International Journal of Evidence & Proof 154–71, 164: 'A couple of advocates also commented that the extent to which intermediaries

v O'Driscoll,[40] it appeared that the defence counsel was concerned that the use of an intermediary would have an undue impact on the evidence.[41] However, the judgment indicates that the intermediary's role was limited to resolving communication issues:

> It is clear from the exchanges between defence counsel and the proposed intermediary in the Central Criminal Court that all involved with the issue envisaged that the intermediary's role would be to intervene where there was a concern about the possibility of confusion or lack of comprehension, and to request that a question be reformulated by counsel. In fact, this is precisely what occurred; there was no occasion when the question was actually formulated and put by the intermediary.[42]

It should be noted that s 14(2) provides that questions 'shall be either in the words used by the questioner or so as to convey to the witness in a way which is appropriate to his age and mental condition the meaning of the questions being asked'; there is no provision for the answers of the witness to be translated or explained by the intermediary for the benefit of the court.[43] It appears to be the practice that the intermediary will ask the questioner to rephrase the question and if difficulties arise, the intermediary may suggest appropriate alternatives, which can be then put by the questioner. It does not seem to be the practice that extensive direct interaction takes place between the intermediary and the complainant beyond practical issues such as requirements to take breaks or checking as to the emotional, psychological and/or physical state of the complainant. The questioning is done by counsel and the intermediary will intervene and interact when necessary but this is kept to a minimum. It appears to be the priority for intermediaries that significant preparatory work is done prior to the trial so that intervention at trial can be kept to a minimum. **[17–39]**

Video Link and the Use of Intermediaries

The use of intermediaries is inextricably linked with that of video link. The relevant section does not state which legislative provision must be used but only that the witness or victim may be granted the support measures where he or she is 'giving, or is to give, evidence through a live television link'.[44] **[17–40]**

The linking of the support measure to that of video link prevents a witness or victim from giving his or her evidence from the body of the court. This may be an issue for any given witness who may not wish to give evidence via video link for a number of reasons – for example, if he or she were a victim of pornography, harassment or 'revenge **[17–41]**

---

intervene relates to counsel's skill rather than the intermediary's overzealousness. When training I do say "if you do your job properly the intermediary won't have to utter a word".'

40 *DPP v O'Driscoll* [2022] IECA 4.

41 ibid [13].

42 ibid [30].

43 Youth Justice and Criminal Evidence Act 1999, s 29, in England and Wales, allows for the intermediary to assist with communication in relation to both the questions and the answers for the benefit of the court:

> '2) The function of an intermediary is to communicate –
> (a) to the witness, questions put to the witness, and
> (b) to any person asking such questions, the answers given by the witness in reply to them, and to explain such questions or answers so far as necessary to enable them to be understood by the witness or person in question.'

44 Criminal Evidence Act, s 14; Criminal Justice Act 1993, s 5B (in relation to the giving of victim impact statements) as inserted by Criminal Procedure Act 2010, s 6.

porn' offences[45] and finds the use of a camera traumatic. Equally, if the witness or victim does not wish to give evidence from an enclosed space, the relevant video link room may not be suitable.

[17–42] In addition, evidence may be 'flattened' by the use of video link and, for certain witnesses, it might be their preference to give evidence physically from a witness box in court and this may result in more powerful and dynamic testimony. A witness may prefer to be physically present in court to give his or her testimony in order to face the defendant, albeit with the assistance of an intermediary.

[17–43] The use of video link with the support measure of intermediaries may also cause practical issues. While there is no reason why the intermediary may not be in the courtroom, in order to perform the role effectively it is reasonable to consider that the intermediary would sit with the witness while he or she is giving evidence. However, the individual circumstances of the case and the witness may influence the procedure adopted by the court. It is important to consider the other personnel who may also be present while the witness gives evidence. The witness minder/court usher will also be in the video link room. In addition, if there are documents or photos to be shown to the witness, in the course of his or her giving evidence, there may also be a member of An Garda Síochána present. Depending on the facilities available, this may then make the technical and physical aspects of giving evidence more problematic.

Jurisdiction in all Courts/Transfer of Proceedings

[17–44] There is no limitation in s 14 of the Criminal Evidence Act 1992 in relation to summary or indictable offences and the provision applies to courts of all jurisdictions. If required, s 17 of the Criminal Evidence Act 1992[46] allows for proceedings under ss 13, 14, 15, 16 and 29 to be transferred to the appropriate court.

Screens and the Use of Intermediaries

[17–45] Section 30 of the Criminal Justice (Victims of Crime) Act 2017 inserted s 14A into the Criminal Evidence Act 1992, placing the use of screens on a legislative basis.[47] There appears to be an inconsistency in the provision as s 14A[48] allows for the use of

---

45 For example, under the Harassment, Harmful Communications and Related Offences Act 2020.

46 Criminal Evidence Act 1992, s 17, Transfer of proceedings:

> 'In any proceedings for an offence in any circuit or district court district in relation to which any of the provisions of sections 13 to 16 or section 29 is not in operation the court concerned may, if in its opinion it is desirable that evidence be given in the proceedings through a live television link or by means of a videorecording or that a screen or other similar device be used in the giving of evidence, by order transfer the proceedings to a circuit or district court district in relation to which those provisions are in operation and, where such an order is made the jurisdiction of the court to which the proceedings have been transferred may be exercised –
>
> (a) in the case of the Circuit Court, by the judge of the circuit concerned, and
>
> (b) in the case of the District Court, by the judge of that court for the time being assigned to the district court district concerned.'

47 See Chapter 27.

48 Criminal Evidence Act 1992, s 14A, Placement of screen etc for giving of evidence:

> '(1) Where a person who is under 18 years of age is to give evidence other than through a live television link in respect of a relevant offence, the court may, on the application of

a screen where a witness is to give evidence 'other than through a live television link' and yet also includes the obligation that a witness giving evidence under the section shall be capable of seeing and hearing and being seen and heard by 'any interpreter, intermediary appointed under section 14' to assist the witness.[49] It is not clear how an appointment for the use of an intermediary under s 14 which requires the use of video link may work with the use of a screen under s 14A where the section outlines that the witness is giving evidence other than through a live television link.

The Use of an Intermediary at Pre-Trial/ Investigative Stages of Proceedings

At present, intermediaries participate in criminal proceedings in the course of preliminary trial hearings, where applications for their appointment are made, and then during the trial itself. Meetings and assessments with the witness will have been conducted prior to engaging with the preliminary trial hearing and the trial process. However, there does not appear to be any current practice of intermediaries attending interviews with An Garda Síochána at an investigative stage. The O'Malley Report[50] and the *Supporting a Victim's Journey*[51] report, which replicates the O'Malley recommendations, envisage the use of intermediaries at an investigative stage. The use **[17–46]**

---

the prosecution or the accused, direct that a screen or other similar device be positioned, in an appropriate place, so as to prevent the witness from seeing the accused when giving evidence, unless the court is satisfied that in all the circumstances of the case such a direction would be contrary to the interests of justice.

(2) Subject to section 14AA, where –

(a) a person who is a victim of an offence, other than a relevant offence, is under 18 years of age and the person is to give evidence, other than through a live television link, in respect of the offence, or

(b) a person who is a victim of any offence has attained the age of 18 years and the person is to give evidence, other than through a live television link, in respect of such an offence, the court may, on the application of the prosecution or the accused, if satisfied that the interests of justice so require, direct that a screen or other similar device be positioned, in an appropriate place, so as to prevent the victim from seeing the accused when giving evidence.

(3) A witness giving evidence under subsection (1) or (2) shall be capable of seeing and hearing and being seen and heard by –

(a) the judge and jury (if any),

(b) legal representatives acting in the proceedings,

(c) any interpreter, intermediary appointed under section 14 or any other person appointed to assist the witness, and shall be capable of being heard by the accused.'

[49] Criminal Evidence Act 1992, s 14A(3).

[50] Dept of Justice and Equality, *Review of Protections for Vulnerable Witnesses in the Investigation and Prosecution of Sexual Offences* (Aug 2020), Summary of Recommendations 108, 138: 'Intermediaries, where needed, should be involved from the earliest stages of the criminal process and, in particular, should be available to assist at Garda interviews of victims, defendants or other potential witnesses who may be vulnerable on account of age or physical or mental disability. … Where at all possible, the same person should serve as intermediary in respect of a particular witness throughout the entire criminal process. An intermediary who has been involved in the Garda interview should continue to function in respect of the witness in question during the trial where one takes place.'

[51] Dept of Justice and Equality, *Supporting a Victim's Journey – A plan to help victims and vulnerable witnesses in sexual violence cases* (October 2020) Intermediaries, Recommendations 7.1 and 7.2, 55.

of intermediaries is mentioned in the *Good Practice Guidelines*, in respect of guidance for the taking of recorded testimony.

Intermediaries and the Use of Recorded Testimony Under s 16(1)(b) of the Criminal Evidence Act 1992/Good Practice Guidelines

[17–47] The *Good Practice Guidelines*, published in 2003, comprises procedural guidance in relation to the recording of evidence under s 16(1)(b) of the Criminal Evidence Act 1992. In relation to the use of interpreters/intermediaries, it states:

> Where the interview team decides to use an interpreter/intermediary, it should clarify at the outset who will lead the interview in terms of maintaining direct communication with the complainant. Where an interpreter is being used, the interviewer should identify his/her own role and maintain appropriate eye contact with the complainant. This will help the complainant understand that he/she should address the interviewer not the interpreter. Where an intermediary is engaged due to the specialist nature of the complainant's communication system or his/her particular needs (e.g. the complainant may be very young or very distressed), it may be more appropriate for the intermediary to lead the interview. In such cases, the presence and role of the interview team member should be clearly agreed at the planning stage. In addition to clarifying the role of an interpreter/intermediary prior to the interview, the legal and confidential requirements should also be discussed and clarified. The consideration of emotional support for the interpreter/intermediary after the interview should also be addressed.
>
> The intermediary/interpreter should be skilled in relaying questions in a precise way so as not to misrepresent the question being asked by the interviewer.[52]

[17–48] Given the significant legislative amendments to both ss 14 and 16(1)(b) of the Criminal Evidence Act 1992 since the *Good Practice Guidelines* were drafted in 2003, revision of the *Guidelines* is required as soon as possible.

Assessment by An Garda Síochána re support measures including intermediary – s 15 Criminal Justice (Victims of Crime) Act 2017

[17–49] Section 15 of the Criminal Justice (Victims of Crime) Act 2017 sets out the obligation of An Garda Síochána to be aware that support measures may be required for a victim, which may include the use of an intermediary.[53] It is the responsibility of a member of An Garda Síochána, when a complaint is made, to consider whether the witness/victim has cognitive or communication needs that will require an intermediary to facilitate communication during the investigation of the offence in line with s 16 of the Criminal Justice (Victims of Crime) Act 2017[54] or s 17 of the Criminal Justice (Victims of Crime) Act 2017.[55] However, there appears to be no legislative provision which states that the assessment can only be done at this stage. If it becomes apparent that the witness requires the assistance of an intermediary it would seem that there

---

52 An Garda Síochána, *Good Practice Guidelines for Persons involved in Video Recording interviews with complainants under 14 years of age (or with intellectual disability) for Evidential Purposes in accordance with Section 16(1)(b) of the Criminal Evidence Act, 1992, in cases involving Sexual and/or Violent Offences* (July 2003) paras 2.65, 2.66.

53 Criminal Justice (Victims of Crime) Act 2017, s 15, Assessment of Victim.

54 ibid s 16, Application of protection measures and special measures during investigations.

55 ibid s 17, Special measures during investigations (interviews).

is nothing to prevent the assessment and application being made at a later stage in proceedings.

In relation to recorded testimony which is recorded under s 16(1)(b) of the Criminal Evidence Act 1992, if an intermediary assists at this stage, an application for his or her presence at trial must be considered at a much later stage, such as when a file has been sent to the Director of Public Prosecutions or when counsel has been briefed by the Chief Prosecution Solicitor. If, at a preliminary trial hearing or at trial, the judge rules against the application for an intermediary, the recorded testimony could then be deemed inadmissible due to any risk of prejudice of the evidence given in the recorded interview. Appropriate training and further procedural guidance are required to ensure that the recorded testimony will be admissible at a later stage in proceedings. [17–50]

Guidance in Relation to Intermediaries in Guidelines for Prosecutors, Office of the Director of Public Prosecutions

The Office of the Director of Public Prosecutions outlines the option of an intermediary in its publication *Guidelines for Prosecutors*.[56] However, it does not contain information as to how the intermediary should be chosen. Nor does it describe the parameters of the interactions between counsel, intermediary and the court. The prosecutor is asked to consider the use of an intermediary in relation to the presentation of the evidence: [17–51]

> l) Where child witnesses are involved, are they likely to be able to give sworn evidence, or evidence in accordance with the criteria in section 27 of the Criminal Evidence Act 1992?; is their evidence in chief available by way of video recording in accordance with section 16 of the Criminal Evidence Act 1992?; how is the experience of a trial including cross examination likely to affect them?; should the children's evidence be presented by way of live television link or with the assistance of an intermediary in accordance with sections 13 and 14 of the 1992 Act?[57]

The University of Limerick has established a postgraduate professional Diploma in Intermediary Studies which will qualify CORU-registered[58] health and social care practitioners to work as Registered Intermediaries for both vulnerable witnesses and vulnerable defendants in Ireland. Graduates will be recognised by the Department of Justice as eligible to be placed on a panel from which the courts can draw to work as an intermediary in the Republic of Ireland. It is possible that updated guidance of the Office of the Director of Public Prosecutions will include information regarding any panel that is to be established. [17–52]

---

56 Office of the Director of Public Prosecutions, *Guidelines for Prosecutors, Giving of Evidence by Live Television Link Through an intermediary and Placement of Screens* (5th edn, December 2019) paras 12.27, 12.28, 12.30, 48, 49. <https://www.dppireland.ie/app/uploads/2021/01/Guidelines-for-Prosecutors-5th-Edition-eng.pdf> accessed 13 October 2023.

57 Office of the Director of Public Prosecutions, *Guidelines for Prosecutors, The Strength of the Evidence* (5th edn, December 2019) para 4.14(l), 15 <https://www.dppireland.ie/app/uploads/2021/01/Guidelines-for-Prosecutors-5th-Edition-eng.pdf> accessed 13 October 2023.

58 CORU is Ireland's multi-profession health and social care regulator. It regulates the individuals who provide health and social care services in Ireland <https://www.coru.ie/> accessed 13 October 2023.

Preliminary Trial Hearings and the Application for an Intermediary

[17–53] An application for an intermediary may be made at a preliminary trial hearing under s 6(8)(b)(v) of the Criminal Procedure Act 2021. However, there is no restriction on an application being made to the trial court where necessity requires this.[59] An application to the use of an intermediary may require the intermediary to give evidence as to how his or her appointment originated, how the assessment with the witness was undertaken,[60] what other reports or documents were used in the assessment and any other relevant questions regarding any report submitted by the intermediary. The intermediary's report may cover aspects of engagement at trial as to what particular difficulties the complainant may have with the trial process and how these may be resolved. Discussion in relation to these aspect of the report may be covered in more detail in a ground rules hearing.

Ground Rules Hearings

[17–54] Preliminary trial hearings may differ slightly from a ground rules hearing in that the trial court may set aside time to ensure that further discussion and rulings may be made as to how the intermediary may interact with the trial court or to determine other facilitations by the trial court.

---

59 See Criminal Procedure Act 2021, s 6 in particular s 6(19).

60 In a preliminary trial hearing, observed by the author, an issue arose as to the location where the assessment had taken place. This had been in a Garda station in the presence of a member of the investigation team. The intermediary noted that this was not uncommon and that conducting assessments in the home of the witness would be avoided. She explained that the presence of a member of An Garda Síochána would be advisable should further disclosures be made. In the *Registered Intermediary Procedural Guidance manual in England and Wales* (Ministry of Justice 2020), guidance is given in respect of the requirement for the police officer who will be conducting the interview to be present: 'The RI should confirm that the police officer who will be conducting the interview (interviewing officer) will be present at the assessment. It is essential that a police officer is present at the assessment at all times. This is to avoid the risk that a disclosure is made to the RI by the witness that would result in their role transitioning to that of a witness themselves. It is also helpful to all parties for the interviewing officer to be present as it assists them in observing the witness's communication skills and needs first-hand. Having observed the witness's communication skills and needs, and the manner in which the RI intervened and managed those communication difficulties, the interviewing officer will better understand the importance of the RI's recommendations. RIs should not be alone with a witness at any point.' (para 3.6) This highlights differences in the practice in Ireland and in England, Wales and Northern Ireland. In the latter jurisdictions, the interviewing police officer is part of the investigating team. In Ireland, if the interview is to be recorded, which would be the case in most cases where an intermediary is involved, the Specialist Interviewer who conducts the recorded interview is not a part of the investigating team. In addition, in England, Wales and Northern Ireland, the general practice appears to be that the intermediary is involved before the interview takes place and this is a much earlier stage than appears to be the practice in Ireland. In Ireland, the intermediary may not have access to or may not see the recorded interview until much later in the criminal process and possibly not until the trial itself.

These issues may be clarified if guidance or practice information becomes available, particularly with the use of intermediaries trained in the University of Limerick for the Professional Diploma – Intermediary Studies <https://www.ul.ie/gps/courses/intermediary-studies-professional-diploma> accessed 13 October 2023. However, the fact remains that the presence of a member of An Garda Síochána may have a direct impact on the reaction of a witness in relation to his or her communication skills and this should be taken into account. This is the case particularly where the circumstances may indicate that the witness may have been involved in criminal activity either related or unrelated to the pertinent offences.

Since its first documented use in Ireland in the case of *DPP v FE (Faisal Ellahi)* in November 2015,[61] Ground rules hearings have become more frequent in Ireland as intermediaries and practitioners have sought to clarify and resolve the manner in which the evidence of the victim or witness could be facilitated. The procedure followed practice in the United Kingdom.[62] **[17–55]**

The purpose of a ground rules hearing is to attempt to clarify, at an earlier stage, how the interaction with the witness will progress at trial and thereby avoid interruption, objections and delays in the course of the trial. It may also assist the vulnerable witness as it ensures that he or she knows what facilitation will be given to him or her. The practice emerged over a period of time and gained legitimacy as an established procedure in cases dealing with vulnerable witnesses. In England and Wales, Criminal Practice Directions now include provision for them[63] and they have been further directed through *R v Lubemba*,[64] a judgment which has been generally followed in Ireland.[65] In *R v Lubemba*, the Court stated: **[17–56]**

> The court is required to take every reasonable step to encourage and facilitate the attendance of vulnerable witnesses and their participation in the trial process. To that end, judges are taught, in accordance with the Criminal Practice Directions, that it is best practice to hold hearings in advance of the trial to ensure the smooth running of the trial, to give any special measures directions and to set the ground rules for the treatment of a vulnerable witness. We would expect a ground rules hearing in every case involving a vulnerable witness, save in very exceptional circumstances. If there are any doubts on how to proceed, guidance should be sought from those who have the responsibility for looking after the witness and or an expert.[66]

The Criminal Procedure Act 2021 provides for any further rulings to be made pre-trial or at any other time during the trial process.[67] Therefore, the practice of ground rules hearings may still continue under the auspices of the Criminal Procedure Act 2021. **[17–57]**

Ground Rules Hearing Where no Application for an Intermediary

A ground rules hearing could also take place where there is no application for an intermediary. The Court of Appeal in *DPP v VE*[68] stated that the views expressed in *R v Lubemba*[69] were apposite in Ireland and referred to the paragraph in *Lubemba* which states that 'it would expect a ground rules hearing in every case involving a vulnerable witness, save in very exceptional circumstances'.[70] The ground rules in the case of *DPP v VE*[71] are comprehensive and would not especially require the presence **[17–58]**

---

61 Caroline Biggs and Miriam Delahunt, 'Prosecutorial Challenges – Vulnerable Witnesses' (2017) 22(1) Bar Review 23, 24.

62 *DPP v VE* [2021] IECA 122 [16]. See also 'Ground Rules Hearings and the Fair Treatment of Vulnerable People in Court' (*The Advocate's Gateway*, 2 September 2019) Toolkit 1 <https://www.theadvocatesgateway.org/> accessed 13 October 2023.

63 PD 3E, General Matters: Ground Rules Hearings to plan the questioning of a vulnerable witness or defendant.

64 *R v JP and R v Lubemba* [2014] EWCA Crim 2064.

65 *DPP v VE* [2021] IECA 122.

66 *R v JP and R v Lubemba* [2014] EWCA Crim 2064 [42].

67 Criminal Procedure Act 2021, ss 6(8) and 6(19).

68 *DPP v VE* [2021] IECA 122.

69 *R v Lubemba* [2014] EWCA Crim 2064.

70 *DPP v VE* [2021] IECA 122 [82]; *R v JP and R v Lubemba* [2014] EWCA Crim 2064 [42].

71 *DPP v VE* [2021] IECA 122.

of an intermediary although an intermediary was appointed in that case.[72] But it is of assistance to any trial for all parties to be aware of the relevant issues, to have an opportunity to discuss them and to have them ruled on so that any issues may be resolved efficiently. Specialist and expert knowledge such as that of an intermediary may be required for personalised assessment of the witness. However, many of the ground rules contained in *DPP v VE*[73] are consistent with the objective of obtaining reliable evidence from any witness by any questioner.

Procedural Guidance not yet Available in Ireland for Intermediaries

[17–59] At present there appears to be no specific procedural guidance in relation to the use of intermediaries in Ireland. This may change with the establishment of a panel of registered intermediaries who have been trained through the University of Limerick.[74] The Irish courts have benefited from procedural guidance in England and Wales and in Northern Ireland.

Procedural Guidance in England and Wales

[17–60] The implementation of the support measure in England and Wales in s 29 of the Youth Justice and Criminal Evidence Act 1999 was reinforced by the publication of consistently updated guidance as to how the measure would be used both at an investigative and trial stage. In 2008 the Office for Criminal Justice Reform (now the Criminal Justice Reform Directorate) published *What's My Story? A Guide to Using Intermediaries to Help Vulnerable Witnesses.*[75] The *Registered Intermediary Procedural Guidance Manual* is a comprehensive piece of procedural guidance which is consistently updated.[76] The Ministry of Justice in England and Wales regularly revises its guidance on interviewing witnesses with the use of special measures in its publication *Achieving Best Evidence in Criminal Proceedings: Guidance on interviewing victims and witnesses, and guidance on using special measures,*[77] which includes comprehensive guidance for multi-agency personnel on the use of support measures for vulnerable witnesses including the use of intermediaries. In addition, the National Crime Agency in England and Wales comprises a Witness Intermediary Team to support police officers who consider

72 At the beginning of the trial, the Court conducted a 'ground rules hearing' to address the manner in which the questioning of the complainant would take place. This was done at the invitation of the prosecution. Counsel for the prosecution referred the trial judge to the case of *R v Lubemba* (discussed in further detail below), a judgment of the Court of Appeal of England and Wales, which refers to the measures which a trial judge may legitimately take to protect a vulnerable witness without impacting adversely on the right of an accused to a fair trial. Naturally the ground rules hearing took place in the absence of the jury: *DPP v VE* [2021] IECA 122 [16].

73 *DPP v VE* [2021] IECA 122.

74 See [17–67]

75 Office for Criminal Justice Reform, *What's My Story? A Guide to Using Intermediaries to Help Vulnerable Witnesses* (2008). The Office for Criminal Justice Reform has since closed.

76 Ministry of Justice, *Registered Intermediary Procedural Guidance Manual* (2020) <https://assets.publishing.service.gov.uk/government/uploads/system/uploads/attachment_data/file/955316/registered-intermediary-procedural-guidance-manual.pdf> accessed 13 October 2023; <https://www.gov.uk/government/publications/achieving-best-evidence-in-criminal-proceedings> accessed 13 October 2023.

77 Ministry of Justice, *Achieving Best Evidence in Criminal Proceedings: Guidance on interviewing victims and witnesses, and guidance on using special measures* (31 January 2022).

that an intermediary may be required at an investigative stage.[78] It assists in matching a Registered Intermediary to the relevant investigative team.[79]

The Advocacy Training Council in conjunction with the NSPCC established an internet resource called *The Advocate's Gateway*,[80] which contains updated legislative and procedural guidance including case law and legislation for anyone dealing with vulnerable witnesses and defendants in the criminal justice system in England, Wales, and Northern Ireland. It is a free resource and the material is consistently revised. Many of the principles and guidance are relevant for Irish courts. [17–61]

Procedural Guidance in Northern Ireland for the Use of Intermediaries

Intermediaries from Northern Ireland can rely on extensive procedural guidance[81] and detailed legislation[82] as well as established training.[83] [17–62]

The relevant provisions relating to the examination of a vulnerable person through an intermediary are Articles 17 and 21BA of the Criminal Evidence (Northern Ireland) Order 1999, as amended by the Justice Act (Northern Ireland) 2011. [17–63]

The Intermediary in Irish Courts

In 2016, the case of *DPP v NR*[84] involved the use of a trained intermediary on English [17–64]

78 The Witness Intermediary Team provides support to police officers and prosecutors in the use of Registered Intermediaries and offers advice on interview strategies for vulnerable and intimidated witnesses. The dedicated team matches Registered Intermediaries to the needs of vulnerable victims and witnesses in order to achieve best evidence.
National Crime Agency (UK) <https://www.nationalcrimeagency.gov.uk/what-we-do/how-we-work/providing-specialist-capabilities-for-law-enforcement/major-crime-investigative-support?; <https://assets.publishing.service.gov.uk/government/uploads/system/uploads/attachment_data/file/955316/registered-intermediary-procedural-guidance-manual.pdf.> accessed 13 October 2023.

79 Joyce Plotnikoff and Richard Woolfson, *Intermediaries in the Criminal Justice System* (Policy Press 2015) is an excellent text comprehensively addressing the subject of intermediaries in the criminal justice system in England, Wales and Northern Ireland.

80 *The Advocate's Gateway* is a free online resource hosted by the Advocacy Training Council and supervised by a committee whose representatives include the Advocacy Training Council, Chartered Institute of Legal Executives, Criminal Bar Association, Crown Prosecution Service Judicial College Kingston University, the Law Society, Ministry of Justice and Solicitors' Association of Higher Courts Advocates: <www.advocatesgateway.org> accessed 13 October 2023.

81 Northern Ireland Registered Intermediary Scheme <https://www.justice-ni.gov.uk/ri> accessed 13 October 2023.

82 Northern Ireland Criminal Evidence (Northern Ireland) Order 1999, Art 17.

83 RIs are professionals with specialist skills in communication. They come from backgrounds such as speech and language therapy and social work. Twenty-seven RIs have been recruited by the DOJ to act in this role. In order to do so, they had to pass Northern Ireland Department of Justice Registered Intermediary accreditation training (Masters level). RIs are bound by a Code of Practice and a Code of Ethics, and are subject to a complaints procedure. They are aware of legal professional privilege and will treat what they hear as confidential, not disclosing anything about the defence case or what has been said to them without the defendant's express consent. Northern Ireland Department of Justice Registered Intermediary Scheme <https://www.justice-ni.gov.uk/ri> accessed 13 October 2023.

84 An English intermediary was employed in assisting the complainant, who was giving evidence via video link from the Old Bailey in England in the case of *DPP v NR* [2021] IECA 121, the

soil, where the complainant was located, albeit assisting an Irish court. The trial of *DPP v VE*,[85] which took place in 2019, appears to be the first reported case of the use of a trained intermediary on Irish soil in an Irish court.[86] *DPP v VE* involved the use of a trained Northern Ireland intermediary physically present and assisting an Irish court.[87]

[17–65] *DPP v VE*[88] is a significant judgment, not only because the original trial involved the first use of a trained intermediary in an Irish court engaging with the rules of evidence in Ireland, but also because the judgment comprehensively examines the development of the treatment of vulnerable witnesses in Ireland. It endorses developments and case law in the United Kingdom and supports their use in Ireland.[89]

Training of Intermediaries

[17–66] As noted above, the Irish courts have consistently benefited from the training and experience of intermediaries from neighbouring jurisdictions.[90] The courts and practitioners have become familiar with the skills and procedures suggested by intermediaries from Northern Ireland and England and their interactions with the courts. *Supporting a Victim's Journey*[91] included plans to establish training and formation of a panel of intermediaries from which the courts can draw, based on the existing legislation, s 14 Criminal Evidence Act 1992 which provides for intermediaries in criminal trials.[92]

[17–67] In May 2022, the Department of Justice announced the anticipated training programme for intermediaries in the Republic of Ireland.[93] The University of Limerick has established a postgraduate professional Diploma in Intermediary Studies which will qualify CORU-registered[94] health and social care practitioners to work as Registered Intermediaries for both vulnerable witnesses and vulnerable defendants in Ireland. Graduates will be recognised by the Department of Justice as eligible to be placed on a panel from which the courts can draw from to work as an intermediary in the Republic of Ireland. Places for the first academic year, 2022–23, were funded by the Department of Justice. To what extent a person with equivalent skills but not trained through the above programme might be included in the panel of registered

trial of which took place over 33 days in April and May 2016. <https://www.theguardian.com/society/2019/mar/04/ruth-marchant-obituary> accessed 13 October 2023.

85 *DPP v VE* [2021] IECA 122.

86 The trial took place in February/March 2019 in the Central Criminal Court in Dublin.

87 *DPP v VE* [2021] IECA 122.

88 ibid.

89 ibid [86]. Ní Raifeartaigh J's judgment endorses the English cases of *R v Barker* [2010] EWCA Crim 4 and *R v Lumbeba and JP* [2014] EWCA Crim 2064.

90 *DPP v VE* [2021] IECA 122; *DPP v FN* [2021] IECA 238; [2022] IESC 22.

91 Dept of Justice and Equality, *Supporting a Victim's Journey – A plan to help victims and vulnerable witnesses in sexual violence cases* (October 2020).

92 Dept of Justice and Equality, *Review of Protections for Vulnerable Witnesses in the Investigation and Prosecution of Sexual Offences* (August 2020) 8.19–8.22, 105–06. Dept of Justice and Equality, *Supporting a Victim's Journey – A plan to help victims and vulnerable witnesses in sexual violence cases* (October 2020) Recommendation 7.1–7.3, 53.

93 Dept of Justice, 'Minister McEntee launches new training programme for professionals who help vulnerable witnesses to give evidence' (4 May 2022).

94 CORU is Ireland's multi-profession health and social care regulator. It regulates the individuals who provide health and social care services in Ireland: <https://www.coru.ie/> accessed 13 October 2023.

intermediaries or could work as an intermediary in the criminal courts if not included on the panel remains uncertain.

Functions of an Intermediary

The appointment of an intermediary may be queried in relation to how they will assist practitioners and the court at trial. The addition of a role which engages so closely to a witness may give rise to concern as to risks of prejudicing with or restricting the evidence or interfering with procedure. However, the role and functions of an intermediary may become apparent during the ground rules hearing where the issues are outlined. An assessment by the intermediary and his or her report to the Court could outline what linguistic or cognitive issues might prevent the witness from giving his or her best evidence. The intermediary may offer suggestions to the Court and practitioners as to how to resolve these. **[17–68]**

In addition, the intermediary, where sitting physically beside the witness, and focusing on the witness, may become aware, where the court or the practitioners do not, when the witness has become upset, lost concentration, needs a break or has not heard the question. In alerting the court to these matters, the intermediary provides a valuable service to the prosecution, defence and the trial judge which may not be performed in the same manner by anyone else in the courtroom. **[17–69]**

Reminder to Counsel of Significant Points of Ground Rules Hearing Re Relevant Witness

Preliminary trial hearings and/or ground rules hearings may take place a significant time before the witness gives evidence. Immediately prior to the witness giving evidence, and in his or her absence and of the jury, the intermediary may remind the court of the particular areas that may cause issues for the vulnerable witness in the course of giving evidence. For example, if the witness has a tendency to become emotionally dysregulated, the intermediary may remind the practitioners to keep a calm, steady tone, and pace. Where the witness is apt to lose focus, the intermediary may remind the court and practitioners to be aware that concentration may be easily lost and if that happens, to gently remind the witness to answer the question and to repeat it if necessary. Through reminders such as these, the intermediary may not need to intervene during the examination and/or cross-examination of a witness, which would be the desired outcome for all concerned. **[17–70]**

Intervention to Rephrase the Question

Generally, where there is continued use of tag questions,[95] where the questions are **[17–71]**

[95] Thomas O'Malley, *Sexual Offences* (Round Hall 2013) para 17.39, 409: 'Much of the psychological research has focused on language-related issues. Children are more likely to give reliable evidence in response to simple, uncomplicated questions phrased in ordinary language. Tag questions in particular should be avoided when questioning young children, principally because of the danger of acquiescence. A tag question consists of a statement, followed by an interrogative, such as: "you went into the kitchen then, didn't you?" Because young children may be reluctant or afraid to contradict an adult, they may acquiesce in such a statement even if they do not agree with it. Long, complicated questions and double negatives should also be avoided.'

overlong or complicated or in any other instance where there is a difficulty with the question, the intermediary may intervene to ask the counsel to rephrase the question. If the practitioner cannot find a way to ask the question in an appropriate way, the intermediary may suggest a phrasing that is appropriate.

[17–72] Section 14(2) of the Criminal Evidence Act 1992 facilitates the modification of questions so that they are appropriate to the witness and can be understood:

> (2) Questions put to a witness through an intermediary under this section shall be either in the words used by the questioner or so as to convey to the witness in a way which is appropriate to his age and mental condition the meaning of the questions being asked.

[17–73] An issue may arise where, theoretically, the question is modified beyond which is desired by counsel. Whether the modification of the question is upheld is a matter which must be determined by the trial judge and, potentially, the Court of Appeal. There may be resistance to traditional cross-examination being modified in any way by many counsel. However, the argument for the modification of questions is that the traditional manner of questioning yields unreliable evidence as well as causing stress and trauma to the witness.

[17–74] The skill of the intermediary to facilitate questions which are easily understood by the witness or victim will take time to become familiar in our courts. However, on seeing how a new manner of questioning may yield positive results for both prosecution and defence counsel, legal practitioners may develop trust in the support measures as well as understanding that preparation is key to the cross-examination of vulnerable witnesses. Intrusion or interference, by the court or by counsel, with the cross-examination of a witness or victim is kept to a minimum in Irish courts. But it is also unlikely that a judge or opposing counsel would allow a questioner to continue to cross examine a witness uninterrupted where the questioning is insulting, irrelevant or speculative. The Bar of Ireland's Code of Conduct prevents a barrister from making statements or asking questions 'which are merely scandalous or are intended only for the purpose of vilifying, insulting or annoying a witness or some other person'.[96]

Multiple Defendants and Multiple Counsel

[17–75] Where there are multiple defendants, respective counsel may feel obliged to repeat questions to ensure that the relevant evidence is put to the witness, and thereby to the jury, in respect of his or her individual client. An intermediary may include in his or her court report, and submit at a ground rules hearing, that repetition be limited. Where this ground rule is sanctioned by the Court, counsel may prepare cross-examination with this in mind in order to avoid repetitive cross-examination. However, the constitutional right to cross-examination, in the context of the cross-examination of vulnerable witnesses, has been underlined in the cases of *DPP v MT*[97] and *DPP v MB*,[98] albeit both cases which did not involve repetitive questioning.

[17–76] Anecdotal evidence suggests that in Ireland where there are multiple defendants,

96 Code of Conduct, Bar Council of Ireland: '5.18. Barristers when conducting a case must not make statements or ask questions which are merely scandalous or are intended only for the purpose of vilifying, insulting or annoying a witness or some other person.'

97 *DPP v MT* [2023] IECA 65 [81].

98 *DPP v MB* [2023] IECA 85 [41]–[42].

counsel are aware that repetitive questioning which is not relevant and which may risk upsetting the witness may be challenged by the trial judge and may be seen by the jury as redundant at best and bullying at worst. Defence counsel may limit questioning or risk challenge by the trial judge where repetitive questioning is not relevant or necessary.[99]

It would be helpful for counsel and judges to have guidance in relation to the prevention of repetitive questioning. Inconsistent practice may give rise to situations where certain counsel are limited in questioning in certain trials where others are not. In England and Wales, the Criminal Practice Directions prevent repetitive questioning of vulnerable witnesses where there are multiple defendants. They state: [17–77]

> If there is more than one accused, the judge should not permit each advocate to repeat the questioning of a vulnerable witness. In advance of the trial, the advocates should divide the topics between them, with the advocate for one accused leading the questioning, and the advocate(s) for the other accused asking only ancillary questions relevant to their client's case, without repeating the questioning that has already taken place.[100]

Communication Points Which May Arise[101]

These points have emerged in ground rules hearings in trials involving intermediaries and are generalised as issues which may arise in trials involving vulnerable witnesses. [17–78]

Compliance of vulnerable witness with persons in authority [17–79]

- The vulnerable witness may be quite compliant and eager to please, particularly in relation to persons in authority. Children tend to see all adults as persons in authority.
- The vulnerable witness could contradict or deny information to appease an adult in order to end the discourse quickly in a manner that made the witness feel safe.
- The vulnerable witness may not feel that he or she can correct mistakes made by an adult. He or she may assume that the adult will always be correct.

Educational proficiencies [17–80]

- Assessment in relevant tests may reveal that the vulnerable witness has particular cognitive or educational requirements, eg he or she may be delayed in terms of spoken language development and his or her understanding may be below that

---

99 In a trial observed by the author in the Central Criminal Court in 2021, where there were multiple accused and several child complainants, defence counsel endeavoured to limit repetition. The issue of repeat questioning had been flagged at a pre-trial hearing where the trial judge had noted that in other trials which involved multiple accused, senior counsel had taken the view that they didn't all have to ask the same questions repeatedly of a witness where answers have been given. The trial judge observed that there may be different perspectives from different accused persons in relation to a matter, but that common sense should prevail in relation to that. He noted that if there was unnecessary repetition, it was up to the trial judge to control it. At trial, counsel engaged with the appointed intermediary to ensure that questioning was carried out in an effective but respectful manner and the objective was to ensure that as little stress or upset was caused to the complainants as possible.
Vivienne Traynor, 'Extraordinary Case Involving Multiple Allegations' RTÉ (6 August 2021) <https://www.rte.ie/news/2021/0806/1239434-abuse-trial-summary/> accessed 13 October 2023.

100 Criminal Practice Directions 2023 England and Wales, para 6.1.10, 50.

101 The author is sincerely grateful to Caroline Cosgrove, a Registered Intermediary in Northern Ireland, for her assistance and expertise in relation to this section.

which would be expected of his age-related peers. However, it may be difficult to perceive this as the witness may mask in order to avoid social awkwardness.

[17–81] Cognitive abilities

- The vulnerable witness's working memory may not be at a level expected of him or her with regard to biological age and educational attainments. An already reduced working memory may be impacted further in stressful circumstances such as a trial environment and due to the pressure of processing complex questions.

[17–82] Emotional concerns

- As a result of delayed educational/language development, the vulnerable witness may fatigue more easily. Fatigue, in addition to high levels of stress, may result in emotional dysregulation where a person experiences high levels of discomfort in a given situation and as a result may become either very distressed or may shut down, go blank and not respond. Breaks may be required to ensure that fatigue does not cause this or affect his or her evidence.
- The vulnerable witness may, himself or herself, wish to have the assistance of an intermediary while giving evidence as there may be a concern that he or she will not understand the question being asked or will need another person there to ensure his or her well being should any issue arise.
- Hypervigilance to threats, even if not actually present, may lead to high emotional distress, causing the vulnerable witness emotional dysregulation.
- Stress and anxiety may cause the vulnerable witness to function at a lower level, making it difficult for him or her to understand the process, and this may be particularly the case for children with underlying difficulties.
- Reassurance that the vulnerable witness is not in trouble may be of assistance in minimising any anxiety on his or her part.
- The vulnerable witness may be concerned that he or she will mislead the court and reassurance that there will be time to give a full answer, and for the vulnerable witness to ask if there is anything that he or she wishes to have explained, may be reassuring.
- The vulnerable witness may wish to be reassured that he or she will have time to explain or to revisit an issue which he or she has not made clear.
- It is important to note that under stress, processing of language and cognitive abilities may drop quite significantly. What may be able to be understood in relaxed circumstances will be very different to what a vulnerable witness will be able to understand in a stressful situation. This would be the same for typically developing children as well as children who have cognitive, developmental or psychological issues.
- A vulnerable witness may not be able to decode facial expressions or tonal pitch. Sensitivity as to how a question may be put such as a raised eyebrow or in an incredulous tone of voice may unwittingly cause stress or concern for a vulnerable witness.

Linguistic Issues

[17–83] Time and spatial issues

- The vulnerable witness may not be able to relate when events occur, such as when school starts or finishes or when a particular television programme is on. He or she may not be able to express how long a lesson or a programme lasts.
- The vulnerable witness may not be able to remember dates or events in the past. A timeline of notable events, eg a series of pictures denoting the houses the witnesses

lived in, or the schools he or she attended, or memorable events such as Holy Communions, Confirmations, Christmases, etc, may be of assistance rather than specific dates.

- The vulnerable witness may have difficulty telling left from right or able to communicate using the points of the compass. Other means of understanding direction such as using landmarks, photographs or visual aids may be required to avoid misunderstanding.

Drawings/Documents Made in the Course of Giving Evidence

In the course of giving evidence, it may become helpful for the witness to draw what he or she is trying to express, eg the layout of a room or building, his or her position in relation to another person. Drawing materials should be made available in the relevant location to facilitate this should it become necessary. The witness may also not be able to say what he or she wishes to say but may wish to write it and show it to the court. With the permission of the court, the intermediary may show and/or read any document to the trial created in the course of the witness' testimony. Any pictures, drawings or documents created while evidence is being given should be preserved and provided to the court for verification and to be made available to the jury. Only documents created during the course of giving evidence and shown to the court and jury should be preserved and handed over.[102] Documents created outside of court may not be admissible. **[17–84]**

Complex linguistic structures to avoid **[17–85]**

- Reversible structures may cause difficulties. Examples of these are: the cup is in the box; the pencil is on the scarf.
- Pronoun binding, ie the use of pronouns linking back to the antecedent nouns, may cause issues. For example, 'The man sees the boy that is pointing at him.' It may be confusing as to who the pronoun 'him' relates to. Using proper nouns continually may assist the vulnerable witness to keep track of who the questioner is referring to, eg instead of 'Was Tom in the kitchen? Were you in the kitchen with him?' use 'Was Tom in the kitchen? Were you in the kitchen with Tom?' Instead of 'What did he say?' use 'What did Tom say?'
- Post modified subjects can be particularly challenging in terms of processing and should be avoided. For example, 'the scarf on the shoe is blue', 'the item the boy is pushing is yellow', 'the ball the duck is on'.
- Centre-embedded sentences (the process of embedding a phrase in the middle of another phrase of the same type) are complex and should be avoided. For example, 'the car the man is in is new', 'the scarf the book is on is blue'.
- Keeping questions very simple and avoiding lengthy and complex questions will improve understanding and expression.
- Avoiding double negatives, eg 'is it true that he was neither cross nor upset?' could be a confusing question. An alternative would be to separate the questions and ask, 'Was he cross?' and 'Was he upset?'
- Reading out long paragraphs and then asking a vulnerable witness, particularly a child, whether he or she agrees or not may cause issues, as it is difficult for the vulnerable witness to keep track of what is being said. Cutting the required sections into smaller pieces and putting simple questions relating to him or her may be easier for the witness to understand.

---

102 *DPP v SA* [2020] IECA 60. Documents created during the course of recorded testimony were deemed to be admissible.

Awareness of Lack of Understanding of Vocabulary

[17–86] Certain words cause difficulty for certain vulnerable witnesses. Vocabulary that has become second nature to legal personnel may be difficult to understand from the perspective of a vulnerable witness. For example, the words 'allegation', 'provoke', 'consent', 'offence', 'charge', 'incident' may be difficult for a vulnerable witness to understand. It is important to have an awareness what words the vulnerable witness may have difficulty understanding. A significant concern is that the vulnerable witness in question may not say when he or she does not understand a particular word or sentence and will let a sentence with a misunderstood word go unchecked.

Tag Questions

[17–87] The issue of 'tag questions' has become more familiar in relation to the confusion that they may cause as well as the unreliability of the answers they may elicit.[103] They are used so often in common speech that it is easy to forget their complexity for a vulnerable witness. Example of tag questions include 'You came on the bus, didn't you?' 'You never saw him, did you?'

Difficulties with Idioms, Metaphors, Jargon and Redundant Phrases

[17–88] Idioms and metaphors can be difficult for certain vulnerable witnesses. For example, 'Can I take you back to …?' or 'We want to fly through this' or 'Let me take you around the room where you were.'

[17–89] Redundant words and phrases may be used when questioners are formulating what they wish to say or to build up to a question. For example, 'I wonder if we could just now have a think about, or can I put it to you ...' This takes time for the vulnerable witness to track and when the actual question is asked, he or she may have forgotten because there has been a preamble which the vulnerable witness is trying to follow.

Signposting Change in Topic

[17–90] Rather than moving on quickly to another topic, signpost the change so that the vulnerable witness can follow the topics of the questions more easily. For example, 'Okay, I've finished talking about the kitchen. I'm going to ask you now about the car.'

Reversible Passives

[17–91] A 'reversible passive' is a passive construction in which the subject can be exchanged with the agent and still leave a correct logical sentence, albeit with the opposite meaning. For example, 'The dog was chased by the fox.' This can cause confusion for certain vulnerable witnesses.

---

[103] See (fn 95).

Processing Difficulties

A particular vulnerable witness may have processing difficulties and may need extra time to respond to a question and it will be important for the questioner to wait the appropriate amount of time for a response from the witness. The court and the questioners should be alerted to the amount of time a vulnerable witness may need to process, formulate his or her response and then articulate that response. **[17–92]**

Re-focusing when Complainant Loses Focus or Disengages

If a witness tends to talk continually in a particular area, he or she may digress unless guided back to the topic by the questioner. The questioner may raise his or her hand, indicating to the witness that he or she should stop. Then the questioner can reassure the witness that he or she 'has given a lot of information' or 'told the questioner a lot'. The questioner may thank the witness if it is appropriate. But the questioner may then say that he or she wishes to go back to the particular point in question that he or she wishes to focus on. **[17–93]**

Breaks may be required to maintain focus and for questions to be repeated. A stressful court setting may aggravate this and aids such as sensory stimulation techniques such as tapping, ie tapping on his or her hand, tapping on the table, using a sensory ball and using aromatherapy (a handkerchief, piece of clothing or soft toy that has a particular smell) may help the vulnerable witness to come back into the present world again. **[17–94]**

Difficulties with Structure

If a vulnerable witness has issues in respect of expression of structure of narrative, or has a tendency to digress on irrelevant details, it may be helpful for the questioner to guide him or her by saying, 'What happened first?,' 'What happened next?' 'Then what happened?' etc in order to give the witness a structure. **[17–95]**

Physical Issues

The vulnerable witness may have physical conditions attached to his or her age or physical state which can impact on the giving of evidence, and which may make it difficult for those questioning him or her to understand easily. For example, a child may not yet be able to form 'R' sounds. Or if the vulnerable witness is nervous, shy or has a soft voice, it may be difficult to hear him or her. In that case, the questioner may take the pressure off the witness by saying, 'My hearing is not very good today, can you say that again?' or, if appropriate, 'the microphone didn't pick that up', reminding him or her to help the court by speaking up. **[17–96]**

Personal Concerns of the Vulnerable Witness

The vulnerable witness may have developed fears, concerns or ideas which can be allayed or dealt with by the court and/or the questioner: **[17–97]**

- The vulnerable witness may be reassured that he or she is not in trouble and is not going to get in trouble by answering the questions.

- The vulnerable witness may be reassured that only persons who need to know about the case are going to hear his or her evidence or read his or her files. However, it is important not to make any promises which cannot be kept or are unrealistic in light of reporting/media factors.
- The vulnerable witness may also be concerned that if he or she makes a mistake, he or she will not be able to rectify it. He or she may be reassured that there will be time to speak and that if he or she wishes to clarify something he or she has said, that will be possible.
- It may be the wish of the vulnerable witness to have an intermediary present in case there is something that he or she does not understand. The desire to have an intermediary present is important and should be made known to the Court.

Organisational Matters Relating to When and How the Witness Gives Evidence

[17–98] The time of day that the witness is best suited to give evidence should be made known to the court. With child complainants, an earlier starting time is usually better as waiting to give evidence later in the day may fatigue the child, which will impact on the quality of the evidence. Alternatively, for some vulnerable witnesses a later starting time may be preferable and this should be accommodated if possible.

[17–99] A pre-trial visit may be useful for the vulnerable witness to get a sense of where he or she will be when giving evidence, to practice with the video link if that is being used. This will also be an opportunity for the witness to ask questions as to any issues which may arise. Counsel will be familiar with the rules against coaching but practical issues and reassurance may be appropriate.[104]

[17–100] Meeting with counsel either face to face or through video link may be helpful so that when the witness begins his or her evidence, there will be a familiar face. It is an option for both prosecution and defence counsel to meet the witness. Photographs of counsel may be supplied to the vulnerable witness so that the face and role of the person is familiar when evidence is being given.

[17–101] The option of use of first names of counsel and the judge is also an important point as it changes the formal atmosphere of the court to one which is more relaxed, which can assist the witness to feel more comfortable.

[17–102] Appropriate consents in relation to the presence of the witness from foster parents, use of his or her files etc must be obtained before the trial.

Intermediary Owes Duty to Court

[17–103] In owing his or her duty to the court, the intermediary takes the following oath or affirms:

> I swear by Almighty God that I shall well and truly put any questions required to be put to the witness(es) in relation to the evidence about to be given and a true explanation

[104] See [25–13]

> give of all such matters and things touching the present charge as shall be required of me to the best of my skill and understanding.[105]

The intermediary owes his or her duty to the court and swears or affirms as such. It is the practice of intermediaries in England, Wales and Northern Ireland to make themselves available to both the prosecution and defence in terms of assistance as to how to phrase questions and to resolve any foreseeable issues. If a ground rules hearing takes place and becomes an order of the court either through agreement or after argument, the ground rules will apply to both defence and prosecution and the intermediary may intervene or advise in relation to the appropriate counsel. **[17–104]**

Intervention by Intermediary if Necessary

If an issue occurs which can be resolved easily, the intermediary may only need to raise his or her hand to remind counsel to adhere to the ground rules. If there is a continued issue, the intermediary may intervene to ask counsel to rephrase or adapt as appropriate. If the intermediary believes there has been a misunderstanding by the witness regarding the question asked, he or she may alert the Court to this fact and may ask counsel to ask the question in another way. The level of involvement of the intermediary at trial will depend on the capacity of the vulnerable witness to engage in criminal proceedings as well as the skill of counsel to ask questions which the witness will understand without difficulty.[106] In the case of *DPP v O'Driscoll*,[107] it appeared that the defence counsel was concerned that the use of an intermediary would have an undue impact on the evidence.[108] It transpired that the intermediary never generated a question independently but only resolved communication issues: **[17–105]**

> It is clear from the exchanges between defence counsel and the proposed intermediary in the Central Criminal Court that all involved with the issue envisaged that the intermediary's role would be to intervene where there was a concern about the possibility of confusion or lack of comprehension, and to request that a question be reformulated by counsel. In fact, this is precisely what occurred; there was no occasion when the question was actually formulated and put by the intermediary.[109]

Intermediaries for Vulnerable Defendants

Background to the use of intermediaries for defendants

The appointment of an intermediary for the accused, allowing the defendant to participate more effectively in proceedings, occurred in England and Wales in *C v Sevenoaks Youth Court*[110] and *R v Dixon*.[111] Section 104 of the Coroners and Justice Act 2009 which will amend the Youth Justice and Criminal Evidence Act 1999 provides for examination through an intermediary of a vulnerable accused, but, at time of publication, it is not yet in force. **[17–106]**

---

105 This oath was prepared by the Courts Services for the High Court in 2008.

106 See (fn 39).

107 *DPP v O'Driscoll* [2022] IECA 4.

108 ibid [13].

109 ibid [30].

110 *C v Sevenoaks Youth Court* [2009] EWHC 3088.

111 *R v Dixon* [2013] EWCA Crim 465; [2014] 1 MHLR 148.

[17–107] As noted previously, it appears Irish legislation excludes the defendant from the measure. While s 14 of the Criminal Evidence Act 1992 states that the application may be made by the prosecution or the defence, the linking of the measure to the support measure of video link causes a difficulty. It would appear that the defendant is not eligible as the use of an intermediary is linked to that of video link and available provisions for video link under s 13 of the Criminal Evidence Act 1992 or s 39 of the Criminal Justice Act 1999 exclude the accused. In any case, the mandatory use of video link with the appointment of an intermediary would limit the effectiveness of his or her functions as will be described below.

[17–108] Other provisions for video link as under Part 4 of the Civil Law and Criminal Law (Miscellaneous Provisions) Act 2020 may not accommodate trials but may accommodate an intermediary for an accused person in pre-trial hearings such as bail.

[17–109] The appointment of intermediaries for defendants in Ireland has been founded on the Constitutional right to a fair trial under Article 38.1 of the Constitution of Ireland. In addition, Article 6 of the European Convention of Human Rights sets out the right to a fair trial as well as participation rights. Articles 47 and 48 of the EU Charter of Fundamental Rights outline the right to an effective remedy, the right to a fair trial, the presumption of innocence and the right to a defence.[112] The EU Directive on the Right to Information in Criminal Proceedings,[113] the UN Standard Minimum Rules for the Administration of Juvenile Justice ('The Beijing Rules'), the UN Convention on the Rights of the Child and the UN Convention on the Rights of Persons with Disabilities also underpin the rights of vulnerable defendants to participate fully in proceedings in which they find themselves.

[17–110] In relation to relevant case law, *V v United Kingdom*[114] was a significant case of the European Court of Human Rights that acknowledged the severe difficulties a vulnerable defendant (in this case, two children aged approximately 11 years of age at time of trial) might have had in fully participating in a trial. In another case, *SC v United Kingdom*,[115] the European Court of Human Rights stated:

> The right of an accused to effective participation in his or her criminal trial generally includes, inter alia, not only the right to be present, but also to hear and follow the proceedings. In the case of a child it is essential that he be dealt with in a manner which takes full account of his age, level of maturity, and intellectual and emotional capacities, and that steps are taken to promote his ability to understand and participate in the

---

[112] EU Charter of Fundamental Rights, Art 47, Right to an effective remedy and to a fair trial: 'Everyone whose rights and freedoms guaranteed by the law of the Union are violated has the right to an effective remedy before a tribunal in compliance with the conditions laid down in this Article. Everyone is entitled to a fair and public hearing within a reasonable time by an independent and impartial tribunal previously established by law. Everyone shall have the possibility of being advised, defended and represented.

Article 48 Presumption of innocence and right of defence 1. Everyone who has been charged shall be presumed innocent until proved guilty according to law. 2. Respect for the rights of the defence of anyone who has been charged shall be guaranteed. Legal aid shall be made available to those who lack sufficient resources in so far as such aid is necessary to ensure effective access to justice.'

[113] Directive 2012/13/EU of the European Parliament and of the Council of 22 May 2012 on the right to information in criminal proceedings.

[114] *V v United Kingdom* (Application no 24888/94).

[115] *SC v the United Kingdom* (2005) 40 EHRR 10.

> proceeding, including conducting the hearing in such a way as to reduce, as far as possible, his feelings of intimidation and inhibition.[116]

The Court accepted that Article 6(1) did not require that a child on trial for a criminal offence should understand or be capable of understanding every point of law or evidential detail. It acknowledged that many adults of normal intelligence are unable fully to comprehend all of the intricacies and exchanges that take place in a courtroom. Article 6(3)c) emphasises the importance of the right to legal representation but effective participation presupposes that the accused has a broad understanding of the nature of the trial process, and of what is at stake for him or her, including the significance of any penalty which may be imposed. **[17–111]**

This case was extensively quoted in *C v Sevenoaks*,[117] where the trial judge, through the inherent jurisdiction of the court, appointed an intermediary for the defendant, a 13-year-old boy who had complex mental health issues but who was still deemed fit to plead. It is significant that the Court referred to the fact that legislation which provided for the appointment of an intermediary for a defendant had been drafted but not commenced. **[17–112]**

Although no legislation exists in Ireland, and has not been proposed, Constitutional, EU and ECHR rights oblige the Irish courts to ensure that a defendant is able to participate in his or her trial and to be able to instruct his or her legal representatives. In addition, the Irish case of *DPP v Harrison*[118] is an extremely important judgment in relation to vulnerable defendants who may have been deemed fit to plead but who may also have issues which will inhibit their participation in the trial process.[119] **[17–113]**

The training in Ireland for intermediaries will encompass assistance for both vulnerable witnesses and defendants.[120] The roles and functions may differ significantly. The intermediary for the vulnerable witness assists in facilitating the evidence of the witness. An intermediary for a defendant may be appointed for the duration of the trial and interact with the defendant and legal representatives throughout the trial. In those respects, the functions of the role may differ. **[17–114]**

---

116 ibid [28].

117 *C v Sevenoaks Youth Court* [2009] EWHC 3088.

118 *DPP v Harrison* [2016] IECA 212.

119 ibid [55]–[56]:

> 'It is not possible to produce an exhaustive list of the many possible ways that a person who meets the statutory criteria in terms of his/her fitness to be tried, but who nonetheless has particular personal mental or physical difficulties, might be assisted and accommodated. Each case will obviously depend upon its own facts.
>
> However, assuming it is possible in a particular case to propose an accommodation or accommodations that may be efficacious to ensure that the accused concerned will receive a fair trial, the only limitation that should be put on such proposals is that they should be reasonably practical; they should be confined to what is strictly necessary, and they should not confer such an unfair advantage on the beneficiary as to render an unfairness to the other side, in this instance the prosecution. We would add that the fact that accommodations might prolong a trial, perhaps significantly, should not be a reason in itself to discount their suitability or practicality.'

120 The programme has a practical skills-based component which ensures those who qualify have the competencies to provide intermediary interventions as part of all aspects of the legal process for both vulnerable witnesses and defendants in the context of Irish legislation: <https://www.ul.ie/gps/intermediary-studies-professional-diploma> accessed 13 October 2023.

[17–115] If the intermediary is appointed for the duration of the evidence of the defendant, the focus is to facilitate the giving of evidence and the resolution of any communication issues. A witness or defendant giving evidence is only in the witness box for a section of the trial. If the intermediary is appointed for the duration of the trial then the role has a different focus. The case law establishes that the role is to facilitate the participation of the vulnerable defendant, and enable him or her to follow proceedings and to instruct his or her legal representatives and in Ireland, it appears that appointments are made for the duration of the trial.

[17–116] Plotnikoff and Woolfson have outlined the significant concerns in relation to the use of intermediaries for defendants.[121] Issues such as whether an intermediary is required during the giving of evidence only or for the duration of the trial, uncertainty as to the nature of the role, the balancing of the duty owed to the client/court as well as lack of oversight are issues which require attention in Ireland.

Intermediaries for defendants in Ireland – current practice

[17–117] Intermediaries appointed in Ireland have come from various disciplines including barristers, social workers and guardian ad litems. They have been appointed in courts of all jurisdictions under the inherent jurisdiction of the court to ensure that the right to a fair trial is protected. In certain cases, where the requirement for an intermediary came to light late in proceedings, the application was generally made on submission of an appropriate medical report. However, more usually, applications for the use of an intermediary have been made through a Notice of Motion and grounding affidavit founded on relevant medical reports. With the commencement of preliminary trial hearings, s 6 Criminal Procedure Act 2021 would appear to be the appropriate procedure to adopt in applications for an intermediary for a defendant. The court may grant an application for an intermediary where there is a particular and significant difficulty in the defendant participating fully in proceedings and giving instructions to his or her legal team. Therefore, not every vulnerable defendant will need to avail of the support measure if he or she does not have any difficulties in this regard. Intermediaries may be appointed to assist the defendant either in respect of a plea or at trial. The nature of the role in each proceeding will depend on the individual needs of the defendant.

[17–118] There is no procedural guidance in relation to the practice of intermediaries for defendants in the courts. However, the role of intermediaries for witnesses and complainants is helpful in this regard. It is submitted that the duty of an intermediary is to the court and that he or she should be impartial and assist the Court in whatever manner possible. It is also submitted that it is not part of the intermediary's role to give legal advice to the defendant. Rather the focus of the role is to convey any legal advice given by the legal team to the defendant in a more comprehensible way and to check that the advice has been satisfactorily understood in order for clear instructions to be given to the legal team. Confidentiality is a prerequisite for an intermediary in the course of proceedings.

[17–119] However, as mentioned, the nature of the role is entirely different from that of an intermediary for a complainant. An intermediary for the prosecution witness is there to facilitate communication when the witness is giving evidence. The role of the intermediary for the defendant is to ensure that the defendant can participate fully in

[121] Joyce Plotnikoff and Richard Woolfson, *Intermediaries in the Criminal Justice System: Improving Communication for Vulnerable Witnesses and Defendants* (Policy Press 2015) ch 13, 247.

the trial process and give instructions to his or her legal team. This may involve giving assistance to facilitate the defendant if he or she decides to give evidence. However, there is no obligation for a defendant to give evidence in a criminal trial and this may not be part of an intermediary's role in a given case. The role of the intermediary for a defendant may focus on ensuring that the defendant understands the nature of the offences, and the trial processes. In order to do so, several meetings may be held with the defendant and his or her family as required prior to the court hearings. It is always advisable that an intermediary never be alone with the defendant to ensure that anything that is said can be verified at a later date. The intermediary will also attend legal consultations and note what is said so that understanding may be checked. In addition, the intermediary may accompany the defendant at trial and take notes, again ensuring that the defendant is following proceedings.

Much of the work is done unseen by the court. However, a significant amount of time may be spent familiarising the defendant with the court processes as well as communicating with the relevant legal practitioners to assist with communication. There is no regulation of intermediaries for defendants in Ireland and responsibility is placed on the courts and practitioner to consider how the intermediary may assist the defendant and to ensure this is taking place. At present, intermediaries in Ireland accompany the defendant throughout the trial if necessary. This is not the case in other jurisdictions where an intermediary for a defendant may only be required if and when the defendant gives evidence.[122] There may be multiple benefits to having an intermediary who accompanies a defendant at trial. The roles of solicitors and counsel do not lend to close supervision of the defendant during the trial. An intermediary may be able to notice and resolve any issues or pick up on any evidential point that may arise particularly where a defendant may be intimidated by the legal personnel. This may be helpful in ensuring that the defendant gives important instructions to the defence legal team. **[17–120]**

Certain points may be raised and agreed, prior to commencement of proceedings, in relation to how the intermediary will interact with the court. This discussion may be part of the overall ground rule hearings of the trial or may be a more informal discussion at the discretion of the court. Topics which may be discussed and resolved include: **[17–121]**

- The duty owed by the intermediary to the court
- The behaviour of the intermediary during court and where he or she will sit
- If an oath is required and how and when it will be taken
- How the court should address the presence of the intermediary to the jury
- How to address the intermediary during proceedings
- Any modifications to the language, timetable or court procedure requested by the intermediary which would assist the defendant
- Any necessary procedures requested by the intermediary should the defendant give evidence
- The parameters of the role of the intermediary eg not to give legal advice, not to discuss the case with anyone not connected to the case
- The payment of the intermediary. This may be an important point in relation to the impartial nature of the role of the intermediary to the court and the duty owed by the intermediary to the court.

It is important that the application for and granting of an intermediary for a defendant **[17–122]**

[122] John Taggart, '"*I am not beholden to anyone. .. I consider myself to be an officer of the court*": *A comparison of the intermediary role in England and Wales and Northern Ireland*' (2021) 25(2) E&P 141–62.

be based on the documented, legitimate requirements of the defendant. If not the value of the role within the criminal courts may be undermined. The role of the intermediary for the defendant is, at present, unsupervised and unregulated except for the court personnel in each trial. It is hoped that the training of intermediaries through the University of Limerick[123] will see new practices and procedures in this area which will place the role on a more established footing.

Intermediaries for Defendants in England and Wales and in Northern Ireland

[17–123] There are very different statutory frameworks regarding the use of intermediaries in England and Wales and in Northern Ireland. In England and Wales, the use of intermediaries for defendants was provided for legislatively but this section has not been commenced as yet. As outlined by Taggart, the position can be contrasted with Northern Ireland where there is provision for intermediaries albeit in a narrower manner at trial, ie intermediaries are available only if the defendant gives evidence.[124] Taggart describes the cultural and procedural differences which to which these two approaches have given rise.[125] He notes that in interviews, while intermediaries in both jurisdictions assert and maintain their impartiality, there may be different approaches to interactions during police interviews and that intermediaries from Northern Ireland appear to refrain from interaction with the police that would be natural to intermediaries from England and Wales.

[17–124] In England and Wales, the legislative use of intermediaries for defendants had been proposed but never commenced under s 33BA of the Youth Justice and Criminal Evidence Act 1999 (as set out under s 104 of the Coroners and Justice Act 2009). However, consistent provision has been made in England and Wales for their use under the inherent jurisdiction of the court.[126]

[17–125] Registered Intermediaries in Northern Ireland assist vulnerable defendants and defence witnesses with communication difficulties, as well as victims and prosecution witnesses. A pilot scheme having been reviewed in November 2014, it was agreed that a further phase of the pilot would be extended to all cases being heard in the Crown Court, and would be undertaken for 12 months beginning 1 April 2015. After this time, the pilot would be re-evaluated to inform decisions in relation to the future direction of the RI Schemes. An application for an intermediary under Article 21BA of the Criminal Evidence (Northern Ireland) Order 1999, as amended by the Justice Act (Northern Ireland) 2011, can be made where their use will enable the defendant to participate

---

123 University of Limerick, Professional Diploma – Intermediary Studies <https://www.ul.ie/gps/courses/intermediary-studies-professional-diploma> accessed 13 October 2023.

124 John Taggart, '"I am not beholden to anyone. .. I consider myself to be an officer of the court": A comparison of the intermediary role in England and Wales and Northern Ireland' (2021) 25(2) E&P 141–62.

125 ibid.

126 See *R (AS) v Great Yarmouth Youth Court* [2011] EWHC 2059 (Admin), [2012] Crim LR 478; *R v H* [2003] EWCA Crim 1208; *R (C) v Sevenoaks Youth Court* [2009] EWHC 3088 (Admin), [2010] 1 All ER 735; *R (D) v Camberwell Green Youth Court* [2005] UKHL 4, [2005] 1 WLR 393, [2005] 2 Cr App R 1; *R (TP) v West London Youth Court* [2005] EWHC 2583 (Admin), [2006] 1 WLR 1219, [2006] 1 Cr App R 25; CPD, 3F3 (October 2020).

effectively in the proceedings as a witness giving oral evidence in court and to ensure a fair trial.[127]

Other Legislative Uses of the Support Measure of Intermediaries

Section 6 of the Criminal Procedure Act 2010[128] allows for a child or a person with an intellectual disability, who is giving a victim impact statement or evidence in respect of a European Arrest warrant, to be facilitated through an intermediary. **[17–126]**

The overlap between ss 5A and 5B reads somewhat confusingly in relation to whether the intermediary can only be used for the giving of evidence in relation to a European Arrest Warrant. The Explanatory Memorandum clarifies this, stating: **[17–127]**

> Section 5 amends the 1993 Act by inserting a new section 5A. The purpose of this section is to allow a child, a person with a mental disorder, or any other person with the leave of the court to make a victim impact statement by means of a live television link, thereby removing the requirement that the person be present in the court. Section 6 amends the 1993 Act by inserting a new section 5B. The purpose of this is to make provision for any questioning of a child or a person with a mental disorder in relation to his or her victim impact statement to be done via an intermediary i.e. a person appointed by the court to act in that capacity. The court may appoint an intermediary where the age or the mental condition of a child or a person with a mental disorder is such that it is in the interests of justice that the questions be put through an intermediary.[129]

The measure is drafted in the same terms as those under s 14 of the Criminal Evidence Act 1992. The scope of the provision and the statutory limitations are essentially the same in that the intermediary is only able to repeat the questions put by the interlocutor to convey the question to the witness in a manner appropriate to his age or mental condition. **[17–128]**

Criminal Justice (Mutual Assistance) Act 2008

Schedule 10A of the Criminal Justice (Mutual Assistance) Act 2008 gives effect (through the Criminal Law (Extraterritorial Jurisdiction) Act 2019),[130] to the 'Istanbul Convention'.[131] 'Article 56 – Measures of Protection' of which states: **[17–129]**

---

127 Criminal Evidence (Northern Ireland) Order 1999, as amended by the Justice Act (Northern Ireland) 2011, Art 21BA.

128 s 5B of the Criminal Justice Act 1993 as inserted by s 6 of the Criminal Procedure Act 2010:

> '(1) Where a child or a person with a mental disorder is giving, or is to give evidence through a live television link, pursuant to section 5A, the court may, on the application of the prosecution or the accused, if satisfied that, having regard to the age or mental condition of the witness, the interests of justice require that any questions to be put to the witness be put through an intermediary, direct that any such questions be so put.
>
> (2) Questions put to a witness through an intermediary under this section shall be either in the words used by the questioner or so as to convey to the witness in a way which is appropriate to his or her age and mental condition, the meaning of the questions being asked.
>
> (3) An intermediary referred to in subsection (1) shall be appointed by the court and shall be a person who, in its opinion, is competent to act as such.'

129 Criminal Procedure Act 2010, Explanatory Memorandum.

130 Criminal Law (Extraterritorial Jurisdiction) Act 2019, s 4.

131 Council of Europe Convention on Preventing and Combating Violence against Women and Domestic Violence held in Istanbul on 11 May 2011.

1. Parties shall take the necessary legislative or other measures to protect the rights and interests of victims, including their special needs as witnesses, at all stages of investigations and judicial proceedings, in particular by:

[...]

d) enabling victims, in a manner consistent with the procedural rules of internal law, to be heard, to supply evidence and have their views, needs and concerns presented, directly *or through an intermediary* (emphasis added), and considered[.]

Custody and access proceedings

[17–130] The Children Act 1997 provides for the use of an intermediary in custody and access proceedings. Section 22, 'Evidence through intermediary', states:

> (1) Where in proceedings to which this Part applies the evidence of a child is being given or [is] to be given through a live television link, the court may, of its own motion or on the application of a party to the proceedings, if satisfied that, having regard to the age or mental condition of the child, any questions to be put to the child should be put through an intermediary, direct that any such question be so put.
>
> (2) Questions put to a child through an intermediary under this section shall be either in the words used by the questioner or in words that convey to the child, in a way that is appropriate to his or her age or mental condition, the meaning of the questions being asked.
>
> (3) An intermediary referred to in subsection (1) shall be appointed by the court and shall be a person who, in its opinion, is competent to act as such.

[17–131] McGrath notes that s 22(1) of the Children Act 1997 is drafted in similar terms to s 14 of the 1992 Act. However, one point of departure is that under s 22(1), the court may direct questions to be put through an intermediary of its own motion. McGrath observes that this reflects the more inquisitorial nature of many child care proceedings.[132]

Suggested Procedure for Use of Intermediary for Prosecution Witness at Trial

Questioning of witness

[17–132] Every case is specific to the facts of the case before the court but these are points that may be relevant as a suggested procedure for the use of an intermediary at trial.

- Court confirms that video link is working.
- Witness is introduced to the judge. Introduction of judge to witness not only for familiarisation purposes but also to satisfy the court that the witness is an eligible and competent one under s 27 Criminal Evidence Act 1992 and as per the test for competence in *O'Sullivan v Hamill* and *DPP v Campion*.[133]
- Registrar has oaths prepared for witness minder and intermediary.
- Intermediary's report has previously been prepared and submitted to court in a ground rules hearing. However, report should be available so that reminders of

---

[132] Declan McGrath and Emily Egan McGrath, *McGrath on Evidence* (3rd edn, Round Hall 2020) paras 3-265 and 3-266, 185.

[133] *O'Sullivan v Hamill* [1998] 2 IR 9; *DPP v Campion* [2018] IESC 35; [2021] 2 IR 1.

particular issues and best means of addressing them are available to the court and to practitioners.

- Where recorded testimony is being played under s 16(1)(b) Criminal Evidence Act 1992, the intermediary will be present with the witness but both will be off screen for the playing of the recording to the jury. Arrangements may have been made for the witness to watch the recording at a previous time.[134] It should be decided if the witness and the intermediary will be watching the recording while it is being played to the jury or if they will be present but not connected by video link to the court.
- Where the witness is giving evidence in chief live in court, the oath or affirmation may be administered depending on whether the witness is eligible as per s 27 Criminal Evidence Act 1992. The trial judge will ensure that sufficient inquiry has been made where the witness is a child or has an intellectual disability to confirm that he or she is a competent witness.[135]
- Video has previously been played to the jury[136] or the witness has given their evidence in chief testimony via video link. If an intermediary is assisting the court, the evidence must be given via video link.
- If recorded testimony has been played, a break in proceedings where the jury are not present may be appropriate to ensure video link is working and witness is ready to give evidence.
- When questioning is to begin, the judge, practitioners and defendant are present but jury is not present yet.
- Video link screen is opened to communicate from video link room to court.
- Any technical issues, eg audibility, framing of witness and intermediary in the screen, are resolved.
- Witness minder is in video link screen and communicates any issues with court.
- Witness minder takes oath or affirms to mind the witness and ensure that the witness does not talk to anyone in the course of giving their evidence.
- Intermediary is present in video link room. (Witness is not present in video link room at this stage.)
- Intermediary takes oath or affirms, '*I swear by Almighty God that I shall well and truly put any questions required to be put to the witness(es) in relation to the evidence about to be given and a true explanation give of all such matters and things touching the present charge as shall be required of me to the best of my skill and understanding.*'[137]
- Intermediary communicates with the judge and prosecution and defence counsel to outline any particular issues or to emphasise matters from the ground rules hearing in respect of the particular witness, eg 'this particular witness has attention issues which can be resolved if counsel gently interrupts and reminds the witness of the question being asked.' If there are any issues from prosecution and defence counsel, this may be an appropriate time to air them.
- Video link is switched off. The witness is brought into the video link room.
- Judge asks for jury to be brought into court.
- Judge gives any necessary direction to jury regarding this witness. Video link should not be open for this as it may take some time. The direction may outline the reasons for the support measures being used. For example, an explanation of the use of video link, an intermediary and how they facilitate the giving of evidence. The judge may explain how and/or when an intermediary may intervene eg if a question is not understood or if the witness may need a break.
- Video link is switched on.
- Judge greets witness who may be introduced to counsel and sworn as appropriate.
- Examination in chief, cross-examination, and re-examination by counsel as appropriate.

---

134 See Chapter 24.

135 *O'Sullivan v Hamill* [1998] 2 IR 9; *DPP v Campion* [2018] IESC 35; [2021] 2 IR 1.

136 See Chapter 24.

137 This oath was prepared by the Courts Services for the High Court in 2008.

- Judge speaks to witness to conclude – eg to thank the witness for attending and to say goodbye to the witness.
- Video link is switched off.
- Any issues then addressed requiring to be made in the presence of the jury.
- Jury leaves.
- Any issues then addressed requiring to be made in the absence of the jury.

Chapter 18

JUDGE'S INTERVENTIONS/ COMMENTS IN THE COURSE OF THE TRIAL

Judge May Ask Questions to Clarify Evidence

In *DPP v DC*[1] the appellant had been convicted of number of sexual offences including rape of his daughter when she was a young child. The trial had taken place when she was just over the age of 18 and her evidence had been given via video link over a period of seven days, five of which comprised cross-examination. The appeal was unsuccessful on a number of grounds, one of which was in relation to excessive judicial intervention. The Court of Appeal outlined that it was appropriate for the trial judge to clarify issues at trial. Edwards J stated: **[18–01]**

> There is nothing improper in a trial judge asking questions that clarify chronology or other aspects of evidence already given – indeed that may be helpful and even essential on occasion if the judge is to ensure a fair trial. The judge is not a mere cypher. We think that the suggestion that the intervention amounted to some form of advocacy in favour of the prosecution is without merit, and indeed to characterise what occurred as some form of cross-examination is entirely wrong. In any event, even if this Court were to be of the view that the relatively short questioning went further than was appropriate, this would not be a basis per se for regarding the trial as having been necessarily unsatisfactory, since any such intervention by a trial judge must be viewed in the context of the trial as a whole. While this trial judge may, perhaps, in a number of questions that she asked, be regarded as having moved slightly beyond clarification of matters which were the immediate subject of the witness's examination or cross-examination, her questions related to relevant matters the elicitation of which could not be open to any possible criticism.[2]

The judgment in *DPP v AH*[3] primarily concerned the issue of excessive judicial intervention in relation to questions by the trial judge. In this case the conviction was quashed. The Court noted that the trial judge may ask questions for reasons of clarification or, beyond that, where there may be issues regarding the nature of the questioning. The issue for the court was whether the interventions were such that they rendered the trial unfair. In giving the judgment of the Court, Kennedy J stated: **[18–02]**

1 *DPP v DC* [2019] IECA 367.
2 *DPP v DC* [2019] IECA 367 [248].
3 *DPP v AH* [2022] IECA 156.

> A judge may question or intervene in a wider range of circumstances than mere clarification; take for example, where the question asked is unfair, where it is asked on a false or inaccurate premise, or where the question seeks to elicit inadmissible evidence. It is the experience of this Court that on occasion, counsel may ask a question which incorporates sub questions and so it becomes almost impossible for a witness to answer the question, and indeed for a jury to know which question is in fact being answered. In those circumstances, or where the question is posed in such a manner that it may not be properly understood, the judge may well have to intervene, always with circumspection and with regard to the fairness of the trial. Care must also be taken to ensure that any intervention does not give the impression of partiality. Whilst it does not arise in this case, it is well established that a judge may also intervene and, indeed, in the view of this Court, should intervene if cross-examination is unduly lengthy or repetitive. The real issue, however, in the present case is whether the interventions of the judge in the examination and cross-examination of the appellant went beyond what may be considered permissible and in effect disrupted the appellant's evidence, rendering the trial unfair. We observe at this point that we deprecate the over-simplification implicit in simply computing the number of interventions and using that as a basis for criticism in and of itself.[4]

[18–03] In this case, the Court held that it did not consider that prolonged and frequent interventions by a judge, in and of themselves, rendered a trial unfair and it stated that each case had to be considered on its own merits. The Court considered that the purpose and nature of the interventions was, in the Court's view, of paramount importance. This was because the rationale underpinning the intervention may inform the fairness or otherwise of the trial. Although many of the trial judge's interventions were made for the purpose of ensuring clarity, or even to ensure audibility, the Court considered that they were such that the conviction should be quashed. Kennedy J observed that:

> We are most reluctant to interfere with the discretion of a trial judge who is best placed to assess the evidence as it unfolds at trial, but we believe that the judge entered the arena to too great a degree, notwithstanding that he did so with the best of motives, such interventions may have given the impression that the judge was, in effect, cross-examining the appellant. We reiterate that frequent or prolonged interventions would not necessarily give rise to an unfair trial, the nature and character of the interventions is that which is the significant issue.[5]

Judicial Intervention Re Repetitive Questioning by Counsel

[18–04] As outlined above, the judgment in *DPP v AH*[6] primarily concerned the issue of excessive judicial intervention in relation to questions by the trial judge. The conviction was ultimately quashed. However, in the course of the judgment, Kennedy J noted that a judge should intervene where cross examination is overly repetitive or lengthy:

> Whilst it does not arise in this case, it is well established that a judge may also intervene and, indeed, in the view of this Court, should intervene if cross-examination is unduly lengthy or repetitive.[7]

[18–05] The case of *DPP v MB*[8] further strengthens this principle, where the Court stated that short, simple, non-repetitive questions should be used. Kennedy J stated:

---

4 ibid [24]–[26].
5 ibid [34].
6 *DPP v AH* [2022] IECA 156.
7 ibid [5].
8 *DPP v MB* [2023] IECA 85.

> In practical terms, when cross-examining a child, questions asked should be short, simple and without repetition. The judge must carefully guard the interests of the child, ensuring the child understands what is being asked but at all times ensuring the right to a fair trial.[9]

Judicial Supervision Re Repetitive Questioning where Multiple Accused/Multiple Complainants

Anecdotal evidence suggests that in Ireland where there are multiple defendants, counsel are aware that repetitive questioning which is not relevant and which may risk upsetting the witness, may be challenged by opposing counsel and/or restricted by the trial judge. In addition, practitioners are aware that repetitive questioning by multiple counsel risks being seen by the jury as redundant at best and bullying at worst. Defence counsel may limit questioning or risk challenge by the trial judge where repetitive questioning is not relevant or necessary. **[18–06]**

In a high-profile trial in the Central Criminal Court[10] which was observed by the author, the case involved multiple accused and several child complainants. During cross-examination, defence counsel endeavoured to limit repetition. The issue of repeat questioning had been flagged at a pre-trial hearing where the trial judge had noted that in other trials, which involved multiple accused, senior counsel had taken the view that they didn't all have to ask the same questions repeatedly of a witness where answers have been given. The trial judge observed that there may be different perspectives from different accused persons in relation to a matter, but that common sense should prevail in relation to that. He noted that if there was unnecessary repetition, it was up to the trial judge to control it. At trial, counsel engaged with the appointed intermediary to ensure that questioning was carried out in an effective but respectful manner and the objective was to ensure that as little stress or upset as possible was caused to the complainants.[11] **[18–07]**

However, the constitutional right to cross-examination, in the context of the cross-examination of vulnerable witnesses, has been underlined in the cases of *DPP v MT*[12] and *DPP v MB*,[13] albeit both cases which did not involve repetitive questioning. The risks associated with repetitive questioning such as unreliable evidence, or undue stress to the witness, may be outlined in the relevant intermediary's report and an appropriate ground rule enforced by the trial judge. While it does not explicitly mention repetitive questioning, the Bar of Ireland's Code of Conduct prevents a barrister from making statements or asking questions 'which are merely scandalous or are intended only for the purpose of vilifying, insulting or annoying a witness or some other person'.[14] **[18–08]**

---

9 ibid [42].

10 Isabel Hayes, 'Munster abuse trial: "It was the quietest house ...There was nothing"' *The Irish Times* (Dublin, 6 August 2021) <https://www.irishtimes.com/news/crime-and-law/courts/criminal-court/munster-abuse-trial-it-was-the-quietest-house-there-was-nothing-1.4641077> accessed 13 October 2023.

11 Vivienne Traynor, 'Extraordinary Case Involving Multiple Allegations' RTÉ (6 August 2021) <https://www.rte.ie/news/2021/0806/1239434-abuse-trial-summary/> accessed 13 October 2023.

12 *DPP v MT* [2023] IECA 65 [81].

13 *DPP v MB* [2023] IECA 85 [41]–[42].

14 Code of Conduct, Bar Council of Ireland 5.18: 'Barristers when conducting a case must not make statements or ask questions which are merely scandalous or are intended only for the purpose of vilifying, insulting or annoying a witness or some other person.'

[18–09] It would be helpful for counsel and judges to have consistent and transparent guidance in relation to the prevention of repetitive questioning. Inconsistent practice may give rise to situations where certain counsel are limited in questioning in certain trials where others are not. In England and Wales the Criminal Practice Directions prevent repetitive questioning of vulnerable witnesses where there are multiple defendants. They state:

> If there is more than one accused, the judge should not permit each advocate to repeat the questioning of a vulnerable witness. In advance of the trial, the advocates should divide the topics between them, with the advocate for one accused leading the questioning, and the advocate(s) for the other accused asking only ancillary questions relevant to their client's case, without repeating the questioning that has already taken place.[15]

Restrictions on Judicial Commentary on the Evidence

[18–10] In *People (DPP) v Donnelly*[16] a ground of appeal included comments by the trial judge in respect of statements admitted as well as in relation to comments to a witness who had given evidence. The Court of Criminal Appeal stated that by referring to the fact that the trial judge had admitted the statement because he believed it to have been made voluntarily, he was in effect giving a direction to the jury. The Court of Criminal Appeal stated that there was no doubt the jury would have treated what was said to them as an opinion held by the judge but nevertheless, there was a danger that it would have been taken to be more than that. The issue as to whether or not the statement was made voluntarily was one which was litigated in the absence of the jury. Accordingly, it was essential that whatever happened in their absence should have been kept from them. This included the conclusion or legal direction made by the trial judge and the reasons for it.

[18–11] The Court of Criminal Appeal also observed a remark made by the trial judge to a young witness when she had finished her evidence when he said, 'You did very well.' The Court of Criminal Appeal stated that such expressions give a wrong impression of the judge's role in the trial and may be taken by the jury as an indication that the judge, with his wide experience of similar cases, regards the witness as being truthful. The Court of Criminal Appeal went on to note that is certainly the trial judge's role to ease the path of a young witness in giving his or her evidence but it is no part of his function, once that evidence has been given, 'to make commendatory remarks which may lead the jury into believing that they have to accept his or her evidence'.[17]

[18–12] In *DPP v LD*[18] the appeal points included a submission that the trial judge had, in her tone and in the comments used during her charge, displayed a commendation and endorsement of the child complainant's evidence. The appeal failed, as the Court considered that the charge in the round was balanced particularly in relation to how the trial judge had outlined the defence position. However, in the course of the judgment Edwards J observed:

> The complaints about the judge's comments in the course of her charge may be summarised as suggesting that in both the language she used, and the tone she adopted, the trial judge would have been, or putting it less strongly, might have been perceived by the jury as endorsing the witness's evidence, and commending it to them. Cases involving

---

15 CPD, England and Wales 2023, para 6.1.10.

16 *People (DPP) v Donnelly*, Court of Criminal Appeal (22 February 1999) 2000 WJSC–CCA 7892.

17 ibid [13]–[15].

18 [2018] IECA 54.

child witnesses represent one area in which judges need to be sure-footed and to step warily if deciding to offer commentary on a complainant's evidence. We consider that that the trial judge was perfectly entitled to comment on the complainant's evidence but that it might have been better if the trial judge had adopted a more conventional style of commentary in this case.[19]

Judge's Charge

Where a support measure of recorded testimony, video link, intermediary, screen or other measure or facilitation for a vulnerable witness is used at trial, the trial judge may consider that it is appropriate to mention their use in the charge to the jury. This is because the use of the support measure may cause prejudice to the defendant, particularly if its use risks a perception that the actions of the defendant have necessitated such protection for the witness. Generally, it has become usual for the judge to mention, in his or her charge, that the Oireachtas has deemed certain witnesses giving evidence worthy of additional supports and that there is no particular significance to be attached to the means of support used at trial. **[18–13]**

The Equal Treatment Bench Book[20] in England and Wales outlines precedents and suggestions in relation to the modification of evidence and relevant information to be given to juries where intermediaries are engaged at trial. The manner in which the judge may describe any modifications or support measures to the jury may be discussed and agreed beforehand with counsel to minimise any subsequent requisitions. **[18–14]**

Where the defendant and/or witness has been facilitated, the judge may wish to outline the exact nature of the support and why it is necessary in order to prevent the jury speculating on any matter in the course of their deliberations. **[18–15]**

[19] ibid [44].

[20] *Equal Treatment Bench Book, England and Wales* (Judicial Council, February 2021 edn, April 2023 revision) 'Information for the jury' paras 180 -181, 86.

CHAPTER 19

INFORMATION TO JURIES

Introduction

While certain legislative provisions have previously provided information to juries, a general legislative provision under Part 3 of the Criminal Procedure Act 2021 was commenced on 28 February 2022. This may be relevant in terms of the transcripts of recorded interviews or any documentation made during the course of an interview with a vulnerable witness or complainant. The trial judge may have to balance the obligation to ensure the jury understands the evidence against the risk of an evidential imbalance. **[19–01]**

Section 12 of the Criminal Procedure Act 2021 states: **[19–02]**

> 12. Provision of information to juries
> Section 12(1) outlines the application of the section which is to any offence being tried on indictment apart from the sections listed which have their own relevant legislation in relation to information to juries. These are:
> (a) section 1078C of the Taxes Consolidation Act 1997
> (b) section 57 of the Criminal Justice (Theft and Fraud Offences) Act 2001
> (c) section 10 of the Competition Act 2002
> (d) section 56 of the Central Bank (Supervision and Enforcement) Act 2013
> (e) section 882 of the Companies Act 2014

Section 12(2) outlines what material may be given to the jury in respect of any or all of this list and in whatever form the judge considers appropriate. **[19–03]**

> (a) any document admitted in evidence at the trial;
> (b) where such transcripts or audio recordings are available:
> (i) the transcript of the opening speeches of counsel or an audio recording of such speeches
> (ii) the transcript of the whole or any part of the evidence given at the trial or an audio recording of such evidence
> (iii) the transcript of the closing speeches of counsel or an audio recording of such speeches
> (iv) the transcript of the trial judge's charge to the jury or an audio recording of such charge
> (c) any charts, diagrams, graphics, schedules or summaries of evidence produced at the trial
> (d) any other document that in the opinion of the trial judge would be of assistance to the jury in its deliberations including, where appropriate, an affidavit by an accountant or other suitably qualified person summarising, in a form which is likely to be comprehended by the jury, any transactions by the accused or other persons which are relevant to the offence.

Section 12(3) provides that if either the prosecution or the accused proposes to apply to the trial judge for an order that a document referred to in subsection (2)(d) shall be **[19–04]** given to the jury, they shall give a copy of the document to the other party in advance of the application and, on the hearing of the application, the trial judge shall take into account any representations made by or on behalf of either party in relation to it.

[19–05] The provision appears to ensure that applications in respect of any information to be given to the jury be done on full notice to the relevant parties. In the normal course of events during the trial process, when the trial judge's charge is completed and the jury is ready to begin its deliberations, there may be some discussion as to what the jury may be given. In the course of its deliberations the jury may also request certain information which on consent[1] or by determination of the trial judge after oral argument may be acceded to. This section places notice of this on a more formal basis rather than just in the interests of justice and normal fair procedures.

[19–06] Section 12(4) provides that where an order that an affidavit be given to the jury in relation to a report under s 12(2)(d),[2] the accountant or other suitably qualified person shall be summoned by the prosecution or the accused, as the case may be, to attend at the trial as an expert witness, and may be required by the trial judge, in an appropriate case, to give evidence in regard to the report and any relevant accounting procedures or principles.

[19–07] The trial judge has discretion as to what information is given to the jury and the factors in relation to the balance of the evidence outlined in *DPP v SA*[3] and *DPP v PB*[4] may be a consideration in relation to the provision of transcripts of recorded evidence.

[19–08] The Criminal Procedure Act 2021 was commenced in its entirety on 28 February 2022 and so there is little case law available at time of publication. Certain case law in relation to similar legislative provisions may give indications as to possible interpretation by the courts. In *DPP v AE*,[5] one of the appeal points related to the trial judge's refusal of the jury's request to rehear the closing speech of counsel. Donnelly J noted that, in submissions, counsel had referred to s. 12 Criminal Procedure Act 2021 (which had not been commenced at the time of the trial). The judgment went on to examine similar legislative provisions such as s 57 of the Criminal Justice (Theft and Fraud Offences) Act 2001, noting that constitutional rights to a fair trial are paramount:

> It is not difficult to see that such a provision may assist in trials that are particularly complex. The arguments of prosecution and defence counsel may be easier to follow by seeing them in written form. That is a specific exception to what appears to be the general practice, potentially amounting to a rule, that those speeches should not be so provided in transcript form at least. Providing a transcript and reading from a transcript may be slightly different, but we do not think that the difference is relevant to what is the longstanding principle: the speeches are not generally repeated to the jury. We do accept however that practice, procedure and even a rule of law, must accommodate the

---

1 In the case of *DPP v FN* [2021] IECA 238, [2022] IESC 22; and in the unreported case of *DPP v SK* (CCDP0124/2020 Dec 2020), defence counsel had consented to the recordings of the examination in chief testimony being deemed exhibits and provided to the jury during their deliberations.

2 s 12(2)(d): 'any other document that in the opinion of the trial judge would be of assistance to the jury in its deliberations including, where appropriate, an affidavit by an accountant or other suitably qualified person summarising, in a form which is likely to be comprehended by the jury, any transactions by the accused or other persons which are relevant to the offence.'

3 *DPP v SA* [2020] IECA 60.

4 *DPP v PB* [2021] IECA 152.

5 *DPP v AE* [2022] IECA 152.

> protection of constitutional rights and therefore ensure that the trial is one in due course of law; a trial must be fair.[6]

The appeal point was unsuccessful, but the conviction was quashed on another point, that of the admission of the memorandum of interviews. **[19–09]**

6 ibid [102].

CHAPTER 20

JURISDICTION

Support Measures Available in Courts of All Jurisdictions

[20–01] Vulnerable witnesses and victims may find themselves in cases which are dealt with in the District Court and appropriate measures will be available to them in that jurisdiction as well. The provisions which facilitate support measures are available to them in every jurisdiction. For example, there is no jurisdictional division for recorded testimony, video link, intermediaries, protection against personal cross-examination or screens under the Criminal Evidence Act 1992 but rather the eligibility for their use depends on relevant offences such as sexual or violent offences, age or intellectual disability. Equally, there is no restriction in terms of jurisdiction under the Criminal Justice (Victims of Crime) Act 2017 but again the eligibility for their use depends on whether the person is a victim of the offence, his or her age and the nature and circumstances of the case.[1]

Prosecution of Sexual Assault Cases in the District Court

[20–02] Sexual assault[2] offences may be prosecuted in the District Court as well as in the Circuit Court and Central Criminal Court.[3] A sexual assault charge may be tried in the District Court provided (1) the judge is of opinion that the facts proved or alleged constitute a minor offence fit to be tried summarily; (2) the DPP consents; and (3) the defendant, on being informed of his or her right to be tried by a jury, does not object to being tried summarily.[4]

[20–03] Section 4 of the Criminal Law (Sexual Offences) Act 2006 provides that the District Court may try a person charged with attempting a sexual act with a person under 15[5] or under 17[6] provided the same three conditions as above are met.[7] Soliciting or

---

1 Criminal Justice (Victims of Crime) Act 2017, s 20, Power to exclude the public; s 21, Questioning in respect of private life of victim.

2 There is no statutory definition for sexual assault. Indecent assault is now termed sexual assault under s 2 of the Criminal Law (Rape) (Amendment) Act 1990. Non-Fatal Offences against the Person Act 1997, s 2, outlines the offence of assault. The Supreme Court decision in *DPP v FN* [2022] IESC 22 provides guidance in relation to the charge to the jury as to what comprises sexual assault.

3 Criminal Law (Rape) Act 1981, s 12.

4 ibid. Thomas O'Malley, *Sexual Offences* (Round Hall 2013) paras 17.09, 5.27 and 4.21.

5 Criminal Law (Sexual Offences) Act 2006, s 2(2).

6 ibid s 3(2).

7 Criminal Law (Sexual Offences) Act 2006, s 4, Summary trial of offences: '(1) The District Court may try summarily a person charged with an offence under section 2(2) or 3(2) if –

importuning a child for the purposes of committing a sexual offence is also triable summarily or on indictment.[8]

[20–04] As O'Malley notes, the Criminal Procedure Act 1967 (s 13) permits the District Court to deal summarily with most indictable offences, apart from serious ones, where the accused wishes to plead guilty and the court is satisfied that he or she understands the nature of the charge and the facts alleged. The prosecutor must consent to the offence being dealt with summarily. The accused may be sent forward to the appropriate court on a signed plea of guilty but, again, only with the prosecutor's consent.

[20–05] Rape, rape contrary to s 4 and aggravated sexual assault may not be dealt with summarily by virtue of s 20 of the Criminal Law (Rape) (Amendment) Act 1990, although a person may be sent forward on a signed plea of guilty to any of those offences.[9]

[20–06] In relation to the restrictions regarding previous sexual history under s 3(1) of the Criminal Law (Rape) Act 1981, the section specifically outlines provisions and appropriate reading of the section should a sexual assault be dealt with in the District Court.[10]

(a) the court is of opinion that the facts alleged constitute a minor offence fit to be tried summarily,
(b) the accused, on being informed by the court of his or her right to be tried with a jury, does not object to being tried summarily for the offence, and
(c) the Director of Public Prosecutions consents to the accused being tried summarily for the offence.

(2) Upon conviction of a person by the District Court of an offence under this section, the person shall be liable to a fine not exceeding €5,000 or to imprisonment for a term not exceeding 12 months or to both.'

8 Criminal Law (Sexual Offences) 1993, s 6, as substituted by Criminal Law (Sexual Offences) (Amendment) Act 2007, s 2.

9 Criminal Procedure Act 1967, s 20:

'(a) Paragraph (a) of subsection (2) of section 13 of the Criminal Procedure Act, 1967, shall not apply in relation to rape, rape under section 4 (within the meaning of the Criminal Law (Rape) (Amendment) Act, 1990) or aggravated sexual assault (within the meaning of the Criminal Law (Rape) (Amendment) Act, 1990).
(b) Notwithstanding paragraph (a), the offences referred to therein shall be deemed, for the purposes of paragraph (b) of the said subsection (2), to be offences to which the said section 13 applies.'

See Thomas O'Malley, *Sexual Offences* (Round Hall 2013) Ch. 17–*The Trial,* Section 1, *Court Jurisdiction,* para 17.10.

10 Criminal Law (Rape) Act 1981, s 3, Restrictions on evidence at trials for rape offences:

'(1) If at a trial any person is for the time being charged with a sexual assault offence to which he pleads not guilty, then, except with the leave of the judge, no evidence shall be adduced and no question shall be asked in cross-examination at the trial, by or on behalf of any accused person at the trial, about any sexual experience (other than that to which the charge relates) of a complainant with any person; and in relation to a sexual assault tried summarily pursuant to section 12 –

(a) subsection (2)(a) shall have effect as if the words 'in the absence of the jury' were omitted,
(b) subsection (2)(b) shall have effect as if for the references to the jury there were substituted references to the court, and (c) this section (other than this paragraph) and subsections (3) and (4) of section 7 shall have effect as if for the references to the judge there were substituted references to the court.

(2) (a) The judge shall not give leave in pursuance of subsection (1) for any evidence or question except on an application made to him, in the absence of the jury, by or on behalf of an accused person.

Section 75 Children Act 2001/s 5 Criminal Law (Rape) Act 1981 – summary trial of sexual assault offences for person under 18

Where an application under s 75 of the Children Act 2001[11] is made for a sexual assault offence[12] to be tried as a summary trial (where the defendant is under 18), s 5 of the Criminal Law (Rape) Act 1981[13] provides for the necessary amendments to be made in relation to jury and judge in a reading of ss 2 and 3 and Criminal Law (Rape) Act 1981, as appropriate. **[20–07]**

It should be noted that the offence of manslaughter, as well as offences which are required to be tried in the Central Criminal Court, are explicitly excluded from an application under s 75 of the Children Act 2001 and may not be dealt with summarily. **[20–08]**

(b) The judge shall give leave if, and only if, he is satisfied that it would be unfair to the accused person to refuse to allow the evidence to be adduced or the question to be asked, that is to say, if he is satisfied that, on the assumption that if the evidence or question was not allowed the jury might reasonably be satisfied beyond reasonable doubt that the accused person is guilty, the effect of allowing the evidence or question might reasonably be that they would not be so satisfied.

(3) If, notwithstanding that the judge has given leave in accordance with this section for any evidence to be adduced or question to be asked in cross-examination, it appears to the judge that any question asked or proposed to be asked (whether in the course of so adducing evidence or of cross-examination) in reliance on the leave which he has given is not or may not be such as may properly be asked in accordance with that leave, he may direct that the question shall not be asked or, if asked, that it shall not be answered except in accordance with his leave given on a fresh application under this section.

(4) Nothing in this section authorises evidence to be adduced or a question to be asked which cannot be adduced or asked apart from this section.'

11 Children Act 2001, s 75: '(1) Subject to subsection (3), the Court may deal summarily with a child charged with any indictable offence, other than an offence which is required to be tried by the Central Criminal Court or manslaughter, unless the Court is of opinion that the offence does not constitute a minor offence fit to be tried summarily or, where the child wishes to plead guilty, to be dealt with summarily.'

12 Criminal Law (Rape) Act 1981, s 1, Interpretation, outlines a 'sexual assault offence' as a rape offence and any of the following, namely, aggravated sexual assault, attempted aggravated sexual assault, sexual assault, attempted sexual assault, aiding, abetting, counselling and procuring aggravated sexual assault, attempted aggravated sexual assault, sexual assault or attempted sexual assault, incitement to aggravated sexual assault or sexual assault and conspiracy to commit any of the foregoing offences.

13 Criminal Law (Rape) Act 1981, s 5, Trials of juveniles:

'Where a person charged with a sexual assault offence is tried for that offence summarily in pursuance of section 75 (which provides for the summary trial in certain cases of persons under the age of 18 years who are charged with indictable offences) of the Children Act, 2001 – (a) sections 2(2) and 3(2)(b) shall have effect as if for the references to the jury there were substituted references to the court, (b) section 3(2)(a) shall have effect as if the words "in the absence of the jury" were omitted, and (c) section 3, subsections (3) and (4) of section 7 and subsections (2), (4) and (5) of section 8 shall have effect as if for the references to the judge there were substituted references to the court.'

CHAPTER 21

PREVIOUS SEXUAL HISTORY/ PRIVATE LIFE – RESTRICTIONS ON EVIDENCE/CROSS-EXAMINATION

Introduction

Legislative provisions allow for protections in relation to questioning relating to the previous sexual history of a complainant under s 3 of the Criminal Law (Rape) Act 1981 and under the Criminal Justice (Victims of Crime) Act 2017, in relation to the private life of the victim (which is unrelated to the offence). **[21–01]**

Section 3 Criminal Law (Rape) Act 1981

Previous sexual history

Section 3 of the Criminal Law (Rape) Act 1981[1] provides that at a trial where a person is charged with a sexual assault offence, then no evidence will be admissible and no **[21–02]**

---

1 Criminal Law (Rape) Act 1981, s 3, Restrictions on evidence at trials for rape offences:

'(1) If at a trial any person is for the time being charged with a sexual assault offence to which he pleads not guilty, then, except with the leave of the judge, no evidence shall be adduced and no question shall be asked in cross-examination at the trial, by or on behalf of any accused person at the trial, about any sexual experience (other than that to which the charge relates) of a complainant with any person; and in relation to a sexual assault tried summarily pursuant to section 12 –

(a) subsection (2)(a) shall have effect as if the words 'in the absence of the jury' were omitted,

(b) subsection (2)(b) shall have effect as if for the references to the jury there were substituted references to the court, and (c) this section (other than this paragraph) and subsections (3) and (4) of section 7 shall have effect as if for the references to the judge there were substituted references to the court.

(2) (a) The judge shall not give leave in pursuance of subsection (1) for any evidence or question except on an application made to him, in the absence of the jury, by or on behalf of an accused person.

(b) The judge shall give leave if, and only if, he is satisfied that it would be unfair to the accused person to refuse to allow the evidence to be adduced or the question to be asked, that is to say, if he is satisfied that, on the assumption that if the evidence or question was not allowed the jury might reasonably be satisfied beyond reasonable doubt that the accused person is guilty, the effect

question asked of the complainant in cross-examination on behalf of any accused about any sexual experience other than that to which the charge relates.[2]

Test Under s 3 Criminal Law (Rape) Act 1981

[21–03] Section 3(2)(b) of the Criminal Law (Rape) Act 1981 provides that the judge shall give leave if, and only if, he or she 'is satisfied that it would be unfair to the accused person to refuse to allow the evidence to be adduced or the question to be asked' and the section further outlines that this means that if he or she is satisfied 'on the assumption that if the evidence or question was not allowed, the jury might reasonably be satisfied beyond reasonable doubt that the accused person is guilty, the effect of allowing the evidence or question might reasonably be that they would not be so satisfied'.

[21–04] Separate legal representation in relation to the application under s 3 is available under s 4A of the Criminal Law (Rape) Act 1981 but at present is limited to the application only. However, anecdotal evidence suggests that many practitioners are present for the questioning as well as the application. Payment to practitioners in respect of separate legal representation is made through the Legal Aid Board.[3] The O'Malley Report suggested that barristers who represent the complainant under applications under s 3 of the Criminal Law (Rape) Act 1981 in respect of evidence regarding previous sexual history should be made by appropriately experienced counsel,[4] noting that this role is often filled by junior counsel.[5] Anecdotally, since then, it appears that senior counsel rather than junior counsel have been briefed in respect of these application.

---

of allowing the evidence or question might reasonably be that they would not be so satisfied.

(3) If, notwithstanding that the judge has given leave in accordance with this section for any evidence to be adduced or question to be asked in cross-examination, it appears to the judge that any question asked or proposed to be asked (whether in the course of so adducing evidence or of cross-examination) in reliance on the leave which he has given is not or may not be such as may properly be asked in accordance with that leave, he may direct that the question shall not be asked or, if asked, that it shall not be answered except in accordance with his leave given on a fresh application under this section.

(4) Nothing in this section authorises evidence to be adduced or a question to be asked which cannot be adduced or asked apart from this section.'

2 Under s 1 of the Criminal Law (Rape) Act 1981 a sexual assault offence means a rape offence and any of the following: aggravated sexual assault; attempted aggravated sexual assault; sexual assault; attempted sexual assault; aiding, abetting, counselling and procuring aggravated sexual assault; attempted aggravated sexual assault; incitement to aggravated sexual assault; or sexual assault; and conspiracy to commit any of the foregoing offences. A rape offence under s 1 of the Act means any of the following: namely, rape; attempted rape; burglary with intent to commit rape; aiding, abetting, counselling and procuring rape; attempted rape or burglary with intent to commit rape; incitement to rape; and, other than in ss 2(2) and 8 of the Act, rape under s 4; attempted rape under s 4; aiding, abetting, counselling and procuring rape under s 4; or attempted rape under s 4; and incitement to rape under s 4.

3 Legal Aid Board *Advice for complainants in rape & certain sexual assault cases* <https://www.legalaidboard.ie/en/our-services/legal-aid-services/common-legal-problems/rape-and-sexual-assault/advice-for-complainants-in-rape-certain-sexual-assault-cases.html> accessed 13 October 2023.

4 Dept of Justice and Equality, *Review of Protections for Vulnerable Witnesses in the Investigation and Prosecution of Sexual Offences* (August 2020) 5; para 5.15, 60.

5 ibid para 6.13, 69.

Proposed Extensions to s 3 Criminal Law (Rape) Act 1981 /s 8 Criminal Law (Sexual Offences and Human Trafficking) Bill 2023

Proposals to widen the provisions are planned under the Criminal Law (Sexual Offences and Human Trafficking) Bill 2022[6] which at time of writing is at an early stage in the legislative process. The presence of separate legal representation will be legislatively provided for the duration of the evidence instead of just the application alone.[7] It will also expand the eligibility for legal representation to include a sexual assault offence, an offence under s 6 of the Criminal Law (Sexual Offences) Act 1993, and an offence under the Criminal Law (Sexual Offences) Act 2006.[8] **[21–05]**

No provision for separate legal representation for appeal

A point to note in relation to legal representation for a complainant under s 3 of the Criminal Law (Rape) Act 1981 is that it appears to be the case that separate legal representation is only provided for at trial and not in any related appeal. Therefore at an appeal hearing where a ground of appeal is predominantly focused on the question of previous sexual history, the complainant is not separately represented. **[21–06]**

People (DPP) v GK

In *People (DPP) v GK*[9] the Court of Criminal Appeal noted the dearth of decided authority at that time in respect of the provision and considered the available judgments in this and neighbouring jurisdictions, including *R v Viola*,[10] where the Court of Criminal Appeal noted that it was common ground that it was wrong to speak of a judge's 'discretion' in this regard. The Court noted that the trial judge must make a 'judgment' as to whether he is satisfied or not in terms of the legislation and once he reaches his judgment of the facts, he has no discretion. If he concludes that it would be unfair to exclude the evidence or question, it has to be admitted and allowed.[11] **[21–07]**

The Court of Criminal Appeal went on to quash the conviction in this case on the basis that questioning on previous sexual history should have been allowed. However, it stressed that the decision was not one which impugned the character of the complainant in any way. The Court noted that had the complainant been given the opportunity of responding to limited questioning about her sexual activity the jury may have been satisfied that those activities were unrelated to the bringing of her complaint against the accused save in limited circumstances as outlined in the evidence before the Court. In his judgment, Kearns J noted that both the jury and the accused were deprived of relevant evidence which clearly could have affected the outcome of the case. **[21–08]**

In an important observation regarding the provision, Kearns J noted that a decision **[21–09]**

---

6 Criminal Law (Sexual Offences and Human Trafficking) Bill 2023, s 8.
This section appears to be implementing recommendations of Dept of Justice and Equality, *Review of Protections for Vulnerable Witnesses in the Investigation and Prosecution of Sexual Offences* (August 2020), 84 and Dept of Justice and Equality, *Supporting a Victim's Journey – A plan to help victims and vulnerable witnesses in sexual violence cases (*October 2020) para 5.1, 5.2, 41 .

7 Criminal Law (Sexual Offences and Human Trafficking) Bill 2023, s 8 (b).

8 Criminal Law (Sexual Offences and Human Trafficking) Bill 2023, s 8 (c).

9 [2007] 2 IR 92.

10 *R v Viola* [1982] 1 WLR 1138.

11 *People (DPP) v GK* [2007] 2 IR 92 [18], 100–01.

to refuse cross-examination may be more readily justified than otherwise. In addition, the younger the complainant the more traumatic the cross-examination of this nature.

> Having regard to the severely restrictive terminology of the statutory provision, the court is of the view that, in general, a decision to refuse to allow cross-examination as to past sexual history may more readily be justified in most cases than the converse. Indeed the Act is quite explicit in so providing. Furthermore, the younger the age of a complainant, the less desirable it is to ever allow cross-examination which may well be extremely traumatic for a complainant of tender years. Where a form of questioning is allowed, it should be confined only to what is strictly necessary and should never be utilised as a form of character assassination of a complainant.[12]

DPP v DD

[21–10] In the case of *DPP v DD*[13] the Court of Appeal had a concern in relation to the trial judge's ruling effectively preventing any questions being raised as to the reasons why the complainant, who was 15 at the time of the alleged offence, was on the contraceptive pill or remained on it despite some adverse medical reaction to the medication. The Court held that there was a possibility that the jury might have been persuaded that a secondary, or a primary, motivation for the taking of the pill or remaining on it, was to have sexual intercourse and that such sexual activity that occurred in the course of her confrontation with the appellant was not the first occasion on which she had engaged in sexual intercourse. The Court held that it was an important credibility issue which ought to have remained open to greater clarification aided by cross-examination and that it was a matter which ought properly to have been left to the jury for its consideration. The Court allowed the appeal and set aside the conviction.

Section 21 Criminal Justice (Victims of Crime) Act 2017

'Questioning in respect of private life of victim'

[21–11] Section 21 of the Criminal Justice (Victims of Crime) Act 2017 allows the courts greater discretion to curtail evidence and questioning in relation to the private life of a victim. In any proceedings relating to an offence, the court 'may give such directions as it considers just and proper regarding any evidence adduced or sought to be deduced and any question asked in cross-examination at the trial which relates to the private life of a victim and is unrelated to the offence'. The court may do so where it is satisfied that (a) the nature or circumstances of the case are such that there is a need to protect a victim of the offence from secondary and repeat victimisation, intimidation, or retaliation; and (b) it would not be contrary to the interests of justice in the case.[14] As interpreted under s 2 of the Act, 'secondary victimisation' means victimisation that occurs indirectly

---

12 ibid [25].

13 *DPP v DD* [2018] IECA 192.

14 Criminal Justice (Victims of Crime) Act 2017, s 21, Questioning in respect of private life of victim:

> 'In any proceedings relating to an offence, where a court is satisfied that –
>
> (a) the nature or circumstances of the case are such that there is a need to protect a victim of the offence from secondary and repeat victimisation, intimidation or retaliation, and
>
> (b) it would not be contrary to the interests of justice in the case, the court may give such directions as it considers just and proper regarding any evidence adduced or sought to be adduced and any question asked in cross-examination at the trial, which relates to the private life of a victim and is unrelated to the offence.

through the response of institutions and individuals to the victim. It remains to be seen how the courts interpret this section but the balancing of the rights of the accused to a fair trial under Article 38.1 of the Constitution may be weighed against the specific reference to evidence or questions relating to the private life of the victim which is 'unrelated to the offence'. The courts customarily curtail irrelevant evidence in a case. The Bar Council Code of Conduct prohibits a barrister from making statements or asking questions 'which are merely scandalous or are intended only for the purpose of vilifying, insulting or annoying a witness or some other person'.[15] However, it is of assistance to the vulnerable victim that a provision outlining parameters in respect of evidence or questioning of the private life of a victim where it is unrelated to the offence has been placed on a legislative basis.

[15] Bar Council of Ireland, *Code of Conduct* (adopted 25 July 2022): '5.18. Barristers when conducting a case must not make statements or ask questions which are merely scandalous or are intended only for the purpose of vilifying, insulting or annoying a witness or some other person.'

CHAPTER 22

PROTECTION AGAINST PERSONAL CROSS-EXAMINATION BY ACCUSED

Introduction

The use of the term 'child examiners' was first suggested by the Irish Law Reform Commission in its Report on Child Sexual Abuse in 1990, as a means to prevent personal cross-examination by the accused.[1] This could be extremely stressful for a complainant or witness, particularly if he or she is related to or knows the questioner. Legislative developments, explored below, now provide that, in certain circumstances, personal cross-examination can be prevented. The court '*shall*' or '*may*' prevent personal cross-examination in certain circumstances depending on the nature of the offence, the age of the witness and the nature of the application. **[22–01]**

Section 14C Criminal Evidence Act 1992 (as Inserted by s 36 Criminal Justice (Sexual Offences) Act 2017)

'Protection against cross-examination by accused'

This section allows the trial judge to prevent person cross-examination by the accused in certain circumstances in relation to certain offences in respect of a child witness or an adult victim. The legislation states: **[22–02]**

> 14C Criminal Evidence Act 1992
>
> (1) Where—
> (a) a person is accused of a relevant offence, and
> (b) a person under the age of 18 years is to give evidence,
> the court shall direct that the accused may not personally cross-examine the witness unless the court is of the opinion that the interests of justice require the accused to conduct the cross-examination personally.
>
> (2) Where—
> (a) a person is accused of a relevant offence, and

[1] Irish Law Reform Commission, *Report on Child Sexual Abuse* (32–1990) para 7.21, 76.

(b) a victim of the relevant offence who has attained the age of 18 years is to give evidence,[2]

the court may direct that the accused may not personally cross- examine the witness unless the court is of the opinion that the interests of justice require the accused to conduct the cross-examination personally.

(2A) The court, in performing its functions under subsection (2), shall have regard to the need to protect the victim from secondary and repeat victimisation, intimidation or retaliation, taking into account—

(a) the nature and circumstances of the case, and
(b) the personal characteristics of the victim.

[22–03] Children benefit from the mandatory nature of s 14(C)1 as well as the broader range of eligible offences. In both cases where such prevention occurs, the defendant will be invited by the court to arrange for a legal representative to act for him or her for the purposes of cross-examining a witness. The court will oblige the defendant to notify it by a certain time as to whether a legal representative is to act in that capacity. If the defendant has not done so, the court shall consider whether it is necessary, in the interests of justice, for the witness to be cross-examined by a legal representative appointed to represent the interests of the accused person. If the court decides it is necessary, in the interests of justice, for the witness to be so cross-examined, the court shall appoint a legal representative (chosen by the court) to cross-examine the witness on behalf of the accused. Where, in a jury trial, an accused person is prevented from cross-examining a witness in person by virtue of this section, the court shall give the jury such warning (if any) as it considers necessary to ensure that the accused person is not prejudiced –

(a) by any inferences that might be drawn from the fact that the accused has been prevented from cross-examining the witness in person, or
(b) where the witness has been cross-examined by a legal representative appointed where the defendant did not choose to be represented by one.

[22–04] Payment for legal representation through the Civil Legal Aid Act 1995 is provided in s 14C(7).

[22–05] It should be noted that s 14C is not contained in s 19 of the Criminal Evidence Act 1992 and so an adult with an intellectual disability will only be able to avail of s 14C (2) and thereby be afforded protection under a narrower range of offences at the discretion of the court.

Section 16 Domestic Violence Act 2018

Protection against cross-examination by applicant or respondent

[22–06] The court shall / may prevent personal cross-examination in relation to certain applications for a specified order unless the interests of justice require it. The court shall prevent personal cross-examination where a child is giving evidence. It may prevent personal cross-examination where an adult is applying for the specified order, is an aggrieved person under s 11,[3] a dependent person or the respondent to the application

[2] Criminal Justice (Miscellaneous Provisions) Act 2023, s 60(b) amending s 14C(2)(a) and (b) was commenced on 1 November 2023 by the Criminal Justice (Miscellaneous Provisions) Act 2023 (Commencement) (No 2) Order 2023 (SI No 525 of 2023), art 3(f).

[3] Under Domestic Violence Act 2018, s 11, an aggrieved person is a person whose safety and welfare

victim. A specified order is outlined in s 2 of the 'Interpretation' of the Act and a safety order, barring order, interim barring order, emergency barring order or protection order, or an order varying or discharging an such an order'.

> Where the witness is under 18
> 16. (1) Where—
> (a) an application is made to a court for a specified order,
> (b) a person under the age of 18 years is to give evidence, and
> (c) the applicant or respondent proposes to cross-examine the person referred to in *paragraph (b)* personally,
>
> the court shall direct that the applicant or the respondent, as the case may be, may not personally cross-examine the witness unless the court is of the opinion that the interests of justice require the applicant or respondent to conduct the cross-examination personally.
>
> Where the witness/alleged victim is an adult
> 16. (2) Where—
> (a) an application is made to a court for a specified order,
> (b) a person who has attained the age of 18 years (being the applicant for the specified order, an aggrieved person under *section 11*, a dependent person or the respondent to that application) is to give evidence, and
> (c) the applicant or respondent proposes to cross-examine the person referred to in *paragraph (b)* personally,
>
> the court may direct that the applicant or the respondent, as the case may be, may not personally cross-examine the witness unless the court is of the opinion that the interests of justice require the applicant or respondent to conduct the cross- examination personally.

Where an applicant or respondent, as the case may be, is prevented from cross-examining a witness, applicant, dependant, aggrieved person or respondent, the court will invite the applicant or respondent to arrange for a legal representative to act for him or her for the purpose of cross-examining the witness, and require the applicant or respondent to notify the court, by the end of such period as it may specify, as to whether a legal representative is to act for him or her for that purpose. If the applicant or respondent has not notified the court that a legal representative is to appear for him or her by the end of the specified period or at all the court shall consider whether it is necessary, in the interests of justice, for the witness to be cross-examined by a legal representative appointed to act for the applicant or respondent for that purpose. If the court decides that it is necessary, in the interests of justice, for the witness to be cross-examined by a legal representative appointed to act for the applicant or respondent for that purpose, the court shall appoint a legal representative (chosen by the court) to cross-examine the witness on behalf of the applicant or respondent. **[22–07]**

Section 32 Criminal Justice (Miscellaneous Provisions) Act 2023[4]

'Protection against cross-examination by applicant or respondent'

Section 32 of the Criminal Justice (Miscellaneous Provisions) Act 2023, when commenced, provides protection against cross-examination where a civil order is being sought against 'relevant conduct'. Section 27 of the Criminal Justice (Miscellaneous Provisions) Act 2023 sets out the definition of 'relevant conduct' as conduct that is likely to cause the applicant or a person connected to the applicant: **[22–08]**

---

is in doubt due to an alleged incident or series of incidents.

4 Criminal Justice (Miscellaneous Provisions) Act 2023, s 32 'Protection against cross-examination by applicant or respondent'.

(a) to fear that violence will be used against the applicant or person or
(b) serious alarm or distress that has a substantial adverse impact on his or her usual day-to-day activities.

[22–09] Where an application is made to a court under s 28 ('Order under section 28'), s 29 ('Variation or discharge of order under section 28') or s 30 ('Renewal of order under section 28') protection against personal cross-examination *shall* or *may* be made by the court depending on the whether the witness is under or over 18.

[22–10] Section 28 of the Civil Legal Aid Act 1995 will be amended by s 65 of the Criminal Justice (Miscellaneous Provisions) Act 2023, which, when commenced, facilitates payment for appropriate legal representation.

CHAPTER 23

PUTTING THE CASE

Origins of the Principle

In Ireland, the requirement to put the case has its origins in the English civil case of *Browne v Dunn*,[1] which established the contention that putting the case is a requirement if that witness is to be 'impeached'. In his judgment, Lord Hershell stated: **[23–01]**

> My Lords, I have always understood that if you intend to impeach a witness you are bound, whilst he is in the box, to give him an opportunity of making any explanation which is open to him; and, as it seems to me, that is not only a rule of professional practice in the conduct of a case; but is essential to fair play and fair dealing with witnesses. Sometimes reflections have been made upon excessive cross-examination of witnesses, and it has been complained of as undue; but it seems to me that a cross-examination of a witness which errs in the direction of excess may be far more fair to him than to leave him without cross-examination, and afterwards to suggest that he is not a witness of truth, I mean upon a point on which it is not otherwise perfectly clear that he has had full notice beforehand that there is an intention to impeach the credibility of the story which he is telling. Of course I do not deny for a moment that there are cases in which that notice has been so distinctly and unmistakably given, and the point upon which he is impeached, and is to be impeached, is so manifest, that it is not necessary to waste time in putting questions to him upon it. All I am saying is that it will not do to impeach the credibility of a witness upon a matter on which he has not had any opportunity of giving an explanation by reason of there having been no suggestion whatever in the course of the case that his story is not accepted.[2]

The legal status of the rule in *Browne v Dunn*[3] was considered by the Supreme Court in *McDonagh v Sunday Newspapers Ltd*[4] in a case of defamation. Charleton J stated: **[23–02]**

> The extent to which fairness requires cross-examination is essentially dependent on how a trial runs. Fairness, however, is what the law requires both in relation to procedures that are dedicated towards achieving a correct conclusion in a trial and in relation to the right of a witness to be given a real opportunity to comment on a verdict the implication of which may only be interpreted as adverse.[5]

In his separate judgment in that case, McKechnie J noted the judgment of Baker J on **[23–03]**

1 *Browne v Dunn* (1894) 6 R 67.
2 ibid (70)–(71).
3 ibid.
4 *McDonagh v Sunday Newspapers* [2018] 2 IR 1.
5 ibid [184], 74.

the issue of putting the case in *DPP v Burke*.[6] In relation to the case of *Browne v Dunn*[7] and the weight that should be given to unchallenged evidence, McKechnie observed:

> It is evident from her judgment that Baker J. was entirely satisfied that *Browne v. Dunn* (1893) 6 R. 67 was part of Irish law, although, and I think rightly so, she had some doubts about where precisely on the legal spectrum it should sit. Disregarding her views on that matter, what is of relevance is her conclusion on how unchallenged evidence should be treated. In rejecting the defence argument that untested evidence must unconditionally be accepted, she stated at para. 44, p. 666, that "the proper approach to unchallenged evidence is to consider the appropriate weight which should be given to such evidence". In this context she was satisfied that such evidence carried greater weight than tested, contradicted evidence. The judge was of the view that *Browne v. Dunn* (1893) 6 R. 67 did not support the argument advanced by the accused, but rather was authority only for the proposition that the credibility of a witness may not be impeached, either in cross-examination or in submissions, if his or her evidence has not been tested in cross-examination. Finally, she was also of the view that there was no requirement, either in practice or in law, as such, that counsel must cross-examine a witness.[8]

[23–04] It should be noted that McKechnie J did differentiate the case of *DPP v Burke*[9] from the defamation case in *McDonagh v Sunday Newspapers Ltd* on the basis that not only was the former a criminal case but it was summary in nature.[10]

[23–05] McKechnie J went on to state:

> What the rule is truly focused on and what it seeks to achieve is to ensure that evidence intended to be impugned is put in issue in a manner or way, whatever that might be, which conveys to all parties and the relevant witnesses that such evidence is being challenged. Is it in dispute or in contention? Is it being contradicted? Simply put, is it in controversy? If so, and in a manner obvious and known to all, then such is sufficient to 'put it in issue'. This therefore is the yardstick. How it is done is not the test: the basis for the rule does not demand more.[11]

Putting the Case – Vulnerable Witnesses

Recent developments in England and Wales

[23–06] The case of *R v Barker* was a milestone judgment in which the Court of Appeal in England and Wales established that the days of deeming a child incompetent due to age were past.[12] That judgment legitimised the evidence of even very young witnesses with

---

6 *DPP v Burke* [2014] IEHC 483, [2014] 2 IR 651.

7 *Browne v Dunn* (1894) 6 R 67.

8 *McDonagh v Sunday Newspapers Ltd* [2018] 2 IR 1 [48]–[49], 19.

9 *DPP v Burke* [2014] IEHC 483, [2014] 2 IR 651.

10 *McDonagh v Sunday Newspapers Ltd* [2018] 2 IR 1 [47], 19.
'Secondly, the High Court was determining a case stated from the District Court pursuant to s. 52 of the Courts (Supplemental Provisions) Act 1961, which process has inherent limitations on the judgment which it can deliver. Thirdly, *Director of Public Prosecutions v. Burke* [2014] IEHC 483, [2014] 2 I.R. 651 was not only a criminal case, but the offences charged were, or were treated as, summary in nature: therefore there was no jury involved. Accordingly, it can only be at the level of principle that the decision feeds into the instant case.'

11 *McDonagh v Sunday Newspapers Ltd* [2018] 2 IR 1 [61], 23.

12 *R v Barker* [2010] EWCA Crim 4:
'33. The former approach was typified by an observation in *R v Wallwork* [1958] 42 CAR 153, when a little girl of 5 years had been called as a witness, and Lord Goddard CJ

the Court of Appeal noting it is the obligation of the courts to facilitate communication. A subsequent decision involving young witnesses, *R v Lubemba*,[13] expressly states that it is for the advocate to adapt to the witness and not the other way round.[14] It also raised doubts as to whether it was necessary to put the case to the witness and if it was that necessary modifications must be made for young or vulnerable witnesses.

> Professional organisations such as the Inns of Court provide training and guidance along similar lines for advocates. It is now generally accepted that if justice is to be done to the vulnerable witness and also to the accused, a radical departure from the traditional style of advocacy will be necessary. Advocates must adapt to the witness, not the other way round. They cannot insist upon any supposed right "to put one's case" or previous inconsistent statements to a vulnerable witness. If there is a right to "put one's case" (about which we have our doubts) it must be modified for young or vulnerable witnesses. It is perfectly possible to ensure the jury are made aware of the defence case and of significant inconsistencies without intimidation or distressing a witness (see for example paragraph 3E.4 of the Criminal Practice Directions).[15]

In England and Wales, there has been what could be termed a significant cultural change with the advent of the national roll out of recorded cross-examination.[16] Questions for the vulnerable witness are now submitted in advance and may be modified to better suit the witness with the assistance of the judge and/or appointed intermediary. As Hoyano notes: **[23–07]**

> Recently a practice has grown up whereby defence advocates have elected not to cross-examine a vulnerable witness, especially a young child, notwithstanding that witness being assessed as competent. Instead the advocate has decided to rely upon the trial judge to direct the jury on the questions which the defence would have put in cross-examination, and to highlight the caution with which the unchallenged Achieving Best Evidence (ABE) interview should be approached. In part this practice has grown up because of a defeatist attitude regarding what can be accomplished in cross-examining such a witness, given that the trial judge will 'blue-pencil' the questions in advance so as not to be too

---

observed: "The court deprecates the calling of a child of this age as a witness … the jury could not attach any value to the evidence of a child of five: it is ridiculous to suppose they could …" That observation was re-emphasised as recently as October 1986 in *R v Wright and Ormerod* [1990] 90 CAR 91, where it was said, in reference to Wallwork: "… the validity of, and good sense behind, that proposition has remained untrammelled in the practice of the criminal court … "

34. Not very much later, in February 1990 in *R v Z* [1990] 2 WB 355, Lord Lane CJ underlined that "… despite those observations … it still remains a matter for the judge's discretion".'

13 *R v Lubemba* [2014] EWCA Crim 2064.

14 ibid [45].

15 ibid. CPD, England and Wales, 2023: '6.1.8 Accommodating the needs of young and/or otherwise vulnerable people may require a radical departure from traditional cross-examination. The form and extent of appropriate cross-examination will vary from case to case. For adult non-vulnerable witnesses an advocate is expected to "put the case" so that the witness will have the opportunity of commenting upon it and/or answering it. When the witness is young or otherwise vulnerable, the court may dispense with the normal practice and impose restrictions on the advocate "putting the case", particularly where there is a risk of a young or otherwise vulnerable witness failing to understand, becoming distressed or acquiescing to leading questions. 6.1.9 Instead of exploring apparent inconsistencies in cross-examination it may, subject to discussion between the judge and the advocate(s), be appropriate for these to be identified to the jury after the witness's evidence. Where appropriate the judge should point out important inconsistencies after (instead of during) the witness's evidence. The judge should also remind the jury of these during summing up. The judge should be alert to alleged inconsistencies that are not in fact inconsistent, or are trivial, and thus do not need to be mentioned.'

16 Youth Justice and Criminal Evidence Act 1999, s 28.

> confrontational; the practice might also be due to defence counsel being relieved not to have to formulate appropriate questions or to be 'stuck' with unfavourable answers.[17]

[23–08] However, as a result of choosing not to cross-examine a witness, a perception may arise that the vulnerable witness is somehow incompetent and his or her testimony unreliable. In *R v RK*[18] the Court of Appeal again addressed the matter and stated:

> In relation to ground 2, we first question what we are told is becoming an increasing practice for defence advocates to decide they will not cross-examine a vulnerable, particularly a child, witness. We understand the concern to protect a child witness and the desire of a defence advocate to avoid any suggestion of confronting a child witness. However, if a child is assessed as competent and the judge agrees the child is competent, we would generally expect the child to be called and cross-examined, with the benefit of the range of special measures we now deploy. There is no reason to distress her or cause her any anxiety and therefore no reason to avoid putting the defence case by simple, short and direct questions. Although this court has in the past doubted the right to put every aspect of the defence case to a vulnerable witness, whatever the circumstances, it has not questioned the general duty to ensure the defence case is put fully and fairly and witnesses challenged, where that is possible.
>
> Furthermore, if the judge approves a decision not to cross examine, it raises the problem of what directions should be given to the jury. The directions should not indicate the child is incompetent when she is competent and should not inadvertently leave the jury with the impression that the child is not worthy of belief. We see some force in Ms Cowe's submission that the judge's directions in this case as to S's lack of maturity and understanding risked giving the jury such an impression, without giving them the best opportunity to assess her.[19]

Putting the case in Ireland

[23–09] The general principle provides that if a matter is not put to the witness then it cannot comprise part of the evidence for the defence and it cannot be relied on in the closing speech of the defence counsel. However, the principle is dependent on the individual circumstances of the case and the issues which may arise. It is important to note that a defence counsel's obligation is to his or her client[20] and in a given set of circumstances, a defence counsel may consider that by cross-examining, a witness may give details which are harmful to the defence. Therefore, a defence counsel may choose not to put the defence case to the witness in cross-examination, particularly where the prosecution case may contain weaknesses favourable to the defendant. To cross examine may mean that the witness will have opportunities to give further details helpful to the prosecution case and a defence counsel may not wish to risk that happening.

[23–10] These issues regarding cross-examination were seen in an article in *The Irish Times* regarding one of the youngest complainants to give evidence in Ireland. 'Zoe' had made disclosures of sexual abuse when she was approximately three years of age, the suspect was charged a year later, and the trial took place approximately two years subsequent to that.

---

17 Laura Hoyano, '*Putting the Case, in Every Case*' (November 2018) Counsel Magazine. (Bar Council of England and Wales).
https://www.counselmagazine.co.uk/articles/putting-the-case-every-case accessed 13 October 2023.

18 *R v RK* [2018] EWCA Crim 603.

19 ibid [27]–[28].

20 Bar Council of Ireland, *Code of Conduct* (adopted 25 July 2022) para 2.6, 11.

> After Zoe's DVD testimony was played, wherein she described Dave's actions, her cross-examination began. She was asked whether she believed in Santa, in the tooth fairy and in the Easter Bunny, but "her complaint was never put to her", says Kate. "What Dave did was never put to her. The defence asked her nothing else because they knew if they did it would have permitted her to tell her story. Silencing her is unforgivable," she says. As is standard procedure in any criminal trial, the prosecution was unable to ask Zoe any questions about what Dave was alleged to have done because the defence had not asked any questions about it in their cross examination.
>
> […]
>
> The couple had taken Zoe to Cari, or Children at Risk in Ireland, before the trial. They explained to Zoe that the court was a place where she would get to tell her story. "I wish they hadn't told her that now, because in the days afterwards she asked why she never got to tell the judge what Dave did," Kate says. "She would have told her story to the jury in a pure way. I think the defence saw how bright and articulate she was and didn't take this risk," Tom adds.[21]

In the case of 'Zoe', her parents appeared to feel that the recorded testimony which was played to the jury was not 'her story'. Yet, the recorded testimony comprises the evidence of the complainant against the accused. It is then the choice of the defence as to whether or indeed how to cross-examine the complainant on this testimony. The manner of cross-examination may be dependent on how the particular evidence meets the proofs required by the charges. As outlined in the article, if an issue is not cross-examined on, it cannot be a subject for re-examination and, therefore, Zoe was not able to give any further details than the account given in her recorded evidence. **[23–11]**

The general principles of *R v Lubemba*[22] in respect of vulnerable witnesses have been affirmed in the case of *DPP v VE*[23] and there has been a move for the criminal courts to adapt to the vulnerable witness rather than the other way around. The courts have endeavoured to ensure that the traditional methods of questioning, involving the use of leading and tag questions, are not employed with vulnerable witnesses. The case of *DPP v MB*[24] underlines the principle. The Court of Appeal stated that short, simple, non-repetitive questions should be used. Where intermediaries are engaged, defence counsel may be required by the court to follow an intervention by the intermediary. Defence counsel may then consider that it might be wiser not to cross-examine where questions may give rise to a possibility that the witness will give information that furthers the prosecution case and harms the defence. This may then place defence counsel in a difficult position, particularly where extremely vulnerable witnesses are involved. **[23–12]**

In *DPP v FN*[25] the appellant appealed on a number of points in relation to a conviction of sexual assault, one of which was that the trial judge erred in determining that the complainant was capable of giving 'an intelligent account and giving evidence at the **[23–13]**

---

21 Sarah-Jane Murphy, 'The story of "Zoe", one of the youngest sex-abuse cases ever heard in Irish courts' *The Irish Times* (Dublin, 24 April 2021) <https://www.irishtimes.com/the-story-of-zoe-oneof- the-youngest-sex-abuse-cases-ever-heard-in-irish-courts-1.4537355> accessed 13 October 2023.

22 *R v Lubemba* [2014] EWCA Crim 2064.

23 *DPP v VE* [2021] IECA 122 [86].

24 *DPP v MB* [2023] IECA 85 [42].

25 *DPP v FN* [2021] IECA 238; [2022] IESC 22. The complainant was approximately six at the time of the offence and eight at the time of trial. Examination in chief evidence was recorded under s 16(1)(b) of the Criminal Evidence Act 1992.

trial'.[26] The complainant was approximately six years of age at the time of the alleged offence and 20 months had elapsed between the recording of his testimony and the trial. Having viewed the recording, the investigating member felt that a further interview should be conducted. However, the mother of the complainant was not agreeable to this suggestion.[27] No further interview was taken and the complainant was not cross-examined. In refusing the appeal point, Birmingham P noted that no cross-examination had taken place and therefore it was not possible to establish whether meaningful cross-examination could not have taken place given the circumstances of the case:

> Unlike some other cases, it was not a question of a young complainant seeking to describe a prolonged pattern of behaviour where the basis [*sic*] narrative could get lost among the detail. It also seems relevant to us that the only account that the jury heard was the account to specialist interviewers. There was no cross-examination so the question of the ability to conduct a meaningful cross-examination being compromised by the lapse of time has not been established, though it is the case where the decision not to cross-examine was taken against the background of a particular timescale. The evidence in chief of the complainant from the meeting with the specialist interviewers was unchallenged, save for an assertion by defence counsel to the jury to the effect that the accused denied outright all allegations made against him in respect of complainant Y.[28]

[23–14] In the case of *DPP v PS*,[29] the difficulties of putting the defence case in respect of vulnerable witnesses were emphasised in relation to the trial judge's charge. The appeal was largely based on the mischaracterisation of the defendant's case by the trial judge in his charge. The defence had been that the sexual offences of the appellant alleged against his daughter had not occurred. In his charge, the trial judge had stated that, as it had never been put to the complainant that she was lying, the defence case must be that she was mistaken. Counsel had requisitioned the trial judge but the subsequent recharge to the jury had exacerbated the situation as the trial judge then stated that the defence counsel was submitting that the complainant was mistaken or lying. This formed the appeal point after conviction. The appellant had argued that defence counsel had done everything to put the case in a respectful way and to ensure not to attack anyone else's character.[30] In giving the judgment of the court, Kennedy J observed that during the judge's charge, a judge will, in general, direct the jury on the issues of fact for their determination, thus defining the issues and in that regard may remind the jury of the salient evidence. She also noted that the manner in which a judge does so is within the discretion of the judge, but the charge must be fair, balanced and impartial.[31] Kennedy J also stated:

> A judge is fully entitled to comment on the evidence, but it must be clear to the jury that they are the deciders of fact and comments should not be expressed which would render the charge unbalanced. A charge must, when considered as a whole, be fair. That is the overarching duty of the trial judge; to ensure fairness.[32]

[23–15] In the course of the judgment, Kennedy J noted the requirement to put the case, as outlined in English case law:

> It is of course a requirement that where it will be suggested to the jury that a witness is

---

26 *DPP v FN* [2021] IECA 238 [2].
27 *DPP v FN* [2021] IECA 238 [9].
28 ibid [26].
29 *DPP v PS* [2021] IECA 311.
30 ibid [16].
31 ibid [13].
32 ibid [14].

> not to be believed, that this is put to the witness in question. As stated by Lord Halsbury in *Browne v. Dunn* (1893) 6 R. 67 at 76–77 and as referred to in McGrath on Evidence second ed. at p.132: –
>
> > "To my mind nothing would be more absolutely unjust than not to cross-examine witnesses upon evidence which they have given, so as to give them notice, and to give them an opportunity often to defend their own character, and, not having given them such an opportunity, to ask the jury afterwards to disbelieve what they have said, although not one question has been directed either to their credit or to the accuracy of the facts they have deposed to."
>
> The text also quotes from the decision of *R v. Fenlon* (1980) 71 Cr App R. 307 at 313 which states: –
>
> > "It is the duty of counsel who intends to suggest that a witness is not telling the truth to make it clear to the witness in cross-examination that he challenges his veracity and to give the witness an opportunity of replying. It need not be done in minute detail, but it is the duty of counsel to make it plain to the witness, albeit he may be a co-defendant, that his evidence is not accepted and in what respects it is not accepted."
>
> Many counsel at the outset of cross-examination of this kind, make it clear to the witness that the allegations are denied, (as occurred in the present case) and during cross-examination, suggest to the witness that the alleged incidents never occurred.[33]

Kennedy J went on to observe: **[23–16]**

> Counsel must make it clear to the witness in any given case that the witness's veracity is under challenge, however, in certain circumstances it is not strictly necessary that the challenge be expressly stated in minute detail. We are persuaded in the circumstances that the judge's comment during the summing-up went beyond the legitimate comment by a judge and undermined the defence case significantly.[34]

The Court determined that the issue had not been rectified by the recharge and quashed the conviction. **[23–17]**

In *DPP v MS*,[35] the defendant appealed his conviction of charges of rape on the basis that the trial judge had erred in law in instructing the jury that a lesser weight should be attached to matters put to the jury by defence counsel as they had not been put to the relevant witnesses during trial. In this case, the complainant had given a description of the rape by her grandfather in a specialist interview. In referring to it in the closing speech, the defence counsel noted details that were not mentioned in the interview but that might have been expected in the circumstances such as vaginal pain, the weight of the defendant and that the complainant had described the offence as a sexual assault rather than rape albeit that she had described the elements of the offence of rape. **[23–18]**

The prosecution counsel had taken issue with this and submitted that that if these points were going to be asserted in the closing speech then they should have been put to the complainant. In her charge, the judge outlined the evidence factually detailing what had been put and what had not been put to the complainant and noted that it was for the jury to decide what weight to give to the evidence. The defence counsel submitted that this would create an impression that there was an obligation on the part of the defence to put certain matters but had not done so. **[23–19]**

---

33 ibid [20]–[22].
34 ibid [26]–[27].
35 *DPP v MS* [2023] IECA 208.

[23–20] The Court of Appeal dismissed the appeal deeming that it was correct the defence counsel could use the evidence given as a means of outlining what was omitted in terms of the detail that might have been expected from the act as outlined. It also added that the judge was restrained in her comments in outlining what actually had been said both in the speech of the defence and in the evidence given and had noted that it was a matter for the jury as to what weight to give the evidence.

[23–21] There was no difficulty with the judges charge and no obligation put on the defence counsel where no obligation actually existed. Giving the judgment of the Court, Birmingham P stated:

> It appears that prosecution counsel hoped for a stronger intervention, whether by way of reprimand or otherwise, than was forthcoming from the trial judge. Had that happened, it might well have given rise to difficulty in the context of the trial, in circumstances where, in our view, defence counsel had not overstepped the line. However, the judge's remarks could scarcely have been more restrained. It seems to us beyond doubt that the judge was entirely within her rights to draw the attention of the jury to the fact that the criticisms of the complainant for not dealing with certain matters in her narrative were in the context that those were not issues raised with her. We do not think it is an answer to that point to say, as defence counsel did, that these were issues canvassed during the course of the specialist interview, and, accordingly, there was no onus on the defence to deal with these issues and the judge should refrain from comment. For our part, we have no doubt that the judge might have chosen to address the issue in less restrained terms, but we are satisfied that the manner in which she did so is not one that can be criticised. Accordingly, we dismiss what is in effect the sole ground of appeal.'[36]

[23–22] Anecdotal evidence in trials, observed by the author, suggests that if defence counsel outline to the trial judge that cross-examination will be modified to ensure that the vulnerable witness is not unduly upset or if certain evidence is put in a limited manner to the complainant but more fully explored with other witnesses, these modifications may then be mentioned by the trial judge in the charge to the jury. This can then ensure that any relevant appeal point will not necessarily fail on the basis that the evidence was not fully challenged. However, in contrast to this, in certain cases, prosecution counsel may also be of the opinion, or be instructed, to challenge these kinds of approaches on the basis that if a matter is not fully explored with the complainant or if the challenge to the evidence is modified in some way through exploration via another witness, this will imply to the jury that the complainant is somehow not competent as a witness. These are issues which require further examination, particularly in light of the development of modifications to the manner of questioning which has been part of the recent initiative in the courts through the use of intermediaries. Perhaps 'the putting of the case' to the witness may be less of a traumatising issue if the manner in which it is put can be modified to suit the relevant witness. But it may also be possible to explore options as putting the case to other witnesses eg parents, social workers, teachers and facilitating that modification through the judge's charge. The courts in Ireland are not at a point similar to England and Wales where cross-examination questions are being submitted to the trial judge for approval in certain circumstances and so comparisons in this regard may have less value. It is open for the courts and practitioners in Ireland to find different means by which these issues may be resolved.

[36] ibid [14]-[15].

CHAPTER 24

RECORDED TESTIMONY

Introduction

The first use of s 16(1)(b) of the Criminal Evidence Act 1992[1] in a criminal prosecution **[24–01]**

[1] Criminal Evidence Act 1992 (CEA 1992), s 16, Videorecording as evidence at trial:
'(1) Subject to subsection (2)
(a) a videorecording of any evidence given, in relation to a relevant offence, by a person under 18 years of age through a live television link in proceedings under Part IA of the Criminal Procedure Act, 1967, and

in Ireland was in 2010.[2] Since then it has been widely used to assist vulnerable witnesses give recorded examination-in-chief testimony at trial. The provision has been extended through legislation such as the Criminal Law (Human Trafficking) (Amendment) Act 2013, the Criminal Law (Sexual Offences) Act 2017, and the Criminal Justice (Victims of Crime) Act 2017.

[24–02] The section provides that a recorded statement by children or persons with mental disorders who are victims or witnesses in relation to certain offences may be admissible as the examination-in-chief testimony of that person. The victim or witness must be available for cross-examination at trial. Cross-examination may be given via video link or from behind a screen under other provisions set out in the 1992 Act and which are available to the witness depending on his or her eligibility.

[24–03] Undoubtedly, the significant advantage of recorded testimony, even in the limited circumstances of s 16(1)(b) of the 1992 Act, is that it allows for the ingredients of the offence to be established ahead of the trial. This means that there will be less risk that a vulnerable witness might not be able to 'swear up' with all the attended evidential and psychological issues that would ensue. With recorded testimony, it is also hoped that, since the taking of evidence is done in a more relaxed environment away from and before the trial, the stress and trauma in recounting the details of the offences alleged are minimised.

Background

[24–04] Efforts to facilitate the evidence of children by allowing them to give their testimony by way of deposition go back to the Children Act 1908.[3] This provision was repealed by the Children Act 2001 but s 255[4] of that Act still allows for a child to give evidence

---

(b) a video recording of any statement made during an interview with a member of the Garda Síochána or any other person who is competent for the purpose –
(i) by a person who is under 18 years of age in relation to an offence of which he or she is a victim, or
(ii) by a person under 18 years of age (being a person other than the accused) in relation to –
(I) a sexual offence, or
(II) an offence under section 3(1), (2) or (3) of the Child Trafficking and Pornography Act 1998, or
(III) an offence under section 2, 4 or 7 of the Criminal Law (Human Trafficking) Act 2008,

shall be admissible at the trial of the offence as evidence of any fact stated therein of which direct oral evidence by him would be admissible:

Provided that, in the case of a video recording mentioned in paragraph (b), the person whose statement was video recorded is available at the trial for cross-examination.' (The original provision was commenced on 15 October 2008.)

2 See Miriam Delahunt, 'Video Evidence and s 16(1)(b) of the Criminal Evidence Act 1992' (2011) 16(1) Bar Review 2.

3 Children Act 1908, ss 28, 29.

4 Children Act 2001, s 255, Power to take deposition of child:
'(1) Without prejudice to section 4F of the Act of 1967, where a judge of the District Court is satisfied on the evidence of a registered medical practitioner that the attendance before a court of any child, in respect of whom an offence under this Part, or any offence mentioned in Schedule 1, is alleged to have been committed, would involve serious danger to the safety, health or wellbeing of the child, the judge may take the evidence either –
(a) by way of sworn deposition, or
(b) in case the evidence is to be given through a live television link pursuant to Part

by way of deposition under the Criminal Procedure Act 1967 process where the child's safety, health or wellbeing is at risk in relation to certain offences. The deposition procedure has not been used to any great extent for children as a facilitation measure for their evidence. It was the commencement and implementation of s 16(1)(b) of the Criminal Evidence Act 1992 which made recorded testimony for vulnerable witnesses widespread and this is a legislative provision which was drafted with the vulnerable witness directly in mind.[5]

Section 16 Criminal Evidence Act 1992

Section 16 of the Criminal Evidence Act 1992 does two things. Section 16(1)(a) provides a means by which a recording of a deposition of a person under 18 through a video link under Part 1A of the Criminal Procedure Act 1967 can be admitted at trial as evidence.[6] Section 16(1)(b) provides for a recording of a statement to be admitted at trial as examination in chief testimony in certain circumstances. **[24–05]**

Section 16 Criminal Evidence Act 1992
Videorecording as evidence at trial
Section 16:
(1) Subject to subsection (2) –
- (a) a videorecording of any evidence given, in relation to a relevant offence, by a person under 18 years of age through a live television link in proceedings under Part IA of the Criminal Procedure Act, 1967, and
- (b) a video recording of any statement made during an interview with a member of the Garda Síochána or any other person who is competent for the purpose –
  - (i) by a person who is under 18 years of age in relation to an offence of which he or she is a victim, or
  - (ii) by a person under 18 years of age (being a person other than the accused) in relation to –
    - (I) a sexual offence, or
    - (II) an offence under section 3(1), (2) or (3) of the Child Trafficking and Pornography Act 1998, or
    - (III) an offence under section 2, 4 or 7 of the Criminal Law (Human Trafficking) Act 2008,

shall be admissible at the trial of the offence as evidence of any fact stated therein of which direct oral evidence by him would be admissible:

III of the Criminal Evidence Act, 1992, or section 39 of the Criminal Justice Act, 1999, through such a link.

(2) The rules mentioned in section 4F(3) of the Act of 1967 shall apply and have effect in relation to the taking of evidence under subsection (1).

(3) A deposition taken under subsection (1) or a videorecording of evidence given by a child under paragraph (b) of that subsection shall be deemed to have been taken under section 4F of the said Act of 1967, and section 4G (admissibility of deposition or videorecording) shall apply and have effect accordingly.

(4) Notwithstanding the provisions of this section, in any criminal proceedings for an offence under this Part or any offence mentioned in Schedule 1, the evidence of a child under 14 years of age may be taken or received otherwise than on oath or affirmation if the court is satisfied that the child is capable of giving an intelligible account of events which are relevant to those proceedings.

(5) If any child whose evidence is taken as aforesaid makes a statement material in the proceedings concerned which he or she knows to be false or does not believe to be true, the child shall be guilty of an offence and on being found guilty shall be liable to be dealt with as if he or she had been guilty of perjury.

5 Dáil Deb 3 March 1992, vol 416, col 1284.
6 See Chapter 6.

Provided that, in the case of a videorecording mentioned in paragraph (b), the person whose statement was videorecorded is available at the trial for cross examination.

(2)

(a) Any such videorecording or any part thereof shall not be admitted in evidence as aforesaid if the court is of opinion that in the interests of justice the videorecording concerned or that part ought not to be so admitted.

(b) In considering whether in the interests of justice such videorecording or any part thereof ought not to be admitted in evidence, the court shall have regard to all the circumstances, including any risk that its admission will result in unfairness to the accused or, if there is more than one, to any of them.

(3) In estimating the weight, if any, to be attached to any statement contained in such a videorecording regard shall be had to all the circumstances from which any inference can reasonably be drawn as to its accuracy or otherwise.

(4) In this section 'statement' includes any representation of fact, whether in words or otherwise.

Sections 16(1)(a) and 16(1)(b) Recordings – 'Shall Be Admissible'

[24–06] The use of the word 'shall' is significant in terms of the obligations to the court to consider the recording admissible unless it is contrary to the interests of justice. In his ruling in the case of *DPP v FE*,[7] Hunt J stated it gave the section a 'mandatory flavour'. This was mentioned in the Court of Appeal judgment of *DPP v JD* where Birmingham J stated[8]:

> It is to be noted that s. 16(1) of the Criminal Evidence Act 1992 provides that a video recording shall be admissible unless the Court is of opinion that in the interests of justice, the video recording ought not to be admitted. In the case of *DPP v. FE* (Bill No. 84/2013), Hunt J. as quoted in the paper "Recorded Evidence for Vulnerable Witnesses, Practical Issues at Trial", delivered by Michael Bowman SC and Dr. Miriam Delahunt BL, at an Irish Criminal Bar Association seminar had said:
>
> > "[t]he use of the word "shall" in the section gives the provisions a directory or mandatory flavour, in that where the age or mental handicap qualifications are met, the relevant evidence shall then be given by the means specified in the section unless it shall not be in the interests of justice to do so."[9]

[24–07] In the case of *DPP v SA*,[10] Kennedy J noted:

> Furthermore, the section is directory in terms, that is to say, such evidence shall be admissible, unless a court is of the opinion that in the interests of justice the video recording or part thereof ought not be admitted.[11]

---

7 Although not a reported judgment, *DPP v FE (Faisal Ellahi)*, November 2015, is an extremely significant case as it involved the first documented use of a 'ground rules hearing'. See Caroline Biggs and Miriam Delahunt, 'Prosecutorial Challenges – Vulnerable Witnesses' (2017) 22(1) Bar Review 23, 24.

8 *DPP v JD* [2018] IECA 232.

9 ibid [7].

10 *DPP v SA* [2020] IECA 60.

11 ibid [48].

Interpretation of 'Victim' Under s 12 Criminal Evidence Act 1992

Part III, 'Evidence in Criminal Proceedings', s 12 of the Criminal Evidence Act 1992, as amended by the Criminal Justice (Victims of Crime) Act 2017 states: [24–08]

> '[V]ictim' means –
> (a) a natural person, other than an accused, who has suffered harm, including physical, mental or emotional harm, or economic loss, which was directly caused by an offence, and
> (b) where the death of a person referred to in paragraph (a) is caused directly by the offence, a family member, provided that the family member concerned has not been charged with, or is not under investigation for, an offence in connection with the death of the person.
>
> (2) The application of this Part is not dependent on the commission of an offence having to be established (nor is it dependent on establishing whether the person concerned suffered any harm caused by an offence).

Eligibility Categories – Recorded Testimony Under s 16(1)(b) Criminal Evidence Act 1992

Section 16(1)(b)(i) – a person under 18 in relation to any offence of which he or she is a victim

Section 16(1)(b)(i): [24–09]

> (1) Subject to subsection (2) –
> a video recording of any statement made during an interview with a member of the Garda Síochána or any other person who is competent for the purpose –
> (i) by a person who is under 18 years of age in relation to an offence of which he or she is a victim, or

The legislation facilitates the recorded evidence of a person under 18 who is the victim of any offence. [24–10]

Section 16(1)(b)(ii) – witness under 18 in relation to certain offences

Section 16(1)(b)(ii): [24–11]

> (1) Subject to subsection (2) –
> (b) a video recording of any statement made during an interview with a member of the Garda Síochána or any other person who is competent for the purpose –
> (ii) by a person under 18 years of age (being a person other than the accused) in relation to –
> (I) a sexual offence,[12] or

---

[12] Criminal Evidence Act 1992, s 2. 'Interpretation'
'"sexual offence" means rape, sexual assault (within the meaning of section 2 of the Criminal Law (Rape) (Amendment) Act 1990), aggravated sexual assault (within the meaning of section 3 of that Act), rape under section 4 of that Act or an offence under—
(a) section 3 or 6 of the Criminal Law Amendment Act 1885,
(b) section 5 of the Criminal Law (Sexual Offences) Act 1993,
(c) section 6 of the Criminal Law (Sexual Offences) Act 1993,
(d) section 1 or 2 of the Punishment of Incest Act 1908,
(e) section 4A or 5A of the Child Trafficking and Pornography Act 1998,

(II) an offence under section 3(1), (2) or (3) of the Child Trafficking and Pornography Act 1998,[13] or
(III) an offence under section 2, 4 or 7 of the Criminal Law (Human Trafficking) Act 2008[14]

Section 16 Criminal Evidence Act 1992/s 19 eligibility due to mental disorder

[24–12] As s 19 applies to s 16, a person with a mental disorder as defined under the Criminal Justice Act 1993 is also eligible.[15] A mental disorder as defined in s 5 of that Act 'includes a mental illness, mental disability, dementia or any disease of the mind'.

[24–13] In *DPP v O'Driscoll*[16] the defence objected both to the use by a prosecution witness of video link under s 13 of the Criminal Evidence Act 1992 and an intermediary under s 14 of the same Act which had been granted by the trial judge. The witness had sustained an acquired brain injury and the Court of Appeal examined whether his condition came under the definition of mental disorder as set out in s 19 of the Criminal Evidence Act 1992. Birmingham P noted:

> While neither party to this appeal opened authority to the Court addressing the proper construction of the term "mental disorder" as it appears in the provisions under consideration, the definition now appearing in s. 5 of the 1993 Act is wide, and falls to be addressed in light of the purpose of those sections in which it appears: "a mental illness, mental disability, dementia or any disease of the mind".[17]

[24–14] In outlining the evidence of the witness' difficulties, the Court of Appeal determined that the acquired brain injury had resulted in a

> subsequent limitation on his powers of comprehension and articulation which, on any version, entitled the trial judge to conclude that [the witness] suffered from a mental disability. The combination of that finding and the evidence that his ability to respond to questions in a court environment would be impaired more than justified the judge in exercising her discretion to enable him give his evidence by video link. The same evidence established the power to direct that his evidence be given with the assistance of an intermediary, and the propriety of exercising that power in the circumstances.[18]

(f) section 249 of The Children Act 2001,
(g) the Criminal Law (Sexual Offences) Act 2006, or
(h) section 3, 4, 5, 6, 7 or 8 of the Criminal Law (Sexual Offences) Act 2017,
excluding an attempt to commit any such offence;'

13 Child Trafficking and Pornography Act 1998, s 3 'Child trafficking and taking, etc., child for sexual exploitation'

14 Criminal Law (Human Trafficking) Act 2008, s 2.–'Trafficking, etc., of children'.
Criminal Law (Human Trafficking) Act 2008,s 4 'Trafficking of persons other than children.'
Criminal Law (Human Trafficking) Act 2008,s 7 'Jurisdiction'.

15 Criminal Evidence Act 1992, s 19: 'Application of Part III to persons with mental handicap.
The references in sections 14, 14B, 15 and 16 to a person under 18 years of age shall include references to a person with a mental disorder, within the meaning of section 5 of the Criminal Justice Act 1993 who has reached the age concerned.'

16 *DPP v O'Driscoll* [2022] IECA 4.

17 ibid [28].

18 ibid [29].

Accused is Ineligible for Recorded Testimony Under s 16 Criminal Evidence Act 1992

Section 16(1)(a) Criminal Evidence Act 1992

Section 16(1)(a) of the Criminal Evidence Act 1992 states: **[24–15]**

> A videorecording of any evidence given, in relation to a relevant offence, by a person under 18 years of age through a live television link in proceedings under Part IA of the Criminal Procedure Act, 1967, [...] shall be admissible at the trial of the offence as evidence of any fact stated therein of which direct oral evidence by him would be admissible:
>
> Provided that, in the case of a videorecording mentioned in paragraph (b), the person whose statement was videorecorded is available at the trial for cross examination[.]
>
> (2) (a) Any such videorecording or any part thereof shall not be admitted in evidence as aforesaid if the court is of opinion that in the interests of justice the videorecording concerned or that part ought not to be so admitted.
>
> (b) In considering whether in the interests of justice such videorecording or any part thereof ought not to be admitted in evidence, the court shall have regard to all the circumstances, including any risk that its admission will result in unfairness to the accused or, if there is more than one, to any of them.
>
> (3) In estimating the weight, if any, to be attached to any statement contained in such a videorecording regard shall be had to all the circumstances from which any inference can reasonably be drawn as to its accuracy or otherwise.
>
> (4) In this section "statement" includes any representation of fact, whether in words or otherwise.

[24–16] At the time of the drafting of s 16(1)(a) of the Criminal Evidence Act 1992, the use of video link at trial was only legislatively available under s 13 of the Criminal Evidence Act 1992 and this provision explicitly excludes the accused.[19] Since then s 39 of the Criminal Justice Act 1999 has been commenced for persons in fear or who have been subject to intimidation but the section also excludes the accused. Therefore it would appear that the accused is excluded under these provisions. However, in recent years, the development of a number of video conference options such as Zoom or Skype or Pexip which facilitate recording could potentially be interpreted as a 'live television link'. Albeit that s 16(1)(a) of the Criminal Evidence Act 1992 is rarely used, it requires clarification as to whether this provision might possibly be available to the accused under the parameters of this section and the Criminal Procedure Act 1967. In addition, s 255 provides that a child may be able to have a deposition of his or her testimony taken and in certain circumstances admitted at trial. This may, in certain circumstances, be appropriate for a child defendant.

Section 16(1)(b) Criminal Evidence Act 1992

[24–17] This section applies either to the victim or to a person 'other than the accused' and the accused is thereby excluded.

---

[19] See Chapter 29

Admission of Recording Under s 16(1)(b) Criminal Evidence Act 1992

[24–18] Section 16(1)(b) now allows for a witness statement to be applied for and admitted as evidence under certain circumstances. A witness statement is one that is generally taken prior to any court proceedings. It is usually but not always taken in a Garda station and will, depending on the age of the witness, be subject to the penalties of s 21(2)(b) of the Criminal Justice Act 1984.[20] This means that the witness, having had the statement read back to him or her and having had an opportunity to amend the statement prior to signing it, will be liable to any penalty if it is discovered that the statement contains elements that are deliberately incorrect or untrue. The age of criminal responsibility in Ireland would suggest that a prosecution under s 21(2)(b) of the Criminal Justice Act 1984 is unlikely.[21]

Who May Conduct the Recording

[24–19] 'A member of the Garda Síochána or any other person who is competent for the purpose' may conduct the recorded interview. A member of An Garda Síochána is automatically qualified. The court, then, has responsibility for deciding who else is competent to conduct the interview, but this must be decided post recording during its application to be considered examination in chief testimony.

[24–20] Since the commencement of s 16(1)(b)[22] of the Criminal Evidence Act 1992 and the admission of recorded testimony under that section, a responsibility to assess and monitor competence is now given to the Specialist Interviewers.[23] These trained interviewers conduct the recorded record examination in chief evidence in anticipation of its admission at trial. The *Good Practice Guidelines*[24] were drafted in 2003 as procedural guidance for use of the s 16(1)(b) of the Criminal Evidence Act 1992.

---

[20] Criminal Justice Act, 1984, s 21(11):

'Where –

(a) a statement is tendered in evidence by virtue of this section, and

(b) the person by whom the statement was made has stated in it anything which he knew to be false or did not believe to be true, he shall be guilty of an offence and shall be liable on summary conviction to a fine not exceeding €2,500 or to imprisonment for a term not exceeding twelve months or to both, or on conviction on indictment to a fine not exceeding €5,000 or to imprisonment for a term not exceeding five years or to both.'

[21] The Children Act 2001, s 52 (as amended by Criminal Justice Act 2006, s 129): 'The age of criminal responsibility is outlined in Section 52 of The Children Act 2001 (as amended by Section 129 of the Criminal Justice Act 2006) and states that the age of criminal responsibility is 12 years. No child under the age of 12 years can be charged with an offence. However, 10- and 11-year-olds may be charged with very serious offences, such as unlawful killing, a rape offence or aggravated sexual assault. The Director of Public Prosecutions must give consent for any child under the age of 14 years to be charged.'

[22] Criminal Evidence Act 1992, s 16, Videorecording as evidence at trial.

[23] A Specialist Interviewer is the term which denotes a member of the garda or a person competent for the purpose who conducts a recorded interview with the appropriate witness for admission at trial at a later date under s 16(1)(b) Criminal Evidence Act 1992.

[24] An Garda Síochána, *Good Practice Guidelines for Persons involved in Video Recording interviews with complainants under 14 years of age (or with intellectual disability) for Evidential Purposes in accordance with Section 16(1)(b) of the Criminal Evidence Act, 1992, in cases involving Sexual and/or Violent Offences* (July 2003).

The policy document *Garda Síochána Policy on the Investigation of Sexual Crime* states: [24–21]

> There is an absolute obligation on investigating members to refer the interviewing of such complainants to trained Specialist Interviewers. Specialist Interviewers have undergone intensive training and are deemed competent to interview such complainants. Members (who are not trained Specialist Interviewers) will not attempt to take a statement from a person who is under 14 years of age or a person with an intellectual disability who complains of a sexual offence or an offence involving violence or threats of violence, except in exceptional urgent circumstances. Such exceptional urgent circumstances involve the imminent risk of loss of life, or injury to the health of any person, harm to the health or welfare of a child or an offender absconding.[25]

Training for Specialist Interviewers is conducted in Templemore Garda College.[26] Members of An Garda Siochana and social workers have been trained to conduct recordings under the legislation. [24–22]

Role of the Specialist Interviewer

The role and functions of the Specialist Interviewer are outlined in the Good Practice Guidelines[27] The Specialist Interviewers work as two-person team and communicate with each other through earpiece and microphone. One Specialist Interviewer conducts the interview with the complainant/witness in the suite and will be visible on camera. The second Specialist Interviewer is situated in a room outside the suite and will be off camera. He or she manages the technological aspects of the interview, such as ensuring it is being recorded correctly as well as checking sound levels etc. In addition, the Second Interview supervises the progress of the interview taking notes as necessary. If there are any questions that need to be asked or if any answers need clarification, the second Specialist Interviewer can raise these as appropriate. [24–23]

The Specialist Interviewer's role is a complex one in that his or her interview with the witness is a statement taken as soon as possible after disclosure. However, the objective in taking it is also that it may serve as examination in chief testimony if the statement is admitted under s 16(1)(b) of the Criminal Evidence Act 1992. The Specialist Interviewer must therefore try and gather as much relevant information as possible but also ensure that no leading questions prejudice any evidence taken. In addition, non- disclosure by the complainant is outlined in the Good Practice Guidelines as an acceptable outcome.[28] [24–24]

The role of the Specialist Interviewer was somewhat addressed in the case of *DPP v* [24–25]

---

25 *Garda Síochána Policy on the Investigation of Sexual Crime, Crimes Against Children and Child Welfare* (2nd edn, 2013) para 32.5, 70.

26 An Garda Síochána *Crime and Specialist Training within An Garda Síochána,* www.garda.ie/en/careers/the-garda-college/crime-and-specialist-training-within-an-garda-siochana.html accessed 13 October 2023.

27 An Garda Síochána, *Good Practice Guidelines for Persons involved in Video Recording Interviews with Complainants under 14 Years of Age (or with Intellectual Disability) for Evidential Purposes in Accordance with Section 16(1)(b) of the Criminal Evidence Act, 1992, in Cases Involving Sexual and/or Violent Offences* (July 2003), para.2.25, 19.

28 An Garda Síochána, *Good Practice Guidelines for Persons involved in Video Recording Interviews with Complainants under 14 Years of Age (or with Intellectual Disability) for Evidential Purposes in Accordance with Section 16(1)(b) of the Criminal Evidence Act, 1992, in Cases Involving Sexual and/or Violent Offences* (July 2003), 20.

MB.[29] The conviction was successfully appealed on the basis that when cross examined at trial, the young complainant had said that the offence of sexual assault had not occurred. In the course of the appeal, the appellant questioned the manner in which the Specialist Interviewers had conducted the recorded interviews. In rejecting this point, Kennedy J stated:

> Insofar as the appellant seeks to make the point that the manner in which the Child Specialist Interviewers conducted the interview with the child was unsatisfactory as it is said there was a general failure to explore or contextualise his complaints and that his younger brother ought to have been interviewed. There is little doubt that the appellant would have complained if indeed the interviewers had explored the allegations further. It seems to us that the interview was conducted in a sensitive and free-flowing manner and no realistic complaint can arise therefrom. Insofar as it is said that the younger boy ought to have been interviewed, he was a child of four years of age who had made no disclosure.[30]

[24–26] Guidance also states that the Specialist Interviewer's duties should not overlap with that of a Family Liaison Officer:

> Where possible Specialist Interviewers will not be engaged as Family Liaison Officers and then only when trained to do so, and will not be used as a Family Liaison Officer in any case where they have conducted an interview. Specialist Interviewers, where possible, should not be nominated for training as Family Liaison Officers.[31]

Consent for Recording

[24–27] The *Good Practice Guidelines* state that a videorecording should only be made with the consent of the complainant. The *Guidelines* state:

> Where a complainant is mature enough to understand the concept, he/she should be given an explanation of the purpose and possible uses of the video recording. In addition, so that the complainant is fully informed to a level appropriate to his/her age and understanding, he/she should be consulted about certain aspects of the planning and preparation for the interview (*viz.* when, where, who *etc.*). A video recording should only be made with the consent of the complainant.
>
> In all cases, it should be explained to the complainant that the video recording may be shown to the court instead of the complainant giving his/her account directly to the court in the event that the case is prosecuted.
>
> When the complainant is not capable of understanding the reasons for making the video recording, the interview team should consult with the parents/carers. However, care should be taken to guard against the possibility of anyone who may be implicated in abuse of the complainant exerting any pressure on the complainant not to give his/her account.[32]

---

29 *DPP v MB* [2023] IECA 85 [42].

30 ibid [62].

31 *Garda Síochána Policy on the Investigation of Sexual Crime, Crimes Against Children and Child Welfare* (2nd edn, 2013) para 33.3.6, 72.

32 An Garda Síochána, *Good Practice Guidelines for Persons involved in Video Recording Interviews with Complainants under 14 Years of Age (or with Intellectual Disability) for Evidential Purposes in Accordance with Section 16(1)(b) of the Criminal Evidence Act, 1992, in Cases Involving Sexual and/or Violent Offences* (July 2003) 'Does the complainant need to agree to be video recorded?' paras 2.34, 2.36, 21.

In the case of *DPP v FN*[33] the complainant was six years of age at the time of the offence and the defendant was 11 years of age. The complainant had been interviewed and his testimony recorded. In the course of the judgment, Birminham P noted: **[24–28]**

> It appears that having viewed the interview, the investigating member, Detective Carol Quinn, felt that a further interview should be conducted, but the mother of the complainant was not agreeable to this suggestion.[34]

There is no information in the judgment as to why this was the case, but no further interview was taken. The judgment also outlines that the complainant attended a Sexual Assault Treatment Unit with his mother after the disclosure had been made, but he refused to be fully medically examined.[35] It is dangerous to speculate as to the reason why but given the age of the complainant, further assessment and questioning may have caused stress and upset. Ultimately, the defendant was convicted on one count of sexual assault but there was a disagreement on a charge of s 4 rape of a second complainant. The appellant was unsuccessful on all grounds of the appeal. **[24–29]**

Witness Must Be Available for Cross-Examination

A condition of s 16(1)(b) is that the witness must be 'available for cross-examination' at trial.[36] The legislation does not require that the complainant be cross-examined but that he or she must be available for cross-examination. There is no definition of the phrase 'available for cross-examination' within the section itself and to what extent the competency of the witness means that he or she is available for cross-examination is a question for the trial judge. **[24–30]**

The term 'available for cross-examination' also appears in other legislation providing for the admission of statements in circumstances where the witness resiles from their statement. Section 16 of the Criminal Justice Act 2006 was intended primarily for use in gangland crime where witnesses may be intimidated or persuaded to retract statements made to the gardaí or others.[37] Its use was challenged in the case of *Rattigan v DPP*[38] on the basis of retrospectivity of the section and its application to the appellant's case.[39] The offence had taken place in 2001 and the trial took place in 2009 after delays which had been the subject of judicial review proceedings. In examining that particular section, the Court of Criminal Appeal noted: **[24–31]**

> A provision such as s 16 therefore provides a partial remedy for a real problem and in doing so removes, or at least reduces, the incentive for anyone to seek to encourage a witness not to testify. While counsel for the applicant argued that the court should approach the section on the basis that it was a very powerful provision since a statement so admitted could not be cross-examined, this is a necessary consequence of the admission of any out of court statement under an exception to the hearsay rule. Indeed, under s 16 the opposing party is in a somewhat better position since the witness must be available for

---

33 *DPP v FN* [2021] IECA 238; [2022] IESC 22.
34 *DPP v FN* [2021] IECA 238 [9].
35 ibid.
36 Criminal Evidence Act 1992, s 16(1).
37 Prior to the commencement of s 16(1)(b) of the Criminal Evidence Act 1992, the 2006 provision was unusually applied in the child sexual abuse case of *DPP v O'Brien* [2011] IR 273.
38 [2013] 2 IR 221.
39 See also Liz Heffernan, *Evidence in Criminal Trials* (2nd edn, Bloomsbury Professional 2020) paras 9.30, 9.31.

> cross-examination, and the opposing party can seek to exploit the witness's uncertainty, or professed lack of memory, if he or she thinks it desirable. That possibility is not available in other exceptions to the hearsay rule. The fact that evidence admitted under the rule may be effective, and even powerful in some cases, is not itself a reason to approach the section with any scepticism.[40]

[24–32] Definitions of the phrase in respect of s 16 of the Criminal Justice Act 2006 have reduced the meaning to physical presence. The phrase 'available for cross-examination' in relation to s 16 of the 2006 Act was defined by the Court of Criminal Appeal in a subsequent application for leave to appeal to the Supreme Court. O'Donnell J stated:

> The concept of making someone available for cross-examination is well understood in the law: it means that a witness is present, and can be called and cross-examined if desired. Whether any such cross-examination takes place, or is useful, is normally a matter for the cross-examining party. It is in truth difficult to see what other interpretation can be given to the words 'available for cross-examination' than that the witness is present and in Court, and can be called, and is therefore available.[41]

[24–33] In respect of s 16(1)(b), the witness would view his or her recorded testimony at a time and place appropriate to the scheduling of the trial.[42] In some cases, this may raise a concern as to what the witness is remembering when being cross-examined, and whether he or she is able to remember the incident itself or only the events as described on the video, as per the English cases of *R v Powell*[43] and *R v Malicki*[44] where these issues arose.

[24–34] This issue has been addressed by the Court of Appeal in the judgment of *DPP v MT*.[45] The Court of Criminal Appeal noted the meaning of 'available for cross-examination' and the differences between s 16 of the Criminal Justice Act 2006 and s 16(1)(b) of the Criminal Evidence Act 1992. Ní Raifeartaigh J noted:

> We consider it important to point out that the context is entirely different to that which obtains in cases arising under s.16 of the Criminal Justice Act 2006. This Court has considered what it means for a witness to be "available for cross-examination" in the context of that particular statutory regime in cases such as *People (DPP) v Rattigan* [2013] 2 IR 221 and *People (DPP) v. D.K. and M.K.* [2021] IECA 32. However, as Murray J. explained in the latter case, the very reason for the introduction of the provision at issue in those cases was to deal with witnesses who refuse to give evidence, including under cross-examination, and that it would therefore undermine the legislative intention if a case were to be withdrawn from a jury on the basis that the witness was refusing to answer questions:
>
>> "It is the purpose of the provision to enable the admission of statements in that very situation.... Nothing in s.16 supports the proposition that it is inoperative in such circumstances and, if it did, the trial Judge would not have made an order under the provision in the first place. For as long as the section remains on the statute

40 *Rattigan v DPP* [2013] 2 IR 221 [229]. The judgment of the Court was delivered by O'Donnell J.

41 *People (DPP) v Rattigan* [2015] IECCA 7 [8].

42 See An Garda Síochána, *Good Practice Guidelines for Persons involved in Video Recording Interviews with Complainants under 14 Years of Age (or with Intellectual Disability) for Evidential Purposes in Accordance with Section 16(1)(b) of the Criminal Evidence Act, 1992, in Cases Involving Sexual and/or Violent Offences* (July 2003) 9; *DPP v VE* [2021] IECA 122 [27]; Caroline Biggs and Miriam Delahunt, 'Prosecutorial Challenges – Vulnerable Witnesses' (2017) 22(1) Bar Review 23, 25.

43 *R v Powell* [2006] 1 CAR 31.

44 *R v Malicki* [2009] EWCA Crim 365.

45 *DPP v MT* [2023] IECA 65.

> book, the issuing of a direction on this basis would fundamentally undermine the legislative framework put in place by the Oireachtas".

> However, the present context is entirely different, and we are of the view that it is important to bear that in mind when considering the intended effect of s.16(1)(b) of the 1992 Act.[46]

How the phrase 'available for cross-examination' is construed under s 16(1)(b) of the 1992 Act may present distinct difficulties for the trial process in circumstances where a complainant or witness may be physically present but perhaps is reluctant to answer any questions or is unable to remember due to a possibly significant delay between the recording of the statement and the subsequent trial. However, it appears that the general standard that the courts have accepted in relation to its definition is quite low. Prior to the case of *DPP v MT*[47] where a witness who has had his or her recorded statement admitted under s 16(1)(b) testified that he or she did not remember, as occurred in *DPP v SA*,[48] the courts seemed to have accepted this, even though meaningful cross-examination is, to all intents and purposes, limited. **[24–35]**

The constitutional right to cross-examination, particularly in the context of the cross-examination of vulnerable witnesses, has been underlined in the cases of *DPP v MT*[49] and *DPP v MB*.[50] In respect of *DPP v MT*,[51] where there had been an interval of approximately five years between the recording of the interview and the complainant being cross-examined, Ní Raifeartaigh J stated: **[24–36]**

> Unfortunately, if delay occurs, for whatever reason, *to the point where the child has little or no recollection of the event(s) in question*, and is relying almost exclusively, or indeed entirely, on what he or she saw on the videorecording, cross-examination loses its fundamental essence. In such a situation i.e., where the child has no remaining memory of the event(s), the right to cross-examine is futile; the child is now answering questions based on what he or she said or saw on the videorecording, not on memories of the event itself.[52]

However, *DPP v MT*[53] may be distinguished from *DPP v SA*[54] as it involved a complainant who stated explicitly in cross-examination that she did not remember the event itself. The difficulties in *DPP v SA*[55] concerned the issue of recall of details surrounding the offences but not a declaration that the offences themselves were not remembered. Section 16(1)(b) of the Criminal Evidence Act 1992 facilitates the evidence of children and persons with an intellectual disability, and memory recall may be particularly difficult for these witnesses. The phrase 'available for cross-examination' should perhaps be approached in a more nuanced fashion although the case law has, as mentioned, accepted a low threshold in respect of the condition of the section. **[24–37]**

In *DPP v SA*[56] the interval between the recording of the statement and the commencement of the trial was approximately seven years. As mentioned previously, **[24–38]**

---

46 ibid [83].
47 *DPP v MT* 2023 IECA 65.
48 *DPP v SA* [2020] IECA 60 [122]–[125].
49 *DPP v MT* [2023] IECA 65 [81].
50 *DPP v MB* [2023] IECA 85 [41]–[42].
51 *DPP v MT* [2023] IECA 65.
52 ibid [81] (emphasis in original).
53 ibid.
54 *DPP v SA* [2020] IECA 60 [122]–[125].
55 *DPP v SA* [2020] IECA 60 [122]–[125].
56 *DPP v SA* [2020] IECA 60.

one of the appeal points was that a significant proportion of the responses of the complainants was that they did not remember or could not recall the time surrounding the offences in question. This is not surprising as the complainants were approximately 10 and 12 years of age when the recordings were taken and 17 and 19 years old respectively when the matter came on for trial.[57] The appeal points failed. Kennedy J stated:

> Moreover, this was a case where the appellant denied the allegations in broad terms. It was not one, as put by the respondent, which was date or event specific. Furthermore, it was common case that he resided with the children and their mother at the relevant locations. It is clear from the transcript of the proceedings before the Central Criminal Court that the cross-examination of each complainant was skilful and fulsome. We are not satisfied that the passage of time rendered the process unfair or impacted negatively on the ability of the appellant to cross-examine the witnesses.[58]

Remembering the Incident / Remembering the s 16(1)(b) Recording

[24–39] The case of *DPP v FN*[59] came on for trial as expediently as possible, involving as it did complainants who were approximately four and six years old and a defendant who was 14 years of age at the time of the alleged incidents. The matter came on for trial approximately 20 months after the alleged sexual offences had taken place and the statements recorded. The jury disagreed in respect of the charge against the younger complainant but returned a guilty verdict in respect of the offence of sexual assault against the older complainant (Y), who was eight years old at the time of trial. The conviction was appealed and in addition to whether the behaviour alleged could be said to be defined as a sexual assault (the offence involved the defendant smacking the bare bottom of the complainant with his hand) the appeal points included the following: first, that the conventional manner of refreshing the memory of such a young child through the playing of the recorded statement would risk him remembering the video and not the incident itself thus rendering cross-examination impossible; and, second, that the trial judge should not have permitted the playing of a DVD of an interview as the direct evidence of the complainant where there had been a significant delay of some 20 months between the making of the recording and the playing of the recording at trial.

[24–40] The Court of Appeal dismissed the appeal. Among the considerations which influenced the Court's conclusion that the delay had not been prejudicial was the fact that no cross-examination had been conducted and so the question of the ability to conduct a meaningful cross-examination being compromised by the lapse of time had not been established. However, it did note that it was the case that the decision not to cross-examine was taken against the background of a particular timescale. The Court stated that, overall, it had not been convinced that the judge fell into error in declining to halt the trial by reason of the lapse of time.[60]

---

57 The delay in the matter coming on for trial had occurred for various reasons, including the defendant being outside the jurisdiction as well as two trial dates not proceeding for procedural reasons: *DPP v SA* [2020] IECA 60 [17]–[18].

58 *DPP v SA* [2020] IECA 60.

59 *DPP v FN* [2021] IECA 238; (The case was appealed to the Supreme Court in relation to the definition of sexual assault *DPP v FN* [2022] IESC 22).

60 *DPP v FN* [2021] IECA 238 [26].

In this case, the specialist interviewer had requested a second interview, but this had been refused by the complainant's mother. In a situation where a second interview was requested, one might speculate that clarity was being sought in relation to the evidence. This was particularly relevant where greater detail of the event might inform any motivation and intent in respect of the nature of the offence. In a situation where the witness is very young, where the nature of the evidence might be problematic, and where a significant amount of time has elapsed, a defence counsel may not wish to cross-examine the witness. Where a witness is not cross-examined, it is for the jury to consider the weight of the evidence which is not challenged. This raises the possibility that the untested evidence will be given more weight simply because it has not been challenged.[61] The fact that a very young witness, who may have particular difficulties remembering, will still be deemed 'available for cross-examination' is problematic. **[24–41]**

This point was also highlighted in the case previously mentioned, *DPP v MT*.[62] The case related to the cross-examination of a child complainant in a sexual offence trial where four-and-a-half years had elapsed between the videorecording of the child's testimony (when she was aged six) and the cross-examination at the trial at which the appellant was convicted (when she was aged 11). The appellant was convicted of one count of sexual assault and sentenced to four years imprisonment. During cross-examination the complainant had conceded that that she had little memory of the incident which was the subject of the charge and was relying upon what she had seen in the video-recording of her interview. As in the cases of *DPP v FN*,[63] *R v Powell*[64] and *R v Malicki*[65] were referred to in the application of the appellant at trial and in the appeal. The issues before the Court were whether in those circumstances the appellant could exercise his lawful entitlement to cross-examine, whether the child's evidence should have been left to the jury, and whether the trial was fair. **[24–42]**

As outlined by Ní Raifeartaigh J, the case raised fundamental questions about the exercise of an accused person's right to cross-examine in circumstances involving a young child and where there is a significant delay between the making of the videorecording of the child's interview and the trial. The Court of Appeal ultimately allowed the appeal and quashed the conviction. In the judgment of the Court, Ní Raifeartaigh J stated: **[24–43]**

> A decision under s.16(1)(b) of the 1992 Act (if there is a challenge to the admissibility of the videorecorded evidence) is of course conducted in the first instance before the child's evidence is played to the jury, but the decision can be re-visited by a trial judge after the witness has been cross-examined (or an attempt to do so has taken place), and there is nothing to prevent a trial judge from ruling the evidence inadmissible at that stage if persuaded that there is a risk of unfairness or that to do so is in the interests of justice (the jurisdiction referred to in Malicki). In a case where the child's evidence is the only evidence of the alleged crime, the practical effect in terms of the ultimate outcome will be the same although by means of a slightly different procedural mechanism to the PO'C jurisdiction. In our view, the second of these mechanisms (i.e. ruling the evidence of the child inadmissible by applying the tests in s.16(1)(b)) is or would have been the appropriate procedural mechanism to be used in the present case.[66]

---

61 *DPP (Kelly) v Burke* [2015] 2 IR 651, 663–64; 666–67.

62 *DPP v MT* [2023] IECA 65.

63 *DPP v FN* [2021] IECA 238; (The case was appealed to the Supreme Court in relation to the definition of sexual assault *DPP v FN* [2022] IESC 22).

64 *R v Powell* [2006] 1 CAR 31.

65 *R v Malicki* [2009] EWCA Crim 365.

66 *DPP v MT* [2023] IECA 65 [98].

Video Recording Inadmissible if Admission is Not in the Interests of Justice /Court to have Regard to all the Circumstances

[24–44] The videorecording will not be admitted if the court is of the opinion that it is not in the interests of justice to do so. In considering this, the court shall have regard to all the circumstances, including any risk that the admission of the videorecording will result in unfairness to the accused.

Inference Which Can Be Reasonably Drawn as to Accuracy

[24–45] Section 16(3) states that:

> In estimating the weight, if any, to be attached to any statement contained in such a video recording regard shall be had to all the circumstances from which any inference can reasonably be drawn as to its accuracy or otherwise.

Statement includes any representation of fact whether in words or otherwise

[24–46] Section 16(4) states:

> In this section "statement" includes any representation of fact, whether in words or otherwise.

Breaches in respect of the recording

[24–47] Unfortunately, there appears to be little relevant reported Irish case law in relation to a test for breaches in respect of the recording. English case law may assist in providing guidance. In *R v Hanton*[67] a young complainant had been asked prejudicial and leading questions during the recording of the recorded evidence in relation to sexual offences allegedly committed by her grandfather. The appellant was convicted and appealed on the basis that the recorded evidence should not have been admitted given the breaches as well as evidential concerns regarding the curtailment of cross-examination of the officer who conducted the interview, how the interview was conducted in relation to the relevant guidance, and the nature of the charge in relation to these issues. The Court of Appeal ruled that the recorded testimony had been admissible but quashed the conviction on the basis that evidence of how it had been taken should have been put before the jury. The test in respect of breaches of the recording of the interview has thus developed from this case:

> Could a reasonable jury properly directed be sure that the witness has given a credible and accurate account on the video-tape, notwithstanding any breaches?[68]

[24–48] The test in *R v Hanton*[69] was upheld in the horrific child cruelty case of *R v Krezolek*.[70] This case involved the death of a four year old child at the hands of his parents. The victim's sister, A, had given recorded evidence which should have been taken in accordance with the relevant guidance. Despite certain breaches of the relevant guidance, her recorded evidence was admitted at trial. The Court of Appeal stated that

67 *R v Hanton* [2005] EWCA Crim 2009. See also [24–60].
68 ibid [10].
69 ibid.
70 *R v Krezolek* [2014] EWCA Crim 2782.

the appellant's counsel's general argument seemed to be based on a false premise that the accounts of children can be subjected to the same kind of forensic analysis as that sometimes applied to adult witnesses. In her judgment Lady Justice Hallett stated:

> That is not the modern approach: see Barker [2010] EWCA Crim 4. Child witnesses are not to be treated as if they are miniature adults. Allowance must be made for the fact that they may well have the kind of difficulties the intermediary observed in A, but that does not render their evidence unreliable and it does not turn them into an incompetent witness.
>
> A was not only a competent witness, she had given a perfectly lucid account on the central issues in the case. One only has to substitute A, an adult, for A, the child, to see the fallacy in Mr Lambert's argument. There may have been passages in her interviews which were open to challenge. Few eye witnesses (whatever their age) tell a completely accurate and reliable story; that does not mean it would be in the interests of justice to exclude the evidence as inaccurate and unreliable. The question "could a reasonable jury properly directed be sure that a witness has given a credible and accurate account on the video tape" does not mean "could a reasonable jury properly directed be sure that every aspect of the account is entirely credible and accurate".[71]

Jurisdiction in All Courts/Transfer of Proceedings

There is no limitation in s 16(1)(b) in relation to summary or indictable offences and the provision applies to courts of all jurisdiction. If required, s 17 of the Criminal Evidence Act 1992[72] allows for proceedings under ss 13, 14, 15, 16 and 29 to be transferred to an appropriate court where any of those sections are not in operation in the originating court. **[24–49]**

Provision for Disclosure under the Section

Section 15 of the Criminal Evidence Act 1992[73] obliges the prosecution to disclose the recording. **[24–50]**

---

[71] ibid [46]–[47].

[72] Criminal Evidence Act 1992, s 17, Transfer of proceedings:

> 'In any proceedings for an offence in any circuit or district court district in relation to which any of the provisions of sections 13 to 16 or section 29 is not in operation the court concerned may, if in its opinion it is desirable that evidence be given in the proceedings through a live television link or by means of a videorecording or that a screen or other similar device be used in the giving of evidence, by order transfer the proceedings to a circuit or district court district in relation to which those provisions are in operation and, where such an order is made the jurisdiction of the court to which the proceedings have been transferred may be exercised –
>
> (a) in the case of the Circuit Court, by the judge of the circuit concerned, and
>
> (b) in the case of the District Court, by the judge of that court for the time being assigned to the district court district concerned.'

[73] Criminal Evidence Act 1992, s 15, Procedure in relation to certain offences:

> '(1) Where –
>
> (a) under Part IA of the Criminal Procedure Act 1967, the prosecutor consents to the sending forward for trial of an accused person,
>
> (b) a person who has made a videorecording under section 16(1)(b), is under 18 years of age on the date consent is given to the accused being sent forward for trial, and
>
> (c) it is proposed that a videorecording of a statement made by the person concerned during an interview as mentioned in section 16(1)(b) shall be given in evidence pursuant to that section,

[24–51] It should also be noted that s 15 of the Criminal Evidence Act 1992 has not been amended to provide for disclosure of recorded evidence in summary matters nor in relation to any person who has had a videorecording taken under the age of 18 but who is then over 18 when consent is given by the DPP to the accused being sent forward for trial.

[24–52] Amendments have been made to this provision under the Criminal Justice (Victims of Crime) Act 2017 but the provision still specifies that it relates to the sending forward of an accused in relation to a person who 'is under 18 years of age on the date consent is given to the accused being sent forward for trial'.

[24–53] This provision may cause confusion and the use of a videorecording as evidence may be challenged where a person is over 18 when the DPP consents to the matter being sent forward.

[24–54] The issue of disclosure is outlined in s 15 of the Act which allows for the accused to view the video prior to the hearing only after the accused has been sent forward for trial under Part 1A of the Criminal Procedure Act 1967. The issue of pre-trial disclosure is thereby only expressly outlined for indictable offences. It is submitted that disclosure concerning District Court matters will still apply under traditional District Court disclosure rules and a 'Gary Doyle Order'.[74] However, as hearings occur more rapidly in the District Court, this may put pressure on appropriate personnel regarding disclosure and editing of recordings.

Linking of Original Provision to s 27 Criminal Evidence Act 1992 /Requirement for Oath

[24–55] The commencement of s 16(1)(b) of the Criminal Evidence Act 1992 was originally intended for child complainants under the age of 14 or persons with an intellectual disability.[75] Under this provision, the recording of a witness statement is taken with

---

(d) it is proposed, pursuant to section 16 (1) (b), that a videorecording of a statement made by that person during an interview as mentioned in that provision shall be given in evidence at the trial, the prosecutor shall, in addition to causing the documents mentioned in section 4B(1) of that Act to be served on the accused –

(i) notify the accused that it is proposed so to give evidence, and

(ii) give the accused an opportunity of seeing the videorecording of the interview.

(2) The judge hearing an application under section 4E of the Criminal Procedure Act 1967 may consider any statement made, in relation to an offence, by a person in a videorecording mentioned in section 16(1)(b) if the person is available for cross-examination at the hearing of the application.

(3) If the accused consents, an edited version of the videorecording of an interview mentioned in section 16(1)(b), may, with leave of the judge hearing an application referred to in subsection (2) of this section, be shown at the hearing of the application, and, in that event, subsection (2) and section 16(1)(b) shall apply in relation to that version as it applies in relation to the original videorecording.'

[74] A 'Gary Doyle Order' is the informal term for disclosure in respect of summary prosecution referred as such after the case of *Director of Public Prosecutions v Gary Doyle* [1994] 2 IR 286. See also Guidelines of the Office of the Director of Public Prosecutions (November 2010) para 9.6, 39.

[75] Under s 19 of the Act, for persons with an intellectual disability who have reached that age. This appears to have tied in with s 27 of the Criminal Evidence Act 1992 which allows for evidence of a child under 14 to be admitted at trial without being sworn or affirmed.

the express intention of it being admitted as examination in chief evidence at trial. It means that a statement taken pre-trial may, after a successful application at trial, be transformed into examination in chief testimony. If it is not admitted, then the question arises if it reverts to a statement as taken under the provisions of s 21(2)(b) of the Criminal Justice Act 1984 even if none of the procedural safeguards attaching to that provision applied at the time it was taken.

The facility for the admission of unsworn testimony for children under s 27 of the Criminal Evidence Act 1992 as originally commenced greatly assisted the child witness in respect of the admission of recorded testimony as it removed a procedural hurdle for the child witness. It meant that the person who conducted the interview, the Specialist Interviewer, did not need to administer an oath before conducting the interview. However, since the extension of the eligibility of the provision under the Criminal Law (Human Trafficking) (Amendment) Act 2013, the Criminal Law (Sexual Offences) Act 2017 and the Criminal Justice (Victims of Crime) Act 2017), the section no longer ties in with s 27 as neatly as it did previously. As mentioned above, the eligibility of the provision now extends to testimony: [24–56]

(i) by a person who is under 18 years of age in relation to an offence of which he or she is a victim, or
(ii) by a person under 18 years of age (being a person other than the accused) in relation to –
   (I) a sexual offence, or
   (II) an offence under section 3(1), (2) or (3) of the Child Trafficking and Pornography Act 1998, or
   (III) an offence under section 2, 4 or 7 of the Criminal Law (Human Trafficking) Act 2008

Child Witness Over 14 but Under 18 when Testimony Recorded

The situation as it relates to eligible persons over 14 and under 18 when they have had their testimony recorded is procedurally difficult. The English case of *R v Sharman*[76] and the Northern Ireland case of *R v N*[77] which followed it, may be relevant here. Both cases outline that the recording of unsworn testimony (when the witness is eligible to give evidence that is unsworn) may be admissible. However, if, at trial, the witness is no longer eligible to give unsworn testimony then the failure to swear that person at trial will be fatal to the admissibility of the videorecorded evidence. The principles of the cases outline that the witness should have been sworn before giving evidence in court. This may be the current solution in Irish courts at present but there is no published guidance or case law to confirm whether this is the case. [24–57]

The admission of the testimony under s 27 of the Criminal Evidence Act 1992 does mean that the evidence is subject to a perjury offence, however unlikely that may be given the age of criminal responsibility in Ireland.[78] Section 27 of the Criminal Evidence Act 1992 has been amended by the Criminal Justice (Perjury and Related Offences) 2021 and is included in Schedule 2 of that Act. [24–58]

76 *R v Sharman* [1998] 1 Cr App R 406.
77 *R v N* [1998] NI 261; [1998] 6 WLUK 361 CA (Crim Div)(NI). See Peter Rook and Robert Ward, *Rook and Ward on Sexual Offences, Law and Practice* (6th edn, Sweet and Maxwell 2021) para 34.37, 1731.
78 Children Act 2001, s 52.

Testimony Recorded Prior to 18 (Originally 14) but Complainant/Witness has Reached 18

[24–59] The upper age limit set by the original legislation was 14 so that a recorded statement could be taken by a person under that age and then applied to be admitted as evidence in chief testimony at trial.

[24–60] In *The People (DPP) v JPR*[79] the accused was charged with the rape of a boy who was seven years of age at the time of the alleged incident in late 2004. A recording under s 16(1)(b) was taken and an application for its admission was made at trial. As Orange has noted[80] the defence had identified a number of possible breaches of the guidelines during the taking of the recorded interview. These included a challenge that the interview had not established that the child complainant understood the difference between truth and lies. The *Guidelines*[81] emphasise the need for the specialist interviewer to establish the child complainant's understanding of truth and lies.[82] However, the judge held that the advice given by the Garda Specialist Interviewer to the child was intended to be age appropriate and that the guidelines did not have to be followed strictly to the letter. The judge expressed concerns that the recording did not show that the child had been warned about the consequences of telling the truth but she was satisfied that there was sufficient evidence to show that the child understood the difference between a truth and a lie and the importance of telling the truth when making the statement. The fact that the judge highlighted this issue is extremely significant. This is notwithstanding the fact that a child under 14 years of age may give his or her testimony unsworn under s 27 of the Criminal Evidence Act 1992. The standard for the admission of unsworn testimony is that the witness who is under 14 years of age is able to give an intelligible account of events which are relevant to the proceedings[83] but s 27(2) of the Act also contains an offence for perjury where the witness gives evidence which he or she knows to be false or does not believe to be true.[84]

---

[79] *The People (DPP) v JPR*, Bill No CC0057/12 (ex temp) (Central Criminal Court, 1 May 2013) (O'Malley J).

[80] Garnet Orange, *Police Powers In Ireland* (Bloomsbury 2013) para 7.38, 121.

[81] An Garda Síochána, *Good Practice Guidelines for Persons involved in Video Recording interviews with complainants under 14 years of age (or with intellectual disability) for Evidential Purposes in accordance with Section 16(1)(b) of the Criminal Evidence Act, 1992, in cases involving Sexual and/or Violent Offences* (July 2003).

They require revision in the face of changing practice. For example, the *Guidelines* state that, should a subsequent recorded interview be required, a request should be made to the DPP. (para 1.30, 14) This has now been revised and a request for a supplemental recorded interview can now be made to the senior investigating officer in the case. (Revision of Policy by Deputy Director, November 2009.)

[82] The guidance for Specialist Interviewers conducting interviews under s 16(1)(b) Criminal Evidence Act 1992 is the *Good Practice Guidelines* (2003) which recommends that it is important to establish a rapport with the complainant to put them at ease, eg discuss hobbies and likes/dislikes. The Specialist Interviewer should also establish the ground rules of the interview, eg if the complainant doesn't understand a question, he or she should say so, and also try and also to establish that the complainant understands the difference between truth and lies. An Garda Síochána, *Good Practice Guidelines for Persons involved in Video Recording interviews with Complainants under 14 years of Age (or with intellectual disability) for Evidential Purposes in accordance with Section 16(1)(b) of the Criminal Evidence Act, 1992, in cases involving Sexual and/or Violent Offences* (July 2003) 27; see also paras 3.9–3.10, 28.

[83] Criminal Evidence Act 1992, s 27, Oath or affirmation not necessary for child etc., witness.

[84] ibid s 27(2): 'If any person whose evidence is received as aforesaid makes a statement material in the proceedings concerned which he knows to be false or does not believe to be true, he shall be guilty of an offence and on conviction shall be liable to be dealt with as if he had been guilty of perjury.'

In *DPP v KD*[85] judicial review was taken before Humphreys J, who rejected the argument that the recording and trial must take place before the witness turned 14 years of age. He stated: **[24–61]**

> In *People (D.P.P.) v. J.P.R.* (Unreported, Central Criminal Court, 1st May, 2013, ex tempore, not circulated), O'Malley J. ruled that s. 16 did not cease to have effect once the child concerned had turned 14 (see Garnet Orange, *Police Powers in Ireland* (Bloomsbury Professional, Dublin and West Sussex, 2014) para. 7.38). This decision was binding on Judge Greally. Furthermore, it is clearly correct.[86]

The matter was appealed[87] and in dismissing the appeal, Birmingham P stated: **[24–62]**

> It is appropriate at this point to consider the complaints concerning the further rejection by the High Court judge of the claim for relief based on complaints concerning the Act of 1992. Again, he felt that the point that was being raised in relation to the correct interpretation of s. 16 of the Act of 1992 was a very straightforward one and one where the answer was clear. Moreover, he felt that when the matter was raised in the Circuit Court there was a relevant and binding authority. I consider that the section could scarcely be clearer and that the trial judge (Judge Greally) was entirely correct in the interpretation that she had placed on the section. The High Court judge was therefore correct in rejecting the statutory interpretation point as failing to meet the arguability test. In the circumstances it was unnecessary to consider whether the Victim's Directive has direct effect.[88]

With the extension of eligibility for s 16(1)(b) of the Criminal Evidence Act 1992 for victims and witnesses under 18, the case is persuasive authority for the principle that the relevant date for eligibility is the time at which the interviews were recorded. **[24–63]**

Inquiry Re Assessment of Witness

DPP v PP[89] indicates that the procedure for the inquiry into the assessment of the witness is quite wide once there is no unfairness in the trial. However, it is preferable to hold the inquiry prior to the evidence being heard: **[24–64]**

> While this Court accepts the respondent's submission that s. 27 of the Act of 1992 does not prescribe the manner or form in which the inquiry should be embarked on, it is the view of this Court that it is preferable that such an inquiry be held prior to placing the evidence before the jury. The question for this Court is whether in the circumstances of this case, the failure to carry out a formal inquiry in advance rendered the trial unsatisfactory.[90]

The case of *DPP v JD*[91] involved a challenge to the admission of the s 16(1)(b) recording in relation to the sexual abuse of a niece by the appellant. The complainant was approximately seven to nine years at the time of the abuse and 12 at the time of the trial. The appellant stated that no warning was given to the complainant before she participated in the recorded interview as to the consequences of telling lies. The Court of Appeal agreed with the comments of the trial judge that a nine-year-old **[24–65]**

---

85 *DPP v KD* [2016] IEHC 21.
86 ibid [12]–[13].
87 *DPP v KD* [2017] IECA 53.
88 ibid [20].
89 [2015] IECA 152.
90 ibid.
91 *DPP v JD* [2018] IECA 232.

would be intimidated by a warning about the consequences of not telling the truth and Birmingham J went on to state that the Gardaí went to very considerable lengths to establish that the complainant knew the difference between truth and lies and was fully aware of the importance of telling the truth.[92] The appellant was unsuccessful on this and all grounds of appeal.

Recordings as Exhibits

[24–66] Cases such as *DPP v PP*[93] and *DPP v SA*[94] have raised issues in relation to the recordings going to the jury room and an imbalance in relation to the weight of the recorded examination in chief testimony as opposed to the cross-examination testimony at trial.

[24–67] In *DPP v PP*[95] a point of appeal included the admission of the DVD recordings under s 16(1)(b) of the 1992 Act as exhibits to the jury room. The trial judge had allowed the evidence to be viewed in the jury room and the Court of Appeal judgment indicates that both the prosecution and the defence had consented to this practice (although the defence counsel had pointed out to the trial judge that the normal procedure was to play the DVD to the jury in the courtroom). On appeal, it was contended that this could have caused a prejudicial imbalance in how the jury weighed the evidence because when the recording was replayed to them the jury would have heard a repetition of the account by the complainant without the benefit of the additional cross-examination evidence. The Court of Appeal noted the submissions made by the appellant and respondent but ultimately did not find that the treatment of the recorded examination-in-chief testimony as exhibits viewable in the jury room caused the trial to be unfair:

> In regard to the s 16 DVD going to the jury in their room, the defence objection during the course of the trial was cursory in nature. There was no need in the circumstances for the jury to be reminded of the cross-examination in the event that they decided to watch the s 16 DVD interview. As this Court has already noted the defendant's cross-examination of the complainant was short focused and limited to general questions about herself and her family, her memory, did she know what pretending meant, had she discussed the case with her mother and then asking her if she had told the truth in the three HSE interviews. There is no question of any injustice resulting from the jury viewing the s 16 DVD in their room along with other exhibits and accordingly the court dismisses this ground of appeal.[96]

[24–68] The case does not offer a definitive ruling on the matter as it appears to turn on its own facts given the nature of the cross-examination in the case. It is worth noting that in subsequent cases the recordings of examination-in-chief testimony have, with the consent of the defence, gone into the jury room as exhibits.[97] Nevertheless, the courts and practitioners should be cognisant of any potential evidential imbalances that may arise in the replaying of testimony.

---

92 ibid [7].

93 *DPP v PP* [2015] IECA 152.

94 *DPP v SA* [2020] IECA 60.

95 *DPP v PP* [2015] IECA 152.

96 ibid [36].

97 *DPP v FN* [2021] IECA 238; [2022] IESC 22. This point is not contained in the judgment. The defence counsel also consented to the recordings going to the jury in the case of *DPP v SK* (CCDP0124/2020 December 2020).

Information to Juries under Criminal Procedure Act 2021

This issue of what may be given to the jury may be considered under s 12 of the Criminal Procedure Act 2021 , 'Provision of information to juries'.[98] Section 12 of the Criminal Procedure Act 2021 greatly expands what may be given to the jury should the judge feel it appropriate. How the courts will generally address any potential imbalance in respect of the evidence of transcripts of any evidence such as recordings of evidence given at trial has yet to be considered.[99] [24–69]

Replaying of Recording at Request of Jury

In the Court of Appeal case of *DPP v SA*[100] a point was raised on appeal in relation to a potential imbalance in the weighing of evidence where the jury had asked for the recorded testimony to be replayed. In that case the jury had been brought back to the courtroom to view the recorded testimony. The defence had argued that without the [24–70]

---

[98] Criminal Procedure Act 2021, Part 3: '12. Provision of information to juries

(1) This section shall apply to any offence being tried on indictment other than an offence to which any of the following provisions apply:

- (a) section 1078C of the Taxes Consolidation Act 1997;
- (b) section 57 of the Criminal Justice (Theft and Fraud Offences) Act 2001;
- (c) section 10 of the Competition Act 2002;
- (d) section 56 of the Central Bank (Supervision and Enforcement) Act 2013;
- (e) section 882 of the Companies Act 2014.

(2) In a trial of an offence to which this section applies, the trial judge may order that copies of any or all of the following documents or materials shall be given to the jury in any form that the judge considers appropriate:

- (a) any document admitted in evidence at the trial;
- (b) where such transcripts or audio recordings are available:
  - (i) the transcript of the opening speeches of counsel or an audio recording of such speeches;
  - (ii) the transcript of the whole or any part of the evidence given at the trial or an audio recording of such evidence;
  - (iii) the transcript of the closing speeches of counsel or an audio recording of such speeches;
  - (iv) the transcript of the trial judge's charge to the jury or an audio recording of such charge;
- (c) any charts, diagrams, graphics, schedules or summaries of evidence produced at the trial;
- (d) any other document that in the opinion of the trial judge would be of assistance to the jury in its deliberations including, where appropriate, an affidavit by an accountant or other suitably qualified person summarising, in a form which is likely to be comprehended by the jury, any transactions by the accused or other persons which are relevant to the offence.

(3) If the prosecution or the accused proposes to apply to the trial judge for an order that a document referred to in subsection (2)(d) shall be given to the jury, the prosecution or the accused, as the case may be, shall give a copy of the document to the other party in advance of the application and, on the hearing of the application, the trial judge shall take into account any representations made by or on behalf of either party in relation to it.

(4) Where the trial judge has made an order that an affidavit referred to in subsection (2)(d) shall be given to the jury, the accountant or other suitably qualified person concerned –

- (a) shall be summoned by the prosecution or the accused, as the case may be, to attend at the trial as an expert witness, and
- (b) may be required by the trial judge, in an appropriate case, to give evidence in regard to the report and any relevant accounting procedures or principles.'

[99] See [24–93].

[100] *DPP v SA* [2020] IECA 60.

trial judge also outlining the cross-examination testimony, an imbalance would ensue. The Court of Appeal stated:

> Where the DVDs are re-played, certain safeguards are in our opinion required to be followed which include the re-playing of the DVD in the courtroom in the presence of the judge and the parties, which should take place without any intervention or interruption. We do not agree with the contention on behalf of the appellant that it was then necessary for the trial judge to summarise again all or part of the cross-examination of the complainants. It is a matter to be determined on the facts and circumstances of each individual case. In the present case the trial judge had carefully summarised the evidence in a fair and balanced manner at the end of a very lengthy trial. Where certain portions of evidence are requested to be repeated by the jury, it is only necessary to give those portions to the jury. Should the jury request further material, it is a matter within the province of the jury to so request.[101]

Clarification Meetings

[24–71] The *Good Practice Guidelines*[102] were drafted in 2003 as procedural guidance for use of the s 16(1)(b) of the Criminal Evidence Act 1992. Clarification meetings are not referred to in the *Good Practice Guidelines* but appear to have evolved as good practice. Clarification meetings are mentioned in *DPP v TV*[103] and *DPP v SA*[104] and generally consist of Specialist Interviewers meeting the complainant to note the disclosures, to confirm eligibility and to arrange the recording of any relevant testimony.

[24–72] In a case reported in *The Irish Times* regarding a very young witness, 'Zoe', who was approximately three years of age at the time of the alleged offence, the sequence of events in terms of what has become known as a 'clarification meeting' is described as what occurred when the parents reported the complainant's disclosures:

> Specially trained gardaí attended the family home two days later. They explained to Kate and Tom (the parents) that they would spend time alone playing with Zoe, and if she made a disclosure about Dave (the suspect), they would begin the formal process. Zoe did so, and the Garda opened an investigation.[105]

[24–73] In the judgment of *DPP v MT*,[106] the Court of Appeal describes the delay in respect of the trial and which may have led to the difficulties in memory recall. The ability to cross-examine was thereby undermined and the conviction was quashed. As part of the timeline of the matter coming on for trial, Ní Raifeartaigh notes:

> In October or November 2016 (the precise date is uncertain), two specialist interviewers attended at the child's home. No notes of this meeting were made or kept. This was described as a "clarification meeting", terminology which has apparently become common

---

[101] ibid [165]–[166].

[102] An Garda Síochána, *Good Practice Guidelines for Persons involved in Video Recording interviews with complainants under 14 years of age (or with intellectual disability) for Evidential Purposes in accordance with Section 16(1)(b) of the Criminal Evidence Act, 1992, in cases involving Sexual and/or Violent Offences* (July 2003).

[103] *DPP v* TV [2017] IECA 200.

[104] *DPP v* SA [2020] IECA 60.

[105] Sarah-Jane Murphy, 'The story of "Zoe", one of the youngest sex-abuse cases ever heard in Irish courts' *The Irish Times* (Dublin, 24 April 2021) <https://www.irishtimes.com/the-story-of-zoe-one-of-the-youngest-sex-abuse-cases-ever-heard-in-irish-courts-1.4537355> accessed 13 October 2023.

[106] *DPP v MT* [2023] IECA 65.

> in this type of case to describe the first meeting of the Gardaí with the complainant. The fact of this meeting was not known to the appellant or his legal team prior to the first trial. (As will be seen, there were three trials: the jury were discharged in the first trial by reason of a failure to disclose the fact of, or any notes concerning, the first clarification meeting referred to; the second trial resulted in a jury discharge because of the pandemic; and the third trial resulted in the conviction of the appellant.)[107]

The failure to make notes during a clarification meeting even where no disclosures were made has become an important evidential issue. [24–74]

> The first trial started on 29th October 2019. The jury was discharged on the second day by reason of the absence of disclosure relating to the clarification meeting, already referred to. Statements were made by the two Gardaí in question, dated 21st November 2019, in which both stated that S made no disclosures at that first clarification meeting.[108]

If the Recording is Not Admitted as Examination in Chief Testimony

There appears to be no reported judgment of a recording not being admitted as examination in chief testimony if an application was made for its admission. As mentioned in *DPP v MT*,[109] the lack of notes in respect of a clarification meeting may cause significant difficulties in relation to a recorded interview but these may be resolved, as in that case, at a later date. If not, or for any other reason, the recording is not admitted, and the issues cannot be resolved at a later date, the transcript of the recording may become the statement of the witness. If this occurs, the reason why the recording has become inadmissible may become an issue at trial. For example, the manner in which the recording was taken may have been prejudicial, eg the use of leading questions, or the use of documents created outside the interview to prompt evidence. There may be technical issues which may cause issues regarding the statement, eg technical problems such as vision or audibility issues. The witness may be able to give testimony but may face increased pressures in terms of having to give examination in chief evidence in accordance with his or her statement. Challenges by defence counsel may then follow in relation to any variance. [24–75]

Issues Regarding the Provision

Editing

Provision for editing of the recording is not explicitly made in the section but only implicit within the phrase 'or any part thereof' or 'that part'. Section 16(2)(a) states: [24–76]

> Any such videorecording or any part thereof shall not be admitted in evidence as aforesaid if the court is of opinion that in the interests of justice the videorecording concerned or that part ought not to be so admitted.[110]

Editing where there is a prejudicial response is outlined in the *Good Practice Guidelines*: [24–77]

---

107 ibid [7].
108 ibid [12].
109 ibid [12].
110 Criminal Evidence Act 1992, s 16(1)(b).

> The answer to a leading question could taint some, or indeed all, of the interview and, therefore, render it partly or wholly inadmissible. Where a leading question has, in fact, been inadvertently asked and a response given, as with other matters it may be necessary, when all parties are present and with the consent of the court, to edit the video recording.[111]

[24–78] Difficulties regarding editing still arise despite the section having been in use for some time. In *DPP v PB*[112] one of the grounds of appeal concerned the manner in which the recording was edited while being played to the jury. The prosecution pressed pause, forward wound and then play. Why this was the case is unclear. However, an edited transcript, as played to the jury, had been provided to the defence, and no objection was raised by the defence when the evidence was being played. The point was unsuccessful.

Verbatim record of salient points

[24–79] After the recording is made, it may or may not be transcribed into document form in order to help various personnel such as prosecution counsel examine the particular case file. It appears that the question of transcripts is a consistent difficulty with regard to cases involving s 16(1)(b) of the Criminal Evidence Act 1992. The length of a recording may be quite long, and longer if there are multiple recordings as in *DPP v TV*[113] and *DPP v SA*.[114]

[24–80] There have been issues regarding the time which must be spent by the Office of the DPP watching the recordings in order to identify the relevant evidence and offences. An agreement has been established between the Specialist Interviewers of An Garda Síochána and the Office of the DPP. In assistance of the prosecution of cases using s 16(1)(b), specialist interviewers prepare a 'Verbatim Record of Salient Points' in relation to what offences and sections of the recording may be relevant. This is enclosed with the recording and sent to the Office of the Director of Public Prosecutions prior to the preparation of the prosecution at trial. Section 16(1)(b) states that a recording under this section shall be admissible, under certain provisions, 'at the trial of the offence as evidence of any fact stated therein of which direct oral evidence would be admissible'.

[24–81] Whether a transcript is made of the relevant sections of the recording or the entire recording, and whether the recording and/or the transcript become part of the Book of Evidence, may be points at issue. However, a reliable transcript is imperative to ensure efficient progress of the case through the criminal justice system. For example, if a defendant wishes to plead early in proceedings and transcript of the recording is not supplied with the Book of Evidence, the prosecution cannot furnish the court with details of the relevant offence(s) and the sentencing will have to be delayed while this information is transcribed. If the matter progresses to trial and a transcript is not provided there may be a delay while one is requested, prepared and verified.

[24–82] Where a recording includes information which is prejudicial to the defendant, this may have to be edited out after agreement between prosecution and defence counsel or after an order by the court. Another significant issue is which agency retains responsibility

---

[111] An Garda Síochána, *Good Practice Guidelines for Persons involved in Video Recording interviews with complainants under 14 years of age (or with intellectual disability) for Evidential Purposes in accordance with Section 16(1)(b) of the Criminal Evidence Act, 1992, in cases involving Sexual and/or Violent Offences* (July 2003) para 4.12.

[112] *DPP v PB* [2021] IECA 152.

[113] *DPP v TV* [2017] IECA 200.

[114] *DPP v SA* [2020] IECA 60.

for the editing of the recording where this is required at trial. Issues regarding editing may cause significant problems as was demonstrated in the case of *People (DPP) v JPR.*[115] While O'Malley J admitted the recording as evidence, the statement was not shown to the jury. Unfortunately, the need to edit it to remove potentially prejudicial comments became an insurmountable obstacle.[116] As a result, the child witness had to come into court to give examination in chief evidence. Editing issues were also seen in *DPP v PB.*[117]

Supplemental questions not provided for in s 16(1)(b) Criminal Evidence Act 1992

The first use of s 16(1)(b) of the Criminal Evidence Act 1992 in the Central Criminal Court took place in 2010 in a case known as *DPP v XY.*[118] The application for a direction was successful for reasons other than the issue of recorded evidence, which had been applied for and deemed admissible at trial. During the application for admission, there was discussion regarding the section in relation to the asking of further questions.[119] Section 16(1)(b) states that that the videorecording 'shall be admissible at the trial of the offence as evidence of any fact stated therein of which direct oral evidence by him would be admissible'. If the videorecorded statement is admitted, it then becomes the examination in chief evidence of the complainant and the words 'direct oral evidence', possibly equating as they do to 'examination in chief' evidence, indicate that the testimony is complete from the prosecution point of view, with no supplemental questions being permissible other than redirect questions arising from any cross-examination. In *DPP v XY*, Mr Justice White commented on the possibility of the complainant having to answer supplementary questions at the hearing and thereby undermining the whole point of the admission of the videorecording as being one of those situations where the law may at times be an ass. Evidential issues may arise which require the prosecution to ask supplemental questions for matters which are not covered on the videorecorded interview and s 16(1)(b) does not provide for this. This is in contrast to the legislation in England and Wales[120] where in certain circumstances, it appears that further questions may be asked. Anecdotal evidence suggests that, in fact, trial judges have permitted the admission of both recorded evidence and additional statements with the witness getting into the witness box to be examined in chief in respect of the additional evidence. This might occur, for example, where the witness has aged out of the eligibility provision for recorded testimony and additional [24–83]

---

[115] *The People (DPP) v JPR*, Bill No CC0057/12 (ex temp) (Central Criminal Court, 1 May 2013) (O'Malley J).

[116] Garnet Orange, *Police Powers in Ireland* (Bloomsbury Publishing 2013) para 7.38, 121.

[117] *DPP v PB* [2021] IECA 152.

[118] See Miriam Delahunt, 'Video Evidence and s.16(1)(b) of the Criminal Evidence Act 1992' (2011) 16(1) Bar Review 2–6, 4. The case of *DPP v XY.*

[119] ibid.

[120] Youth Justice and Criminal Evidence Act 1999, s 27:

> '(5) Where a recording is admitted under this section: –
> (a) the witness must be called by the party tendering it in evidence, unless –
> (i) a special measures direction provides for the witness's evidence on cross-examination to be given in any recording admissible under section 28, or
> (ii) the parties to the proceedings have agreed as mentioned in subsection (4)(a)(ii); and
> (b) the witness may not without the permission of the court give evidence in chief otherwise than by means of the recording as to any matter which, in the opinion of the court, is dealt with in the witness's recorded testimony.'

Therefore s 27(5)(b) seems to indicate that with the permission of the court, the witness may give evidence in chief otherwise than by means of the recording as to any matter, which in the opinion of the court, is not dealt with in the witness's recorded testimony.

statements have been taken. There appears to be no published rulings or judgments as yet in relation to this point. A situation where the witness is examined in chief in the witness box as well as having recorded testimony admitted at trial raises a number of issues. The prosecution case will have the advantage of having evidence taken at a time closer to the incident in addition to further opportunities for clarification as appropriate. However, the defence will not have had an opportunity to cross examine at the same time as the recording was taken so there will be an imbalance in terms of memory recall which disadvantages the defence. Also, if the witness can give evidence from the witness box what is the reason for the admission of the recorded testimony? The admission of recorded testimony is an exception to the hearsay rule and is provided for, under certain circumstances, to facilitate the evidence of vulnerable witnesses. If a witness is able to be examined in chief in the witness box to give additional evidence which wasn't recorded, does this devalue the use of the provision? In addition, without legislative parameters or procedural guidance, inconsistencies may arise in any given court regarding the use of recorded evidence as well as additional examination in chief testimony from the witness box. A general, transparent practice should be established to ensure that all witnesses, defendants and practitioners can rely on how the evidence should be admitted.

Multiple recordings

[24–84] There seems to be no explicit restriction in the legislation, guidance or case law as to the number of interviews that may be taken. The issue of multiple interviews is significant as repetitive questioning may cause prejudice to the defendant. The risks involved are highlighted in *Achieving Best Evidence*, the guidance in England and Wales, which states:

> In some circumstances it might be necessary to conduct the interview over more than one session (for example: in complicated cases; where allegations of multiple offences are involved; where the witness is elderly and frail; where the witness is traumatised or where the witness is taking medication likely to make them sleepy). These sessions might be separated by a matter of hours or, if necessary, could take place over a number of days. When this occurs, care must be taken to avoid repetition of the same focused questions over time, which could lead to unreliable or inconsistent responding in some witnesses and interviews being ruled inadmissible by the court.[121]

[24–85] The *Good Practice Guidelines* state that once the videorecording has been completed further questioning should not take place unless the gardaí are fully satisfied, if necessary, after consultation with the Director of Public Prosecutions, that it is desirable to elicit further information and that any supplementary statements should also be videorecorded.[122] It appears that a request for a supplemental recorded interview can now be made to the senior investigating officer in the case.[123]

[24–86] In *DPP v TV*,[124] where three recorded interviews had taken place, a ground of appeal

---

[121] Ministry of Justice, *Achieving Best Evidence in Criminal Proceedings: Guidance on Interviewing Victims and Witnesses, and Guidance on Using Special Measures* (National Chiefs' Police Council January 2022) 'Planning and Preparation' 'Duration of the Interview (including Pace, Breaks and the Possibility of more than One Session)' para 2.236, 70.

[122] An Garda Síochána, *Good Practice Guidelines for Persons involved in Video Recording interviews with complainants under 14 years of age (or with intellectual disability) for Evidential Purposes in accordance with Section 16(1)(b) of the Criminal Evidence Act, 1992, in cases involving Sexual and/ or Violent Offences* (July 2003) 'Supplementary Statements' para 1.30, 14.

[123] *Revision of Policy by Deputy Director of Public Prosecutions* (4 November 2009).

[124] *DPP v TV* [2017] IECA 200.

involved a submission that prejudicial material had been put to the witness, thus making the recordings inadmissible. In relation to the third interview, the objection was based on the fact that a period of many months had expired since the second interview, and that the third interview did not arise as a result of any new disclosures being made, but rather on the basis of a request from the prosecution. The complainant was shown the recording of the first and second interviews prior to the third interview.

The Court of Appeal dismissed the appeal, stating that there had been no difficulty in respect of the admissibility of the recordings. In relation to the admissibility of the third recording, Mahon J stated: **[24–87]**

> The learned trial judge ruled, correctly in this court's view, that there was nothing wrong in the complainant being shown the content of the first and second interview in advance of her third interview. He said:–
>
> > There [sic] were perfectly entitled to show the tapes because that was for her the equivalent of giving her statement. They left it at no more than asking her whether they would wish to clarify or add anything and she didn't do so."[125]

In the case of *DPP v SA*,[126] five recorded interviews took place, and one was ruled inadmissible at trial. On appeal, the appellant contended that the remaining recorded interviews had been taken in prejudicial circumstances, and should not have been admitted as evidence particularly in light of the long interval between the recording of the testimony and the trial (approximately six-and-a-half years). In giving the ruling of the Court, Kennedy J dismissed the appeal stating, on this point: **[24–88]**

> The provisions of the Act provide safeguards for an accused person and a trial court must be diligent to ensure that the evidence not be admitted if the court is of the opinion that in the interests of justice the video recording or part thereof ought not to be admitted and in this regard, the court must also have regard to all the circumstances to include any risk of unfairness to the accused person if it be admitted.
>
> We are satisfied for the reasons stated above that the criticisms made on behalf of the appellant regarding the admission of the DVDs are without foundation and that the trial judge did not err in admitting the DVDs of interview in evidence. The trial judge took scrupulous care in the manner in which he addressed the issues which arose.[127]

Audibility and the use of transcripts

A jury may request a transcript for the recorded testimony. This may be due to audibility issues[128] or merely because it is felt that a written record will be helpful in not only following the testimony but also during deliberation.[129] When issues have arisen in relation to clarification, the trial judge has generally gone through his or her note of the relevant testimony again and clarified any issues that might have arisen. **[24–89]**

In the unreported case of *DPP v FE*,[130] a small portion of the transcript of the recording (where audio was poor) was made available to the jury but in controlled circumstances **[24–90]**

---

125 ibid [36]–[37].
126 *DPP v SA* [2020] IECA 60.
127 ibid [89]–[90].
128 *DPP v PB* [2021] IECA 152.
129 *DPP v SA* [2020] IECA 60.
130 Caroline Biggs and Miriam Delahunt, 'Prosecutorial Challenges – Vulnerable Witnesses' (2017) 22(1) Bar Review 23, 24.

(ie the portion was made available while the DVD was being played, but was withdrawn from the jury immediately after the DVD was played) according to the principles outlined in English case law.[131]

[24–91] In *DPP v PB*,[132] the audio quality of the recording was so poor that the Court of Appeal noted that consideration was given to giving the jury a transcript. Ultimately, this did not happen but during deliberations, the jury asked for one. The trial judge refused on the basis that neither the transcript, nor the video, was part of the evidence. The video was replayed in court and viewed by the jury.[133] The appellant challenged on the basis that the trial judge had erred in allowing the recording of the complainant's evidence to be played back to the jury and that doing so without repeating the complainant's cross-examination caused an imbalance in the evidence. The Court of Appeal was referred to a similar situation in *DPP v SA*[134] (in which a similar challenge was rejected), and noted that in this instance:

> In a situation where sound quality difficulties attached to the direct examination, but no such difficulties attached to the cross-examination, and where the two events took place in quite different contexts, one an interview suite in a Garda station conducted by specialist Garda interviews and the other in a courtroom cross-examination, albeit conducted by video link, requiring the jury to view both when they had expressed no desire to do so would not have been an effective exercise in communication which is, first and foremost, what a judge's charge and interaction with the jury is meant to be about.[135]

[24–92] It may be noted that transcripts for juries are not mentioned in the *Good Practice Guidelines*.[136]

[24–93] English cases including *R v Baird*[137] *R v Welstead*,[138] *R v Popescu*[139] and *R v Sardar*[140] note the potential imbalance of the weight of evidence where a jury had a transcript of the recorded testimony. Discussing these cases Archbold notes the procedure best followed where a transcript is required:

> (a) great care must be taken before a jury are given the transcript of an interview at all, even whilst the video-recording of the interview is being shown; this should only be done if there is good reason for it (e.g. the evidence would be difficult to follow on screen, or the audio quality is poor);
> (b) if the transcript is given to the jury, the judge must warn them to take care to examine the video as it is shown, not least because of the importance of the demeanour of the witness in giving evidence;
> (c) other than in exceptional circumstances, the transcript should be withdrawn from the jury once the evidence-in-chief has been given; if the jury are to retain the transcript during cross-examination, this possibility must be given positive thought before it

---

131 Noted in the article ('fn 27') as being *R v Welstead* [1996] 1 Cr App R 59 CA; *R v Popescu* [2011] Crim LR 227 CA.; *R v Sardar* [2012] EWCA Crim 134.

132 *DPP v PB* [2021] IECA 152.

133 ibid [46].

134 *DPP v SA* [2020] IECA 60.

135 *DPP v PB* [2021] IECA 152 [53]–[54].

136 An Garda Síochána, *Good Practice Guidelines for Persons involved in Video Recording interviews with complainants under 14 years of age (or with intellectual disability) for Evidential Purposes in accordance with Section 16(1)(b) of the Criminal Evidence Act, 1992, in cases involving Sexual and/ or Violent Offences* (July 2003) paras 3.8–3.10, 28.

137 *R v Baird* [2007] EWCA Crim 2887.

138 *R v Welstead* [1996] 1 Cr App R 59 CA.

139 *R v Popescu* [2011] Crim LR 227 CA.

140 *R v Sardar* [2012] EWCA Crim 134.

is done; and the reasons why the jury are being permitted to retain the transcript should be explained to them;

(d) if the transcript is retained during cross-examination, then it should normally be recovered once the witness has finished his evidence;

(e) retention by the jury of the transcript after the witness has finished must be for a good reason;

(f) exceptional circumstances apart, the jury should not be permitted to retire with the transcript; those exceptional circumstances will usually only be present if the defence positively want the jury to retire with the transcript, and the judge is satisfied that there are good reasons why they should do so; and the summing up must explain why the jury are being allowed the transcript and the limited use to which they must put it, viz. to aid them to understand the evidence-in-chief of the relevant witness, and, if it be the case, that the defence want the jury to retain the transcript; if this course is taken, then it is incumbent on the judge to ensure that the cross-examination and re-examination of the witness are fully summed up to the jury, and the jury must be specifically reminded that they must take all that evidence into consideration in their deliberations, and must not be over-reliant upon the evidence-in-chief.

The court made clear that a decision to provide the jury with a transcript, or to allow the jury to retain it during cross-examination or after the conclusion of the witness's evidence or to retire with it should only be done after the issue has been discussed with counsel in the absence of the jury.[141]

Criminal Procedure Rules 2020 and *Criminal Practice Directions*[142] in England and Wales generally outline that any transcript given to the jury be removed from the jurors when the recording has finished. **[24–94]**

In Ireland, s 12 of the Criminal Procedure Act 2021 now provides the facilitation of transcripts to juries in certain circumstances. English judgments may have an influence on how this is dealt with. However, trial judges in Irish trials have generally, where a transcript is requested, either resolved any audibility issues,[143] read out the relevant evidence from their own note or the transcript[144] or, as outlined above, replayed the relevant portion of the recording.[145] **[24–95]**

---

[141] *Archbold: Criminal Pleading Evidence and Practice* (ed PJ Richardson) (Sweet & Maxwell 2024) para 8.87, 1544.

[142] Criminal Practice Direction VI (Trial) 26L:

'Juries: Jury access to exhibits and evidence in retirement 4-495a

26L.1 At the end of the summing up it is also important that the judge informs the jury that any exhibits they wish to have will be made available to them.

26L.2 Judges should invite submissions from the advocates as to what material the jury should retire with and what material before them should be removed, such as the transcript of an ABE interview (which should usually be removed from the jury as soon as the recording has been played.)

26L.3 Judges will also need to inform the jury of the opportunity to view certain audio, DVD or CCTV evidence that has been played (excluding, for example ABE interviews). If possible, it may be appropriate for the jury to be able to view any such material in the jury room alone, such as on a sterile laptop, so that they can discuss it freely; this will be a matter for the judge's discretion, following discussion with counsel.'

[143] See Miriam Delahunt, 'Video Evidence and s 16(1)(b) of the Criminal Evidence Act 1992' (2011) 16(1) Bar Review 2.

[144] *DPP v VE* [2021] IECA 122; *DPP v SA* [2020] IECA 60.

[145] *DPP v PB* [2021] IECA 152.

Refreshing memory/viewing recording at trial

[24–96] Although now in need of revision, the *Good Practice Guidelines* state:

> In all cases where a video recording is to be viewed by the court and it is proposed to cross examine and/or re-examine the complainant, it is recommended that arrangements be made to ensure that the complainant can view the recording on the monitor in the witness room when it is being shown it to the court and to the jury.[146]

[24–97] There is no procedure outlined in the *Good Practice Guidelines* in terms of the witness watching his or her recorded testimony prior to giving evidence. Practice has evolved that the recordings are viewed in the company of a person, usually a member of An Garda Síochána at an appropriate time and location. The Garda will not be involved with the investigation of the case and will be the same gender as the witness. The Garda should take a note of any incident that occurred or any comment that was made by the witness and be prepared to give a statement and evidence if so required.

[24–98] How the witness views the recording whether before or during the trial may be agreed in a preliminary trial hearing or ground rules hearing prior to trial.

Competency issues arising from split recorded testimony

[24–99] The competency of vulnerable witnesses is a theme that runs through the trial process and may be raised at any time in the course of their giving evidence. Delay will occur when evidence is divided into recorded and live evidence and the extent of that delay may potentially exacerbate the concern regarding competency. Cases such as *R v Powell*[147] and *R v Malicki*[148] suggest that a substantial delay between recording the giving of evidence and giving evidence at trial may raise suggestions about the ongoing competency of the witness. While the recording of testimony allows for evidence to be taken closer to the time of the incident, evidence of younger witnesses or witnesses with an intellectual disability, who may be competent at the time of the recording of examination in chief evidence may, by the time of giving live cross-examination evidence at trial, be deemed to be incompetent.

[24–100] Up until s 30 of the Children Act 1908, the test for competency was linked to the ability of the child witness to swear an oath[149] and this gave rise to particular difficulties in respect of a judge's opinion as to what the child's understanding of truth, falsehood and damnation might be.[150] In Ireland, s 27 of the Criminal Evidence Act 1992 has simplified the process. It allows a child under the age of 14 to give testimony without that evidence being sworn or affirmed. It outlines a competency test for the child witness. It provides an offence of perjury should false evidence be given and it allows persons with an intellectual disability who have reached the age of 14 to avail of the provisions with the section.

---

146 An Garda Síochána, *Good Practice Guidelines for Persons involved in Video Recording interviews with complainants under 14 years of age (or with intellectual disability) for Evidential Purposes in accordance with Section 16(1)(b) of the Criminal Evidence Act, 1992, in cases involving Sexual and/ or Violent Offences* (July 2003) 'XV Cross Examination' 9.

147 *R v Powell* [2006] 1 CAR 31.

148 *R v Malicki* [2009] EWCA Crim 365.

149 *R v Holmes* (1861) 175 ER 1286.

150 The evolution in respect of the taking of the oath and the origins of the dispensation under s 27 of the Criminal Evidence Act 1992 is detailed in Irish Law Reform Commission, *Oaths and Affirmations* (34–1990).

The competency test for child witnesses is essentially that the witness should be capable of giving an intelligible account of events that are relevant to the proceedings.[151] In England and Wales, the test under s 53 of the Youth Justice and Criminal Evidence Act 1999,[152] for any witness, is that the witness should be able to understand what the court is saying to him or her and the court should be able to understand what the witness is saying to the court. **[24–101]**

The cases of *R v Powell*[153] and *R v Malicki*[154] highlight the difficulties relating to competency that may stem from a delay between the time of the incident and the recording of the statement, or a delay between the recording of the statement and the case coming to trial. In *R v Powell*,[155] after considering a videorecording of the child's evidence, as well as evidence of the officer responsible for the interview and expert evidence, the trial judge decided that a girl of three-and-a-half years of age was competent to give evidence in a case involving sexual abuse. The Court of Appeal upheld that the trial judge's initial decision was justified. However, the Court went on to consider the related question of whether the child's competency should have been revisited later at trial when the cross-examination of the child raised serious doubts as to whether she was 'simply not intelligible in the context of the case'.[156] **[24–102]**

The Court of Appeal held that the trial judge should have re-assessed the child's competency at that stage and furthermore that the judge should have found the child to be incompetent. This would have led inevitably to the trial judge dismissing the charges. In *R v Malicki*,[157] the complainant was four years and eight months of age at the date of the alleged indecent assault. The video interviews suggested she was competent at that time and after cross-examination at trial the question of her competence was re-visited. In cross-examination the complainant had detailed a recollection of the incident, but it was 'impossible to discern whether she was actually remembering the incident herself or simply recalling her video, which she had just seen twice: once on the Friday before the Monday of the trial, and once at the trial before she was cross-examined'.[158] It was suggested by the defendant that the problem of cross-examining the child arose from the fact that it was not possible to ask whether 'her being licked was a recollection of a question put to her by the police officer on the video rather than **[24–103]**

151 Criminal Evidence Act 1992, s 27.

152 Youth Justice and Criminal Evidence Act 1999, s 53, Competence of witnesses to give evidence:

'(1) At every stage in criminal proceedings all persons are (whatever their age) competent to give evidence.

(2) Subsection (1) has effect subject to subsections (3) and (4).

(3) A person is not competent to give evidence in criminal proceedings if it appears to the court that he is not a person who is able to –

(a) understand questions put to him as a witness, and

(b) give answers to them which can be understood.

(4) A person charged in criminal proceedings is not competent to give evidence in the proceedings for the prosecution (whether he is the only person, or is one of two or more persons, charged in the proceedings).

(5) In subsection (4) the reference to a person charged in criminal proceedings does not include a person who is not, or is no longer, liable to be convicted of any offence in the proceedings (whether as a result of pleading guilty or for any other reason).'

153 *R v Powell* [2006] 1 CAR 31.

154 *R v Malicki* [2009] EWCA Crim 365.

155 *R v Powell* [2006] 1 CAR 31.

156 ibid.

157 *R v Malicki* [2009] EWCA Crim 365.

158 ibid [15].

a direct recollection of the event itself'.[159] The Court identified two problems arising from the delay: first that a child of such a young age would not have any accurate recollection of events which took place 14 months earlier; and, secondly, a matter of greater concern was that she might merely be recollecting what was said on the video and incapable of distinguishing between that account and the underlying events themselves. These considerations led the Court of Appeal to conclude that the evidence should have been excluded under the relevant legislation[160] and 'stopped because of the lapse of time'. Although the interview took place relatively soon after the incident, the trial itself followed some 14 months later and this extended time frame was sufficient to give rise to concern regarding competency.

[24–104] The difficulties of splitting the evidence between pre-recorded examination in chief evidence and live cross-examination evidence give rise to these unique competency concerns. It is submitted that challenges similar to those raised in *R v Powell*[161] and *R v Malicki*[162] would be upheld in Ireland, thus allowing the advantage of the admission of evidence of even very young victims to be lost where, if the testimony had been recorded in full prior to trial, competency issues would not have arisen.

[24–105] A further difficulty in splitting the child's evidence between the pre-trial and trial phases is the absence of examination in chief as a lead-in to cross-examination evidence. Where the evidence is recorded close to the time of the incident and there is a delay between the recording and the coming on for trial of the offence, the vulnerable witness must then face the difficulty of immediate cross-examination at trial. 'Parachuting' the child into the trial itself and requesting him or her to undergo cross-examination without any lead-in through examination-in-chief questioning may heighten the level of stress experienced by the witness. The Irish Law Reform Commission noted:

> The process of giving oral evidence in court may actually help the child. The prosecutor can bring the child through his or her evidence thereby giving the child time to settle down, and to get used to the courtroom atmosphere and to answering questions put by a lawyer.[163]

[24–106] Bernard Richmond QC, who acted as counsel for the defence in *R v Barker*,[164] has noted the difficulties in cross-examining young children:

> One of the main problems for those who defend in cases involving young complainants or witnesses is one of *attuning* ourselves to the witness. The "achieving best evidence"

---

[159] ibid.

[160] Police and Criminal Evidence Act 1984, s 78, Exclusion of unfair evidence:

> '(1) In any proceedings the court may refuse to allow evidence on which the prosecution proposes to rely to be given if it appears to the court that, having regard to all the circumstances, including the circumstances in which the evidence was obtained, the admission of the evidence would have such an adverse effect on the fairness of the proceedings that the court ought not to admit it.
>
> (2) Nothing in this section shall prejudice any rule of law requiring a court to exclude evidence.'

[161] *R v Powell* [2006] 1 CAR 31.

[162] *R v Malicki* [2009] EWCA Crim 365.

[163] The Law Reform Commission of Victoria, Australia, similarly observed: 'Otherwise the child is immediately confronted by the defence counsel's cross-examination and may find it difficult to testify effectively.' Law Reform Commission of Victoria, *Report No. 18, Sexual Offences Against Children* (1988) para 275, as mentioned in Irish Law Reform Commission, *Consultation Paper on Child Sexual Abuse* (CP2–1989) 158.

[164] *R v Barker* [2010] EWCA Crim 4.

> interview[165] is not particularly useful in that regard – it is often conducted many months previously; in an atmosphere where the child is made as comfortable as possible; the surroundings permit the child and questioner to interact as naturally as possible; and the interviewer has doubtless either met the child before or spent some time familiarizing him/herself with the needs of the child.[166]

Full recorded testimony, ie recording of examination in chief, cross-examination and re-examination evidence, has now been rolled out nationwide under s 28 of the Youth Justice and Criminal Evidence Act.[167] The section was not commenced until 2013 and was evaluated on a pilot project basis.[168] The delay in commencement was possibly due to the protests from the Criminal Bar Association in England and Wales on the basis of difficulties of third-party disclosure at an early stage in proceedings and the clash between the 'mere credibility rule' and public interest immunity.[169] Spencer suggests that it was attributable to implementation difficulties on the part of the Home Office.[170] **[24–107]**

However, one of the catalysts for implementation of s 28 of the Youth Justice and Criminal Evidence Act 1999 was the high-profile reporting of cases where vulnerable witnesses suffered extreme trauma during the trial process.[171] In commencing the section and implementing pilot projects, the Secretary of State for Justice, Chris Grayling, said: **[24–108]**

> The particularly hostile treatment of victims and witnesses in court has nothing to do with fairness or justice. I am adamant we must put a stop to this, but without compromising everyone's right to a fair trial.[172]

Initially established through a pilot scheme in three areas – Leeds, Liverpool and Kingston-upon-Thames – implementation of the initiative has now been rolled out **[24–109]**

---

165 The interview taken under Youth Justice and Criminal Evidence Act 1999, s 27 is known as 'the ABE interview' or 'the Achieving Best Evidence interview'. While similar to the provisions of s 16(1)(b) Criminal Evidence Act 1992, the eligibility for the provision is wider as child witnesses in all criminal proceedings are eligible to have their evidence recorded. Youth Justice and Criminal Evidence Act 1999, s 16 outlines the parameters for eligibility for special measures for vulnerable witnesses.

166 Bernard Richmond, '*Cross Examining Young Witnesses*' Criminal Law & Justice Weekly (2011) 175 JPN 69.

167 Youth Justice and Criminal Evidence Act 1999, s 28, Video recorded cross-examination or re-examination.

168 See Andrew Ford, *'Pre-Record, Not fade away – Section 28 of the Youth Justice and Criminal Evidence Act (March 2015)'* Counsel (Bar Council of England and Wales); David Wurtzel, '*Pre-Recorded Cross-examination and the Questioning of Vulnerable Witnesses in the Criminal Justice System*', (Dec 2014) Counsel (Bar Council of England and Wales).

169 Laura Hoyano and Caroline Keenan, *Child Abuse Law and Policy Across Boundaries* (Oxford University Press 2010) lv. This matter was previously addressed in the hardback edition of Laura Hoyano and Caroline Keenan, *Child Abuse Law and Policy Across Boundaries* (Oxford University Press 2007) 552.

170 JR Spencer, 'Conclusions: If Section 28 is Workable, Will it Solve all the Problems that Arise from the Cross-examination of Children' in John R Spencer and Michael E Lamb (eds), *Children and Cross-Examination: Time To Change the Rules?* (Hart Publishing 2012) 172.

171 Owen Bowcott, 'Pre-recorded evidence to spare vulnerable victims court ordeal' *The Guardian* (London, 11 June 2013): 'Rather than having to delay recalling horrific experiences until a trial takes place, thereby prolonging the trauma, those who have suffered serious attacks will be helped to put the memories behind them at an earlier stage. The move follows several high-profile cases – such as that of the violinist Frances Andrade, who killed herself after giving evidence in court about historic indecent assaults – that have raised questions about how victims should be treated.' <http://www.theguardian.com/law/2013/jun/11/pre-recorded-evidence-victims-court?CMP=twt_gu> accessed 13 October 2023.

172 ibid.

nationwide. While full recorded evidence was examined in the 'O'Malley Report', it was not recommended in Ireland at present due to disclosure and other issues which, according to the report, would need to be addressed before the measure could be introduced.[173]

Application for a Direction

[24–110] The taking of evidence via recorded testimony under s 16(1)(b) of the Criminal Evidence Act 1992 disconnects the examination in chief evidence to the trial. In addition, the delay that is inherent in the trial process may cause particular issues for the vulnerable witness. While inconsistencies and credibility are generally deemed matters for the jury, the point at which the evidence is such that it would be unfair for the matter to be put before the jury is a difficult one for the trial judge.

[24–111] The application for a direction, whether on the basis of *R v Galbraith*,[174] *DPP v M*,[175] or *DPP v PO'C*[176] at the close of the prosecution case, is more generally dealt with elsewhere.[177] In relation to vulnerable witnesses, recent cases have dealt with the issues involved in the strength of the evidence where there had been issues regarding memory recall or where the complainant stated in cross-examination that the offences did not occur.

[24–112] The case of *DPP v MB*[178] involved allegations of sexual abuse of a child of approximately seven years of age by a babysitter. During cross-examination the child said that the offence alleged to have occurred hadn't happened. The defence made an application for a direction, which was unsuccessful, and the appellant was subsequently convicted. In granting the appeal, Kennedy J said:

> A judge must consider all of the evidence in determining whether to withdraw a case from the jury, and the trial judge did so in the present case. It is an exceptional measure to withdraw a case from the jury. However, in our view, in the circumstances of this case, the answers given by the complainant were to questions central to the allegations, in fact, directly concerning the events which gave rise to the allegations and contradicted

[173] Dept of Justice and Equality, *Review of Protections for Vulnerable Witnesses in the Investigation and Prosecution of Sexual Offences* (August 2020) para 6.28: 'Accordingly, for a number of reasons, including the issue just mentioned in connection with disclosure, we do not recommend at this point that pre-recorded cross-examination or re-examination be introduced. We are also conscious of a number of other potential problems that were mentioned by the Bar Council in its submission to the Working Group. These include possible issues with technology, a potential reduction in the jury's ability to "read" a witness's body language, whether video testimony might create emotional distance between the witness and the jury, and possibly lack the immediacy and persuasiveness of live testimony. We do, however, acknowledge that strong arguments have been made, by academic experts and others, in favour of introducing such a practice. Our recommendation is based solely on practical considerations rather than any opposition in principle. If the point is reached where these practical issues can be effectively addressed, pre-recorded cross-examination and re-examination may well become feasible, though any potential constitutional impediments would need to be carefully examined before a final decision is taken on the matter.'

[174] *R v Galbraith* [1981] 1 WLR 1039.

[175] *DPP v M* [2015] IECA 65.

[176] *DPP v PO'C* [2006] 3 IR 238.

[177] See Thomas O'Malley, *The Criminal Process* (Round Hall 2009); Declan McGrath and Emily Egan McGrath, *McGrath on Evidence* (3rd edn, Round Hall 2020); Liz Heffernan, *Evidence in Criminal Trials* (2nd edn, Bloomsbury 2020).

[178] *DPP v MB* [2023] IECA 85.

> his direct testimony. This was not a situation of inconsistencies arising on the evidence, this was quite different, where, in truth, the answer given as to whether the offending occurred was a simple "no." We wish to make it clear that where the child's response to questions was that he was unsure of certain things, this would not necessarily have been sufficient to direct a jury to return verdicts of not guilty, but those responses, together with the responses [sic] "no" brings the case into the exceptional category.[179]

The judgment also notes the importance of re-examination where there is any confusion. However, while re-examination had taken place in this instance, it did not resolve the issue. Kennedy J observed: **[24–113]**

> In our view, re-examination is especially important in the context of a child witness whose direct testimony is adduced by way of video recorded interview. Re-examination may have the effect of clarifying an unsatisfactory situation one way or the other. Whilst re-examination took place in the present case, it did not sufficiently rehabilitate the witness to confirm that the events complained of took place.[180]

In *DPP v MT*[181] the complainant stated during cross-examination that she did not remember the alleged offence. It was alleged to have taken place when she was approximately six and the trial took place when she was approximately 11 years of age. At the close of the prosecution case, the appellant made an application based on the decision in *People (DPP) v PO'C*[182] in relation to the inability to receive a fair trial on the basis of delay, which was refused by the trial judge. The Court of Appeal quashed the conviction on the basis that no rulings by the trial judge could have cured the fact that delay had undermined the right of the appellant to cross-examine the complainant. Giving the judgment of the court, Ní Raifeartaigh J stated: **[24–114]**

> Having regard to the totality of the evidence and circumstances, the Court is satisfied that there was a risk of an unfair trial. In our adversarial system of criminal justice as currently constituted, it is not sufficient that there be clear and coherent evidence-in-chief from the child complainant (which there undoubtedly was, via the videorecording): there must be some realistic opportunity to cross-examine in order to afford an accused person his constitutional right to cross-examine. The Court has concluded that where the witness' memory was impaired to the degree described by the child complainant herself in this case, any attempt to cross-examine the child was effectively an exercise in futility and there was therefore a real risk that the trial was unfair which could not be cured, no matter what warnings the jury might be given.[183]

In relation to the issue of memory, the case of *DPP v PB*[184] is relevant in that the Court determined that issues of memory recall were matters for the jury. Amongst several appeal points, the appellant challenged how the trial judge dealt with the complainant's difficulties in remembering details of events. The prosecution placed this in the context of the circumstances of the complainant's younger life, which had involved various interactions with social services. Ultimately, the appeal failed both on this and other points. **[24–115]**

> It seems to us that one cannot lose sight of the fact that the jury saw both the direct examination and cross-examination and observed for themselves how often the

---

179 ibid [58]–[59].
180 ibid [53].
181 *DPP v MT* [2023] IECA 65.
182 *DPP v PO'C* [2006] 3 IR 238.
183 *DPP v MT* [2023] IECA 65 [97].
184 *DPP v PB* [2021] IECA 152.

complainant responded to questions by saying that she did not remember. They were then further reminded of this, as one would expect, during the course of the defence closing argument and the judge made specific mention of it in the course of his charge. Having said that, we do think there is much force in the argument made by the Director that such was the extent of the young complainant's interaction with medics and social workers, that it was not surprising that she would have difficulty recalling particular interactions and what was said on particular occasions. It is the nature of things that individuals recall standout events, or once-off events, but may have difficulty in remembering the details of a particular event if events of that nature were frequent or routine. For this young complainant, contact and interaction with professionals of one variety or another was very routine indeed. We have not been persuaded that the judge's handling of this issue was other than satisfactory.[185]

[24–116] **Suggested procedure in relation to recorded testimony**

- View the recording to confirm that any transcript is correct and that there are no audibility/technical issues.
- Agree edits to the recording to excise any sections which may be prejudicial.
- Check how the editing of the recording will be made and ensure that all parties consent to the final edit.
- The prosecution may liaise with the investigating officer to create a new recording with the edited testimony. It is important to ensure that this format works in the courtroom facilities available.
- Ensure that the courtroom has working facilities for the format of recording that is being played to the court.
- Ensure that the master copy will be available should the intended copy not play correctly, be lost etc.
- Ensure that the recording works. Ensure also that if cross-examination evidence is to be given via video link, that the playing of the recording and the video link facilities both work in harmony, ie that the complainant is able to view the video as it is being played to the jury.
- Ensure that there is a member of the Information Technology Department available to assist at any time, in case unforeseen issues arise.
- Where a vulnerable witness is giving evidence, confirm what their particular needs are in relation to what is best to facilitate them, eg what time of day is best for them to give evidence, how many breaks they may need. These aspects may be assessed if an intermediary has been appointed and the intermediary will inform the court of these aspects through the ground rules hearing.
- If an intermediary has not been appointed, then the prosecution counsel should gain as much information as possible about the complainant as to their physical needs that will allow them to give their best evidence e.g. time of day, eating, snacks, breaks. The court can be informed of this to schedule how the evidence can be given. For example, many children find it easier to concentrate in the morning. So if the recording of their evidence in chief evidence is played to the jury the day or afternoon previously, then the first task of the following day should be the examination in chief evidence. Any difficulty or delay to this should be anticipated and resolved, including any defence or prosecution applications or any rulings that are required from the trial judge.
- In the course of the playing of the recording, it is important to ensure that any audibility issues are resolved. Preparation for audibility issues is advised. This may involve an application for transcripts to be provided as appropriate.
- When the cross-examination is ready to be given, the trial judge may pause proceedings and allow the jury to leave in order to ensure that the witness is available and ready to give evidence via video link or in court.

[185] ibid [33].

Chapter 25

REFRESHING THE WITNESS' MEMORY

Introduction

Given the interval of time between the taking of a written statement by a member of An Garda Síochána and the date when a witness gets into the witness box to give evidence, the witness is allowed to refresh his or her memory by being able to look at his or her original statement. The normal procedure is to have the witness be given his or her statement prior to trial or hearing so that his or her memory can be refreshed. Coaching of a witness is not permitted.[1] In addition, a witness may not learn off his or her statement and recite the contents of the statement in court. The Court of Appeal case of *People (DPP) v Donnelly*[2] involved a charge of sexual assault against a complainant, who was almost 13 years of age at the time of the offence and approximately 14 and half at the time of trial. The complainant was given her statement prior to trial and, in cross-examination via video link, conceded that she had learned off her statement. This point was appealed but the Court of Appeal rejected it, stating: **[25–01]**

> There is clearly a danger that if a witness seeks to learn the contents of his or her statement by heart then when such witness gives evidence in court it may not be about what occurred but about what such witness had said in the statement had occurred. This would clearly be wrong. Nevertheless it is a matter which if raised can be dealt with by the trial judge as in fact it was. So far as the practice is concerned there is no reason why witnesses including young witnesses who are going to give evidence on video link not be shown their statements in advance.[3]

With the introduction of recorded evidence, other issues have come to light in terms of how the witness' memory is refreshed and what impact that may have on their evidence. While it is commonly understood that the giving of evidence is not a memory test, the viewing of a video which contains footage of the witness giving detail of the alleged offence much closer in time to the alleged incidents may have a bearing on the **[25–02]**

1 *GO'R v DPP* [2011] IEHC 318; [2012] 1 IR 193. See also Bar Council of Ireland, *Code of Conduct* (adopted 25 July 2022) para 5.11, 21: 'Barristers may not coach a witness in regard to the evidence to be given.'

2 *People (DPP) v Donnelly*, Court of Criminal Appeal (22 February 1999) 2000 WJSC–CCA 7892.

3 ibid.

emotional state of the witness and, it could be argued, have a more powerful effect, by the very nature of the medium, of influencing the witness not to remember the incident as it occurred but to remember the contents of the video itself. The latter is evidentially problematic.

[25–03] In Ireland, if the recorded evidence is admitted, even as an edited version, it comprises the examination in chief of the witness. The details of the event will be recorded close to the time of the alleged incident and this is the purpose and advantage of recorded evidence. However, for very young witnesses and for certain persons with an intellectual disability, memory recall may deteriorate significantly with time. Refreshing the memory of the witness by watching the video may mean that the witness, when it comes to cross-examination, may be remembering the events as related on the video. If he or she had to get into the witness box for examination in chief, having had his or her memory refreshed, he or she would have to give an independent voluntary answer to any questions asked at a greater time period after the offence. That may or may not be different from what might have been said closer to the time of the incident but both prosecution and defence will be dealing with a witness with the same level of memory recall in terms of examination in chief and cross-examination evidence.

[25–04] In the case of recorded testimony, if admitted, a significant part of the testimony has been given already. When it comes to cross-examination the information of the relevant offence has been heard by the court, the jury and the witness and, with any interval of time, that evidence may take priority while other information is less fresh in the mind of the witness. A particular difficulty may arise when it comes to younger witnesses or witnesses with an intellectual disability in terms of whether they are remembering the details of the statement or the actual incident itself.

[25–05] The danger is that aspect of what a very young child is remembering in respect of their competence and, regarding recorded evidence, this has been examined in English cases mentioned such as *R v Powell*[4] and *R v Malicki*[5] which have been referenced in Irish appeal cases such as *DPP v FN*[6] and *DPP v MT*.[7] With written statements, as McGrath notes, the English Court of Appeal case *R v Westwell*[8] held that the fact that a witness has refreshed his or her memory may go to the weight to be attached to his or her evidence rather than admissibility. McGrath notes, thus, that :

> in a criminal case, injustice may be caused to the accused if the jury are not informed that this has occurred. This is also important because the accused is entitled to obtain a copy of and cross-examine on the previous statement. It is therefore desirable that, if the prosecution is aware that witnesses have seen the statements, they should inform the defence of this fact. However, a failure to do so will not, of itself, be a ground for acquittal or setting aside a conviction.[9]

[25–06] The defence should be made aware that the witness' memory has been refreshed, albeit by whatever means, either through reading the statement or watching the recording. When the evidence is given, it is the responsibility of the defence to flag and for the

4 *R v Powell* [2006] EWCA Crim 3.
5 *R v Malicki* [2009] EWCA Crim 365.
6 *DPP v FN* [2021] IECA 238; [2022] IESC 22.
7 *DPP v MT* [2023] IECA 65.
8 *R v Westwell* [1976] 2 All ER 812.
9 Declan McGrath and Emily Egan McGrath, *McGrath on Evidence* (3rd edn, Round Hall 2020) para 3–192, 161. *Owen v Edwards* (1983) 77 Cr App R 191; *Worley v Bentley* [1976] 2 All ER 449.

judge and/or jury (or appeal court) to determine if the witness was remembering his or her statement or the incident itself. This is a difficult issue but it appears the courts are more willing to accommodate these difficulties and allow the evidence to be admitted unless there is a clear breach of the defendant's constitutional rights.

Recorded Testimony

The *Good Practice Guidelines* state: **[25–07]**

> In all cases where a video recording is to be viewed by the court and it is proposed to cross examine and/or re-examine the complainant, it is recommended that arrangements be made to ensure that the complainant can view the recording on the monitor in the witness room when it is being shown it to the court and to the jury.[10]

However, generally to avoid distress, the witness may be able to watch the DVD in a suitable environment with appropriate accompaniment at a time prior to the trial, if agreed by the court, through counsel, or through both via a ground rules hearing. There is no procedure outlined in the *Good Practice Guidelines* in terms of the witness watching his or her recorded testimony prior to giving evidence. Practice has evolved that the recordings are viewed in the company of a person, usually a member of An Garda Síochána, not involved with the investigation of the case. The Garda should preferably be the same gender as the witness as the Garda will be alone with the witness while he or she views the recording. The Garda should take a note of any incident that occurred or any comment that was made by the witness and be prepared to give a statement and evidence if so required. Issues should be anticipated and resolved where necessary. In a case reported in the *Irish Times* concerning a very young witness, the stress caused by technical issues is clear: **[25–08]**

> The couple cite a litany of things that made Zoe's experience at court much more difficult than anticipated. Initially, there was no room available for her to view her DVD evidence before it was shown to the jury. After a frantic search one was found.
>
> The technology in the courtroom broke down repeatedly so Zoe had to leave the video link room and return to it numerous times. 'All that expensive marble, and the IT is substandard,' Kate says.[11]

When Giving Testimony at Trial from the Witness Box

The case of *People (DPP) v Donnelly* outlines the evidential principle that a witness should not learn off his or her statement by heart.[12] **[25–09]**

---

[10] An Garda Síochána, *Good Practice Guidelines for Persons involved in Video Recording interviews with complainants under 14 years of age (or with intellectual disability) for Evidential Purposes in accordance with Section 16(1)(b) of the Criminal Evidence Act, 1992, in cases involving Sexual and/or Violent Offences* (July 2003) 9.

[11] Sarah-Jane Murphy, 'The story of "Zoe", one of the youngest sex-abuse cases ever heard in Irish courts' *The Irish Times* (Dublin, 24 April 2021) <https://www.irishtimes.com/the-story-of-zoe-one-of-the-youngest-sex-abuse-cases-ever-heard-in-irish-courts-1.4537355> accessed 13 October 2023.

[12] *People (DPP) v Donnelly*, Court of Criminal Appeal (22 February 1999). 2000 WJSC–CCA 7892. See [25–01].

[25–10] Although not a case involving vulnerable witnesses, the case of *DPP v Quinn*[13] may be relevant particularly where a witness may have educational or cognitive difficulties. The case involved a case of assault and, while giving evidence, the witness' mind had gone blank on the witness stand. The trial judge allowed the witness to have his memory refreshed through the reading of his witness statement in circumstances where the witness said he had read it two days previously but had forgotten to bring it with him on the morning of his evidence. The witness had also conceded that he had difficulties with reading. The Court of Appeal dismissed this ground of appeal but the conviction was quashed on other evidential points. On this point however, Sheehan J stated:

> In respect of ground (3)(b) (the ground in respect of the ruling that the statement could be read to the witness), it is worth reiterating that a witness is always entitled to have a copy of his or her witness statement and to read over it prior to giving evidence. This Court is satisfied that the trial judge's decision to allow Robert Ryan's statement of evidence to be read over to him by the solicitor for the Director of Public Prosecutions in the presence of the appellant's solicitor was an appropriate ruling in circumstances where it had emerged that he had a problem with reading.[14]

[25–11] The refreshing of memory may go to the weight to be attached to the evidence.[15] In *DPP v Quinn*[16] the circumstances of the memory issues were outlined in the trial judge's charge to the jury and she directed that the jury must bear this in mind when they were deciding the weight to be attached to this witness' evidence.[17]

Witness Should Have Time to Consider Documents Furnished in Cross-Examination

[25–12] In the case of *DPP v DC*,[18] the evidence of the complainant, in relation to sexual offences, was given by video link over seven days at the trial, five of which comprised cross-examination. One of the points of appeal was in relation to the ruling of the trial judge that the complainant was entitled to what the appellant had characterised as 'advance notice of the material upon which she was being cross-examined' and that this had adverse effects on the fairness of the cross-examination or its effectiveness. It was suggested that this allowed the complainant to anticipate what matters might be canvassed and that with respect to any material which was inconsistent with her evidence she was 'better placed to prepare or revise answers' to make them more favourable to her in the eyes of the jury. In disallowing this point, and the appeal in general, Edwards J stated:

> The search for truth in a trial can only be assisted by ensuring that a witness has an adequate opportunity to answer questions in an informed manner. If documents are proffered to a witness for her consideration, she is entitled to an opportunity to peruse and consider them: it is far better, in many instances, if the witness is furnished with such materials either before entering the witness box or, if proffered in the witness box, afforded an opportunity to leave the box and consider them. Obviously, the witness box is not the ideal place to consider documents calmly and an insistence that that course be

13 *DPP v Quinn* [2015] IECA 308.
14 ibid [8.12].
15 *R v Westwell* [1976] 2 All ER 812.
16 *DPP v Quinn* [2015] IECA 308 [8.12].
17 *DPP v Quinn* [2015] IECA 308 [7.6].
18 *DPP v DC* [2019] IECA 367 [245].

> adopted might well engender lengthy and unnecessary delays, be unfair to the witness, and render the evidence elicited less reliable. Having regard to the length of cross-examination this was an obvious case for affording an opportunity to the witness to consider matters otherwise than in the witness box. It is correct to say that a witness, being furnished with documents in advance, will have had the optimum opportunity to consider them. We cannot see how there could be any right vested in an accused in the context of affording him a fair trial to insist on a right, in effect, to deprive a witness of this opportunity; or, in a sense, to ambush a witness and seek immediate answers on a document of complexity or length. Accordingly, we reject this complaint.[19]

No Coaching of Witnesses

The *Code of Conduct* adopted by the Bar Council of Ireland prohibits the coaching of witnesses by barristers.[20] In addition, the case of *GO'R*,[21] referring to the analogous English case *R v Momadou*,[22] is authority in Ireland for the principle that witnesses should not be coached. However, the judgment outlines the balance that should be drawn between non-coaching and professional interaction before a witness gives evidence at trial. Charleton J stated: **[25–13]**

> Trained solicitors and barristers involved in pre trial consultations will avoid any suggestion to a witness that a particular emphasis is needed in evidence, much less suggest that a witness should embroider or invent facts. The nature of this process, if professionally conducted, is neutral. It does no more than focus potential evidence and it avoids directing its content. Formal enquiry in preparation for trial is necessary and appropriate: it can help expose strengths and weaknesses to the professional lawyers representing a client; this, when conducted in this neutral form, aids a fair assessment prior to court, possible settlement of a case and its proper prosecution at trial. Witnesses are never to be directed as to the content of their evidence. It would fundamentally undermine the trial process were it to be allowed to become fictional whereby each side is presenting invented facts based on direction as to what may assist their case. No criminal trial process, consistent with that principle of the obligation of truthfulness, can be presented by the defence whereby the case which is regarded as suitable for a successful challenge to the prosecution is put, in distinction to the case made in consultation by the accused and his or her witnesses. It must be recognised, as well, that some witnesses may need more than usual assurance and in the instance of some expert witnesses, for instance university academics, more used to the presentation of a discursive rehearsal of a subject, these may be assisted as to the best form in which their evidence may become focussed. It is not wrong, therefore, to direct those witnesses as to the issues in question in the case and the manner in which their view may be appropriately presented through being shorn of rambling side references and irrelevant musings or tangential material.[23]

No Discussion Amongst Witnesses Prior to Giving Evidence

The case of *GO'R*[24] is also authority in Ireland for the principle that there should be no discussion between witnesses prior to giving evidence. In that judgment, Charleton J **[25–14]**

---

19 ibid.

20 Bar Council of Ireland, *Code of Conduct* (25 July 2022).

21 *GO'R v DPP* [2011] IEHC 368, [2012] 1 IR 193.

22 *R v Momadou* [2005] 1 WLR 3442.

23 *GO'R v DPP* [2011] IEHC 368; [2012] 1 IR 193, 201, 202.

24 *GO'R v DPP* [2011] IEHC 368; [2012] 1 IR 193. See also *R v Skinner* (1993) 99 Cr APP r 212, 216; *R v Richardson* (1971) 2 QB 484, 490.

agreed with the comments in *R v Marmodu*[25] that, while pre-trial familiarisation was helpful, discussions which may lead to a witness modifying his or her testimony were prohibited.[26]

No Discussion with Barristers During Cross-Examination

[25–15] It is the practice of trial judges to warn a witness, in a break in their cross-examination, not to discuss his or her evidence with anyone. This will avoid any contamination of the evidence. In addition, barristers are prohibited from conferring with a witness unless there is consent with the barrister on the other side or the trial judge.

> Barristers shall not confer with a witness while such witness is under cross examination without prior leave of the other parties or the Court.[27]

[25] *R v Momadou* [2005] 1 WLR 3442.

[26] *GO'R v DPP* [2011] IEHC 368; [2012] 1 IR 193 [21].

[27] Bar Council of Ireland, *Code of Conduct* (25 July 2022) para 5.12.

CHAPTER 26

RIGHT TO CROSS-EXAMINE

Introduction

In *White v Ireland*[1] the defendant was awaiting trial for sexual offences against a child and the complainant was to give evidence via video link under s 13 of the Criminal Evidence Act 1992. The defendant sought a declaration that s 13 was repugnant to the Constitution and also an injunction to prevent its use at trial. His application was grounded in the contention that the use of live video link under s 13(1)(a) for witnesses under 17 years of age[2] constituted an infringement of his right to cross-examine and confront his accuser in open court.[3] In order to determine whether the defendant's constitutional rights were being breached, Kinlen J examined the right to a trial in due course of law under Article 38.1 of the Constitution of Ireland as well as the right of every citizen to be treated equally under Article 40. **[26–01]**

Kinlen J examined the principles set out in *State (Healy) v Donoghue*,[4] where Gannon J had affirmed that among the natural rights of an individual whose conduct is impugned and whose freedom is put in jeopardy are: **[26–02]**

> the rights to be adequately informed of the nature and substance of the accusation, to have the matter tried in his presence by an impartial and independent court or arbitrator, to hear and test by examination the evidence offered by or on behalf of his accuser, to be allowed to give or call evidence in his defence, and to be heard in argument or submission before judgment be given.[5]

In *Donnelly v Ireland*[6] the Supreme Court held that the use of video link did not restrict the right of an accused person to a fair trial, including the right to cross-examine, as established by *In Re Haughey*[7] and *State (Healy) v Donoghue*.[8] *In Re Haughey*[9] outlined the basic requirements which must be afforded to every person accused of a 'serious offence',[10] including that of cross-examination; it did not include an express right to confront a witness.[11] **[26–03]**

---

1 *White v Ireland* [1995] 2 IR 268.
2 The age of eligibility at the time of the proceedings prior to the amendment of the Act by s 257 of the Children Act 2001, which raised the threshold to 18 years of age.
3 *White v Ireland* [1995] 2 IR 268, 275.
4 *State (Healy) v Donoghue* [1976] IR 325.
5 ibid 335.
6 *Donnelly v Ireland* [1998] 1 IR 321.
7 *In re Haughey* [1971] IR 217.
8 *State (Healy) v Donoghue* [1976] IR 325.
9 *In re Haughey* [1971] IR 217.
10 *Donnelly v Ireland* [1998] 1 IR 321, 330 (HC).
11 *In re Haughey* [1971] IR 217, 263.

[26–04] However, the questioning must be relevant and a distinction as to the latitude afforded to the questioner will be made regarding questions as to the facts in issue and that of credibility. In P*eople (DPP) v Piotrowski*,[12] it was held that a trial judge would have greater latitude to intervene and control cross-examination in the case of the latter:

> The defence is, of course, entitled to some latitude in pursuing issues concerning the credibility of important prosecution evidence. However, it is also true that the trial judge has an important role in ensuring that the case is confined to questions which are at least of sufficient relevance to the issues which the jury has to decide to make their pursuit material. If the issues being pursued by cross-examination are directly relevant to the facts of the case in the sense of the facts which are alleged to constitute the offence charged or the guilt of the accused in respect of that offence, then wide latitude must be allowed. Where the issues raised simply go to general credibility not directly connected with the offence but connected with matters which may have some indirect bearing on the credibility of witnesses in relation to the offence, then it seems to this Court that the trial judge is entitled to exercise a greater degree of control over the extent to which such issues can be pursued.[13]

Right to Cross-Examine Where Significant Delay Between Offence and Trial

[26–05] The right to cross-examine, particularly in relation to vulnerable witnesses, where there is a delay between the time of the offence and the trial was considered in *DPP v MT*.[14] The case related to the cross-examination of a child complainant in a sexual offence trial. Four-and-a-half years had elapsed between the videorecording of the child's testimony (when she was aged six) and the cross-examination at the trial at which the appellant was convicted (when she was aged 11). The appellant was convicted of the one count of sexual assault and sentenced to four years imprisonment. During cross-examination the complainant had conceded that that she had little memory of the incident which was the subject of the charge and was relying upon what she had seen in the video-recording of her interview. The issues before the Court were whether in those circumstances the appellant could exercise his lawful entitlement to cross-examine, whether the child's evidence should have been left to the jury, and whether the trial was fair. As outlined by Ní Raifeartaigh J, the case raised fundamental questions about the exercise of an accused person's right to cross-examine in circumstances involving a young child and where there is a significant delay between the making of the videorecording of the child's interview and the trial. This is a situation that unfortunately arises relatively frequently in Ireland. Ultimately the Court allowed the appeal and quashed the conviction, Ní Raifeartaigh J stating:

> Having regard to the totality of the evidence and circumstances, the Court is satisfied that there was a risk of an unfair trial. In our adversarial system of criminal justice as currently constituted, it is not sufficient that there be clear and coherent evidence-in-chief from the child complainant (which there undoubtedly was, via the videorecording): there must be some realistic opportunity to cross-examine in order to afford an accused person his constitutional right to cross-examine. The Court has concluded that where the witness' memory was impaired to the degree described by the child complainant herself in this case, any attempt to cross-examine the child was effectively an exercise in futility

[12] *DPP v Piotrowski* [2014] IECCA 17.

[13] ibid [8.3].

[14] *DPP v MT* [2023] IECA 65.

> and there was therefore a real risk that the trial was unfair which could not be cured, no matter what warnings the jury might be given.[15]

In the case of *DPP v MB*[16] the child complainant said during cross-examination that the offence hadn't happened and yet an application for a direction was unsuccessful. Quashing the conviction, the Court of Appeal stated: **[26–06]**

> The rights of victims are protected by Article 40.3 of the Constitution and Article 42A.1 of the Constitution refers to the natural and imprescriptible rights of a child and guarantees to protect and vindicate those rights as far as practicable. In practical terms, when cross-examining a child, questions asked should be short, simple and without repetition. The judge must carefully guard the interests of the child, ensuring the child understands what is being asked but at all times ensuring the right to a fair trial.[17]

The Court also noted the significance of re-examination in correcting any uncertainty and also noted that re-examination may involve a witness being asked to explain and clarify an answer given and may be used to rehabilitate a witness. **[26–07]**

In relation to recorded testimony and the issue of delay, the Court observed: **[26–08]**

> In our view, re-examination is especially important in the context of a child witness whose direct testimony is adduced by way of video recorded interview. Re-examination may have the effect of clarifying an unsatisfactory situation one way or the other. Whilst re-examination took place in the present case, it did not sufficiently rehabilitate the witness to confirm that the events complained of took place.
>
> Each case is of course fact dependent. In the experience of this Court, difficulty in recall is not an unusual feature of cases where a witness statement is taken by video link and the cross examination takes place sometime thereafter. It is obvious that these trials should, where possible, be prioritised. In some instances, the insufficiency of recall will be starker than in others, there is no one size fits all, sometimes there will be an absence of recall regarding the specifics of an incident, but the child confirms some details of the incident. Sometimes, it may be an inability to recall one incident whilst recalling others or the detail of an incident may differ somewhat. Without being prescriptive, in those situations, the absence of specifics may impact on the credibility of the witness, and can safely be left to a trial judge to determine whether the lack of recall renders a trial unfair. The courts must strike a balance between ensuring a child gives their best evidence whilst ensuring a person's right to a fair trial is honoured.[18]

---

[15] ibid [97].
[16] *DPP v MB* [2023] IECA 85.
[17] ibid [42].
[18] ibid [53]–[54].

Chapter 27

SCREENS

Background

It could be argued that the use of screens has been permissible in Ireland on a common law basis since the decision in *R v Smellie*.[1] The defendant was accused of neglect and ill-treatment of his daughter, who was approximately 11 years of age. Before she gave evidence, the defendant was directed, on the instructions of the Court, to sit on the stairs leading out of the dock and was thereby out of sight but not out of hearing of the complainant. The trial court had determined that his presence would 'terrify his daughter'. The defendant was convicted, and his appeal dismissed. Lord Coleridge stated: **[27–01]**

> If the judge considers that the presence of the prisoner will intimidate a witness there is nothing to prevent him from securing the ends of justice by removing the former from the presence of the latter.[2]

Section 14A Criminal Evidence Act 1992

Section 30(d) of the Criminal Justice (Victims of Crime) Act 2017 put the use of screens on a statutory footing through the insertion of s 14A of the Criminal Evidence Act 1992.[3] The section was commenced on 30 May 2018 and states: **[27–02]**

---

1 *R v Smellie* (1919) 14 Cr App R 128 (CA).

2 ibid.

3 Criminal Evidence Act 1992, s 14A as inserted by Criminal Justice (Victims of Crime) Act 2017, s 30(d). At time of writing s30(d) Criminal Justice (Victims of Crime) Act 2017 is only commenced for the Central Criminal Court, the Dublin Circuit Criminal Court and the Dublin Metropolitan District of the District Court.

14A. (1) Where a person who is under 18 years of age is to give evidence other than through a live television link in respect of a relevant offence, the court may, on the application of the prosecution or the accused, direct that a screen or other similar device be positioned, in an appropriate place, so as to prevent the witness from seeing the accused when giving evidence, unless the court is satisfied that in all the circumstances of the case such a direction would be contrary to the interests of justice.

(2) Subject to section 14AA, where –

(a) a person who is a victim of an offence, other than a relevant offence, is under 18 years of age and the person is to give evidence, other than through a live television link, in respect of the offence, or

(b) a person who is a victim of any offence has attained the age of 18 years and the person is to give evidence, other than through a live television link, in respect of such an offence, the court may, on the application of the prosecution or the accused, if satisfied that the interests of justice so require, direct that a screen or other similar device be positioned, in an appropriate place, so as to prevent the victim from seeing the accused when giving evidence.

(3) A witness giving evidence under subsection (1) or (2) shall be capable of seeing and hearing and being seen and heard by –

(a) the judge and jury (if any),

(b) legal representatives acting in the proceedings,

(c) any interpreter, intermediary appointed under section 14 or any other person appointed to assist the witness,

and shall be capable of being heard by the accused.

Who is Eligible

[27–03] The eligibility for the use of a screen relates to whether the witness is under 18, is a victim and/or the offence is a relevant offence subject to s 14AA of the Criminal Evidence Act 1992.[4]

- Section 14A(1) – A witness (ie victim or witness) under 18 in relation to a relevant offence subject to s 14AA.
- Section 14A(2)(a) – A victim under 18 in relation to an offence other than a relevant offence subject to s 14AA.

---

[4] Criminal Evidence Act 1992, s 12(1):

'"relevant offence" means –

(a) a sexual offence;

(b) an offence involving violence or the threat of violence to a person;

(ba) an offence under section 10 (amended by section 23 of the Criminal Justice (Miscellaneous Provisions) Act 2023) of the NonFatal Offences against the Person Act 1997;

(c) an offence under section 3, 4, 5 or 6 of the Child Trafficking and Pornography Act 1998;

(d) an offence under section 2, 4 or 7 of the Criminal Law (Human Trafficking) Act 2008;

(da) an offence under section 33, 38 or 39 of the Domestic Violence Act 2018;

(e) an offence consisting of attempting or conspiring to commit, or of aiding or abetting, counselling, procuring or inciting the commission of, an offence mentioned in paragraph (a), (b), (c), (d) or (da).'

Criminal Justice (Miscellaneous Provisions) Act 2023, s 60 now extends 'relevant offence' to include 'harassment or stalking' under s.10 Non Fatal Offences Against the Person Act 1997. When commenced, it will also include s 44 'Order' under Criminal Justice (Miscellaneous Provisions) Act 2023, s 28.

- Section 14A(2)(b) – An adult victim who is over 18 in relation to any offence subject to s 14AA.

Who is Excluded

Who is excluded includes: **[27–04]**

- A witness who is not a victim under 18 to an offence other than a relevant offence, eg neglect, cruelty, an offence under the Harassment, Harmful Communications and Related Offences Act 2020, depending on the circumstances of the case e.g. whether it involves violence or the threat of violence..
- An adult witness, who is not a victim, in relation to any offence. This includes an adult with an intellectual disability as s 14A is not included in s 19 Criminal Evidence Act 1992[5]
- The defendant.

While not expressly stating that the defendant is excluded, s 14A(1) states: **[27–05]**

> 14A(1) Where a person who is under 18 years of age is to give evidence other than through a live television link in respect of a relevant offence, the court may, on the application of the prosecution or the accused, direct that a screen or other similar device be positioned, in an appropriate place, so as to prevent the witness from seeing the accused when giving evidence, unless the court is satisfied that in all the circumstances of the case such a direction would be contrary to the interests of justice.

The legislation notes that the screen is to be positioned to prevent the witness from seeing the accused when giving evidence, which may be interpreted that the section excludes the defendant. However, the prosecution and defence may apply for a screen for any prosecution or defence witness as appropriate. **[27–06]**

Section 14A(2)(a) and (b) explicitly state the 'victim'. However, there is nothing to prevent the court, if necessary, facilitating the use of a screen of its own inherent jurisdiction with the objective of minimising the stress for the defendant in order to obtain the best evidence possible. Edwards J in *DPP v Harrison* stated that practical measures may be used to facilitate a vulnerable defendant, each case depending on its own facts.[6] **[27–07]**

Inherent Jurisdiction for Witnesses and Victims

The case of *R v Smellie*[7] may be helpful in facilitating the court's inherent jurisdiction to allow for the use of screens where the legislation does not explicitly provide for it. In addition, the principles of *Donnelly v Ireland*[8] may support such an application. That case involved an unsuccessful challenge to the use of video link which had recently been provided for in the Criminal Evidence Act 1992. The Supreme Court outlined **[27–08]**

---

5 s 14A (the use of screens), is not included under Criminal Evidence Act 1992, s 19. s 19 allows for persons over 18 with a mental disorder within the meaning of s 5 of the Criminal Justice Act 1993 to avail of certain support measures. These are s 14 (the use of intermediaries), s 14B (the removal of wigs and gowns for persons under 18), s 15 (procedure and disclosure in relation to recorded evidence), and s 16 (recorded evidence).

6 *DPP v Harrison* [2016] IECA 212 [54]-[56].

7 *R v Smellie* (1919) 14 Cr App R 128 (CA).

8 *Donnelly v Ireland* [1998] 1 IR 321.

that, while there is a right of a defendant to challenge the testimony of the accuser, the Court was satisfied that the assessment of the credibility of all the testimony in the prosecution case, including the testimony of child witnesses, did not require that the witness be obliged to give evidence in the physical presence of the accused person. The Court held that there was no such constitutional right to physical confrontation and that modifications could be made to assist vulnerable witnesses once there was no interference with the right to cross-examination.[9]

Reported Case Law and the Use of Screens

[27–09] There is little reported case law in respect of screens, but it is notable that in the case of *DPP v AE*,[10] the trial of which took place in April 2021, the complainant gave evidence from behind a screen. The complainant was 33 years of age and was the brother of the defendant who was accused of rape and charges of assault. The judgment refers to the support measures, which were not the subject of a ground of appeal, in relation to the summary of the evidence.

[27–10] Donnelly J stated:

> C (the complainant) explained the delay in making a complaint was because he " was ashamed of [his] life" and that he was still in fear of the appellant. Special measures were employed even though he was 33 at the time of the trial and he gave his evidence from behind a screen.[11]

[27–11] While not commonly used, the use of screens may be a lesser interference than other support measures to the defendant's right to challenge the testimony of the vulnerable witness. The principles outlined in *Donnelly v Ireland*[12] may be of assistance for vulnerable witnesses in relation to an application for the support measure.

Application for the Use of a Screen

[27–12] In relation to s 14A of the Criminal Evidence Act 1992, the application can be made by the prosecution or the accused. It appears, therefore, that it is not possible for the court, of its own motion, to make the order.

[27–13] The application may be made at a preliminary trial hearing under s 6 (8)(b)(v) of the Criminal Procedure Act 2021[13] or during the trial. However, in respect of supporting evidence as to why a screen should be used for victims of an offence, a s 15 of the Criminal Justice (Victims of Crime) Act 2017 assessment by a member of An Garda Síochána may support the application. While s 15 relates only to victims, the eligibility criteria within the categories indicate that the vulnerabilities attached to age, to the

---

9 ibid 358 (SC): 'Once it is established that an accused person has no constitutional right to have a witness give evidence in his presence and in effect "confront" him, then the circumstances in which evidence is given other than in his presence is a matter for the Oireachtas.'

10 *DPP v AE* [2022] IECA 152 [11].

11 ibid [11].

12 *Donnelly v Ireland* [1998] 1 IR 321. See also *DPP v GM* [2023] IECA 151 para [27–18].

13 Criminal Procedure Act 2021, s 6(8)(b)(v):

> 'Without prejudice to the generality of subsection (7), the trial court may, at a preliminary trial hearing, make any one or more of the following orders: [...] (v) section 13, 14, 14A, 14C, 19A or 29 of the Act of 1992'.

nature of the offences as well as to the fact that the evidence will be given by a victim of the alleged offence are significant in themselves.

Jurisdiction in All Courts/Transfer of Proceedings

There is no limitation in s 14A of the Criminal Evidence Act 1992 in relation to summary or indictable offences and the provision applies to courts of all jurisdiction. If required, s 17 of the Criminal Evidence Act 1992[14] allows for proceedings under ss 13, 14, 14A, 15, 16 and 29 to be transferred to the appropriate court. **[27–14]**

Test for the Use of a Screen

The test for s 14A(1) is that the court may (therefore is not obliged to) grant the use of the screen unless it is satisfied that in all the circumstances of the case such a direction would be contrary to the interests of justice. **[27–15]**

The test for s 14A(2) is that the court may (therefore is not obliged to), if satisfied that the interests of justice so require, grant the use of the screen subject to s 14AA(c). This provision states that the court, in deciding: **[27–16]**

> whether, under section 14A(2), the interests of justice require that it direct that a screen or other similar device be positioned, in an appropriate place, so as to prevent the victim from seeing the accused when giving evidence, shall have regard to the need to protect the victim from secondary and repeat victimisation, intimidation or retaliation, taking into account –
> (i) the nature and circumstances of the case, and
> (ii) the personal characteristics of the victim.

Secondary victimisation is interpreted in the Criminal Justice (Victims of Crime) Act 2017 as 'victimisation that occurs indirectly through the response of institutions and individuals to the victim'.[15] **[27–17]**

There is no definition of the 'interests of justice' in the legislation. However, the case of *DPP v GM*[16] outlines how the court may consider the granting of the support measures. In this case, the complainant, the former wife of the appellant, had given evidence from behind a screen in relation to 16 charges of rape under s 4 of the Criminal Law (Rape) (Amendment) Act 1990. An assessment had been carried out by the investigating Garda under s 15 of the Criminal Justice (Victims of Crime) Act **[27–18]**

---

14 Criminal Evidence Act 1992, s 17, Transfer of proceedings:
'In any proceedings for an offence in any circuit or district court district in relation to which any of the provisions of sections 13 to 16 or section 29 is not in operation the court concerned may, if in its opinion it is desirable that evidence be given in the proceedings through a live television link or by means of a videorecording or that a screen or other similar device be used in the giving of evidence, by order transfer the proceedings to a circuit or district court district in relation to which those provisions are in operation and, where such an order is made the jurisdiction of the court to which the proceedings have been transferred may be exercised –
(a) in the case of the Circuit Court, by the judge of the circuit concerned, and
(b) in the case of the District Court, by the judge of that court for the time being assigned to the district court district concerned.'

15 Criminal Justice (Victims of Crime) Act 2017, s 2, Interpretation.

16 *DPP v GM* [2023] IECA 151.

2017, who had recommended the use of the screen so that the complainant could give 'coherent evidence'. The appellant appealed his conviction on a number of grounds, including the fact that the complainant had given evidence from behind a screen. The Court of Appeal dismissed all grounds of appeal. In relation to the use of screens, Kennedy J referred to the Supreme Court case of *Donnelly v Ireland*[17] in the course of the judgment, and stated:

> Applications for special measures require an evidential basis, such applications are not granted as a matter of course. It is clear from the statute that as assessment of each individual alleged victim is required, it is not sufficient in itself that a complainant is an alleged victim, there must [be] some factor or factors which point towards a vulnerability on the part of the victim over and above that of being a complainant. Each case will require careful assessment by a trial judge on foot of evidence. On occasion, there may well be expert testimony. The purpose of the legislation is to protect the victim which must, of course, be balanced with the right of an accused to a fair trial.
>
> It is well established that an accused does not have a right to confront his/her accuser but has a right to cross-examine in order to ensure a fair trial. The presence of a screen however, does not remove the right to cross-examine. An analogy may be made with evidence by video link, placing a witness at a remove from the accused and from cross-examining counsel, however, evidence by video link is now a well-trodden path and cannot be said to place an accused's right to a fair trial in jeopardy. The use of video link for child witnesses is therefore instructive; *Donnelly v Ireland* [1998] 1 IR 321 concerned a challenge to the constitutionality of s. 13(1)(a) of the Criminal Evidence Act, 1992, regarding the use of a video link to enable children to give evidence. The Supreme Court found, inter alia that the use of this measure did not impinge on an accused's right to a fair trial which incorporates the right to cross-examine. As stated, special measures are not automatic, a discretion is vested in the trial judge to determine whether it is in the interests of justice to grant such permission, thus protecting the rights of an accused. The court in considering how to exercise its discretion, must strike the correct balance between the competing interests; that of the need to protect a vulnerable complainant and the overarching right of an accused's right to a fair trial.[18]

[27–19] In examining the appellant's contention that the use of the screen would be prejudicial, Kennedy J noted that the test for the support measure is whether the interests of justice require it. Discretion vests in the trial judge to determine whether the support measure may be used, thus safeguarding the right to a fair trial. In relation to whether the measure may be deemed prejudicial, Kennedy J noted that it could be argued that the use of video link is prejudicial but:

> society recognises the need to protect vulnerable witnesses, which may include a child witness or an adult witness for various reasons. A screen will only be granted if it is required in the interests of justice upon determination by the court of trial.[19]

Reason for a Screen

[27–20] The question may be asked why a screen is a preferable support measure instead of video link. For personal reasons, the witness may prefer to be physically present in the courtroom but may still need assistance to ensure that he or she is not overwhelmed by stress or anxiety while giving evidence. In terms of the quality of the evidence, the

---

17 *Donnelly v Ireland* [1998] 1 IR 321.
18 *DPP v GM* [2023] IECA 151 [55]–[57].
19 ibid [58]–[59].

physical presence of the vulnerable witness in court may prevent the 'deadening' effect which the use of video link could otherwise produce.[20] The screen may assist the witness to give the best evidence possible while minimising the difficulties for the witness giving evidence as outlined in the test under s 14AA of the Criminal Evidence Act 1992.

Screens and the Use of an Intermediary

The use of intermediaries under s 14 of the Criminal Evidence Act 1992 is linked to witnesses and victims giving evidence through video link. This section has not been amended to allow for the use of screens as an alternative. This is despite the fact that s 14A(3)(c) states: **[27–21]**

> (3) A witness giving evidence under subsection (1) or (2) shall be capable of seeing and hearing and being seen and heard by –
> (a) the judge and jury (if any),
> (b) legal representatives acting in the proceedings,
> (c) any interpreter, intermediary appointed under section 14 or any other person appointed to assist the witness,
>
> and shall be capable of being heard by the accused.[21]

Linking of Screens to Identification of Accused at Trial[22]

Section 18 of the Criminal Evidence Act 1992 allows for a witness of a relevant offence or a victim of any other offence other than a relevant offence who gives evidence through the use of video link under s 13 or a screen or other similar device under s 14A to identify the accused if he or she knew them previously, unless the court, in the interests of justice, directs otherwise. If the witness or victim identified the accused in the course of an identification parade, the identification in court can be done through a third party. **[27–22]**

In the case of victims who are giving evidence through a screen, as Heffernan notes, this will presuppose that the court has considered the test in s 14AA before granting the use of the special measure but that the entitlement not to have to identify the accused **[27–23]**

---

[20] Charleton J has observed that while video link can be extremely beneficial, it can also be problematic as it could create a distance between the victim and the jury which was less helpful. He also remarked, however, that without video link, on occasion, there would be no witness. Charleton J, 'Chairman's Opening Speech' (The Law Reform Commission Annual Conference 2011: Sexual Offences and Capacity) 6 <http://www.lawreform.ie/_fileupload/misc/AC11/CharletonJ.pdf> accessed 13 October 2023.

[21] Criminal Evidence Act 1992, s 14A(3)(c).

[22] Criminal Evidence Act 1992, s 18, Identification evidence:

> 'Where a person (in this section referred to as 'the witness') –
> (a) gives evidence in respect of a relevant offence, or
> (b) gives evidence in respect of any other offence of which he or she is a victim,
>
> through a live television link pursuant to section 13(1) or (1A) or using a screen or other similar device pursuant to section 14A, then –
> (i) in case evidence is given that the accused was known to the witness before the date on which the offence is alleged to have been committed, the witness shall not be required to identify the accused at the trial of the offence, unless the court in the interests of justice directs otherwise, and
> (ii) in any other case, evidence by a person other than the witness that the witness identified the accused at an identification parade as being the offender shall be admissible as evidence that the accused was so identified.'

arises automatically through the use of the screen and not on the basis of any further discretionary determination by the trial judge.[23]

Intention of the Legislation

[27–24] The aim of s 14A is to direct that a screen or a similar device be positioned in an appropriate place, so as to prevent the witness or victim from seeing the accused when giving evidence. Section 14A(3) states that a witness giving evidence shall be capable of seeing and hearing and being seen and heard by the judge and jury (if any), legal representatives, interpreter, intermediary appointed under s 14 of the Criminal Evidence Act 1992 or any other person appointed to assist the witness, and shall be capable of being heard by the accused.

[27–25] The technical issues negotiating this will depend on the geography of the court. The use of video cameras and video screens may be used to allow the relevant parties to be able to see the witness while he or she gives evidence. The intention of the legislation is that the witness giving evidence does not see the accused when giving evidence. The accused may or may not be able to see the witness, perhaps through the use of a video screen, but this intention is not specified in the section. The witness may have a difficulty knowing that he or she may be seen by the accused even if he or she cannot see the accused and this should be raised ahead of the testimony being given.

Screen for Anonymity

[27–26] Section 55 of the Criminal Justice (Miscellaneous Provisions) Act 2023, sets out a general anonymity provision for witnesses in criminal proceedings. When commenced, the section will provide 'anonymity measures' which the court may apply to provide anonymity for the witness. As part of those measures, s 55(d) states that: 'that the witness shall be screened to an extent specified by the court.'

Procedure

[27–27] The application may be made at a preliminary trial hearing under s 6(8)(b)(v) of the Criminal Procedure Act 2021 or during the trial, preferably well in advance of the witness giving evidence so that any practical difficulties may be resolved in advance. It should be noted, s 30(d) of the Criminal Justice (Victims of Crime) Act 2017, which provides for s 14A of the Criminal Evidence Act 1992, has not at the time of writing been commenced other than for the Central Criminal Court, the Dublin Circuit Criminal Court and the Dublin Metropolitan District of the District Court. Therefore, the provision for screens outside Dublin may be used on an inherent jurisdiction basis as outlined above.

[27–28] The screens that have been used in the Dublin courts are similar to roll-up screens used for film projectors. When the time comes for the witness to give evidence, one can be placed in front of the dock. Rather than the witness having to walk into court and pass the defendant, the court could be cleared of everyone, including the defendant. The witness can then be seated behind the screen, the video cameras turned on (as

[23] Liz Heffernan, *Evidence in Criminal Trials* (2nd edn, Bloomsbury 2020) 6.47, 277.

necessary if a camera and screens within the courtroom are facilitating the jury seeing the witness) and positioned appropriately. At this point, the judge, jury, defendant and all other parties can then be alerted by the judge's judicial assistant and/or member of An Garda Síochána to return to the court. As the physical layout of the courts differ on a nationwide basis, it will be for the judge and legal representatives to consider, with the intention of the legislation in mind, as to how best to proceed. When the witness has finished giving evidence, the procedures allowing him or her to leave the court without seeing the defendant will need to be considered and the court may have to be cleared again to ensure that the witness does not have to be in close proximity to the defendant when leaving the courtroom.

CHAPTER 28

SENTENCING

Introduction

The general topic of sentencing is covered more comprehensively elsewhere.[1] However, certain recent developments are important to note in terms of current sentencing issues relating to both vulnerable defendants and witnesses. The difficulties in terms of imposing suspended sentences on children have been highlighted in the courts.[2] These issues had been previously circumvented in other cases[3] but the sentencing of children in relation to long sentences for serious offences remains problematic. The **[28–01]**

1 Thomas O'Malley, *Sentencing Law and Practice* (3rd edn, Round Hall 2016) ch 9, 'Young Offenders'.

2 Mary Carolan, 'Teenager's murder conviction exposes failure of legislation to grant essential powers to courts'.

The lack of provisions in the Children Act to allow the courts review or suspend sentences imposed on minors for serious crimes means judge faces 'all or nothing' choice' *The Irish Times* (Dublin, 10 February 2023) <https://www.irishtimes.com/crime-law/courts/2023/02/10/teens-murder-conviction-exposes-failure-of-legislation-to-grant-essential-powers-to-courts/> accessed 13 October 2023.

3 Conor Gallagher and Eoin Reynolds 'Ana Kriégel murder: Boy A sentenced to life, Boy B sentenced to 15 years Sentence for Boy A to be reviewed in 12 years; sentence for Boy B is due for review in 8 years' *The Irish Times* (Dublin, 5 November 2019) <https://www.irishtimes.com/news/crime-and-law/courts/criminal-court/ana-Kriégel-murder-boy-a-sentenced-to-life-boy-b-sentenced-to-15-years-1.4072944> accessed 13 October 2023.

Irish Law Reform Commission, in its *Report on Suspended Sentences*, has suggested a detention and supervision order may only be used in circumstances where the child offender will turn 18 during the currency of the sentence.[4] However, in *DPP v DMcD* the Court of Appeal noted that there were diverging views on the issue:

> While there was reference to s. 151 of the Children's Act which provides for detention and supervision orders which results in half of the specified period of detention being served in detention, and the remaining half being spent in the community under supervision, there was no real detailed analysis of the relevance or applicability of the section. We are aware from other cases that we are dealing with at present that there is a divergence of view as to whether the section has any relevance in a situation where the person before the Court would be turning 18 years old during the period of actual detention. This would be of considerable significance in the context of the present case because the sentence hearing took place within a fortnight of the appellant's 18th birthday.[5]

[28–02] Suspended sentences under s 99 of the Criminal Justice Act 2006 have been deemed to be impermissible in the sentencing of children as s 99 does not provide for 'detention' but only 'imprisonment'.[6]

[28–03] In relation to suspended sentences and their inapplicability to the sentencing of child defendants, the *Report on Suspended Sentences* stated:

> The Commission recommends that the practice of reviewable sentences of detention be continued, but that it be put on a statutory footing so as to bring clarity and certainty as to the legal basis of this sentencing option.[7]

[28–04] Legislative efforts to resolve this issue as well as solutions to the restrictions of mandatory life imprisonment for murder for child defendants have been made, but whether these will come to fruition remains to be seen.[8]

[28–05] In addition to the above, since the commencement of the Parole Act 2019, the view of victims in relation to the potential release or otherwise of persons in custody has been put on a legislative basis.

The Sentencing of Child Defendants

[28–06] The sentencing of a child defendant will clearly depend on the nature of the offences and the age and maturity of the child. Part 9 'Powers of Courts in Relation to Child Offenders' of the Children Act 2001 outlines the courts' powers in relation to children who are convicted of a criminal offence. Certain significant sections of the Act are noted here in more detail:

---

4 Irish Law Reform Commission, *Report on Suspended Sentences* (123–2020) para 7.5.

5 *DPP v DMcD* [2020] IECA 149.

6 *DPP v AS* [2017] IECA 310.

7 Irish Law Reform Commission, *Report on Suspended Sentences* (123–2020) para 7.5.

8 Criminal Justice (Juvenile Offenders) Bill 2023 will provide: 'An Act to amend the Criminal Justice Act 1990 to provide for non-mandatory life sentences for juvenile offenders in cases of treason and murder, to expand the provisions of section 99 of the Criminal Justice Act 2006 relating to suspended sentences to include juvenile offenders, and to amend The Children Act 2001 to allow judicial discretion in setting the terms of a detention and supervision order.'

Section 96 Children Act 2001

'Principles relating to exercise of criminal jurisdiction over children'

The section outlines the principles that the court should consider when sentencing a child, including that children have the same rights and freedoms as adults and a right to be heard and to participate in any proceedings of the court that can affect them. It also outlines that criminal proceedings shall not be used solely to provide any assistance or service need to care for or protect a child. The section also outlines that it is desirable, wherever possible: **[28–07]**

(a) to allow the education, training or employment of children to proceed without interruption,
(b) to preserve and strengthen the relationship between children and their parents and other family members,
(c) to foster the ability of families to develop their own means of dealing with offending by their children, and
(d) to allow children reside in their own homes.

It provides that any sentence should not restrict the normal life of a child and should allow him or her to continue with educational and leisure pursuits. Most significantly, the section states that a period of detention should be imposed only as a measure of last resort. **[28–08]**

Section 98 Children Act 2001

'Orders on finding of guilt'

This section outlines the orders that a court may make where it is satisfied of the guilt of a child without prejudice to its general powers. It may reprimand the child or deal with the case by making one or more than one of the following orders: **[28–09]**

(a) a conditional discharge order,
(b) an order that the child pay a fine or costs,
(c) an order that the parent or guardian be bound over,
(d) a compensation order,
(e) a parental supervision order,
(f) an order that the parent or guardian pay compensation,
(g) an order imposing a community sanction,
(h) an order (the making of which may be deferred pursuant to s 144) that the child be detained in a children detention school,
(i) a detention and supervision order.

Section 99 Children Act 2001

'Probation officer's report'

This section states that the sentencing court may request a probation report and *shall* (emphasis added) request one where the court is considering detention, thereby making this section one of the provisions that will be lost if the sentencing of a child takes place after he or she turns 18. **[28–10]**

Sections 100–114 Children Act 2001

[28–11] These sections deal with reports in relation to the sentencing of the child; ss 108–10 relate to the payment of fines, ss 111–14 outline involvement of parents and guardians in relation to supervision orders, compensation by parent or guardian, as well as binding over of parent or guardian.

Section 115 Children Act 2001

Community sanctions

[28–12] This section outlines the orders which may be made by a court on being satisfied that a child is guilty of an offence:

(a) in the case of a child of 16 or 17 years of age, a community service order under s 3 of the Act of 1983,
(b) an order under s 118 (a day centre order),
(c) an order under s 2 of the Act of 1907 (a probation order),
(d) an order under s 124 (a probation (training or activities) order),
(e) an order under s 125 (a probation (intensive supervision) order),
(f) an order under s 126 (a probation (residential supervision) order),
(g) an order under s 129 (a suitable person (care and supervision) order),
(h) an order under s 131 (a mentor (family support) order),
(i) an order under s 133 (a restriction on movement order), or
(j) an order under s 137 (a dual order).

[28–13] Sections 116–39 relate to the orders which may be made under s 115.

Section 140 Children Act 2001

'Effect of subsequent period of detention'

[28–14] Section 140 provides that a community sanction which is in force will cease when a child commences a period of detention for another offence.

Section 141 Children Act 2001

'Regulations'

[28–15] This section outlines the regulations that may be made by the court in relation to community sanctions.

Section 142 Children Act 2001

Detention orders[9]

[28–16] This section outlines that the court may, in accordance with Part 9, impose a period of detention in a children detention school through a children detention order.

---

9 Children Act 2001, s 142: 'A court may, in accordance with this Part, by order (in this Part referred to as a "children detention order") impose on a child a period of detention in a children detention school specified in the order.'

Section 143 Children Act 2001

'Restriction on detention orders'

This section outlines that the court shall not make an order imposing a period of detention on a child unless it is satisfied that detention is the only suitable way of dealing with the child and that a place in a children detention school is available for him or her. In addition, where such an order is made, the court must give its reasons for doing so in open court. **[28–17]**

Section 144 Children Act 2001

'Deferment of detention order'

Section 144 allows a court, given certain circumstances, to defer making a detention order. Under s 144(5) of the Children Act 2001, the court shall state in open court: **[28–18]**

(a) the period of detention that is being deferred,
(b) the date of the resumed court hearing, and
(c) that the court will take into account at that hearing the information in the probation and welfare officer's report concerning the child's conduct in the meantime and the other matters mentioned in subsection (7)(b).

Under s 144(6) and s 144 (7) of the Children Act 2001, the court shall also explain in open court, in appropriate language why the detention order is being deferred and for what period. It shall also outline any of the conditions which should be complied referred to under s 117 of the Children Act. Section 144(7) states: **[28–19]**

(7) (*a*) The probation and welfare officer under whose supervision the child has been placed shall prepare a report on the child for consideration by the court at the resumed hearing.
(*b*) The report shall contain information on the child's conduct after the finding of guilt, including the extent to which the child has complied with any conditions suggested by the court, on any change in the child's circumstances and on any reparation by the child to the victim, together with any other information which the officer considers to be relevant.
(*c*) The officer shall make all reasonable endeavours to ensure that the report is lodged with the clerk or other proper officer of the court at least 4 working days before the date of the resumed hearing.

(8) The resumed court hearing shall take place not later than one year from the date of the adjourned hearing and may take place notwithstanding that the child has attained the age of 18 years in the meantime.

(9) At the resumed hearing the court shall consider the report prepared by the probation and welfare officer and, if the court thinks it necessary, hear evidence from the officer and shall by order –
(a) impose the period of detention which it had deferred or any shorter period,
(b) suspend the whole or any portion of a period of detention so imposed, or
(c) impose a community sanction appropriate to the age of the child concerned, and shall explain to the child in open court the reasons for its decision in language that the child understands.

Section 145 Children Act 2001

'Alternative to detention where no place available in children detention school'

[28–20] This section allows the court, in certain circumstances, to make a community sanction where a detention order is to be made but no place in a children detention school is available.

Section 146 Children Act 2001

'Finding of guilt during deferment'

[28–21] This section provides that where a court has deferred the making of a children detention order in relation to a child pursuant to s 144 it may make the order before the expiration of the period of deferment if during that period the child is found guilty of any offence. The court may issue a summons to require the child to appear before it and issue a warrant where the child does not do so.

Section 148 Children Act 2001

'Document to be produced to Director of children detention school'

[28–22] This section provides that the order providing for the detention of the child must accompany him or her and be delivered to the Director of the relevant school.

Section 149 Children Act 2001

'Period of detention in children detention school'

[28–23] This section outlines that where a child is found guilty of an offence in the Children Court, any term of detention in a children detention school imposed for the offence shall not be for a period longer than the term of detention or imprisonment which the court could impose on an adult who commits such an offence.

Section 151 Children Act 2001

'Detention and Supervision'

[28–24] Section 151 deals with the issue of detention and supervision orders (but this is limited to children who will be under 18 for the duration of the order).[10] Temporary release and remission are dealt with as well within the section[11] subject to the same condition.

Section 155 Children Act 2001

'Persons who attain 18 years of age while detained'

This section provides that where a person is detained in a children detention school on foot of a children detention order following conviction for an offence, and the person's 18th birthday will occur before the period of detention specified in the order expires, that person shall serve any period of detention remaining to be served on the relevant date in a place of detention provided under s 2 of the Prisons Act 1970, or prison. However, if a person is engaged in a course of education or training in the children detention school, or the period of detention remaining to be served by a person in the children detention school on the relevant date is six months or less, the Director of the children detention school may determine that the person shall continue to be detained in the children detention school for a period not exceeding six months from the relevant date. [28–25]

---

10 Irish Law Reform Commission, *Report on Suspended Sentences* (123–2020) para 7.36: 'However, when read in its entirety, it appears that section 151 was intended to be used only in circumstances where the child will remain under 18 for the duration of the sentence, including the supervision element of the sentence.'
para 7.44: 'These decisions highlight the practical difficulties with the operation of section 151 of the 2001 Act. In theory, a detention and supervision order can be seen as a useful approximation of the part-suspended sentence in the context of child offenders. However, in practice, the fact that the offender must be a child for the duration of the sentence, including the period of supervision, is problematic. This peculiarity of the legislation effectively serves to debar its application in the case of children being sentenced for serious offences as the child offender will almost invariably have turned 18 during the currency of the sentence.'

11 Children Act 2001, s 151, Detention and supervision:
> '(1) Where a court is satisfied that detention is the only suitable way of dealing with a child [...], it may, instead of making a children detention order, make a detention and supervision order. (2) A detention and supervision order shall provide for detention in a children detention school followed by supervision in the community. (3) Subject to subsection (4), half of the period for which a detention and supervision order is in force shall be spent by the child in detention in a children detention school and half under supervision in the community. (4) Where the child is released from detention on earning remission of sentence by industry or good conduct or on being given temporary release under section 2 or 3 of the Act of 1960, supervision of the child in the community under the order shall be deemed to commence on the child's release. (5) The supervision provided for in this section shall be by a probation and welfare officer. (6) A detention and supervision order, in so far as it relates to detention, shall be deemed for all purposes to be a children detention order. (7) A detention and supervision order may specify such of the conditions provided for in section 117 as the court considers necessary for helping to ensure that the child concerned would be of good behaviour and for reducing the likelihood of the child's committing any further offences. (8) Section 130 shall apply, with any necessary modifications, to non-compliance with a detention and supervision order, or with any condition to which it is subject, as if for the references to an order in that section there were substituted references to a detention and supervision order.'

Section 156 Children Act 2001

'Restriction on punishment of children'

[28–26] This section is significant as it states that no court shall pass a sentence of imprisonment on a child or commit a child to prison. Since the judgment of *DPP v AS*,[12] suspended sentences under s 99 of the Criminal Justice Act 2006 have been deemed to be impermissible in the sentencing of children as s 99 does not provide for 'detention' but only 'imprisonment'.[13]

General Principles – Sentencing of Children

[28–27] General principles in the sentencing of children in the Children Court have been outlined in the following cases. Welfare considerations are a significant consideration in relation to any sentence imposed.

Cases involving children – special duty to be dealt with as expeditiously as possible

[28–28] The Irish courts have repeatedly outlined that cases involving children should be dealt with as expeditiously as possible. This has been outlined in *BF v DPP*[14] where Geoghan J stated:

> It was of the utmost importance that if it was decided to proceed with charges, there should be no delay so that a trial would take place while memories were fresh and while the appellant was reasonably close to the age at which he is alleged to have committed the offences. A trial of an adult in respect of an offence which he committed as a child, and particularly a sexual offence, takes on a wholly different character from a trial of a child who has committed such offences while a child. This is true quite independently of the different penal provisions applicable to a child or young person, a point also relied on by the appellant. There was, in my view, a special obligation of expedition in this case, but that obligation was not complied with in that the extradition proceedings were allowed to take an excessive length of time, and this delay appears to be inexplicable.[15]

[28–29] As the Irish Law Reform Commission has noted,[16] this principle was also set out in *Cullen v DPP*[17] where it was held that, in cases involving child offenders: 'there is a "special duty" on the part of the State authorities, over and above the normal duty of expedition, to ensure the speedy trial of [the child]'. *Donoghue v DPP*[18] also emphasises the special duty on the State authorities, over and above the normal duty of expedition, to ensure a speedy trial, having regard to the sensitivities involved, as reflected in the statutory provisions. What might be excusable delay in the case of an adult in any given case might not be acceptable in the case of the prosecution of a child.

---

12 *DPP v AS* [2017] IECA 310.

13 ibid.

14 *BF v DPP* [2001] 1 IR 656.

15 ibid 664.

16 Irish Law Reform Commission, *Report on Suspended Sentences* (123–2020) para 7.10.

17 *Cullen v DPP* [2014] IESC 59.

18 *Donoghue v DPP* [2014] 2 IR 762.

DPP v TC[19]

Welfare concerns should predominate at sentencing stage

As noted in the Irish Law Reform Commission's Report on Suspended Sentences, in *DPP v TC,* Judge O'Connor pointed out that '[j]ustice and welfare concerns are issues in any juvenile sentencing in criminal law matters', and that while pre-trial procedures ought to be governed primarily by justice considerations, welfare considerations should predominate once a child has been found guilty of an offence, ie at the sentencing stage.[20] **[28–30]**

DPP v AB[21]

Individual circumstances of the child are significant

In the case of *DPP v AB*, which involved a child who had been charged with various offences while housed in a special care unit, O'Connor J noted: **[28–31]**

> Sentencing in the Children Court is not done in isolation and is dependent on many factors. On the one hand the court, in complying with the legislative and judicial requirements should, where possible, strive for consistency. On the other hand, the particular circumstances of a child frequently require an individualised response. Within this framework it is important to be realistic as to what the child is capable of and what can be achieved by a sentence. In reconciling the various issues, the court may apply a different type of sentence for similar crimes to different children but in doing so the court will explain its reasons in making that decision.[22]

Age of offender at time of offence/sentencing

Efficiency and promptness are crucial in relation to children in the criminal justice system. The writers of the Irish Law Reform Commission *Report on Suspended Sentences* have stated 'when sentencing child offenders, there must be a close temporal nexus between the wrongdoing and the punishment',[23] and also, 'it is a reasonably well established principle of sentencing that when an adult is being sentenced for an offence committed during childhood, the penalty that the offender would have received if sentenced immediately after the offence was committed, is a matter which can be taken into account for this purpose'.[24] The report notes that in *R v Ghafoor*, the English Court of Appeal set out the rationale for this approach as follows: **[28–32]**

> The starting point is the sentence that the defendant would have been likely to receive if he had been sentenced at the date of the commission of the offence. It has been described as "a powerful factor". That is for the obvious reason that ... the philosophy of restricting sentencing powers in relation to young persons reflects both (a) society's acceptance that young offenders are less responsible for their actions and therefore less culpable than adults, and (b) the recognition that, in consequence, sentencing them should place greater emphasis on rehabilitation, and less on retribution and deterrence than in the case of adults.[25]

---

19 *DPP v TC* [2017] IEDC 7.
20 Irish Law Reform Commission, *Report on Suspended Sentences* (123–2020) para 7.9.
21 *DPP v AB* [2017] IEDC 12.
22 ibid [46].
23 Irish Law Reform Commission, *Report on Suspended Sentences* (123–2020) para 7.56.
24 ibid para 7.13.
25 *R v Ghafoor* [2002] EWCA Crim 1857 [31].

[28–33] The report highlights that this principle has been approved in the Irish courts, notably in *MS v DPP*[26] and *DPP v JH*.[27] In *DPP v JH*, the appellant was convicted of two counts of rape and two of sexual assault. At the time of conviction and sentence, the defendant was 23, whereas he was 15 at the time of the offence and the complainant 11 years of age. He received a two-year sentence in respect of the sexual assault counts and a four-year sentence in respect of the rape counts, to run concurrently. On appeal against severity, the Court of Appeal agreed that the sentencing judge had not given sufficient weight to his young age and lack of maturity at the time of the offence. It quashed the sentence, setting a headline sentence of two-and-a-half years, imposing a sentence of 18 months' imprisonment, with the final six months suspended for a period of one year.[28]

Suspended sentences under s 99 Criminal Justice Act 2006 not permissible for detention of children

[28–34] As mentioned above, since the judgment of *DPP v AS*,[29] suspended sentences under s 99 of the Criminal Justice Act 2006 have been deemed to be impermissible in the sentencing of children.[30] This is due to a number of factors:

- Under s 156 of the Children Act 2001 a child can not be sentenced to a term of imprisonment.
- The definition of 'imprisonment' under s 98 of the Criminal Justice Act does include certain detention facilities under s 2 of the Prisons Act 1970 (which empowers the Minister to provide places other than prisons for the detention of offenders for the purpose of promoting their rehabilitation). The relevant regulations under s 3 of the Prisons Act 1970 do not include Oberstown Children Detention School.
- Regulations made under s 32 of the Children (Amendment) Act 2015 state that children who are subject to a detention order are to be sent to Oberstown Children Detention Campus.[31]

[28–35] The judgment of Edwards J in the consultative case of *DPP v AS*[32] considered these issues and determined that suspended sentences under s 99 of the Criminal Justice Act 2006 do not apply to children.[33]

[28–36] While a detention and supervision order may be made under s 151 of the Children Act 2001, s 130 outlines the provisions for non-compliance with a care and supervision order and s 144(9) facilitates the deferment of a detention order. Under the latter, a court may impose a sentence similar to that of a suspended sentence. However, Edwards J noted that the Children Act 2001 did not contain an express power to suspend a sentence other than that contained in s 144(9) and that he had no reason to believe that this was other than a deliberate policy choice by the legislature. He stated:

> I have carefully considered the entire scheme of the Act of 2001, as well as its long title and its detailed provisions and having done so I am not persuaded by the arguments advanced by the prosecutor. In particular, I find the absence of an express power to

26 *MS v DPP* [2018] IEHC 285 [39].
27 *DPP v JH* [2017] IECA 206.
28 Irish Law Reform Commission, *Report on Suspended Sentences* (123–2020) para 7.14.
29 *DPP v AS* [2017] IECA 310.
30 ibid.
31 SI No 108/2017 – Children (Amendment) Act 2015 (s 32(5)) Order 2017.
32 *DPP v AS* [2017] IECA 310.
33 Irish Law Reform Commission, *Report on Suspended Sentences* (123–2020) paras 7.21–7.22.

> impose a suspended sentence other than in the circumstances set forth in s. 144(9) to be of significance. I am satisfied that no basis exists for implication of the power that the prosecutor invites us to imply. The Act is clear in its terms and I have no reason to believe that the failure to provide for an express general power to suspend sentences of detention in either a children detention school or in a children detention centre was other than a deliberate policy choice by the legislature. The Act is neither ambiguous nor does a literal interpretation lead to an absurdity. There is no basis for affording it the purposive or teleological interpretation that the prosecutor would have us do.[34]

In imposing a detention order on a child, the court must be satisfied that detention is the only way of dealing with the child and that a place is available for him or her. The court must also give its reasons in open court for making the order.[35] **[28–37]**

As highlighted by the Irish Law Reform Commission in its *Report on Suspended Sentences*, a detention and supervision order cannot be used in circumstances where the child offender will turn 18 during the currency of the sentence.[36] **[28–38]**

> The Commission recommends that the practice of reviewable sentences of detention be continued, but that it be put on a statutory footing so as to bring clarity and certainty as to the legal basis of this sentencing option.[37]

DPP v DG (Darren Goodwin)

Review mechanism in lieu of suspended sentence – 'light at the end of the tunnel'

The review mechanism was approved in *DPP v DG*,[38] where long sentences for children were deemed to fall into a special category. **[28–39]**

> Children or very young offenders convicted of serious offences which would normally involve lengthy custodial sentences must be considered as falling into a special category insofar as there is a special onus on the Court to have regard to their rehabilitation and welfare for the future because of their young age at the time and the reasons outlined above. In one sense counsel for the appellant is correct that there should be *'a light at the end of the tunnel'* for the appellant. However, in the Court's view the learned trial judge provided for this in determining that the sentence imposed should be reviewed by the Court in the year 2014, ten years after he had been taken into custody in connection with the offence. For young persons like the appellant who fall into the special category referred to above the provision for a later review of the sentence imposed may be appropriate when it is inappropriate for other categories of cases. Moreover, the imposition of a sentence, in this instance a life sentence, subject to a review by the Court, does not in any way impinge on the autonomous power of the Executive to exercise clemency or to provide for special or early release pursuant to statutory powers as and when the relevant authorities deem appropriate.[39]

---

34 *DPP v AS* [2017] IECA 310 [33].

35 The Children Act 2001, Restriction on detention orders, s 143:

> '(1) The court shall not make an order imposing a period of detention on a child unless it is satisfied that detention is the only suitable way of dealing with the child and that a place in a children detention school is available for him or her.
>
> (2) Where an order is made under subsection (1), the court making the order shall give its reasons for doing so in open court.'

36 Irish Law Reform Commission, *Report on Suspended Sentences* (123–2020) para 7.5.

37 ibid.

38 *DPP v DG (Darren Goodwin)* [2005] IECCA 75.

39 ibid [24].

DPP v MS (A Minor)

'Merit in review mechanism'

[28–40] In *DPP v MS (A Minor)* the sentence in respect of attempted murder was deemed to be unduly lenient by the Court of Appeal given the seriousness of the offence and the fact that it included significant pre-meditation. The Court deemed the sentence of 11 years to be appropriate in the circumstances given the young age of the defendant (15 years and two months) at the time of the offence, the absence of previous convictions and his significant mental health difficulties. However, the Court of Appeal extended the review date by two years. Birmingham P stated:

> We see merit in the review mechanism. The existence of a review date means that there is a target date for the young respondent to work towards. On that review date, there will be a number of options open to the judge conducting the review. One possibility is that the review might not result in the release of the respondent. Another possibility is that the judge might decide to suspend the balance of the sentence then unserved, either from that point, or from some date in the future. The option would also be available to the judge to provide that the balance of the sentence would be suspended for a period in excess of the sentence remaining to be served, so, by way of example, if there was to be a review at a time when two years of the sentence was unserved, the judge might decide to suspend the balance of the sentence, either from that day, or, perhaps, from a date six months later, and to stipulate that the sentence would be suspended for a period of, say four or five years, on condition that he would specify including that the respondent be of good behaviour during any remaining period custody and for the specified period post release.[40]

[28–41] Birmingham P also noted:

> Having considered the matter, it seems to us that a review offers the best prospects of a managed, supervised and guided reintroduction to society. Clearly, this is a difficult case and there are no easy solutions. No outcome is entirely straightforward, but it seems to us that making provision for a review is the least worst option.[41]

Deferred sentencing under s 144 Children Act 2001

[28–42] In the case of *DPP v Cian O'Leary*[42] the sentencing judge had stated a consultative case where the original sentencing hearing had commenced when the defendant was 17 years of age but had been adjourned until after he had reached 18 years of age. Wishing to impose a deferred detention order under s 144 of the Children Act 2001, the sentencing judge was informed by Birmingham P that the only possible sentence was probation under s 2 of the Probation of Offenders Act 1907. It was not possible to impose a deferred detention nor a suspended sentence.

[28–43] The questions posed in the consultative case were:

> (i) What are the options available to the court in sentencing the defendant, Mr O'Leary?
> (ii) Does the court have any power to sentence the defendant in light of s 144(11) of The Children Act 2001, in circumstances where the resumed hearing date nominated under s 145(5) has now passed?
> (iii) Where the deferment date occurred when the defendant was a child, but the resumed hearing date occurred when the defendant was 18 years of age, does the court have

---

40 *DPP v MS (A minor)* [2020] IECA 178 [8].

41 ibid [10].

42 *DPP v Cian O'Leary* [2023] IECA 48.

the jurisdiction to impose a period of detention under s 144(9) Children Act on the defendant?

(iv) Where the deferment date occurred when the defendant was a child, but the resumed hearing date occurred when the defendant was an adult, does the court have the jurisdiction to suspend the whole or a portion of the period of detention on the defendant?

(v) If the answer to (iv) is yes, do the provisions of s 99 of the Criminal Justice Act 2006 govern the suspension of the period of detention?

(vi) In the alternative, if the answer to (iv) is no, does the court have an inherent jurisdiction to impose terms and conditions on the suspended period of detention?[43]

The defendant had submitted there was no difficulty in making a detention order and that the Circuit Court was incorrect in its considerations of how a sentence of detention would be implemented, something, which it was said, was exclusively a matter for the executive. The Director of Public Prosecutions took the position that the person before the court had turned 18, was an adult, and said that, accordingly, the court had the full range of powers available to it, as are available when an adult is before the court for sentence. **[28–44]**

The Court of Appeal held that the effect of s 144 of the Children Act 2001 is to provide the court with a menu of a restricted choice of options. It also held that the custodial options available pursuant to statute were the imposition of the period of detention which had been deferred, or a shorter period, with the option to suspend any period of detention in whole or in part; the section does not provide a basis for imposing a longer period of detention and it does not provide for the imposition of a period of imprisonment. The Court noted that the section adverts to the possibility of the deferred hearing taking place after the child has turned 18, but no additional options are made available to the court for dealing with a young person in that situation. The Court held that the only option available to a court is to consider a community sanction; however, while s 115 of the Children Act 2001 has some 10 community sanctions, all but one of these, a probation order under s 2 of the Probation Act 1907, were unavailable, either because the defendant was not a child of 16/17 years, or was not a child. **[28–45]**

The Court answered the questions posed as follows: **[28–46]**

(i) The only option available to the Court is to make an order pursuant to s. 2 of the Probation Act 1907.

(ii) The Court does not have any power to sentence, apart from the making of a probation order pursuant to s. 2 of the Probation Act 1907.

(iii) In the circumstances described, the Court does not have a power to impose a detention order.

(iv) In circumstances where the Court does not have power to impose a detention order, the question of suspension in whole or in part does not arise.

(v) In circumstances where the Court does not have a jurisdiction to impose a detention order, the question of suspension in whole or in part pursuant to any inherent jurisdiction of the Court does not arise.

(vi) In circumstances where the Court does not have the power to impose a detention order, the question of imposing terms and conditions on the suspended period of detention does not arise.[44]

---

[43] ibid [1].

[44] ibid [24].

Review of certain sentences by Director of Public Prosecutions / severity appeals

Difficulties of retrial/sentencing post successful review where child defendant has turned 18

[28–47] Prior to the commencement of s 61 of the Criminal Justice (Miscellaneous Provisions) Act 2023 on 1 August 2023, where a child defendant was sentenced under the provisions of the Children Act 2001 and the sentence was appealed and found to be unduly lenient (under s 2 of the Criminal Justice Act 1993) when the defendant had turned 18, the Court of Appeal was restricted in its options. It could not re-sentence the defendant as the provisions under the Children Act 2001 were no longer available to the Court nor could the Court sentence the defendant as an adult as s 2 of the Criminal Justice Act 1993 states that the Court must resentence the defendant as they would have under the provisions available to the defendant at the time of sentencing. This was outlined in the case of *DPP v PMcC*[45] which involved an undue leniency appeal and the Irish Law Reform Commission's *Report on Suspended Sentences* noted the issue:

> The Court, concluding that it was an "inconvenient interpretation" it was "not absurd", consequently held that it could not engage in anything but a literal interpretation of section 2(3) of the 1993 Act. This tied the Court's hands in such a way that it could not impose an alternative sentence, so it had to simultaneously find that the sentence was unduly lenient and let it stand. The Court suggested that this oversight be examined by the Oireachtas and remedied through appropriate statutory amendment.[46]

[28–48] The situation of resentencing, where the defendant has turned 18 post undue leniency appeal by the Director of Public Prosecutions under s 2 of the Criminal Justice Act 1993, has now been addressed through s 61(1) of the Criminal Justice (Miscellaneous Provisions) Act 2023 which amends the 1993 Act. Section 2(5) and s 2(6) of the Criminal Justice Act 1993 now states:

> (5) Where the convicted person in relation to whom an application under this section is made is a person who was under the age of 18 years when the sentence was imposed on him by the sentencing court concerned and he has attained the age of 18 years on or before the date on which the application is determined by the Court, the reference in subsection (3)(a) to a sentence which could have been imposed on him by the sentencing court concerned shall be construed as a reference to a sentence which could have been imposed on him by the sentencing court concerned had he attained that age at the time when the sentence was so imposed.
>
> (6) Where subsection (5) applies and the application under this section is in respect of a sentence imposed on a person convicted of treason or murder before the person has attained the age of 18 years, the Court may, notwithstanding section 2 of the Criminal Justice Act 1990, impose such sentence as it considers appropriate.

[28–49] Section 61(2) goes on to provide that the amendments of s 2 of the Criminal Justice Act 1993 shall apply in respect of an application under that section that:

> (a) is brought on or after the date of the coming into operation of this section, or
> (b) has been brought before the date of the coming into operation of this section where final judgment has not been given before that date.

---

[45] *DPP v PMcC* [2018] IECA 309.

[46] Irish Law Reform Commission, *Report on Suspended Sentences* (123–2020) para 7.65.

Appeal against severity of sentence where child has turned 18 post appeal

The difficulties in sentencing a child who is very shortly to be an adult were seen in the case of *DPP v DMcD*.[47] The sentencing judge had referred to s 151 of the Children Act 2001 but had concerns as to whether it was appropriate where the defendant was about to turn 18 and he wished to ensure an engagement with the Probation Services. In an appeal against severity of sentence, in the course of the judgment, the Court of Appeal stated: **[28–50]**

> While there was reference to s. 151 of the Children's Act which provides for detention and supervision orders which results in half of the specified period of detention being served in detention, and the remaining half being spent in the community under supervision, there was no real detailed analysis of the relevance or applicability of the section. We are aware from other cases that we are dealing with at present that there is a divergence of view as to whether the section has any relevance in a situation where the person before the Court would be turning 18 years old during the period of actual detention. This would be of considerable significance in the context of the present case because the sentence hearing took place within a fortnight of the appellant's 18th birthday.[48]

The Court held that, given that the judge was so obviously and clearly anxious to be in a position to provide for the continuing involvement of the Probation Service following the appellant's release into the community, that the judge had erred, at least to the extent of not specifically considering the option of deferring finalisation so as to open up the possibility of part-suspension. The Court imposed a sentence of four years imprisonment (four years detention having been imposed by the sentencing judge) and suspended the final eight months. The Court was now in a position to do so, the defendant having turned 18 years of age. **[28–51]**

In *DPP v RL*[49] the Court of Appeal, on being asked not to consider *DPP v DMcD* a precedent in relation to a severity appeal, stated that it did not consider it as a significant precedent as the question of constraints, if any, to which the Court was subject, was not the subject of argument or submissions.[50] Rather, the Court considered the case of *DPP v PMcC*[51] as significant and did not consider overruling its decision in that case. The Court determined that it was constrained by the relevant legislative sections in relation to how it could re-sentence the defendant who was 17 when originally sentenced but now 18 at time of the appeal. **[28–52]**

> We recognise the force of the arguments advanced by the parties, but nonetheless, we must conclude that what is being urged on us is that we should rewrite the legislation. It seems to us that what both sides contend for is simply a step too far. A further fact to be considered is that following the course of action urged would necessarily involve overturning the decision of this Court in *PMcC*. If the stage had been reached where we had been convinced by the arguments we had heard, we would not have been deterred from overturning *PMcC*. However, that stage has not been reached. Another question that arises is what order the Court can or should make. In that regard, it seems that the choice is a binary one: the Court can quash the sentence imposed in the court below and make no further order; or the Court can decline to quash the sentence and reject the appeal. We fully recognise that is far from an ideal situation; it is certainly inconvenient, to use

47 *DPP v DMcD* [2020] IECA 149.
48 ibid [5].
49 *DPP v RL* [2023] IECA 47.
50 ibid [6].
51 *DPP v PMcC* [2018] IECA 309.

> the language of Edwards J. in *PMcC.* However, we believe the language of the statute is clear and compels us to follow this course.[52]

[28–53] As the Court was not minded to overrule its decision in *DPP v PMcC*,[53] it invited the parties to make submissions in respect of the appeal against severity and whether the sentenced imposed should be allowed stand or should be quashed.[54] In the subsequent judgment, *DPP v Reece Lambert*,[55] the Court of Appeal noted the focussed consideration the sentencing judge gave to the relevant factors.[56] It dismissed the appeal, noting that, in all the circumstances, the sentence that was imposed did not fall outside the available range for offending of such seriousness and that it did not identify an error in principle.

[28–54] Section 62 of the Criminal Justice (Miscellaneous Provisions) Act 2023, commenced on 1 August 2023, addresses the situation where a child has turned 18 post appeal. Section 3 of the Criminal Procedure Act 1993 and s 3(9), (10) and (11) now state:

> (9) For the purposes of subsection (1)(d), where the appellant is a person who—
> (a) was under the age of 18 years when he was convicted and sentenced at the trial, and
> (b) has attained the age of 18 years on or before the date on which the appeal is determined by the Court, the sentence that may be imposed on the person by the Court pursuant to subparagraph (ii) of subsection (1)(d) for some other offence and in substitution for the sentence imposed at the trial shall not be deemed to be a sentence of greater severity by reason only of the fact that the sentence could not have been imposed on the person at the trial given that the person was under the age of 18 years at the time of sentencing.
>
> (10) For the purposes of subsection (2), where the convicted person in relation to whom an appeal against sentence is brought is a person who was under the age of 18 years when the sentence was imposed on them by the court of trial and the person has attained the age of 18 years on or before the date on which the appeal is determined by the Court, the reference in that subsection to a sentence or order which could have been imposed on the convicted person for the offence at the court of trial shall be construed as a reference to a sentence or order which could have been imposed on the convicted person for the offence at the court of trial had he attained that age at the time when the sentence or order was so imposed.
>
> (11) Where subsection (10) applies and the appeal against sentence is in respect of a sentence imposed on a person convicted of treason or murder before the person has attained the age of 18 years, the Court may, notwithstanding section 2 of the Criminal Justice Act 1990, impose such sentence or order as it considers appropriate.".

[28–55] Section 62(2) of the Criminal Justice (Miscellaneous Provisions) Act 2023 states that the amendments of s 3 of the Criminal Procedure Act 1993 shall apply in respect of—

> (a) an appeal under subsection (1) of that section against conviction of an offence, and
> (b) an appeal under subsection (2) of that section against sentence for an offence— where the appeal—
> (i) is brought on or after the date of the coming into operation of this section, or
> (ii) has been brought before the date of the coming into operation of this section where final judgment has not been given before that date.

---

52 *DPP v RL* [2023] IECA 47 [14].
53 *DPP v PMcC* [2018] IECA 309.
54 *DPP v RL* [2023] IECA 47 [14].
55 *DPP v Reece Lambert* [2023] IECA 124.
56 ibid.

Life sentence for child defendants possible in respect of murder

The Irish Law Reform Commission noted the difficulties which arise in terms of the use of the word imprisonment in the mandatory sentence of life imprisonment for murder in s 2 of the Criminal Justice Act 1990. **[28–56]**

> More generally, the Commission notes that the 2001 Act does not provide much guidance in terms of the approach to be taken when sentencing child offenders convicted of murder who remain under 18 at the date of conviction / sentence. By virtue of the fact that a child may never be sentenced to a sentence of imprisonment,[57] it seems clear that the mandatory sentence of life imprisonment provided for in section 2 of the 1990 Act cannot apply to child offenders. Further, section 142 of The Children Act 2001 provides the court with a general power to "impose on a child a period of detention in a children detention school or a children detention centre." This general power to impose a period of detention, it seems, enables a sentencing court to sentence a child convicted of murder to life if the court deems it appropriate in the circumstances. Older decisions of the Irish courts decided prior to the enactment of The Children Act 2001 support this assertion.[58]

The Commission observed that in the sentencing of Boy A and Boy B, both of whom had been convicted of the murder of Ana Kriégel, the sentencing judge noted that it was open to him to impose a life sentence, but that it was not mandatory in the case of child offenders. Boy A had been convicted of murder and aggravated sexual assault, while Boy B, an accomplice in the offence, was also convicted of murder. McDermott J sentenced Boy A to life with an in-built review after 12 years, and sentenced Boy B to fifteen years with a review after eight years.[59] **[28–57]**

The Irish Law Reform Commission Report on Suspended Sentences[60] states that it seems clear from previous that a sentencing court may impose any sentence of detention, including life, on a child offender convicted of murder. However, the Commission notes that s 9 of the Children (Amendment) Act 2015, when commenced, will put the above on a more solid statutory footing. Section 9 provides that the period of detention that a sentencing court may impose upon the child offender 'shall not exceed the term of detention or imprisonment that the court could have imposed on a person of full age and capacity who is convicted of such an offence'. **[28–58]**

Other legislative efforts to resolve this, as well as the issue of suspended sentences and detention orders, have been made through the Criminal Justice (Juvenile Offenders) Bill 2023, which will provide for **[28–59]**

> non-mandatory life sentences for juvenile offenders in cases of treason and murder, to expand the provisions of section 99 of the Criminal Justice Act 2006 relating to suspended sentences to include juvenile offenders, and to amend The Children Act 2001 to allow judicial discretion in setting the terms of a detention and supervision order.[61]

---

57 The Children Act 2001, s 156.

58 *State (O) v O'Brien* [1973] IR 50 and *The People (DPP) v VW* (a minor) (Court of Criminal Appeal, 3 March 1998). See Thomas O'Malley, *Sentencing Law and Practice* (3rd edn, Round Hall 2016) para 9.57; Irish Law Reform Commission, *Report on Suspended Sentences* (123–2020) para 7.17.

59 Irish Law Reform Commission, *Report on Suspended Sentences* (123–2020) para 7.17; Conor Gallagher, 'Ana Kriégel Murder: Boy A sentenced to life, Boy B sentenced to 15 years' *The Irish Times* (Dublin 5 November 2019) <https://www.irishtimes.com/news/crime-and-law/courts/criminalcourt/ana-Kriégel-murder-boy-a-sentenced-to-life-boy-b-sentenced-to-15-years-1.4072944> accessed on 13 October 2023.

60 Irish Law Reform Commission, *Report on Suspended Sentences* (123–2020) para 7.18.

61 Criminal Justice (Juvenile Offenders) Bill 2023.

Spent convictions

[28–60] While generally spent convictions are available through the Criminal Justice (Spent Convictions and Certain Disclosures) Act 2016, the concept by which a child would be able to pursue future opportunities without the disadvantage of a criminal record was included in the Children Act 2001 and is available subject to certain conditions.

[28–61] Section 258 of the Children Act 2001 allows for spent convictions for certain offences for which a child has been found guilty where:

(a) the offence was committed before the person attained the age of 18 years,
(b) the offence is not an offence required to be tried by the Central Criminal Court,
(c) a period of not less than three years has elapsed since the finding of guilt, and
(d) the person has not been dealt with for an offence in that three-year period.

[28–62] Dunne J noted this in the Supreme Court case of *Donoghue v DPP*[62]:

> Birmingham J. noted that had the case come before the court when it ought to have done that Mr. Donoghue would have benefited from the provisions of s. 93 of the Act, as substituted by s. 139 of the Criminal Justice Act 2006, which provides for anonymity in respect of a child defendant. The trial judge was of the view that that section was particularly significant when considered in combination with the provisions of s. 258 of the Act allowing for convictions to be spent after three years in certain circumstances.
>
> As Birmingham J. observed:–
>
> > 'The ability to expunge the record of conviction is particularly valuable if the original conviction did not and could not receive publicity.'

[28–63] As with spent offences under the Criminal Justice (Spent Convictions and Certain Disclosures) Act 2016, while an individual may be deemed to have no criminal record in Ireland, disclosure of convictions may be required depending on the immigration laws of a foreign country.

Child or adult at time of sentencing

[28–64] The Irish Law Reform Commission Report on Suspended Sentences[63] notes that relevant age of the child for the purposes of sentencing is potentially problematic: is it the date of the offending behaviour, or the date of conviction/sentence? It refers to England and Wales where the rule is that a person will be sentenced according to their age at the date of conviction (which will often also be the day of sentence). However, it also observes that this rule was identified by reference to statutory provisions that have no analogue in Irish law.

[28–65] O'Malley has thus observed that, in an Irish context, the matter must be approached by reference to first principles when construing the Children Act 2001. On this basis, he posits that, since various penalty provisions of Part 9 of the 2001 Act refer to 'the child' and 'parents or guardians' throughout, that would not be necessary in the case of an adult offender, the Act necessarily implies that those under the age of 18 at the date of conviction must be sentenced as children.[64] O'Malley also states that the English authorities have held, with whom the Irish court 'must doubtless agree', that an

---

62 *Donoghue v DPP* [2014] 2 IR 762, 768–69.

63 Irish Law Reform Commission, *Report on Suspended Sentences* (123–2020) para 7.12.

64 Thomas O'Malley, *Sentencing Law and Practice* (3rd edn, Round Hall 2016) para 9.16.

offender's culpability must be assessed by reference to his or her circumstances, including age, at the time of the offence. In *R v Ghafoor*, the English Court of Appeal said:

> The approach to be adopted where a defendant crosses the relevant age threshold between the date of the commission of the offence and the date of conviction should now be clear. The starting point is the sentence that the defendant would have been likely to receive if he had been sentenced at the date of the commission of the offence. It has been described as 'a powerful factor'. That is for the obvious reason that … the philosophy of restricting sentencing powers in relation to young persons reflects both (a) society's acceptance that young offenders are less responsible for their actions and therefore less culpable than adults, and (b) the recognition that, in consequence, sentencing them should place greater emphasis on rehabilitation, and less on retribution and deterrence than in the case of adults. It should be noted that the 'starting point' is not the *maximum* sentence that could lawfully have been imposed, but the sentence that the offender would have been likely to receive.[65]

Operational issues

The Irish Youth Justice Service (IYJS) operates as an executive office located in the Department of Children and Youth Affairs (DCYA). The IYJS has responsibility for leading and driving reform in the area of youth justice; its objective is to improve delivery of youth justice services and reduce youth offending. **[28–66]**

There are two divisions within IYJS: the Children Detention Schools Unit of the Department of Children and Youth Affairs, which is responsible for legislation and policy in respect of children detention schools, and the Youth Crime Policy and Programmes Division of the Department of Justice and Equality, which deals with youth crime policy, oversight and funding of the 105 Garda youth diversion projects nationwide.[66] **[28–67]**

Sex Offender's Register

A child who has been convicted of a sexual offence[67] will be placed on the Sex Offender's List.[68] **[28–68]**

---

65 *R v Ghafoor* (1995) 16 Cr App R (S) 246. See also *DPP v TD* [2021] IECA 289 and *DPP v OGP* [2023] IECA 259.

66 Irish Youth Justice Service, <http://www.iyjs.ie/> accessed 13 October 2023.

67 'Sexual offence' is outlined in the Schedule of the Sex Offenders Act 2001.

68 Sex Offenders Act 2001, s 7, Persons subject to the requirements of this Part:

> '(1) Without prejudice to subsection (2) and section 13 and 16(7), a person is subject to the requirements of this Part if he or she is convicted of a sexual offence after the commencement of this Part.
>
> (2) A person is also subject to the requirements of this Part if he or she has been convicted of a sexual offence before the commencement of this Part and, at that commencement, either – (a) the sentence to be imposed on the person in respect of the offence has yet to be determined, or (b) a sentence has been imposed on the person in respect of the offence and – (i) the person is serving the sentence in prison, (ii) the person is temporarily released under section 2 or 3 of the Criminal Justice Act, 1960, or (iii) the sentence is otherwise still in force or current.'

The Sex Offenders (Amendment) Act 2023 amends the Sex Offenders Act 2001 in relation to notification requirements of persons subject to Part 2 of that Act as well as increased powers of An Garda Síochána for the taking and retention of fingerprints, palm prints and photographs.

[28–69] Section 8(4) outlines the period of time for which a person under 18 must remain on the register:

> If – (*a*) a sentence is imposed on a person in respect of a sexual offence, and
> (*b*) at the time of sentencing the person is aged under 18 years,
> *subsection (3)* shall have effect in relation to that person as if for the references to 10 years, 7 years and 5 years in that subsection there were substituted references to 5 years, 3½ years and 2½ years, respectively.

[28–70] Where the prosecution of a case is delayed, the impact in respect of the relevant provision may be significant. *MS v DPP*[69] McDermott J noted the loss of the reduction in the time periods under s 8 Sex Offenders Act 2001.[70] Reference was also made to the loss of the reduction of the time period in *Forde v DPP*.[71]

Diversion programme

[28–71] The Youth Diversion Programme is set out in Part 4 of the Children Act 2001. Also known as the juvenile diversion programme, if a person under 18 comes to the attention of An Garda Síochána because of their behaviour, they may be dealt with otherwise than through the courts. Garda Juvenile Liaison Officers (JLOs) deal with young people and their families in relation to crime-prevention, the operation of the diversion programme and all other areas involving young people and the criminal justice system. Each Garda Division in Ireland has JLOs and they are obliged to interact with young people at risk and to liaise with teachers, Tusla staff, school attendance officers and other gardaí in their local area. The Diversion Programme allows for a caution to be administered by An Garda Síochána instead of the child being prosecuted. The child, where appropriate, is placed under the supervision of a JLO.[72]

Section 258 Children Act 2001 – spent convictions / relevant date

[28–72] In relation to spent convictions under s 258 of the Children Act 2001,[73] in the Court of Appeal judgment in *DPP v LE*, Birmingham P noted that the date of the offence is the relevant date in relation to s 258:

> The qualifying criterion for the procedural protections provided for under the Children Act 2001 is the age of the accused as of the date of the trial of the offences (as opposed to his or her age as of the date when the alleged offences are said to have occurred). Thus, an alleged offender who has transitioned from being a "child" (as defined) to an adult between (i) the date on which the offences are said to have occurred, and (ii) the date of the hearing and determination of criminal charges arising from those alleged offences, cannot avail of most of the procedural protections under the Act. The principal exception is in respect of the right to have the record of a criminal conviction expunged under Section 258 of The Children Act 2001 where the relevant date is the date of the offence. This would mean that if the appellant was tried and convicted of an offence as a minor, then she could later have that conviction expunged.[74]

---

69 *MS v DPP* [2018] IEHC 285.

70 ibid [35].

71 *Forde v DPP* [2017] IEHC 799 [30].

72 Garda Youth Diversion Bureau, An Garda Síochána <https://www.garda.ie/en/crime-prevention/community-engagement/community-engagement-offices/garda-youth-diversion-bureau/> accessed 13 October 2023.

73 See [28–60] 'Spent Convictions'.

74 *DPP v LE* [2020] IECA 101 [3].

If the offence was committed prior to the age of 18, the child defendant will still have the benefit of the section. However, the clock of the required three years will only start running from the date of the finding of guilt.[75] Therefore it could be argued that any prosecutorial delay will still cause a prejudice to the child defendant, particularly when aligned with the loss of anonymity under s 93 of the Children Act 2001. **[28–73]**

Dunne J noted this in the Supreme Court case of *Donoghue v DPP*: **[28–74]**

> Birmingham J. noted that had the case come before the court when it ought to have done that Mr. Donoghue would have benefited from the provisions of s. 93 of the Act, as substituted by s. 139 of the Criminal Justice Act 2006, which provides for anonymity in respect of a child defendant. The trial judge was of the view that that section was particularly significant when considered in combination with the provisions of s. 258 of the Act allowing for convictions to be spent after three years in certain circumstances. As Birmingham J. observed:–
>
> > "The ability to expunge the record of conviction is particularly valuable if the original conviction did not and could not receive publicity."[76]

Sentencing Issues – Victims

Certain aspects in respect of sentencing may be relevant to certain victims such as the nature of his or her relationship with the accused, the giving of victim impact statements, being heard in relation to parole hearings and involvement with restorative justice schemes. These disparate areas are examined below. **[28–75]**

Section 40 Domestic Violence Act 2018

Intimate relationship as aggravating factor[77] in sentencing of certain offences

Section 40 of the Domestic Violence Act 2018 provides that the fact that the injured **[28–76]**

---

75 Children Act 2001, s 258 (1)(c).

76 *Donoghue v DPP* [2014] 2 IR 762, 768–69 [16].

77 Domestic Violence Act 2018, s 40, Relationship between defendant and victim as aggravating factor in sentencing for certain offences:

> '(1) Where a court is determining the sentence to be imposed on a person for a relevant offence, the fact that the offence was committed by the person against a relevant person shall be treated, for the purpose of determining the sentence, as an aggravating factor.
>
> (2) Subject to subsection (3), where subsection (1) applies the court shall impose a sentence which is greater than that which would have been imposed if the person against whom the offence was committed was not a relevant person.
>
> (3) Subsection (2) shall not apply where the court considers that there are exceptional circumstances justifying it not applying that subsection.
>
> (4) The sentence imposed as a result of the application of subsection (2) shall not be greater than the maximum sentence permissible for the relevant offence concerned.
>
> (5) In this section –
>
> "Act of 1990" means the Criminal Law (Rape) (Amendment) Act 1990;
>
> "relevant offence" means –
>
> (a) an offence under sections 2 to 15 of the Non-Fatal Offences against the Person Act 1997,
>
> (aa) an offence under section 2 or 3 of the Harassment, Harmful Communications and Related Offences Act 2020,
>
> (b) any offence which involves violence or a threat of violence to a person other than an offence –
>
> (i) referred to in paragraph (a), or
>
> (ii) under section 39,

party and the defendant or a 'relevant person' are in an intimate relationship is an aggravating factor.

[28–77] Relevant person means:

(a) is the spouse or civil partner of that other person, or
(b) is not the spouse or civil partner of that other person and is not related to that other person within a prohibited degree of relationship but is or was in an intimate relationship with that other person.

[28–78] Intimate relationship appears not to be defined within the Act.

[28–79] A relevant offence means:

(a) an offence under sections 2 to 15 of the Non-Fatal Offences against the Person Act 1997
(aa) an offence under section 2 or 3 of the Harassment, Harmful Communications and Related Offences Act 2020
(b) any offence which involves violence or a threat of violence to a person other than an offence –
(i) referred to in paragraph (a), or
(ii) under section 39,
(c) rape,
(d) rape under section 4 of the Criminal Law (Rape) (Amendment) Act 1990
(e) sexual assault within the meaning of section 2 of the Criminal Law (Rape) (Amendment) Act 1990
(f) aggravated sexual assault within the meaning of section 3 of the Criminal Law (Rape) (Amendment) Act 1990
(g) an offence consisting of attempting or conspiring to commit, or aiding or abetting, counselling or procuring or inciting the commission of, an offence referred to in paragraph (a), (aa), (b), (c), (d), (e) or (f)

[28–80] The Court of Appeal judgment *in DPP v Daniel Kane*,[78] the first prosecution in respect of coercive control,[79] observed that the sentencing judge had properly applied s 40 in that case as an intimate relationship is a constituent element of the offence itself and so cannot be an aggravating factor. Kennedy J noted:

The judge also considered as an aggravating factor, that the appellant and the injured

---

(c) rape,
(d) rape under section 4 of the Act of 1990,
(e) sexual assault within the meaning of section 2 of the Act of 1990,
(f) aggravated sexual assault within the meaning of section 3 of the Act of 1990,
(g) an offence consisting of attempting or conspiring to commit, or aiding or abetting, counselling or procuring or inciting the commission of, an offence referred to in paragraph (a), (aa), (b), (c), (d), (e) or (f)

(6) In this section, a person is a "relevant person" in respect of another person if he or she –
(a) is the spouse or civil partner of that other person, or
(b) is not the spouse or civil partner of that other person and is not related to that other person within a prohibited degree of relationship but is or was in an intimate relationship with that other person.'

78 *DPP v Daniel Kane* [2023] IECA 86.

79 Paul Neilan, 'Court upholds 10½-year sentence for first coercive control conviction in Ireland: Daniel Kane (54) lost his appeal against sentence for repeatedly assaulting, threatening, intimidating and humiliating partner' *The Irish Times* (30 March 2023) <https://www.irishtimes.com/crime-law/courts/2023/03/30/court-upholds-10-and-a-half-year-sentence-for-first-coercive-control-conviction-in-ireland/> accessed 13 October 2023.

party were in an intimate relationship, however, it is clear from her opening remarks on sentencing that she properly applied s. 40 of the 2018 Act only to the assault offences, as s. 40(5)(b)(ii) excludes an offence under s. 39 as a relevant offence. This is so, as an intimate relationship is a constituent element of the offence of coercive control and so cannot constitute an aggravating factor.[80]

Victim impact statements

On conviction, subject to the nature of the harm done to a natural person, a 'victim impact statement' may be required for sentencing. The term 'victim impact statement' is not found in the relevant legislation. The title of s 5 of the Criminal Justice Act 1993 is 'Effect of certain offences on persons in respect of whom committed'. However, the more commonly used term is that of 'victim impact statement' or 'report'. A victim impact statement could originally be provided given in relation to sexual or violent offences.[81] However, the EU 'Victims Directive'[82] introduced a wider obligation on the courts to offer the victim (and their friends and family if the victim had been killed) an opportunity to inform the court as to how the offence or offences had affected him or her. The Criminal Justice (Victims of Crime) Act 2017, as the domestic legislation giving effect to the EU Victim's Directive, expanded the remit of victim impact statements through the amendments of s 5 of the Criminal Justice Act 1993. Where a child under 14 or a person with a 'mental disorder'[83] has been affected by an offence and wishes to give a victim impact statement, a family member may do so on his or her behalf. **[28–81]**

The Criminal Justice Act 1993 has been amended by the Criminal Procedure Act 2010 to allow for the giving of a victim impact statement through video link or through an intermediary.[84] The wording of these sections are very similar to the relevant sections in the Criminal Evidence Act 1992.[85] **[28–82]**

The Parole Act 2019

The Parole Act 2019 was commenced on 30 July 2021, placing the granting of parole on a statutory footing.[86] It established the Parole Board on 30 July 2021, which is an independent statutory body that considers applications for parole from prisoners serving life sentences once the prisoners concerned have served at least 12 years of their sentence.[87] Parole involves release from prison under certain conditions. If granted parole, the person must follow all the conditions of their parole order. They are still serving a life sentence, but in the community. The person may be returned to prison if they re-offend or break any of the conditions of the parole order. **[28–83]**

---

80 *DPP v Daniel Kane* [2023] IECA 86 [31].

81 Criminal Justice Act 1993, s 5.

82 Directive 2012/29/EU of The European Parliament and of the Council (25 October 2012) Establishing minimum standards on the rights, support and protection of victims of crime, and replacing Council Framework Decision 2001/220/JHA.

83 Mental disorder is defined in s 5 Criminal Justice Act 1993 as including a mental illness, mental disability, dementia or any disease of the mind.

84 See [29–06].

85 Criminal Evidence Act 1992, ss 13, 14.

86 Dept of Justice 'Minister Humphreys establishes new Parole Board and increases time life prisoners must serve before being considered for parole' 11 August 2021 <https://www.gov.ie/en/press-release/d8f3f-minister-humphreys-establishes-new-parole-board-and-increases-time-life-prisoners-must-serve-before-being-considered-for-parole/> accessed 13 October 2023.

87 The Parole Board <www.gov.ie/paroleboard> accessed 13 October 2023.

[28–84] The Parole Act 2019 allows submissions by victims or family members to be made to the Board which must be taken into account in relation to the parole of a prisoner.[88] It also obliges the Board to communicate information and decisions to victims or family members as appropriate.

[28–85] The Parole Act 2019 defines a 'victim' as:

> 1. A person who has suffered harm, including physical, mental or emotional harm or economic loss, which was directly caused by a criminal offence for which the prisoner is serving a term of life imprisonment;
>
> 2. The family members of a person whose death was directly caused by a criminal offence and who have suffered harm including physical, mental, or emotional harm, or economic loss as a direct result of that crime.

[28–86] Under the Act a 'family member' is:

- a spouse, civil partner, or cohabitant of the victim;
- a child or step-child of the victim;
- a parent or grandparent of the victim;
- a brother, sister, half brother or half sister of the victim;
- a grandchild of the victim;
- an aunt, uncle, nephew, or niece of the victim;
- any other person who was dependent on the victim;
- a sufficiently close connection to warrant being treated as a family member by the Board.

[28–87] A family member will not be entitled to the rights provided to victims by the Act if they have been charged with or are under investigation for the death of the victim. The Parole Board has a Legal Aid Scheme in place and can arrange for legal assistance for registered victims free of charge, even if they have financial resources to pay for it. The Parole Board will arrange this prior to the victim/family member making his or her submission. The victim/family member may choose his or her own legal representation and this may be paid for under the Legal Aid Scheme. The legal representative may accompany the victim/family member to the meeting of the Board.

Restorative justice

[28–88] The concept of restorative justice in relation to sexual offences was extensively explored in research carried out in UCD and detailed in *Sexual Trauma and Abuse: Restorative and Transformative Possibilities?*[89] The challenges in relation to restorative justice in respect of sexual offences are complex as the risk of repeating the original traumatic event is significant. However, continual investigations into the area are being explored. In *Supporting A Victim's Journey*, the Dept of Justice outlined a mapping exercise in respect of restorative justice.[90] *Restorative Justice: Strategies for Change (RJS4C)* outlines

[88] Jennifer O'Connell, 'Husband of murdered woman "relieved" as killer refused parole 27 years later' *The Irish Times* (Dublin 23 March 2023). <https://www.irishtimes.com/crime-law/courts/2023/03/25/husband-of-murdered-woman-relieved-as-killer-refused-parole-27-years-later/> accessed 13 October 2023.

[89] Dr Marie Keenan, *Sexual Trauma and Abuse: Restorative and Transformative Possibilities? A Collaborative Study on the potential of Restorative Justice in Sexual Crime in Ireland.* (27th November 2014, School of Applied Social Science, University College Dublin, Ireland).

[90] Dept of Justice and Equality, *Supporting a Victim's Journey – A plan to help victims and vulnerable witnesses in sexual violence cases* (October 2020). 64.

the progress of these initiatives in Ireland.[91] In collaboration with nine other European countries, Ireland is participating in a new cross-European venture :

- — to contribute towards refocusing European criminal justice systems, agencies, policies and practices around restorative principles and processes and
- — to determine how the Council of Europe Recommendation CM/Rec (2018) concerning restorative justice in criminal matters could be used to support this work.[92]

In August 2023, the Dept of Justice published its policy paper, *Promoting and Supporting the Provision of Restorative Justice at all stages of the Criminal Justice System* which outlines the parameters and goals of restorative justice in the criminal justice system in the future.[93] **[28–89]**

Criminal Justice (Victims of Crime) Act 2017 – information regarding a restorative justice scheme where available

Section 7 of the Criminal Justice (Victims of Crime) Act 2017 states that on first contact, the victim will be given information in respect of a restorative justice scheme where available. The definition of 'restorative justice scheme' is outlined in s 2 of the Act, which states that a 'restorative justice scheme' means any scheme administered for the time being under which, with the consent of each of them, a victim and an offender or alleged offender engage with each other to resolve, with the assistance of an impartial third party, matters arising from the offence or alleged offence. **[28–90]**

The parameters of restorative justice are to be found in s 26 of the Criminal Justice (Victims of Crime) Act 2017, which outlines: **[28–91]**

> (1) In respect of any offence or alleged offence, a body or other person shall administer a restorative justice scheme (in this section referred to as a 'scheme') only if the requirements of this section are complied with.
>
> (2) The offender or alleged offender shall – (a) acknowledge the basic facts of the offence committed or offence alleged to have been committed, as the case may be, against the victim, and (b) give his or her free and informed consent to participating in the scheme.
>
> (3) The victim shall – (a) receive full and unbiased information about –
> (i) the scheme and the potential outcomes of participating in the scheme
> (ii) the procedures for supervising and implementing any agreement that may be reached between the parties in the context of the scheme, and
> (iii) his or her right to withdraw at any time his or her consent to participating in the scheme,
>
> and (b) having received such information, give his or her free and informed consent to participating in the scheme.
>
> (4) Where a scheme is administered – (a) any agreement between the parties reached in the context of the scheme shall only be so reached on the basis of the free and informed

---

91 Restorative Justice Strategies for Change Ireland, https://restorativejustice.ie/about/ accessed 13 October 2023.

92 The Probation Service <http://www.probation.ie/EN/PB/WebPages/WP19000022> accessed 15 May 2023. Restorative Justice: Strategies for Change – Ireland <https://restorativejustice.ie/> accessed 13 October 2023.

93 Dept of Justice, *Promoting and Supporting the Provision of Restorative Justice at all stages of the Criminal Justice System,* (8 August 2023). Promoting and supporting the provision of Restorative Justice at all stages of the criminal justice system (www.gov.ie)> accessed 13 October 2023.

consent of each of the parties, (b) an agreement reached in the manner referred to in paragraph (a) may, with the consent of both parties, be taken into account by a court in any criminal proceedings relating to the offence or alleged offence which is the subject of the parties' participation in the scheme, and (c) any discussions between the parties which form part of their participation in the scheme and which are not conducted in public shall not be disclosed, save with the agreement of the parties or as required by law.

(5) The body or person which or who administers a scheme shall – (a) prior to the commencement of the parties' participation in the scheme inform them of each of the matters referred to in subsection (4), (b) be satisfied that the victim's participation in the scheme is in the interests of the victim, and (c) in administering the scheme, have regard to the need to safeguard the victim from secondary and repeat victimisation, intimidation or retaliation.

(6) Nothing in this section shall affect the operation of Parts 4 and 8 of the Act of 2001.

Sections 26 and 32A Children Act 2001

Presence of victim at formal caution/Diversion Programme conference

[28–92] In relation to young offenders, s 26 of the Children Act 2001[94] provides for the presence of the victim at the formal caution of the child while in relation to Part 4, and the Diversion Programme, s 32A of the Children Act 2001 provides for the attendance at the conference by the victim.[95]

---

94 Children Act 2001, s 26, Presence of victim at formal caution:

'(1) The Director may invite any victim whose views in relation to the child's criminal or anti-social behaviour have been considered pursuant to section 23(4) to be present at the administration of a formal caution. (1A) Where the Director invites a victim to be present at the administration of a formal caution pursuant to subsection (1), he or she shall ensure that the victim –40 (a) is provided with full and unbiased information about the process of administering a formal caution and the potential outcomes of the process under this Act, and (b) is informed that he or she may withdraw at any time his or her consent to being so present. (2) Where any victim is so present, there shall be a discussion among those present about the child's criminal or anti-social behaviour. (2A) The member of the Garda Síochána administering the formal caution shall, where a victim is present at the administration of the caution, have regard to the need to safeguard the victim from secondary and repeat victimisation, intimidation or retaliation while the victim is so present. (3) The member of the Garda Síochána administering the formal caution may invite the child – (a) to apologise, whether orally or in writing or both, to the victim, and (b) where appropriate, to make financial or other reparation to him or her.'

95 Children Act 2001, s 32A, Attendance at conference by victim:

'(1) Where the facilitator invites a victim to be present at a conference pursuant to section 32(4), he or she shall ensure that the victim – (a) is provided with full and unbiased information about – (i) the process relating to a conference, (ii) the potential outcomes of the process under this Act, and (iii) the procedures for monitoring the implementation of, and compliance with, an action plan, and (b) is informed that he or she may withdraw at any time his or her consent to being so present. (2) The facilitator shall, where a victim is present at a conference, have regard to the need to safeguard the victim from secondary and repeat victimisation, intimidation or retaliation while the victim is so present.'

CHAPTER 29

VIDEO LINK

Introduction

[29–01] The support measure of video link allows the vulnerable witness to be physically distant from the courtroom but to be able to see the trial judge and the relevant questioner. It also allows the witness to be seen by those in the courtroom, including the jury and the defendant.[1] It thus minimises the stress for the witness, facilitating better evidence and hopefully reduces the trauma which might arise from a stressful court environment. The use of video link has become a familiar and widespread support measure in Ireland[2] and its use has expanded following the pandemic.[3] The introduction of video link in criminal proceedings led to constitutional challenges and to a Supreme Court judgment which still has an impact on how the courts consider the use of support measures for vulnerable witnesses.[4]

[29–02] There are a number of provisions facilitating the use of video link by a witness. Some may be designed with a focus on the more vulnerable witness, such as s 13 of the Criminal Evidence Act 1992 or s 39 of the Criminal Justice Act 1999. Others may facilitate the giving of evidence from outside the State in criminal proceedings, eg, s 29 of the Criminal Evidence Act 1992 or s 67 of the Criminal Justice (Mutual Assistance) Act 2008. Provisions also exist which facilitate the limited use of video link for defendants in the course of certain criminal proceedings.[5] However, there is no provision which facilitates the giving of evidence by a defendant in the course of a criminal trial. It is possible that the general principles outlined in *DPP v Harrison*[6] would allow the court to grant the support measure for a defendant to facilitate the giving of evidence via video link.

Legislative Provisions

[29–03] The available legislative provisions include:

Section 13 of the Criminal Evidence Act 1992 allows for a child or an adult with the leave of the court, to give evidence within or outside the State, via video link in

1 Irish Law Reform Commission, *Report on Child Sexual Abuse* (32–1990).
2 *DPP v Osei and Opoku* [2022] IECA 61 [14].
3 Civil Law and Criminal Law (Miscellaneous Provisions) Act 2020.
4 *Donnelly v Ireland* [1998] 1 IR 321.
5 Civil Law and Criminal Law (Miscellaneous Provisions) Act 2020.
6 *DPP v Harrison* [2016] IECA 212.

relation to a relevant offence. A victim may give evidence via video link in relation to an offence other than a relevant offence subject to s 14AA.

> 13. –(1) In any proceedings (including proceedings under section 4E or 4F of the Criminal Procedure Act, 1967) for a relevant offence a person other than the accused may give evidence, whether from within or outside the State, through a live television link –
> (a) if the person is under 18 years of age, unless the court sees good reason to the contrary,
> (b) in any other case, with the leave of the court.
>
> (1A) In any proceedings (including proceedings under section 4E or 4F of the Criminal Procedure Act 1967) relating to an offence, other than a relevant offence, a court may, subject to section 14AA, grant leave for a victim of the offence to give evidence, whether from within or outside the State, through a live television link.
>
> (2) Evidence given under subsection (1) or (1A) shall be videorecorded.

[29–04] Under s 14AA of the Criminal Evidence Act 1992, when deciding whether to grant the use of video link, the court shall have regard to the need to protect the victim from secondary and repeat victimisation, intimidation or retaliation, taking into account (i) the nature and circumstances of the case, and (ii) the personal characteristics of the victim.[7] Secondary victimisation is interpreted in s 2 of the Criminal Justice (Victims of Crime) Act 2017 as 'victimisation that occurs indirectly through the response of institutions and individuals to the victim'.

[29–05] Section 5A of the Criminal Justice Act 1993 allows for a child or person with a mental disorder, or any other person with the leave of the court, to give a victim impact statement through video link.[8]

[29–06] Section 39 of the Criminal Justice Act 1999 provides for the use of video link for offences on indictment where the witness may be in fear or intimidation.

[29–07] Section 255 of the Children Act 2001 provides that a District Court judge may allow a child victim to avail of video link under s 13 of the Criminal Evidence Act 1992 or s 39 of the Criminal Justice Act 1999 when giving evidence through deposition under the Criminal Procedure Act 1967 where the safety, health or well being of a child may be at risk.[9]

---

[7] Criminal Evidence Act 1992, s 14AA, Matters to be taken into account under ss 13, 14 and 14A regarding victims:

> 'The court, in deciding –
> (a) whether to grant leave under section 13(1A) for a victim to give evidence through a live television link,
> (b) whether, under section 14(1A), the interests of justice require that it direct that questions be put to the victim through an intermediary, or
> (c) whether, under section 14A(2), the interests of justice require that it direct that a screen or other similar device be positioned, in an appropriate place, so as to prevent the victim from seeing the accused when giving evidence,
>
> shall have regard to the need to protect the victim from secondary and repeat victimisation, intimidation or retaliation, taking into account –
> (i) the nature and circumstances of the case, and
> (ii) the personal characteristics of the victim.

[8] Criminal Justice Act 1993, s 5B also allows for the use of an intermediary during the giving of a victim impact statement.

[9] The Children Act 2001:

> '255. – (1) Without prejudice to section 4F of the Act of 1967, where a judge of the District

Section 39 of the Criminal Justice (Miscellaneous Provisions) Act 2023, when commenced, allows for evidence to be given via video link where appropriate in applications under Part 5 of the Act in relation to civil orders against relevant conduct. **[29–08]**

Section 27 of the Criminal Justice (Miscellaneous Provisions) Act 2023 sets out the definition of 'relevant conduct' as conduct that is likely to cause the applicant or a person connected to the applicant: **[29–09]**

(a) to fear that violence will be used against the applicant or person or
(b) serious alarm or distress that has a substantial adverse impact on his or her usual day-to-day activities.

There are no legislative provisions for defendants to attend or give evidence via video link at trial. Section 25 of the Civil Law and Criminal Law (Miscellaneous Provisions) Act 2020 allows for the use of video link for persons in custody to communicate with the court for certain proceedings. Section 5 of the Civil Law and Criminal Law (Miscellaneous Provisions) Act repealed ss 33 and 34 of the Prisons Act 2007, which had previously provided for certain matters to be dealt with via video link where the defendant was in custody or detention, ie 'remand centre, or a children detention school, within the meaning of the Children Act 2001' if there was consent by the defendant to do so. It is possible that the general principles outlined in *DPP v Harrison*[10] would allow a court to grant the support measure for a defendant to attend trial or facilitate the giving of evidence via video link. In *DPP v Harrison*,[11] the defendant had been found fit to plead while the Court of Appeal noted that he had vulnerabilities which could have been facilitated through the trial. **[29–10]**

While this work is focused on criminal proceedings, certain civil law proceedings may sometimes overlap with criminal proceedings, particularly in respect of issues such as violation of barring orders etc and custody proceedings. **[29–11]**

Section 25 of the Domestic Violence Act 2018 provides for evidence to be given through video link for civil proceedings. It may also be noted that in relation to criminal offences, s 13 Criminal Evidence Act 1992 was amended by s 44 Domestic Violence Act 2018 and the use of video may be granted in relation to offences under ss 33, 38 or 39 of the Domestic Violence Act 2018: namely, s 33 contravention of a safety order, a barring order, an interim barring order, an emergency barring order or a protection order; s 38 the offence of forced marriage; and s 39 the offence of coercive control. (Note there is no mention in the section of 'within or outside the State'.) **[29–12]**

Court is satisfied on the evidence of a registered medical practitioner that the attendance before a court of any child, in respect of whom an offence under this Part, or any offence mentioned in Schedule 1, is alleged to have been committed, would involve serious danger to the safety, health or wellbeing of the child, the judge may take the evidence either – (a) by way of sworn deposition, or (b) in case the evidence is to be given through a live television link pursuant to Part III of the Criminal Evidence Act, 1992, or section 39 of the Criminal Justice Act, 1999, through such a link. (2) The rules mentioned in section 4F(3) of the Act of 1967 shall apply and have effect in relation to the taking of evidence under subsection (1). (3) A deposition taken under subsection (1) or a videorecording of evidence given by a child under paragraph (b) of that subsection shall be deemed to have been taken under section 4F of the said Act of 1967, and section 4G (admissibility of deposition or videorecording) shall apply and have effect accordingly.'

[10] *DPP v Harrison* [2016] IECA 212.

[11] ibid.

[29–13] Section 21 of the Children Act 1997 allows for a child, whether from within or outside the State, to give evidence in civil proceedings before any court, concerning the welfare of the child[12] through video link. Section 28 of the Children Act 1997 provides for the dispensation of oath/affirmation as well as a perjury provision (s 28(2)) which is contained in Schedule 2 of the Criminal Justice (Perjury and Related Offences) Act 2021.

[29–14] Section 35 of the Employment Permits Act 2006 allows, with the leave of the court, for a person, other than the accused, to give evidence in any proceedings for an offence under the 2006 Act or the Employment Permits Act 2003, through video link if the person is outside the State.

[29–15] Section 29 of the Criminal Evidence Act 1992 allows for a person, other than the accused or the person seeking extradition, to give evidence in any criminal proceeding, or proceedings under the Extradition Acts, 1965 to 2001, via video link. The section is entitled 'Evidence through television link by persons outside State'. Section 24 of the Extradition (European Union Conventions) Act 2001 amended the original provision, which stated 'in any criminal proceedings a person other than the accused who is outside the State may, with the leave of the court, give evidence through a live television link' and inserted the current provision which omits 'from outside the State' and states:

> in any criminal proceedings or proceedings under the Extradition Acts, 1965 to 2001, a person other than the accused or the person whose extradition is being sought, as the case may be, may, with the leave of the court, give evidence through a live television link.[13]

[29–16] Section 67 of the Criminal Justice (Mutual Assistance) Act 2008 allows for a witness to give evidence in criminal proceedings through video link from a designated State.

Background to the Measure of Video Link

[29–17] In its *Report on Child Sexual Abuse*[14] the Law Reform Commission advocated the use of live link[15] and the support measure was enacted under s 13 of the Criminal Evidence Act 1992.[16] Section 13 allows for the use of 'a live television link' in relation to a 'relevant offence'[17] in any court, District or otherwise, where the person is under 18 years of

---

12 Children Act 1997, s 20, Application of Part III.

13 Criminal Evidence Act 1992, s 29 as amended by Extradition (European Union Conventions) Act 2001, s 24.

14 Irish Law Reform Commission, *Report on Child Sexual Abuse* (32–1990) 70–72, 94.

15 ibid para 7.08: 'The use of a live TV link enables one to locate the child outside the courtroom in a comfortable and congenial environment while everyone in the courtroom will be able to observe the child giving her evidence.'

16 Criminal Evidence Act 1992, s 13 was commenced on 15 February 1993 through the Criminal Evidence Act 1992 (Commencement) Order 1993 (SI No 38 of 1993) initially for the Central Criminal Court and the Dublin Circuit Criminal Court.

17 Criminal Evidence Act 1992, s 12(1)

"Relevant offence' means –

(a) a sexual offence;

(b) an offence involving violence or the threat of violence to a person;

(ba) an offence under section 10 (amended by section 23 of the Criminal Justice (Miscellaneous Provisions) Act 2023) of the NonFatal Offences against the Person Act 1997;

(c) an offence under section 3, 4, 5 or 6 of the Child Trafficking and Pornography Act 1998;

age, unless the court sees good reason to the contrary and, in any other case, with the leave of the court. The provision has remained one of the most commonly used provisions for the use of video link. The section has been expanded by the Criminal Justice (Victims of Crime) Act 2017. Under s 13(1A) of the Act, the support measure may also be used by a victim of an offence other than a relevant offence in line with the factors outlined in s 14AA of the Criminal Evidence Act 1992.

While either a defence or prosecution witness may apply for use of the support measure, the defendant is explicitly excluded from availing of it. It may be used in proceedings under s 4E of the Criminal Procedure Act 1967 where the accused is applying to have the charges dismissed. It may also be used under s 4F of the Criminal Procedure Act 1967 where evidence is taken prior to trial on deposition. [29–18]

Constitutionality of video link

There were two significant constitutional challenges to the support measure. The first challenge was *White v Ireland*[18] where judicial review proceedings were taken in the High Court. Judicial review proceedings were also taken in the High Court in *Donnelly v Ireland*[19] and that decision was then appealed to the Supreme Court.[20] The decision in *Donnelly* referred to and approved the judgment in *White*. Both constitutional challenges to the use of the support measure ultimately failed but the judgments provide an opportunity to understand how the courts interpret the legislation and delineate its practical applications. [29–19]

The Supreme Court determined that once it is established that an accused person has no constitutional right to have a witness give evidence in his presence then the circumstances in which evidence is given other than in his presence is a matter for the Oireachtas. The Court reiterated the importance of upholding the rights of the defendant in observing: [29–20]

> It is well established in our constitutional jurisprudence that an accused person's right to a fair trial is one of the most fundamental constitutional rights accorded to persons and that in so far as it is possible or desirable to construct a hierarchy of constitutional rights it is a superior right.[21]

The introduction of support measures other than video link which may assist the child witness at trial may be examined through the principles of the judgment in *Donnelly v Ireland*,[22] which could be said to be the starting point for the implementation of [29–21]

(d) an offence under section 2, 4 or 7 of the Criminal Law (Human Trafficking) Act 2008;
(da) an offence under section 33, 38 or 39 of the Domestic Violence Act 2018;
(e) an offence consisting of attempting or conspiring to commit, or of aiding or abetting, counselling, procuring or inciting the commission of, an offence mentioned in paragraph (a), (b), [(c), (d) or (da).'

Criminal Justice (Miscellaneous Provisions) Act 2023, s 60, now extends 'relevant offence' to include 'harassment or stalking' under Non Fatal Offences Against the Person Act 1997, s 10. When commenced, it will also include s 44 'Order' under Criminal Justice (Miscellaneous Provisions) Act 2023, s 28.

18 *White v Ireland* [1995] 2 IR 268.
19 *Donnelly v Ireland* [1998] 1 IR 321.
20 ibid.
21 ibid 348 (SC).
22 *Donnelly v Ireland* 1 IR 321; [1998] 1 ILRM 402 (SC).

any other support measures that the Oireachtas may establish. In a comprehensive judgment outlining the development of measures designed to facilitate the giving of evidence by vulnerable witnesses, Ní Raifeartaigh J stated in *DPP v VE*:

> The right to cross-examine witnesses undoubtedly inheres in the concept of a fair trial pursuant to Article 38(1) of the Constitution (and for that matter, Article 6 of the European Convention on Human Rights). In *State (Healy) v. Donoghue*, Gannon J. identified among the trial rights of an accused the right "to hear and test by examination the evidence offered by or on behalf of his accuser", while in the same case on appeal, O'Higgins C.J. said that words "in due course of law" make it "mandatory that every criminal trial shall be conducted in accordance with the concept of justice, that the procedures applied shall be fair, and that the person accused shall be afforded every opportunity to defend himself". Nonetheless, O'Higgins C.J. also went on to say: – "The general view of what is fair and proper in relation to criminal trials has always been the subject of change and development. Rules of evidence and rules of procedure gradually evolved as notions of fairness developed". These words were cited by Hamilton C.J. in Donnelly v. Ireland, a case in which the Supreme Court upheld the constitutionality of s 13 of the 1992 Act (video link evidence) in the face of a challenge grounded upon the constitutional right to cross-examination.[23]

Video link – 'flattening' the evidence

[29–22] While Kinlen J in *White v Ireland*[24] considered that the technology would allow the jury a great facility for examining the body language and demeanour of the child witness, some defence counsel do not object to the use of video link as it may 'flatten' the emotional impact of the testimony.[25] This issue has been flagged by Charleton J who has suggested extra judicially that the further one gets from the live appearance of a person 'telling their story' in court,[26] the more the prosecution case may be weakened[27] There is no legislative provision for the vulnerable witness to express a preference for the manner in which evidence is given. In England and Wales, the relevant provision allows for the views of the witness to be taken into account.[28]

---

23 *DPP v VE* [2021] IECA 122 [66].

24 *White v Ireland* [1995] 2 IR 268 [281].

25 'There is some slender empirical support for the widespread belief in the legal professions in all our comparative jurisdictions that the video technology distances the jury from the complainant, making it more difficult to assess credibility.' Laura Hoyano and Caroline Keenan, *Child Abuse, Law and Policy Across Boundaries* (Oxford University Press 2010) 643.

26 Charleton J, 'Chairman's Opening Speech' (The Law Reform Commission Annual Conference 2011: Sexual Offences and Capacity) 6 <http://www.lawreform.ie/_fileupload/misc/AC11/CharletonJ.pdf> accessed 13 October 2023.

27 ibid. Charleton J has observed that while video link can be extremely beneficial, it can also be problematic as it could create a distance between the victim and the jury which was less helpful. He also remarked, however, that without video link, on occasion, there would be no witness.

28 Youth Justice and Criminal Evidence Act 1999, s 16, Witnesses eligible for assistance on grounds of age or incapacity:

> '(1) For the purposes of this Chapter a witness in criminal proceedings (other than the accused) is eligible for assistance by virtue of this section –
> (a) if under the age of at the time of the hearing; or
> (b) if the court considers that the quality of evidence given by the witness is likely to be diminished by reason of any circumstances falling within subsection (2).
> (2) The circumstances falling within this subsection are –
> (a) that the witness –
> (i) suffers from mental disorder within the meaning of the M1Mental Health Act 1983, or
> (ii) otherwise has a significant impairment of intelligence and social functioning;

Recent case law outlined a challenge in respect of evidence being given via a screen due to alleged deficiencies in this manner of giving testimony. In *DPP v PB*,[29] where a challenge was made in relation to the admission of recorded testimony and the subsequent cross-examination via video link, Birmingham P stated: **[29–23]**

> Neither are we persuaded by the argument that the cross-examination should not have proceeded by way of video link. There was statutory authorisation for what occurred and, in our view, this is sufficient to dispose of this ground of appeal.[30]

Concerns have been cited in respect of the possible detachment of full recorded evidence, ie examination in chief, cross-examination and re-examination evidence. The O'Malley Report has referenced submissions from the Bar Council to its Working Group in relation to the difficulties of losing the immediacy of live evidence in respect of recorded evidence.[31] The report mentions the concern whether video testimony might create emotional distance between the witness and the jury. **[29–24]**

'[W]ith the leave of the court'

DPP v Ronald McManus (AKA Ronald Dunbar) – adult witness

Section 13(1)(b) allows the use of the measure to be used 'in any other case, with the leave of the court'.[32] The case of *DPP v Ronald McManus (AKA Ronald Dunbar)*[33] provides some guidance from the Court of Criminal Appeal regarding the factors **[29–25]**

(b) that the witness has a physical disability or is suffering from a physical disorder.
(3) In subsection (1)(a) "the time of the hearing", in relation to a witness, means the time when it falls to the court to make a determination for the purposes of section 19(2) in relation to the witness.
(4) In determining whether a witness falls within subsection (1)(b) the court must consider any views expressed by the witness.
(5) In this Chapter references to the quality of a witness's evidence are to its quality in terms of completeness, coherence and accuracy; and for this purpose "coherence" refers to a witness's ability in giving evidence to give answers which address the questions put to the witness and can be understood both individually and collectively.'

29 *DPP v PB* [2021] IECA 152.

30 ibid [28].

31 Dept of Justice and Equality, *Review of Protections for Vulnerable Witnesses in the Investigation and Prosecution of Sexual Offences* (August 2020) para 6.28: 'Accordingly, for a number of reasons, including the issue just mentioned in connection with disclosure, we do not recommend at this point that pre-recorded cross-examination or re-examination be introduced. We are also conscious of a number of other potential problems that were mentioned by the Bar Council in its submission to the Working Group. These include possible issues with technology, a potential reduction in the jury's ability to "read" a witness's body language, whether video testimony might create emotional distance between the witness and the jury, and possibly lack the immediacy and persuasiveness of live testimony. We do, however, acknowledge that strong arguments have been made, by academic experts and others, in favour of introducing such a practice. Our recommendation is based solely on practical considerations rather than any opposition in principle. If the point is reached where these practical issues can be effectively addressed, pre-recorded cross-examination and re-examination may well become feasible, though any potential constitutional impediments would need to be carefully examined before a final decision is taken on the matter.'

32 *Donnelly v Ireland* [1998] 1 IR 321, 357 (SC) (Hamilton CJ): 'The accused person's right to a fair trial is further protected by the fact that it is open to the court not to permit the giving of evidence by a young person through a live television link if the accused person establishes that "there is good reason to the contrary" and that the leave of the court is required before any other person may give evidence in this manner. A judge considering either of these issues will be obliged to have regard to the accused person's right to a fair trial.'

33 *DPP v Ronald McManus (AKA Ronald Dunbar)* [2011] IECCA 32.

the court will consider in allowing a witness to give evidence via video link. The case involved the use of video link under s 13(1)(b) of the Criminal Evidence Act 1992 by a female witness who had just turned 18 and who was to give evidence against the accused, her father, in a murder trial.

[29–26] The defendant appealed his conviction *inter alia* on the ground that the learned trial judge had erred in fact and law in allowing the witness, a person over 18 years of age, to give evidence by way of video link. He submitted that when a witness gives evidence in the ordinary course of events, ie from the body of the court, a jury has the greatest possible opportunity to assess the demeanour, deportment and reaction of such a witness in examination and cross-examination. The appellant also submitted that departure from the standard procedure could be only be lawfully made on the basis of 'strong evidence'. The application for video link was based on evidence by a social worker who stated that the witness was afraid that she would freeze while giving evidence and that she would be unable to confront her father face to face. In addition, the witness did not wish to give evidence in front of a crowd.

[29–27] The Court of Criminal Appeal stated that, regarding s 13(1)(b) which allows the use of video link with the leave of the court, 'no conditions are imposed in respect of that leave, and no restriction is set down in respect of the exercise by the trial judge of his discretion'.[34] The Court outlined the factors which had warranted the use of the provision. These included (i) the witness had certain communication difficulties, ii) she had only just turned 18 years of age, (iii) she was giving evidence in a murder trial against her own father about events that occurred when she was 15 years of age, and (iv) she was, on the evidence of her social worker, a vulnerable person. The Court stated that the defendant was not restricted in his defence by the use of the support measure and had been able to cross-examine the witness at length in accordance with the principles in *State (Healy) v Donoghue.*[35] Ultimately, the Court found that there had been no evidence adduced on behalf of the defendant on which it could be found that there had been a real or serious risk of an unfair trial by reason of the trial judge exercising his discretion to allow the use of video link. On that and other grounds, the appeal was dismissed.

[29–28] The judgment enforces the point made by the Supreme Court in *Donnelly*[36] that once fair procedures have been afforded the accused and have been overseen by the trial judge, then the use of video link may facilitate the witness to give his or her testimony. The CCA did not specify what criteria would be necessary for the support measure to be used. For example, would it be necessary to use video link if the witness would be hindered in giving evidence by being physically present in court? Alternatively, would it be necessary if he or she could not give evidence at all without the use of the video link? Echoing the judgment in *Donnelly,*[37] the Court did not refer to these operational issues once it was satisfied that the use of the support measure did not breach fair procedures in principle.

[29–29] While s 13(1)(b) gives the court wide latitude in relation to the granting of the support measure, the case of *DPP v Ronald McManus (AKA Ronald Dunbar)*[38] may indicate that

---

[34] ibid.

[35] *State (Healy) v Donoghue* [1976] IR 325.

[36] *Donnelly v Ireland* [1998] I IR 321.

[37] ibid.

[38] *DPP v Ronald McManus (AKA Ronald Dunbar)* [2011] IECCA 32.

the courts are reluctant to allow the use of the support measure unless there is good reason to do so and that s 13(1)(b) is not a provision which will be used indiscriminately.

A similar situation arose in the case of *DPP v EC*[39] where the prosecution had successfully applied to the trial judge to be allowed for a complainant, K, who was one of three children of the appellant whom he had been accused of sexually abusing, to give evidence via video link when she was no longer 18. The defence objected as they wished to be able to cross-examine this complainant from the witness box. The application was made pursuant to s 13(1)(b) of the Criminal Evidence Act 1992, and was supported by the evidence of a psychiatrist who stated that K was extremely vulnerable and that the court procedure was very traumatic and stressful for her. The psychiatrist further stated: **[29–30]**

> K is often suicidal and has a history of multiple overdoses and chronic deliberate self-harm. The entire court proceeding naturally is making her more vulnerable at this point in time. I'm extremely worried for her mental health and her safety in terms of, again, deliberate self-harm or suicide attempts and general coping. During the course of this trial she is extremely concerned about having to face the accused in the courtroom setting. She's very avoidant consistently of verbalising even or discussing matters with — relating to the accused and memories of the alleged abuse even in session with me over the years. She has had no contact with him for many years and to have her face him or not to be given the opportunity to give her evidence via video link, in my opinion, would be endangering her life further, and that is my opinion.[40]

In dismissing this and all other appeal points, Edwards J stated: **[29–31]**

> It was submitted in the written submissions filed on behalf of the appellant, although only pressed lightly in oral submissions at the appeal hearing, that there were not sufficient grounds to allow the video link application. In our view that contention is simply untenable in the light of the testimony given by the psychiatrist. We are satisfied that the trial judge's decision to allow K to testify via a video link was made within the scope of his legitimate and lawful discretion having regard to the terms of the statute and having regard to the evidence that he had received.[41]

DPP v Osei and Opoku – adult complainant

The Court of Appeal also dealt with the granting of the support measure of video link for a complainant over 18 under s 13(1)(b) of the Criminal Evidence Act 1992 in *DPP v Osei and Opoku*.[42] In this case, the witness did not suffer from significant psychological issues or an intellectual disability but was residing in Australia and for this as well as for work and emotional reasons, the prosecution applied that she be allowed to give evidence via video link.[43] The Court of Appeal referred back to the original challenges to the use of video link and how the courts had become more accustomed to its use, noting that it did not inhibit cross-examination of the complainant nor her being seen by the jury. Birmingham P stated: **[29–32]**

> Since those early days, we have all become much more familiar with the technology and its use. When it is used, accused persons are not inhibited in any way from cross examining the witness. In this case, the witness in question, the complainant, was cross examined

39 *DPP v EC* [2016] IECA 150.
40 ibid [111].
41 *DPP v EC* [2016] IECA 150 [115].
42 *DPP v Osei and Opoku* [2022] IECA 61.
43 ibid [12].

> at some length by senior counsel on behalf of each accused. The jury could see her as she gave her evidence, and jurors, as well as the accused and their legal teams, were in a position to assess her demeanour as she gave her evidence.[44]

[29–33] The Court of Appeal stated that it did not believe that the accused was in any way prejudiced because the complainant gave evidence via video link and was satisfied that the trial judge exercised his discretion to grant the measure in a proper manner.

DPP v Goidan – adult complainant[45]

[29–34] In *DPP v Goidan*[46] one of the appeal points concerned the giving of evidence by the complainant under s 13(1)(b) of the Criminal Evidence Act 1992 when, at short notice, she was not able to travel from her home country to attend court in Ireland. The appellant objections to the s 13 application were based on the need for *viva voce* evidence to ensure a fair trial, the absence of notice, the lack of sufficient reason for her (the complainant's) absence, and the apparent failure of the Gardaí to enquire as to her availability beyond the week ahead.[47]

[29–35] Giving the judgment of the Court, McCarthy J noted that the norm will remain the giving of evidence *viva voce*, but observed that where there was a coherent and rational basis for the reason for the complainant not attending, evidence could be given via video link:

> The Supreme Court in *Donnelly v Ireland* [1998] 1 IR 321 considered whether or not the right to cross examine a witness in order to be effective and to give the accused person the opportunity to defend himself adequately required that the witness should give evidence in his or her presence and that the witness when giving evidence should physically confront him. This was rejected and hence no procedural unfairness need be feared when evidence is given in this way.
>
> There is no basis for saying there is any infringement of the right to constitutional justice by virtue of the fact that a witness is heard remotely or by video link in accordance with *Donnelly*. Accordingly, it is a matter within the discretion of the judge and on a matter of this kind she is in the best position to make a judgment as to whether it is permissible to hear a witness in this way. The norm will of course remain that evidence will be given *viva voce* in person in court. Where there is a coherent and rational basis, as here, on the evidence as to why the witness could not attend, the judge properly exercised her discretion in permitting the evidence to be given in this way.[48]

Video link under s 13 Criminal Evidence Act 1992 no longer included in s 19 Criminal Evidence Act 1992 – application re mental disorder

[29–36] When commenced, the provision was available to persons under 17 as well as to persons with an intellectual disability.[49] Section 19, which allowed persons with an intellectual

---

44 ibid [14].

45 *DPP v Goidan* [2022] IECA 202.

46 ibid.

47 ibid [27].

48 ibid [28]–[29].

49 Criminal Evidence Act 1992, s 19:

> 'The references in sections 13(1)(a), 14(1)(b), 15(1)(b) and 16(1)(a) to a person under 17 years of age and the reference in section 16(1)(b) to a person under 14 years of age shall include references to a person with mental handicap who has reached the age concerned.'

This section was amended by Children Act 2001, s 257 to increase the age eligibility to 18.

disability to avail of certain support measures, included s 13(1)(a). However, s 30(l) of the Criminal Justice (Victims of Crime) Act 2017 amended s 19:

(i) by the substitution of "sections 14, 14B, 15 and 16" for "sections 13(1)(a), 14(1)(b), 15(1)(b) and 16(1)(a) and (b)(ii)",
(ii) by the deletion of "and the reference in section 16(1)(b)(i) to a person under 14 years of age", and
(iii) by the substitution of "a mental disorder, within the meaning of section 5 of the Criminal Justice Act 1993," for "mental handicap".

The section therefore no longer includes s 13[50] and so a person with an intellectual disability is not automatically eligible under s 3(1)(a) of the Act. The provision under s 13(1)(b) is now the appropriate section for a person with an intellectual disability who wishes to avail of video link. **[29–37]**

Prior to that amendment, the case of *O'D v DPP*[51] was significant as the granting of the support measure of video link risked prejudicing the jury where an evidential aspect related to the intellectual disability of the complainants. In *O'D v DPP*[52] this was deemed to be prejudicial to the accused in light of the requirement to first establish whether the complainants were mentally impaired in respect of capacity to consent, a requirement under the offence allegedly committed (s 5 of the Criminal Justice (Sexual Offences) Act 1993) the offence of having sexual intercourse with a mentally impaired person. **[29–38]**

DPP v O'Driscoll – adult witness/mental disorder

The case of *DPP v O'Driscoll*[53] involved the use of video link under s 13(1)(b) of the Criminal Evidence Act 1992 where a prosecution witness had an acquired brain injury and counsel applied for the use of video link under s 13(1)(b) and the use of an intermediary under s 14 of the Criminal Evidence Act. Both measures were granted by the trial judge and after conviction, the defendant appealed on the grounds that the trial judge had erred where there had been no necessity for their use at trial. The appeal was dismissed on the basis that the granting of the measures had been appropriate in the circumstances.[54] **[29–39]**

In relation to the use of video link, the Court of Appeal noted that there was no disadvantage to the appellant in the prosecution witness giving evidence via video link. The witness had suffered a serious brain injury, required on-going assistance with many aspects of day-to-day living, and the evidence which had been accepted by the trial judge showed that his delivery of responses to questions could be arrested under the stress of a live confrontation. Referring to the change in criteria regarding the eligibility of a person under s 19 of the Act, the Court stated: **[29–40]**

> Critically, while it is obviously not necessary that a witness suffer a mental disorder before the Court can exercise its broadly worded discretion to permit that witness to

---

50 ibid. 'The references in sections 14, 14B, 15 and 16 to a person under 18 years of age shall include references to a person with a mental disorder, within the meaning of section 5 of the Criminal Justice Act 1993 who has reached the age concerned.'
Mental disorder under s.5 Criminal Justice Act 1993 includes a mental illness, mental disability, dementia or any disease of the mind'.

51 *O'D v DPP and Judge Patricia Ryan* [2009] IEHC 559.

52 ibid.

53 *DPP v O'Driscoll* [2022] IECA 4.

54 ibid [31]–[32].

> give evidence by video link, the fact that the trial judge determined that Mr. Foley's (the witness) medical profile did come within the definition of 'mental disorder' was critically relevant to the exercise of that discretion.[55]

[29–41] The judgment states that s 19 of the Criminal Evidence Act 1992 includes s 13(1)(a), which involves the use of video link for children under 18.[56] As mentioned above, video link under s 13 was removed from s 19 through the Criminal Justice (Victims of Crime) Act 2017 when s 30 of that Act was commenced on 30 May 2018. The section now states:

> The references in sections 14, 14B, 15 and 16 to a person under 18 years of age shall include references to a person with a mental disorder, within the meaning of section 5 of the Criminal Justice Act 1993 who has reached the age concerned.

[29–42] However, the ruling appears to have been made on the basis that s 13 was not included in s 19, therefore the principles of the judgment are not impacted.

Section 13(2) Criminal Evidence Act 1992

'Evidence shall be video recorded'

Recording the witness while being cross-examined via video link

[29–43] Note should be taken of the case in Galway where the jury had to be discharged when it was realised that the cross-examination evidence which was taken via video link was not being videorecorded.[57] In light of the increased use of Zoom, Skype and Pexip technology for use in courtrooms to facilitate the giving of evidence, it should be remembered that the evidence should be recorded as stipulated under this legislation.

Physical installation of facilities in courthouses

[29–44] All counties now have video technologies installed. Prior to the pandemic video link was installed in 15 counties. As part of the Courts Services modernisation plans, the remaining 11 counties have now been brought on stream.

[29–45] The gradual increase in the installation of video link facilities is reflected in periodic commencement orders allowing for the giving of live video link evidence in the relevant courts. For example, the commencement order in respect of video link in the Special Criminal Court under s 13 of the Criminal Evidence Act 1992 was effected in June 2022.[58] If video link facilities are not available, for whatever reason, proceedings may be transferred[59] to an appropriate courtroom where such facilities are available.

---

[55] *DPP v O'Driscoll* [2022] IECA 4 [26].

[56] ibid [4]. s 19 provides, under the title 'Application of Part III to persons with mental handicap': 'The references in sections 13(1)(a), 14(1)(b), 15(1)(b) and 16(1)(a) and (b)(ii) to a person under 18 years of age … shall include references to a person with a mental disorder within the meaning of section 5 of the Criminal Justice Act 1993, who has reached the age concerned.'

[57] Ann Healy '*Trial of mother for cruelty to eight children collapses. Jury told technical difficulties were to blame as video link evidence had not been recorded*' The Irish Times (Dublin 3 December 2015) <http://www.irishtimes.com/news/crime-and-law/courts/circuit-court/trial-of-mother-for-cruelty-to-eight-children-collapses-1.2453152> accessed 13 October 2023.

[58] Special Criminal Court Criminal Evidence Act 1992 (s 13) (Commencement) Order 2022 (SI 308/2022) Art 2 30 June 2022.

[59] Criminal Evidence Act 1992, s 17, provides for the transfer of proceedings if facilities are not

Jurisdiction in all courts/Transfer of proceedings

There is no limitation in s 13 of the Criminal Evidence Act 1992 in relation to summary or indictable offences and the provision applies to courts of all jurisdiction. If required, s 17 of the Criminal Evidence Act 1992[60] allows for proceedings under ss 13, 14, 15, 16 and 29 to be transferred to the appropriate court. **[29–46]**

Necessity for use of video link with the support measure of intermediary

Section 14 of the Criminal Evidence Act 1992 states that the support measure of an intermediary may be granted subject to certain factors where a witness under s 14(1) or a victim under s 14(1)(A) is giving evidence via a live television link. Additionally, s 5(B) of the Criminal Justice Act 1993 allows for the granting of the support of intermediary during the giving of a victim impact statement where the person is giving evidence via a live television link. The granting of video link appears to be an essential requirement. **[29–47]**

Suggested procedure for use of video link at trial

Every case is specific to the facts of the case before the court but this is a suggested procedure for the use of video link at trial. **[29–48]**

- Depending on age and intellectual disability of witness, the witness has previously been introduced to the judge, not only for introduction purposes but also to satisfy the court that the witness is an eligible and competent one under s 27 Criminal Evidence Act 1992 and as per the test for competence in *O'Sullivan v Hamill* and *DPP v Campion*.[61]
- It is confirmed that video link is working.
- Any documents which are required for examination in chief or cross-examination to be sent to video link room.
- If paper and pens are required for witness, these should be provided in video link room.
- Registrar has oath prepared for witness minder and / or intermediary as required.

Examination in chief and/or Cross-Examination of Witness

- Where recorded testimony is being played under s 16(1)(b) of the Criminal Evidence Act 1992, arrangements may have been made for the witness to watch the recording at a previous time. Prior to cross-examination, it should be decided if and how the witness will be watching the recording while it is being played to the jury. **[29–49]**
- Where the witness is giving evidence live, via video link, the oath or affirmation may

---

available in the original district and if it is 'desirable' that evidence be given through a live television link or by videorecording.

60 Criminal Evidence Act 1992, s 17, Transfer of proceedings:

> 'In any proceedings for an offence in any circuit or district court district in relation to which any of the provisions of sections 13 to 16 or section 29 is not in operation the court concerned may, if in its opinion it is desirable that evidence be given in the proceedings through a live television link or by means of a videorecording or that a screen or other similar device be used in the giving of evidence, by order transfer the proceedings to a circuit or district court district in relation to which those provisions are in operation and, where such an order is made the jurisdiction of the court to which the proceedings have been transferred may be exercised –
>
> (a) in the case of the Circuit Court, by the judge of the circuit concerned, and
>
> (b) in the case of the District Court, by the judge of that court for the time being assigned to the district court district concerned.'

61 *O'Sullivan v Hamill* [1998] 2 IR 9; *DPP v Campion* [2018] IESC 35; [2021] 2 IR 1[136].

be administered depending on whether the witness is eligible as per s 27 Criminal Evidence Act 1992. It is the responsibility of the trial judge to ensure that sufficient inquiry has been made where the witness is a child or has an intellectual disability that he or she is a competent witness.[62]

- If recorded testimony has been played, there may be a break between the playing of the recorded testimony and the start of cross-examination. However, this is not necessarily the case and the witness may wish to continue immediately.
- Where video link is being used for examination in chief and cross-examination or just cross-examination (where recorded evidence has been played as examination in chief testimony), it is suggested that the jury not be present while the video link connection is set up.
- Judge is present – jury is not present yet.
- Video link screen is opened to communicate from video link room to court.
- Any technical issues, eg audibility, framing of witness in the screen, are resolved.
- Confirmation that any documents, papers, pens etc required for examination in chief or cross-examination have been sent to video link room.
- Witness minder is in video link screen and communicates any issues with court.
- Witness may not be present in video link room at this stage but may be waiting just outside the video link room.
- Witness minder takes oath or affirms to mind the witness and ensure that the witness does not talk to anyone in the course of giving their evidence.
- Video link is switched off.
- Judge asks for jury to be brought into court.
- Judge gives any necessary direction to jury regarding this witness and the use of video link. Video link should not be open for this as it may take some time. The direction may outline the reasons for the support measures being used.
- Video link is switched on.
- Judge greets witness who is sworn as appropriate and introduced to counsel.
- Examination in chief, cross-examination and re-examination by counsel as required with appropriate breaks as per suggestions by counsel and trial judge.
- Any documents referred to or created during evidence to be collected and brought to the court.
- Judge speaks to witness to conclude – eg to thank and say goodbye to the witness.
- Video link is switched off.
- Any issues required to be made in the presence of the jury are then addressed.
- Jury leaves.
- Any issues required to be made in the absence of the jury are then addressed.

---

[62] *O'Sullivan v Hamill* [1998] 2 IR 9. See Chapter 9.

Chapter 30

WIGS AND GOWNS

Persons with an Intellectual Disability/ Child Witnesses/Complainants

Section 14B of the Criminal Evidence Act 1992 provides for the removal of wigs and gowns when a vulnerable witness is giving evidence: **[30–01]**

> Where a person who is under 18 years of age –
> (a) is giving evidence in respect of a relevant offence, or
> (b) is giving evidence in respect of any other offence of which he or she is a victim,
> neither the judge nor the barrister or solicitor concerned in the examination of the witness shall wear a wig or gown.

For adults who have reached 18, and who have an intellectual disability, s 19 of the Criminal Evidence Act 1992 applies to s 14B for persons with a mental disorder, within the meaning of s 5 of the Criminal Justice Act 1993. A mental disorder, as defined in s 5 of the Act, 'includes a mental illness, mental disability, dementia or any disease of the mind'. **[30–02]**

Section 14B was inserted into the Act by s 30(f) of the Criminal Justice (Victims of Crime) Act 2017[1] as a stand-alone support measure. Previously, legislative provision for no wigs or gowns to be worn during the giving of evidence via a live television link was included under s 13 of the Criminal Evidence Act 1992 and has now been deleted by s 35 of the Criminal Law (Sexual Offences) Act 2017. **[30–03]**

The format of 'persons under 18 giving evidence in respect of a relevant offence or giving evidence in respect of any other offence of which he or she is a victim' is confusing, as are many similar sections in the Criminal Evidence Act 1992. It would appear to then mean that a child who is giving evidence as a witness (not a victim) in proceedings which are not related to a relevant offence, eg neglect, will not be able to avail of the section. **[30–04]**

Should it be felt appropriate for the judge and counsel not to robe, it is possible that the trial judge will order, through the inherent jurisdiction of the court, on his or her own motion or on the application of the prosecution counsel, that no wigs or gowns or worn. While the legislation stipulates only wigs or gowns will not be worn, it is common practice, given the individual circumstances, that not only are no tabs (specific collars worn by barristers) are worn but also senior counsel and judges will not wear **[30–05]**

---

1 Inserted (30 May 2018) by Criminal Justice (Victims of Crime) Act 2017 (28/2017), s 30(f), SI No 173/2018.

senior counsel and judicial attire but will wear everyday suits.[2] This may depend on the age of the child or wishes of the witness, and factors such as how long the evidence may take influence the decision.

Child Defendants

[30–06] Practice Directions in the Dublin Metropolitan District Court provide that no robes, wigs or tabs will be worn in the Children Court.[3] Section 71 of the Children Act 2001 outlines definition of the Children Court.

[30–07] While the provision is legislatively defined in respect of the Children Act in tandem with the practice Direction for Dublin Metropolitan District Court, it is the practice that in all jurisdictions of the court and in all geographical jurisdictions, the judge and practitioners will not 'robe up'. This may be by agreement or by order of the court on application by the prosecution counsel or state solicitor.

[30–08] The dispensing of robes, wigs and tabs for witnesses and defendants may form part of the orders in an appropriate preliminary hearing under the Criminal Procedure Act 2021.[4]

[30–09] The wearing of suits by all parties and the dispensing with wigs, gown and tabs has been common practice for cases involving child defendants in the Circuit and Central Criminal Courts. For the duration of the trial of *DPP v Boy A and Boy B* in the Central Criminal Court in 2019, in relation to the murder of Ana Kriégel, the counsel and judge wore suits and no wigs, gowns or tabs were worn.[5]

---

2 Caroline Biggs and Miriam Delahunt, '*Prosecutorial Challenges – Vulnerable Witnesses*' (2017) 22(1) Bar Review 25.

> 'Counsel did not wear gowns, wigs and tabs, and counsel and the judge wore suits for the duration of the complainant's testimony'

3 Dublin Metropolitan District Court, *Practice Direction* (DC 04 No 20): 'Tabs, robes and wigs should not be worn in court'.

4 Criminal Procedure Act 2021, s 6(8)(f): 'The trial court, in holding a preliminary trial hearing, may make such orders with regard to the conduct of the preliminary trial hearing as it considers appropriate and in accordance with the interests of justice, including with regard to the making of submissions in writing.'

5 See Miriam Delahunt, '*The Trial of Children in the Central Criminal Court*' (2020) 25(1) Bar Review 20.

PART IV

GENERAL ISSUES

CHAPTER 31

DELAY

Introduction

The issue of delay has been a constant factor for many years in relation to vulnerable witnesses and defendants in the criminal justice system and one that has been exacerbated by the Covid-19 pandemic. Delay as a factor in pre-trial issues for vulnerable defendants is dealt with elsewhere in this book. In relation to vulnerable witnesses, reported cases may reflect the issues that face witnesses, practitioners and the judiciary in Ireland. Defendants in custody will take priority in terms of a matter getting on for trial. A defendant on bail may have issues trying to get a matter on for trial expediently while also trying to ensure that disclosure have been fully addressed. **[31–01]**

The *Courts Service Annual Report* outline the difficulties facing the management of trial lists across Ireland: **[31–02]**

> Waiting times for criminal cases vary, depending on whether the accused is on bail or in custody; on whether the plea is 'guilty' or 'not guilty'; on whether the trial is scheduled to last two days or two weeks. In most Circuit Courts outside Dublin, the majority of guilty pleas will be dealt with at the next criminal session – making the waiting time approximately three months. Defendants who are in custody take precedence so their trials are dealt with first, followed by trials of those who are on bail. Waiting times in Dublin Circuit Court have been impacted in recent years by the number of so-called 'white collar' cases taken by the State in the wake of the financial collapse that followed the global recession in 2008. The complicated nature of the evidence in these cases together with the number of witnesses called and the additional legal argument required has lengthened the trials with a resulting impact on the number of trial courts available for other cases. Measures introduced to address this situation include the allocation of the additional judges (subject to the availability of courtrooms) and the listing of only one long trial at any one time.[1]

Waiting times are outlined in the Report[2] but the issues which might prevent a trial getting on are varied, such as unavailability of judges, witnesses or courtrooms in addition to issues such as disclosure. The *Review of Protections for Vulnerable Witnesses in the Investigation and Prosecution of Sexual Offences* (the 'O'Malley Report') examined the issue of delay[3] and put forward suggestions as to how to reduce it, including an increase in the appointment of judges and a review of sentence discounts for guilty pleas. In addition, one of the issues in relation to the trials of sexual offences often relates to disclosure: **[31–03]**

1 *Courts Service Annual Report* (2022).
2 ibid 112–122.
3 Dept of Justice and Equality, *Review of Protections for Vulnerable Witnesses in the Investigation and Prosecution of Sexual Offences* (August 2020) 110.

> Completion of disclosure can be delayed in sexual offence prosecutions because relevant material must be sought from other agencies and bodies. As discussed elsewhere in the report, the burden of evaluating increasing volumes of electronic data retrieved from phones and other devices for relevance and redacting irrelevant personal information to protect privacy is placing a significant burden on the prosecution. Disclosure may come in tranches, right up to the beginning of the trial and sometimes, indeed, after the trial has begun. We hope that our recommendations in relation to disclosure will help to expedite the process.[4]

[31–04] The recommendations are being followed up by the Department of Justice.[5] Legislation for preliminary trial hearings has already been commenced[6] and an increase in the appointment of judges has been achieved.[7] In relation to disclosure, the *Supporting a Victim's Journey* report includes a recommendation to place a positive obligation on all statutory or public bodies, voluntary bodies and independent counsellors holding counselling records to furnish those records promptly to the Director of Public Prosecutions once requested to do so.[8]

[31–05] The Court Proceedings (Delays) Bill 2023 has been published in tandem with the Regulatory Impact Analysis, which examined the approaches to resolving the issues regarding delay in the justice system.[9] The Bill sets out:

> An Act to provide for the right of persons who are party to proceedings, where such proceedings are not concluded within a reasonable time, to seek a declaration of that fact and, in certain cases, compensation and, for that purpose to make provision for the making by such persons of applications for such a declaration and compensation and for the appointment of a Chief Court Delays Assessor and Court Delays Assessors to assess such applications; to provide for the making, in certain circumstances, of an application to the Circuit Court for such a declaration and compensation; and to provide for related matters.

[31–06] The Bill includes criminal proceedings although there is no definition as to who is a party to proceedings (eg does the victim have any say in the issue of delay in a case?) and there seems to be no specific provision for children.

[31–07] While these efforts may effect real change, criminal trials must still continue to address the issues of delay on a daily basis. Delay is particularly problematic for vulnerable witnesses and defendants in terms of difficulties of memory recall as well as the inhibition on life developments.

[31–08] Until the judgment of *DPP v MT*,[10] there appears to have been no successful argument

---

4 ibid para 6.24.

5 Dept of Justice and Equality, *Supporting a Victim's Journey – A plan to help victims and vulnerable witnesses in sexual violence cases* (October 2020) 'Reducing Delay – Recommendation 8.1' 56.

6 Criminal Procedure Act 2021 was commenced on 28 February 2022 through the Criminal Procedure Act 2021 (Commencement) Order 2022 (SI No 79/2022) rt 2.

7 Mary Carolan, 'Appointment of significant number of extra judges to be recommended by new top-level report: Increase likely to be linked to more efficient working practices, including more court sittings and shorter vacations' *The Irish Times* (Dublin 23 February 2023) <https://www.irishtimes.com/crime-law/courts/2023/02/23/significant-increase-in-number-of-judges-to-be-recommended/> accessed 13 October 2023.

8 Dept of Justice and Equality, *Supporting a Victim's Journey – A plan to help victims and vulnerable witnesses in sexual violence cases* (October 2020) para 5.8.

9 Court Proceedings (Delays) Bill 2023, *Regulatory Impact Analysis* (January 2023).

10 *DPP v MT* [2023] IECA 65.

in relation to how a lengthy interval of time between the recording of testimony and the trial itself may have affected the evidence in the case. In *DPP v MT*,[11] the Court of Appeal describes the delay in respect of the trial which may have led to the difficulties in memory recall which ultimately led to difficulties in cross-examination. The conviction was quashed as the fact that the complainant could not remember the incident itself meant that the right to cross-examination was undermined. Ní Raifeartaigh J emphasised that where the complainant, who was six at the time of the offence and 11 years of age at time of trial, was unable to remember the incident, the issue was not one of competency, but regard had to be had to the difficulty of memory recall. The judgment referred to the delay as a significant factor in this case. The judgment also referred to the cases of *DPP v TV*[12] and *DPP v SA*[13] where the intervals between the recording of the interview and the trial getting on were approximately four years and six-and-a-half years. Various factors including late disclosure, unavailability of judges, the suspect being out of the country although not charged, were the factors in the reasons for the delay in the latter case. Challenges in respect of the ability to cross-examine due to the prolonged interval between the taking of the recorded testimony and the trial failed.

In *DPP v FN*,[14] the appellant appealed on a number of points in relation to a conviction of sexual assault, one of which was that the trial judge erred in determining that the complainant was capable of giving an intelligent account and therefore giving evidence at the trial. The complainant was approximately six years of age at the time of the alleged offence and 20 months had elapsed between the recording of his testimony and the trial. In refusing the appeal point, Birmingham P noted that no cross-examination had taken place and therefore it was not possible to establish whether meaningful cross-examination could not have taken place: **[31–09]**

> In our view, there can be no doubt about the fact that cases involving very young complainants, and/or very young accused persons should be prioritised. This is all the more so when both complainants and the accused are very young. However, in the present case, we have not been persuaded that there was any prejudice arising from the delay. At one level, the allegation was a very straightforward one with a contemporaneous complaint. Unlike some other cases, it was not a question of a young complainant seeking to describe a prolonged pattern of behaviour where the basis [sic] narrative could get lost among the detail. It also seems relevant to us that the only account that the jury heard was the account to specialist interviewers. There was no cross-examination so the question of the ability to conduct a meaningful cross-examination being compromised by the lapse of time has not been established, though it is the case where the decision not to cross-examine was taken against the background of a particular timescale. The evidence in chief of the complainant from the meeting with the specialist interviewers was unchallenged, save for an assertion by defence counsel to the jury to the effect that the accused denied outright all allegations made against him in respect of complainant Y. Insofar as an alternative explanation for the incident was canvassed, that what occurred was in the context of chastisement, a theory for which there was no evidential basis, the appellant was not prevented from pursuing that theory by the passage of time. Overall, we have not been convinced that the judge fell into error in declining to halt the trial by reason of the lapse of time and we dismiss this ground of appeal.[15]

---

11 ibid.

12 *DPP v VE* [2021] IECA 122 [80].

13 *DPP v SA* [2020] IECA 60.

14 *DPP v FN* [2021] IECA 238; [2022] IESC 22.

15 *DPP v FN* [2021] IECA 238 [26]; [2022] IESC 22.

[31–10] In the case of *DPP v PB*,[16] a corroboration warning was given where there had been difficulties in memory recall and inconsistencies in the evidence of the witness. Approximately four years had passed between the taking of the witness' evidence under s 16(1)(b) of the Criminal Evidence Act 1992 (July 2010) and the matter coming on for trial (February 2014), and an earlier trial had ended in disagreement. The complainant was approximately 13-and-a-half when the examination in chief evidence was taken and approximately 17-and-a-half when the second trial resulted in a conviction. The defendant appealed on a number of points, one of which was that the corroboration warning had not been adequate in relation to the evidence in the case. The Court of Appeal dismissed this and all points, stating that the corroboration warning was, in the circumstances of the case, more than adequate.[17] It may be noted that in refusing a ground of appeal in relation to an application to stay the indictment, the Court of Appeal judgment distinguished this case from cases of historic sex abuse. Birmingham P stated:

> As will be apparent, this was not the usual delay application that not infrequently arises in what are sometimes referred to as historic sex cases. This was not a case where there had been really major delay. There was a complaint to Gardaí, leading to the complainant being interviewed by specialist Garda interviewers within approximately two years after the abuse ended and after various orders were made under the Childcare Acts.[18]

[31–11] A factor of the delay between the making of complaints and the recording of interviews was the retraction of the allegations by the complainant. The Court of Appeal observed that the prosecution contended that this was due to the pressure by the defendant. While there may have been no unusual reasons for delay in terms of interval between the offences and the trials in this matter, the difference in a child giving evidence at the age of approximately 17 about events that had taken place approximately six years previously remains significant in terms of the evidence placed before a jury.

[31–12] Were recording of full testimony including examination in chief, cross-examination and re-examination a reality, negative impact both on the witnesses and on the evidence would be minimised. In England and Wales, recorded cross-examination under s 28 of the Youth Justice and Criminal Evidence Act 1999 has been piloted and rolled out on a national basis.[19] While examined in the 'O'Malley Report', full recorded testimony was not recommended due to disclosure and other issues which, according to the report, would need to be addressed before the measure could be introduced.[20]

---

16 *DPP v PB* [2021] IECA 152.

17 ibid [38]–[39].

18 ibid [7].

19 'Case Management in Criminal Cases When a Witness or a Defendant is Vulnerable' (*The Advocate's Gateway*, 2 September 2019) Toolkit 1a <https://www.theadvocatesgateway.org/_files/ugd/1074f0_cbed7b4162c8468aa9cd7dc3c4ddffb6.pdf> accessed 13 October 2023.

20 Dept of Justice and Equality, *Review of Protections for Vulnerable Witnesses in the Investigation and Prosecution of Sexual Offences* (August 2020) para 6.28: 'Accordingly, for a number of reasons, including the issue just mentioned in connection with disclosure, we do not recommend at this point that pre-recorded cross-examination or re-examination be introduced. We are also conscious of a number of other potential problems that were mentioned by the Bar Council in its submission to the Working Group. These include possible issues with technology, a potential reduction in the jury's ability to "read" a witness's body language, whether video testimony might create emotional distance between the witness and the jury, and possibly lack the immediacy and persuasiveness of live testimony. We do, however, acknowledge that strong arguments have been made, by academic experts and others, in favour of introducing such a practice. Our recommendation is based solely on practical considerations rather than any opposition in principle. If the point is reached where these practical issues can be effectively addressed, pre-recorded cross-examination

In the above-mentioned case of *DPP v FN*[21] the trial concerned complainants aged four years old and six years old and a defendant who was 14 years of age at the time of the alleged incidents. The matter came on for trial approximately 20 months after the alleged sexual offences had occurred and the statements recorded. The trial of Boy A and Boy B in the Central Criminal Court started slightly less than one year after the death of Ana Kriégel.[22] Where it is possible, priorities can be made to minimise delay where young witnesses and defendants are involved in criminal trials. A general objective to ensure cases involving extremely vulnerable witnesses and defendants could assist. For example, in England and Wales, the Young Witness Initiative is a protocol between the police, Crown Prosecution Service (CPS) and His Majesty's Courts and Tribunals Service (HMCTS) to fast-track cases involving a witness who is under the age of 10.[23] In Northern Ireland, a fast track pilot project allows for expedience of cases for witnesses involved in criminal cases who are under 13.[24] **[31–13]**

and re-examination may well become feasible, though any potential constitutional impediments would need to be carefully examined before a final decision is taken on the matter.'

21 *DPP v FN* [2021] IECA 238; [2022] IESC 22.

22 Miriam Delahunt, 'The Trial of Children in the Central Criminal Court' (2020) 25(1) Bar Review 19.

23 Crown Prosecution Service, *Under 10s protocol*

> 'The Young Witness Initiative is a protocol between the police, Crown Prosecution Service (CPS) and Her Majesty's Courts and Tribunals Service (HMCTS) to fast-track cases involving a witness who is under the age of 10. The aim is to bring these cases to trial much more quickly to give the child witness the best chance of remembering the incident and to make the criminal justice process less stressful for them. The protocol only applies to cases charged on or after 1 April 2015.'

<https://www.cps.gov.uk/legal-guidance/special-measures> accessed 13 October 2023.

24 The Law Society of Northern Ireland ,*Criminal Practitioners With Cases In The Fast Track Pilot Court*, https://www.lawsoc-ni.org/fast-track-pilot-court-for-witnesses-under-13years-in-laganside accessed 13 October 2023

Chapter 32

DISABILITY AND THE COURTS

Introduction

[32–01] The focus of this work has been on the relevant legislation and case law for eligibility for assistance and support for victims, witnesses and defendants who are vulnerable due to age, intellectual disability and the nature of the offence before the courts. Persons who have difficulties within the courts due to a physical disability such as visual impairment, deafness or mobility issues may be assisted through the Courts Services in terms of access and accommodation in the courtroom. Certain legislative rights have been established through the Disability Act 2005, the Irish Sign Language Act 2017 and the Criminal Justice (Victims of Crime) Act 2017 which oblige the courts to accommodate persons with a disability in relation to their individual needs. A person may also be assisted through a specific direction of the trial judge in terms of the individual physical needs of the person to engage with the trial. While the case of *DPP v Harrison*[1] focused on the needs of a defendant with an acquired brain injury, it outlined a general accommodation by the courts in order to assist the individual needs of persons who come before them.[2]

[32–02] Although a comprehensive analysis of the issues in relation to disabilities and the criminal justice system is outside the scope of this work, it is worth noting certain research and initiatives which have been completed in relation to access to the justice system for persons with disabilities.

National Disability Authority

[32–03] The National Disability Authority is an independent statutory body that provides information and advice to the government on policy and practice relevant to the lives of persons with disabilities. In 2012 it commissioned University College Cork and the Centre for Criminal Justice and Human Rights (CCJHR) to conduct research on access to justice for people with disabilities as victims of crime in Ireland.[3] The research indicates much remains to be done to improve participation by people with disability in the criminal justice system. In June 2020, the National Disability Authority published an Independent Advice Paper on the use of intermediaries in relation to

1 *DPP v Harrison* [2016] IECA 212.

2 *ibid* [54] –[56].

3 Claire Edwards, Gillian Harold and Shane Kilcommins, '*Access to Justice for People with Disabilities as Victims of Crime in Ireland*' (University College Cork, February 2012) <https://nda.ie/publications/access-to-justice-for-people-with-disabilities-as-victims-of-crime-in-ireland> accessed 13 October 2023.

persons in the Irish justice system who may have communication difficulties. The use of intermediaries for both witnesses and defendants, albeit with required legislative changes, was recommended.[4]

The Courts Services

[32–04] The *Courts Service Annual Report* notes:

> The Service achieved the status of 'Ability Company' in the 'Environmental Accessibility' category of the O2 Ability Awards 2010. The award followed an assessment of the Service on a range of factors including policies relating to disability, accessibility and organisational commitment, and an examination of the Criminal Courts of Justice.[5]

[32–05] The *Courts Service Annual Report* has consistently outlined reviews, in conjunction with the Office of Public Works, of accessibility to court buildings across the jurisdiction to ensure that access is compliant with disability legislation.[6] In addition, in 2021, the *Courts Service Annual Report* outlined the JAM Card initiative.

> As part of a collaborative project with our justice sector colleagues, the Coroner's Court, the Irish Prison Services, and the Courts Service secured funding from the Public Service Innovation Fund 2021 to support our organisation becoming JAM Card friendly. A JAM Card allows people with a learning difficulty, autism, or a communication barrier to tell others that they need 'Just A Minute' discreetly and easily. Those with a communication barrier are often reluctant or unable to tell others about their condition. JAM Card allows this to happen in a simple, effective non-verbal manner. This initiative was launched in September 2021 across the three agencies and anyone with a communication barrier can now present a physical JAM Card or electronic JAM Card via an app in any of our public service offices to request an additional amount of time to deal with their query. Our commitment to become a JAM Card friendly organisation sends out a clear message of inclusion, access, and quality customer service to all our users. This initiative is another example of how the Courts Service continues to develop a human centred approach, putting users at the centre of our innovation efforts.[7]

---

4 National Disability Authority <https://nda.ie/publications/nda-advice-paper-the-use-of-intermediaries-in-the-irish-justice-system> accessed 13 October 2023.

5 *Courts Service Annual Report* (2010) 39.

6 *Courts Service Annual Report* (2014) 28; (2015) 32; (2016) 35; (2017) 40; (2018) 38.

7 *Courts Service Annual Report* (2021) 26 <https://www.courts.ie/annual-report> accessed 13 October 2023.

Chapter 33

SEPARATION OF DEFENDANT AND VICTIM

Introduction

A frequent difficulty for victims is that, in the course of court proceedings, they may come across the defendant or alleged defendant in the building where the court is situated. This may cause distress and upset which may in turn affect the quality of the evidence given. Section 33 of the Criminal Justice (Victims of Crime) Act 2017 addresses this difficulty by amending the Court Services Act 1998. **[33–01]**

Section 2 of the Court Services Act 1998, now outlines the word 'victim' which is given the same meaning as in s 2 of the Criminal Justice (Victims of Crime) Act 2017 ie a natural person who has suffered harm, including physical, mental or emotional harm or economic loss, which was directly caused by an offence. **[33–02]**

Section 33 also inserts s 5A ('Victims of crime') into the Court Services Act 1998 so it now reads: **[33–03]**

> Section 5A: In carrying out its functions under paragraphs (d) ('provide, manage and maintain court buildings') and (e) ('provide facilities for users of the courts') of section 5, the Service shall ensure that—
>
> (a) in so far as is practicable, provision is made during the course of criminal proceedings which are conducted in a court building referred to in section 5(d) for the separation of an offender or an alleged offender and his or her parents, relatives and friends from a victim and his or her parents, relatives and friends such that contact between the parties may be avoided except where necessary for the purposes of the criminal proceedings concerned, and
>
> (b) a separate waiting area for victims who are involved in criminal proceedings is provided in any building which—
>
> (i) is built after the commencement of this section, and
>
> (ii) at the time that it is built, is intended to be used as a court building.

The section was commenced on the 27 November 2017 and while it is a positive aspiration, given the size and layout of certain courthouses in the country, it is still a significant issue which both defendants and victims and their families and friends must deal with in the course of court proceedings for some time to come. **[33–04]**

FURTHER READING

Frank Feehan QC and Caroline Harris , *Vulnerable Witnesses within Family and Criminal Proceedings: Protections, Safeguards and Sanctions* (Bloomsbury Professional 2019).

Barbara Mitchels Children and Vulnerable Witnesses in Court Proceedings (Wildy, Simmonds and Hill Publishing 2016).

Prof. Penny Cooper and Linda Hunting (eds.) *Addressing Vulnerability in Justice Systems* (Wildy, Simmonds and Hill Publishing 2016).

Joyce Plotnikoff and Richard Woolfson, *Intermediaries in the Criminal Justice System: Improving Communication for Vulnerable Witnesses and Defendants* (Policy Press 2015).

John R Spencer, Michael E Lamb (eds), *Children and Cross-Examination – Time to Change The Rules?* (Hart 2012).

Michael E Lamb et al (eds), *Children's Testimony – A Handbook of Psychological Research and Forensic Practice* (2nd edn, Wiley-Blackwell 2011).

Michael E Lamb, Irit Hershkowitz, Yael Orbach, and Philip W Esplin, *Tell Me What Happened – Structured Investigative Interviews of Child Victims and Witnesses* (Wiley 2010).

INDEX